The cool genius who is
Naruto's rival... This series
is a gag manga about that
Sasuke! Please enjoy this
new version of Sasuke acting
like an idiot.

—Kenji Taira, 2016

NARUTO: Chibi Sasuke's Sharingan Legend

SHONEN JUMP MANGA EDITION

VOLUME 1

STORY AND ART BY KENJI TAIRA

Translation: Amanda Haley
Touch-Up Art & Lettering: Thea Willis, Snir Aharon
Design: Yukiko Whitley
Editor: Alexis Kirsch

UCHIHA SASUKE NO SHARIN GANDEN © 2014 by Masashi Kishimoto, Kenji Taira
All rights reserved.
First published in Japan in 2014 by SHUEISHA Inc., Tokyo.
English translation rights arranged by SHUEISHA Inc.

The stories, characters and incidents mentioned in
this publication are entirely fictional.

Printed in the U.S.A.

Published by VIZ Media, LLC
P.O. Box 77010
San Francisco, CA 94107

10 9 8 7 6 5 4 3 2 1
First printing, September 2017

viz.com

shonenjump.com

NARUTO

Chibi Sasuke's Sharingan Legend

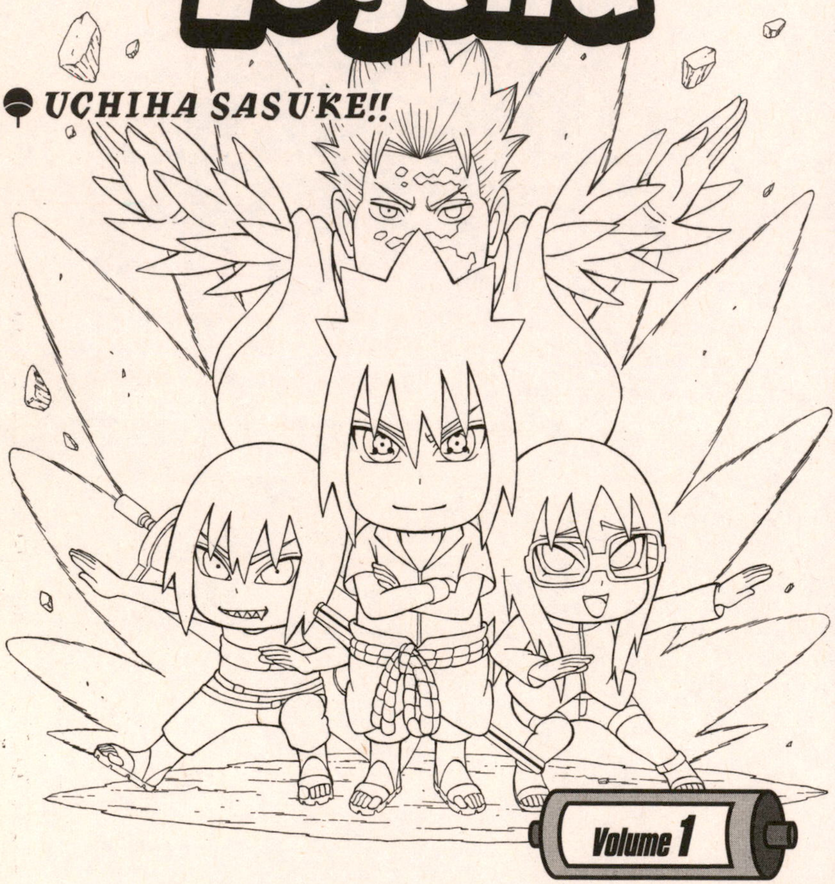
UCHIHA SASUKE!!
Volume 1

Based on Naruto by **Masashi Kishimoto** Story and Art by **Kenji Taira**

CHARACTERS

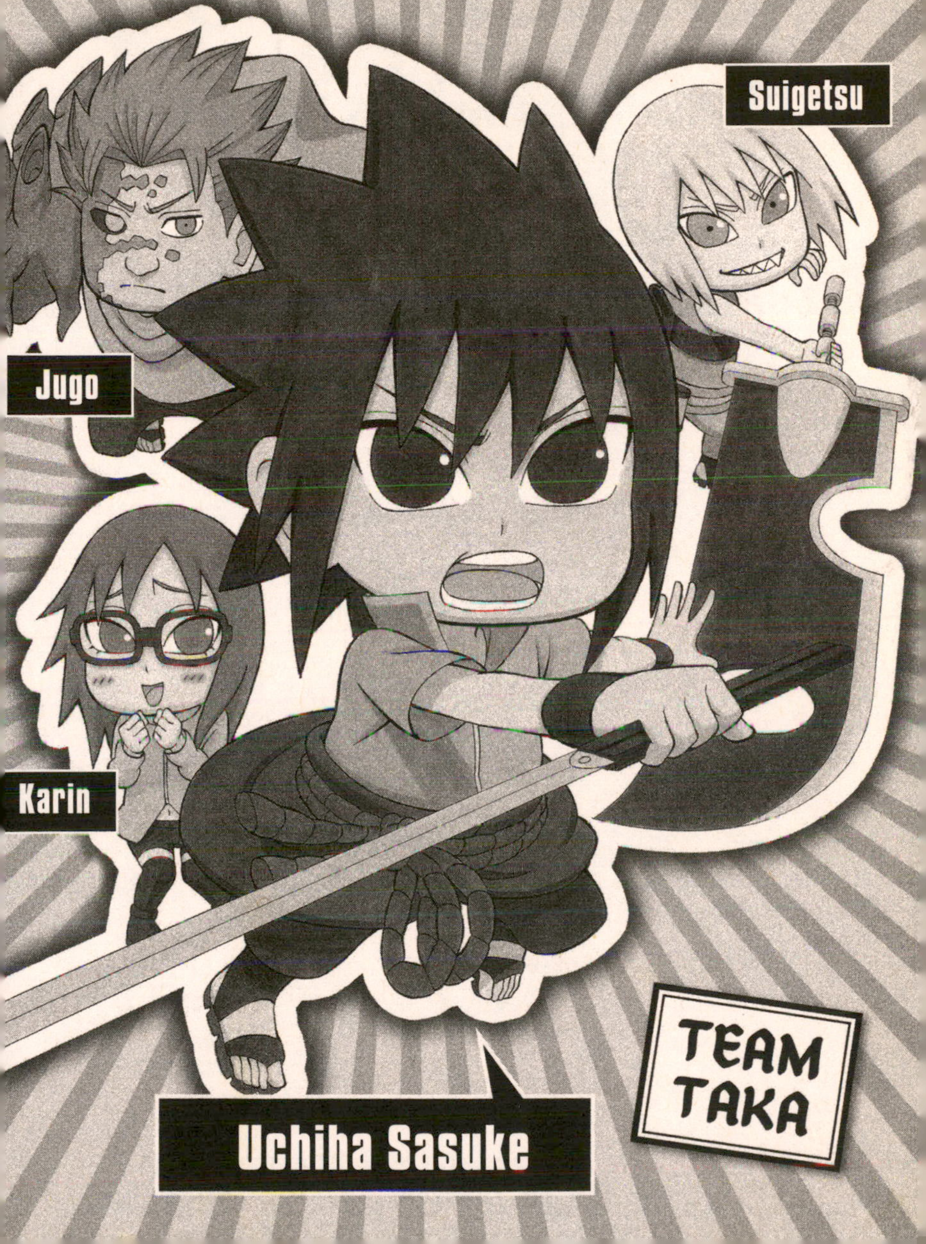

Suigetsu
Jugo
Karin
TEAM TAKA
Uchiha Sasuke

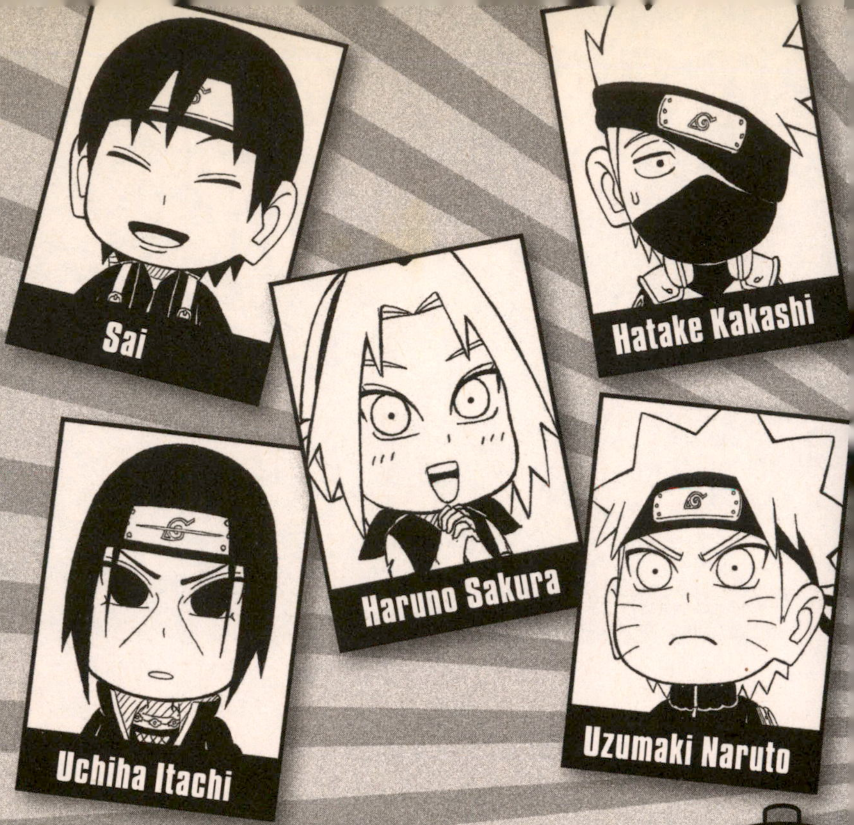
Hatake Kakashi
Sai
Haruno Sakura
Uzumaki Naruto
Uchiha Itachi

OUR STORY

Uchiha Sasuke was once a ninja of Konohagakure Village, until he parted ways with Naruto, Sakura and the others. Now he travels as a rogue shinobi with Suigetsu, Karin and Jugo. Together, they are Team Taka. Sasuke devotes every day to the search for his big brother, Itachi. Will he ever achieve his objective? Either way, Sasuke's long journey is bound to be eventful!

NARUTO Chibi Sasuke's Sharingan Legend

VOL. 1
UCHIHA SASUKE!!

CONTENTS

CHAPTER 1: UCHIHA SASUKE!!

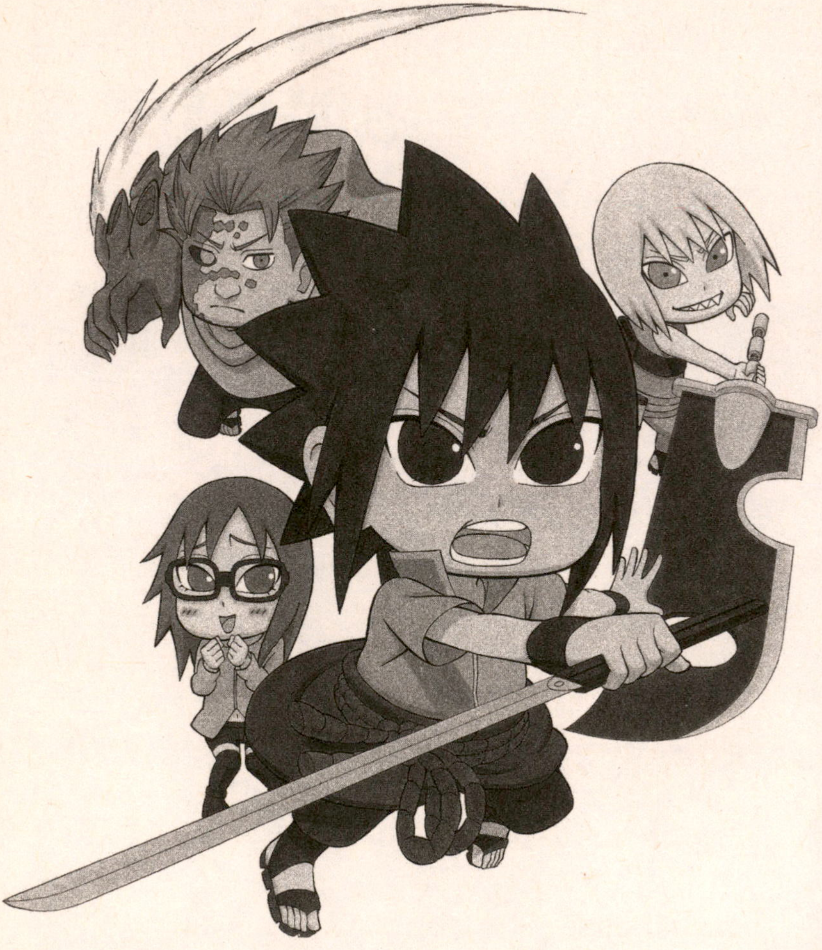

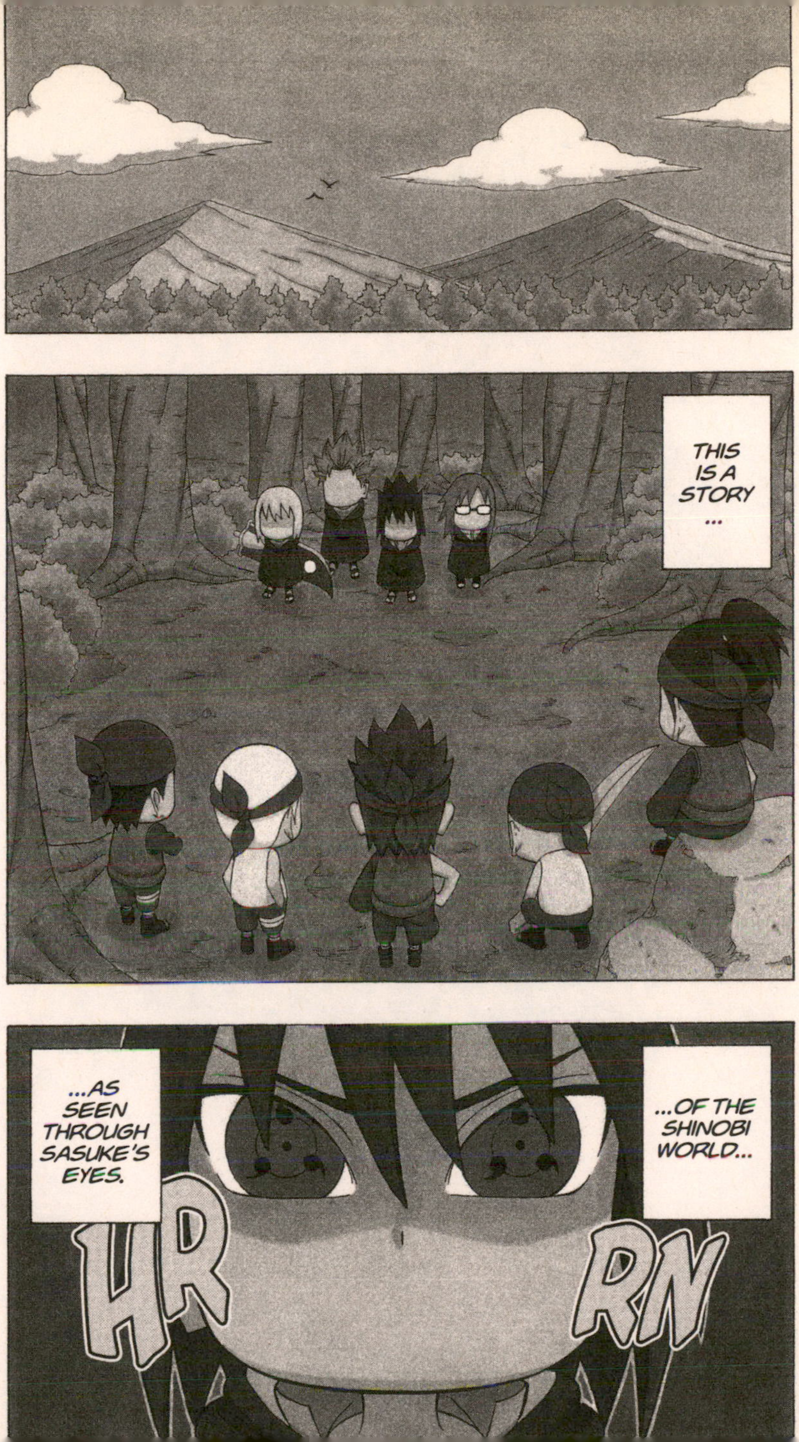
THIS IS A STORY...
...OF THE SHINOBI WORLD...
...AS SEEN THROUGH SASUKE'S EYES.
HRRN

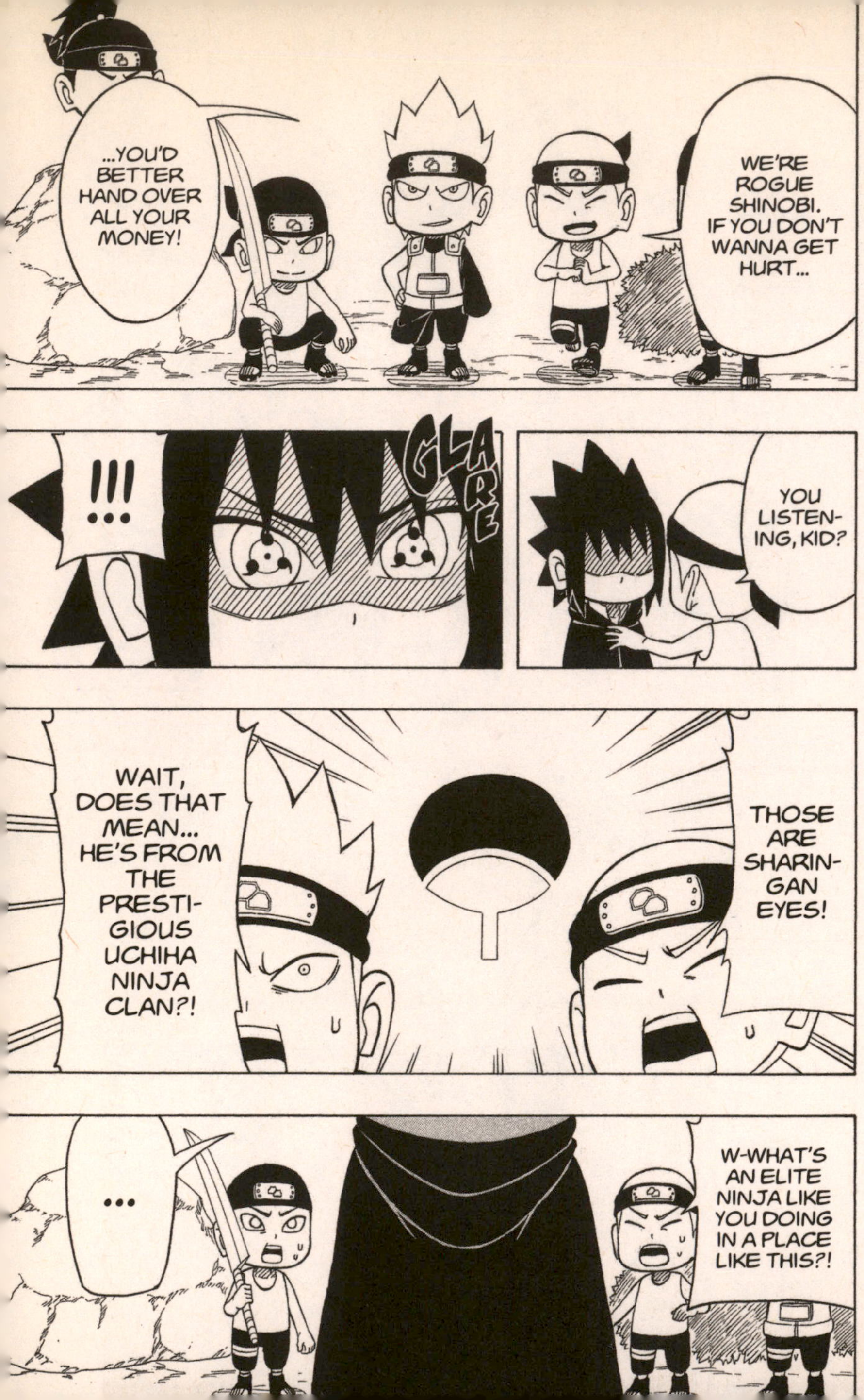
WE'RE ROGUE SHINOBI. IF YOU DON'T WANNA GET HURT...
...YOU'D BETTER HAND OVER ALL YOUR MONEY!
YOU LISTENING, KID?
GLARE
!!! ...
THOSE ARE SHARINGAN EYES!
WAIT, DOES THAT MEAN... HE'S FROM THE PRESTIGIOUS UCHIHA NINJA CLAN?!
W-WHAT'S AN ELITE NINJA LIKE YOU DOING IN A PLACE LIKE THIS?!
...

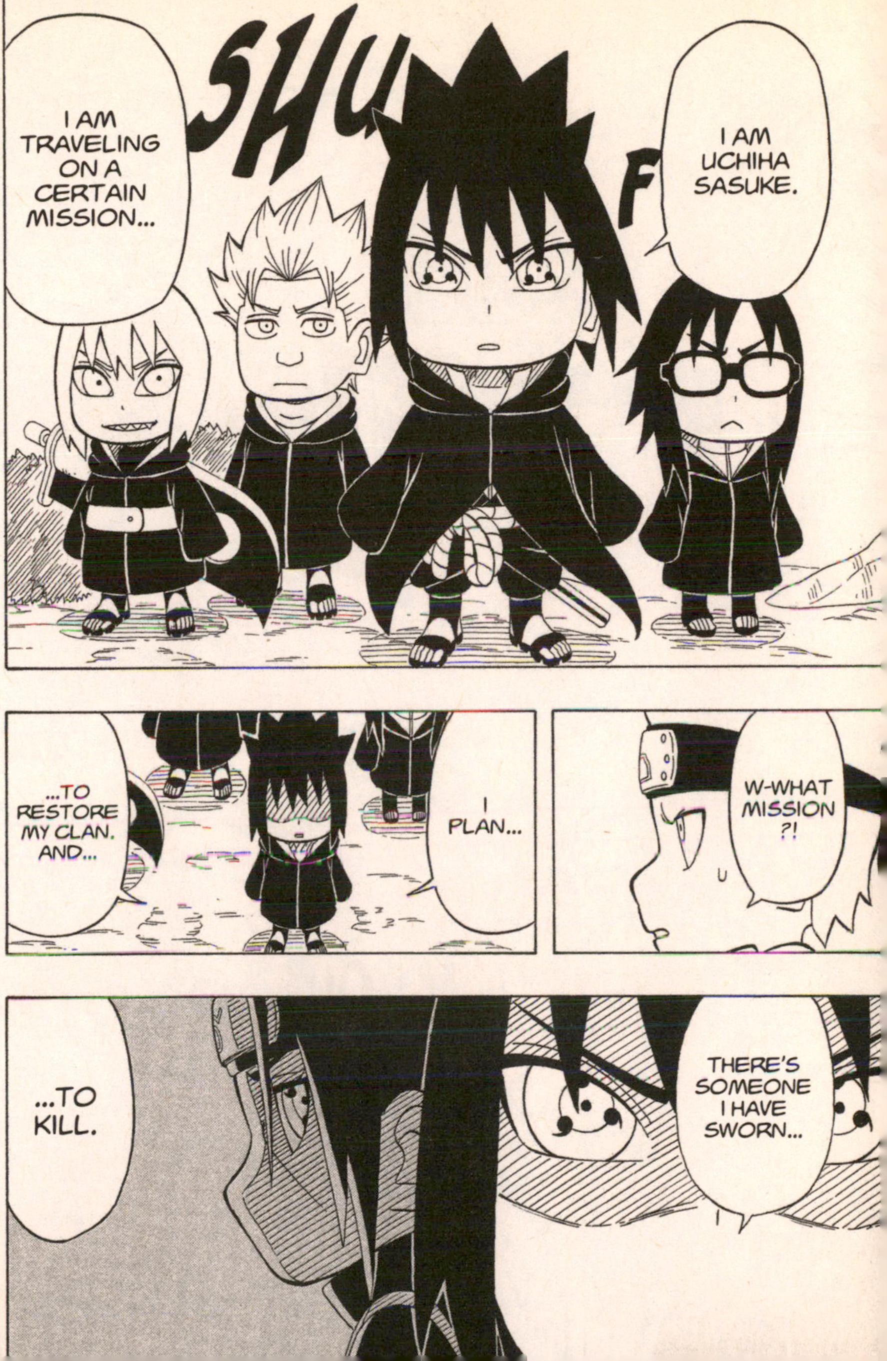
I AM UCHIHA SASUKE.
SHUF
I AM TRAVELING ON A CERTAIN MISSION...
W-WHAT MISSION ?!
I PLAN...
...TO RESTORE MY CLAN. AND...
THERE'S SOMEONE I HAVE SWORN...
...TO KILL.

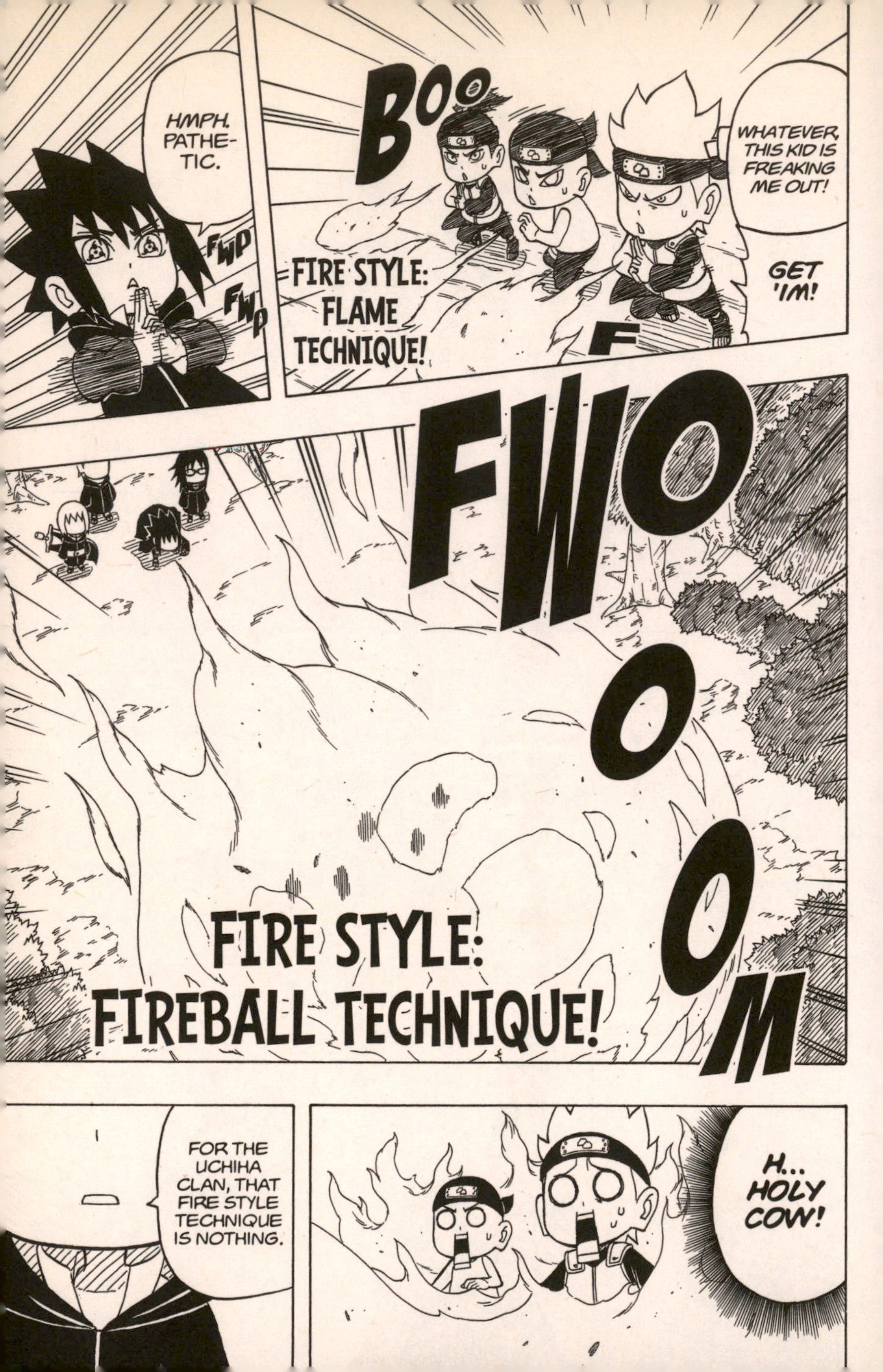
WHATEVER, THIS KID IS FREAKING ME OUT!
GET 'IM!
BOO
FIRE STYLE: FLAME TECHNIQUE!
HMPH. PATHETIC.
FWP
FWP
F
FWOOOOM
FIRE STYLE: FIREBALL TECHNIQUE!
H... HOLY COW!
FOR THE UCHIHA CLAN, THAT FIRE STYLE TECHNIQUE IS NOTHING.

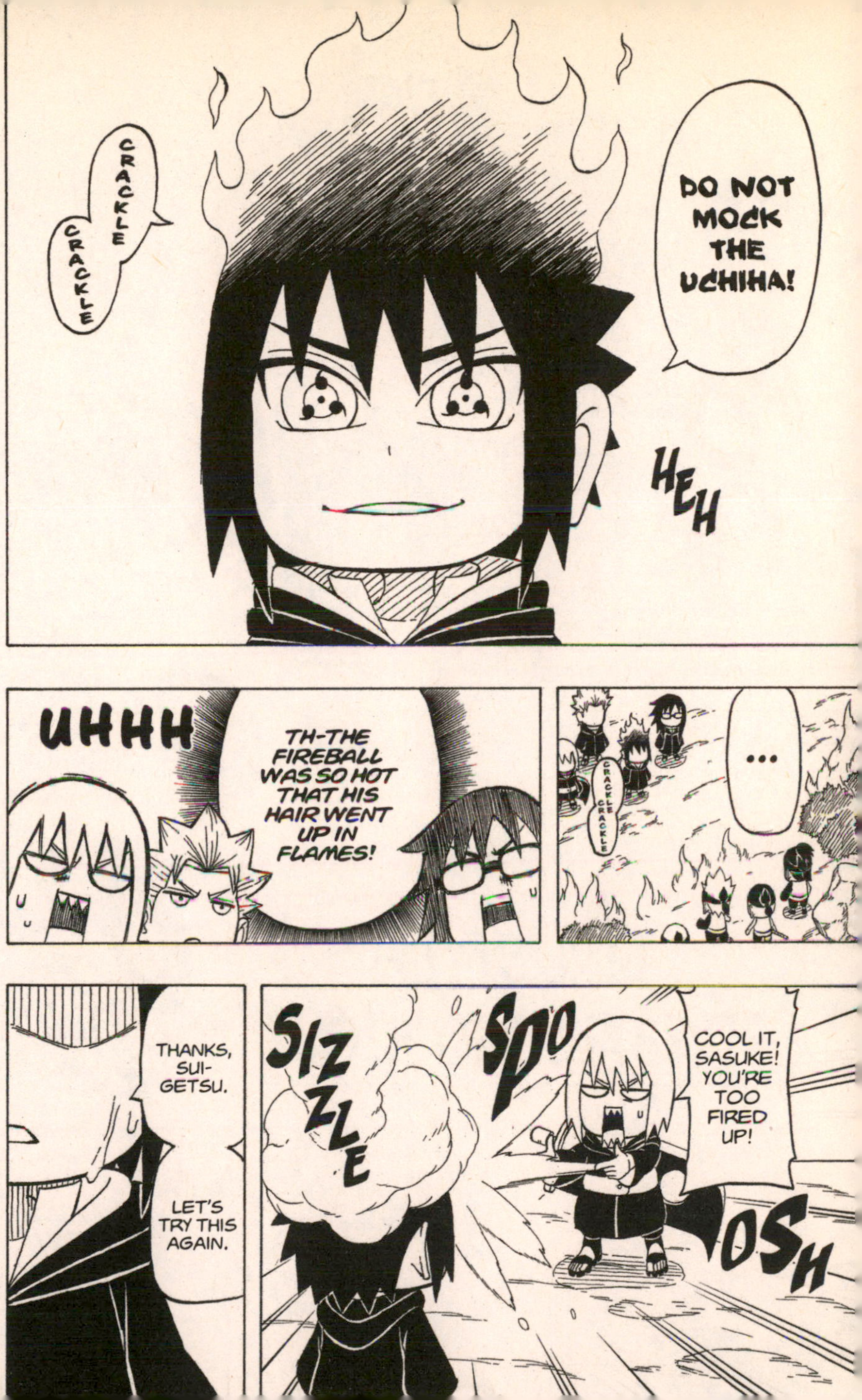
DO NOT MOCK THE UCHIHA!
HEH
CRACKLE CRACKLE
...
CRACKLE CRACKLE
TH-THE FIREBALL WAS SO HOT THAT HIS HAIR WENT UP IN FLAMES!
UHHH
COOL IT, SASUKE! YOU'RE TOO FIRED UP!
SPOOSH
SIZZLE
THANKS, SUIGETSU.
LET'S TRY THIS AGAIN.

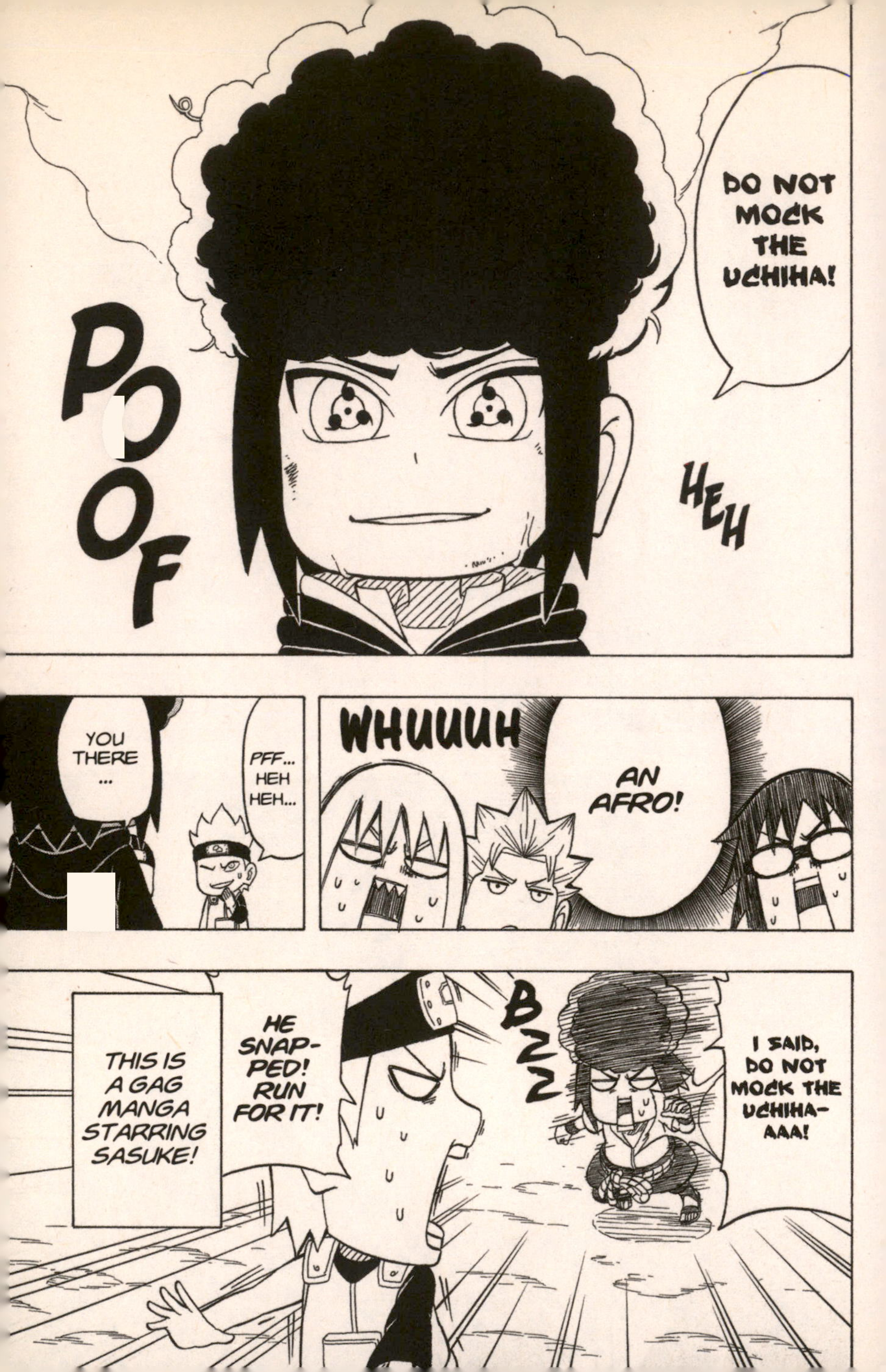
DO NOT MOCK THE UCHIHA!
HEH
POOF
AN AFRO!
WHUUUH
PFF... HEH HEH...
YOU THERE ...
I SAID, DO NOT MOCK THE UCHIHA-AAA!
BZZ
HE SNAP-PED! RUN FOR IT!
THIS IS A GAG MANGA STARRING SASUKE!

REVENGE

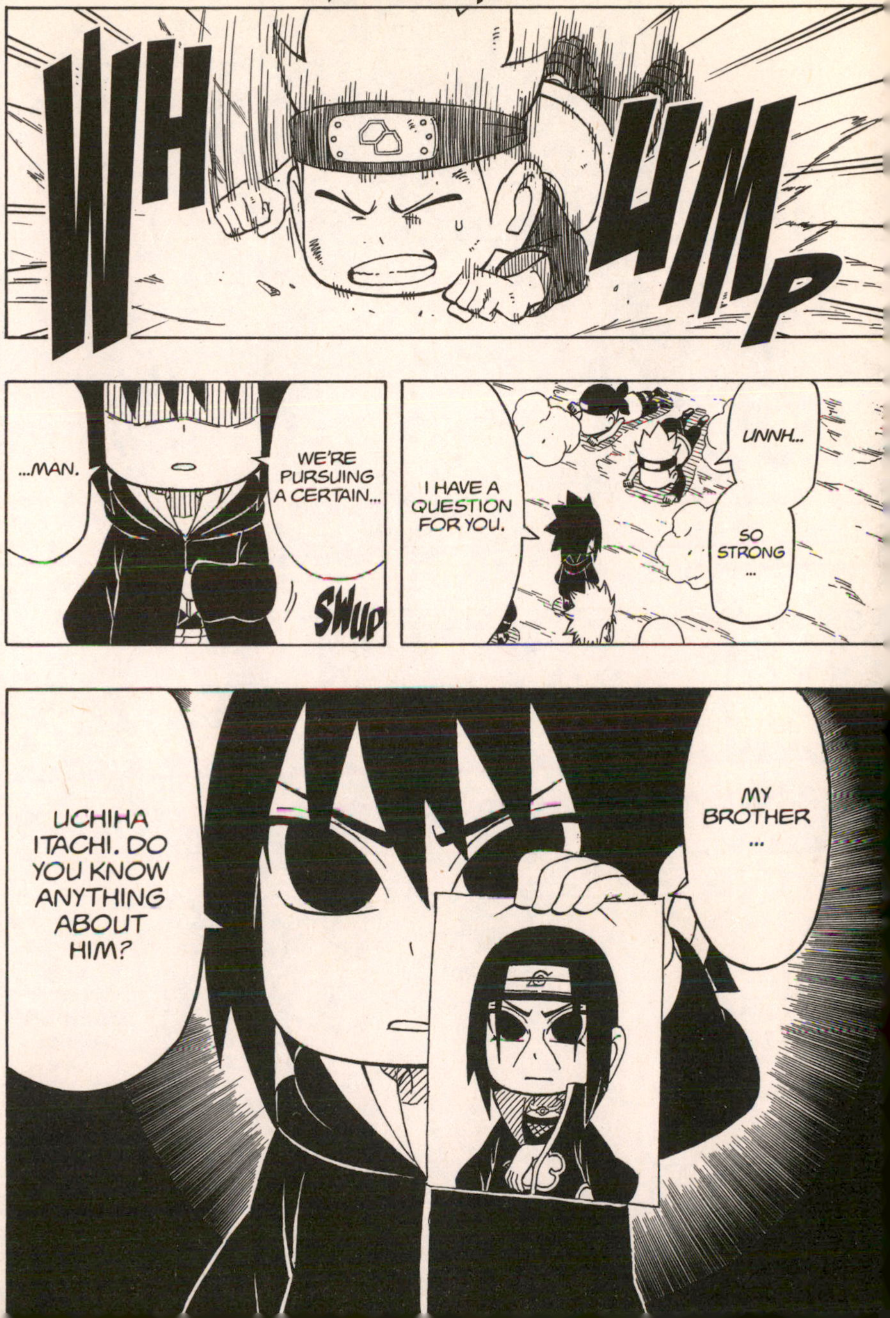
WHUMP
UNNH...
SO STRONG ...
I HAVE A QUESTION FOR YOU.
WE'RE PURSUING A CERTAIN...
...MAN.
SWUP
MY BROTHER ...
UCHIHA ITACHI. DO YOU KNOW ANYTHING ABOUT HIM?

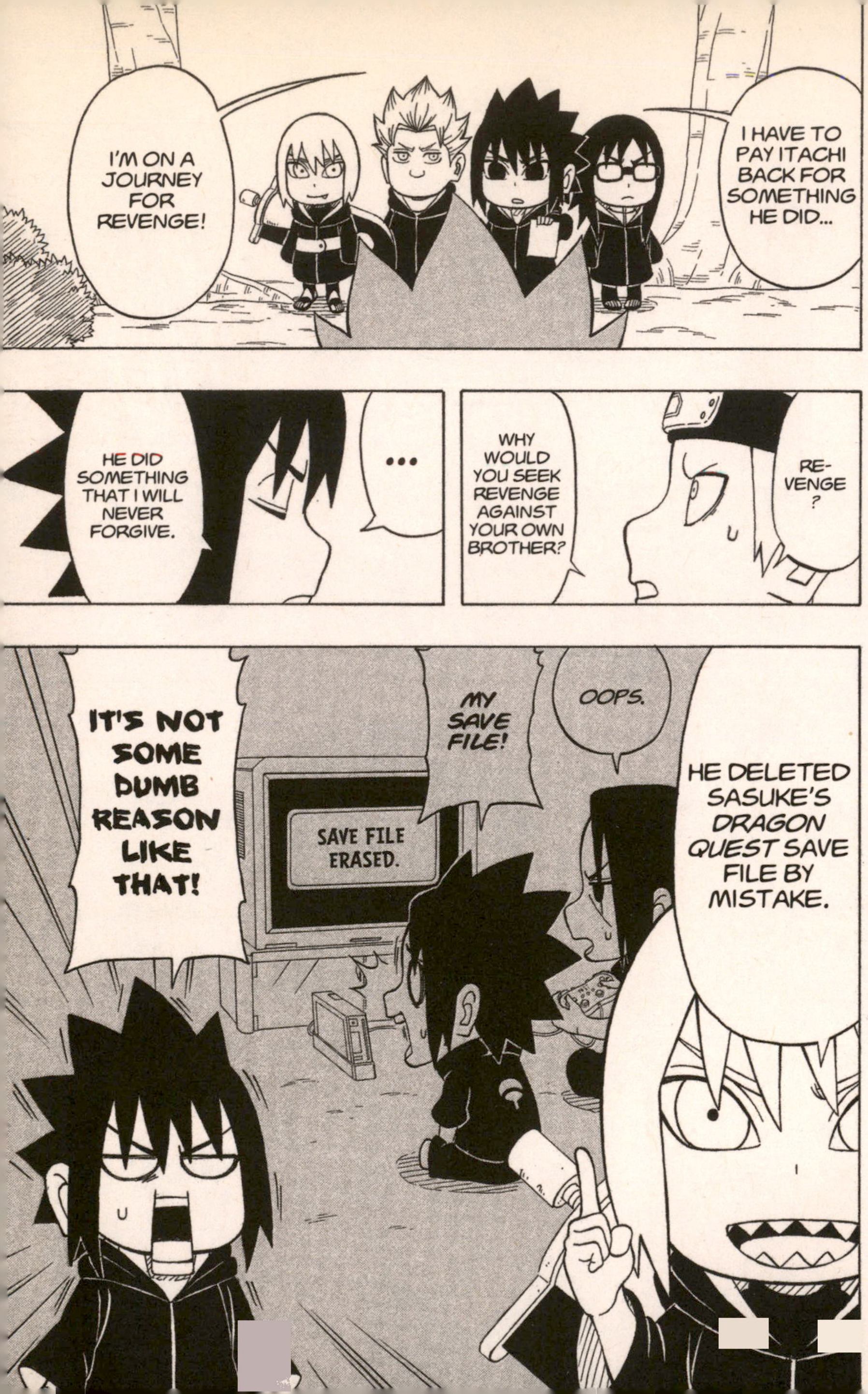
I HAVE TO PAY ITACHI BACK FOR SOMETHING HE DID...
I'M ON A JOURNEY FOR REVENGE!
RE-VENGE?
WHY WOULD YOU SEEK REVENGE AGAINST YOUR OWN BROTHER?
...
HE DID SOMETHING THAT I WILL NEVER FORGIVE.
HE DELETED SASUKE'S *DRAGON QUEST* SAVE FILE BY MISTAKE.
OOPS.
MY SAVE FILE!
SAVE FILE ERASED.
IT'S NOT SOME DUMB REASON LIKE THAT!

TAKA

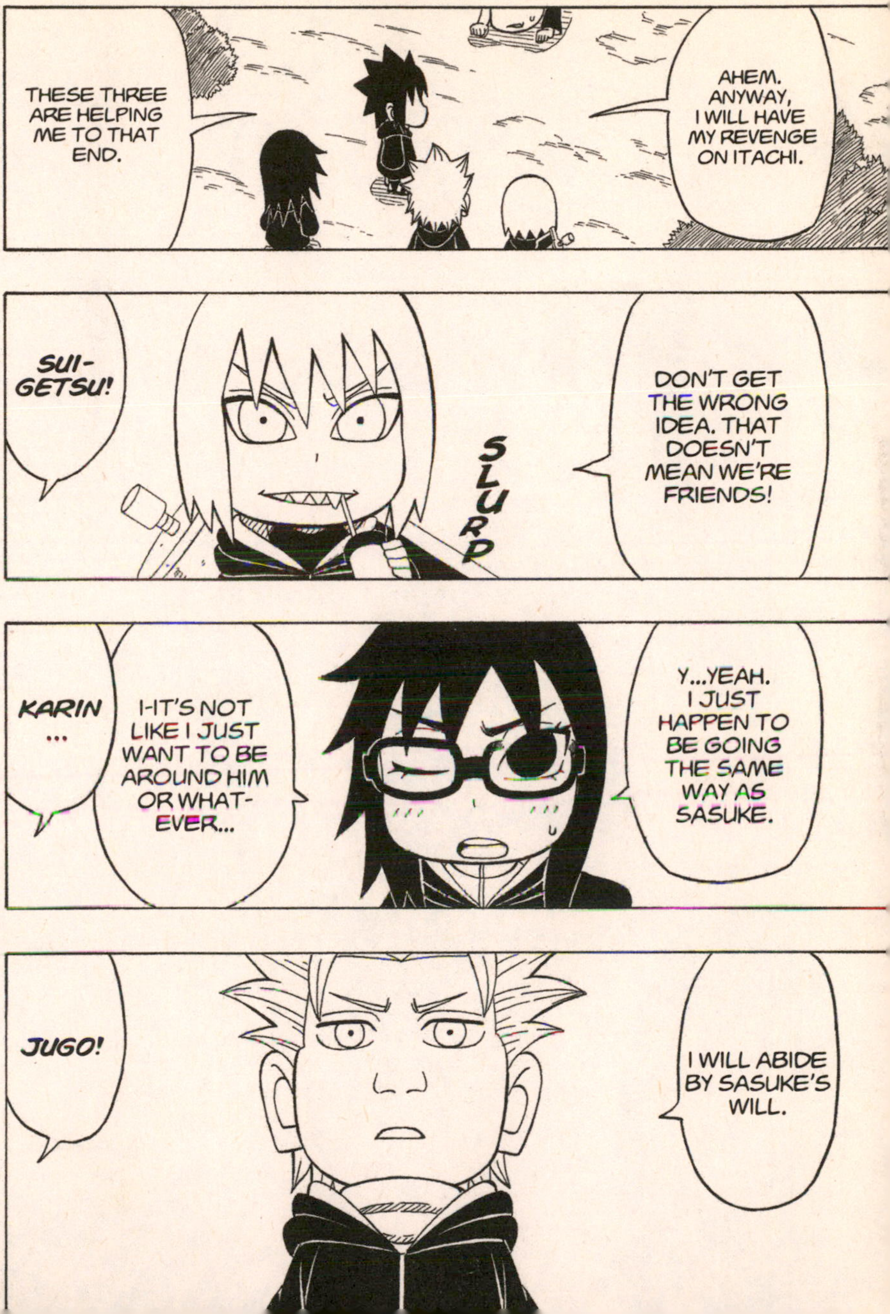

AHEM. ANYWAY, I WILL HAVE MY REVENGE ON ITACHI.
THESE THREE ARE HELPING ME TO THAT END.
DON'T GET THE WRONG IDEA. THAT DOESN'T MEAN WE'RE FRIENDS!
SLURP
SUI-GETSU!
Y...YEAH. I JUST HAPPEN TO BE GOING THE SAME WAY AS SASUKE.
I-IT'S NOT LIKE I JUST WANT TO BE AROUND HIM OR WHAT-EVER...
KARIN...
I WILL ABIDE BY SASUKE'S WILL.
JUGO!

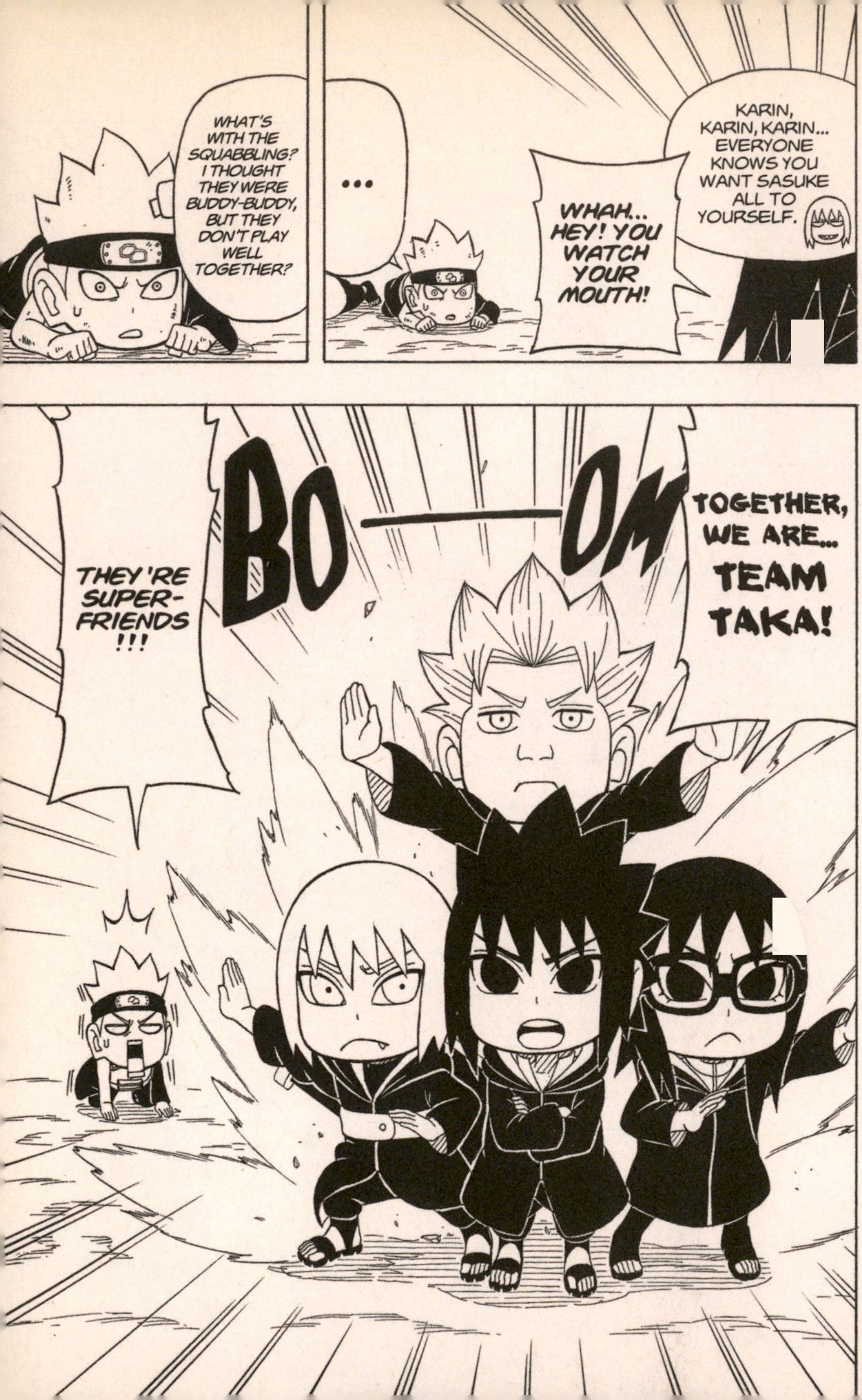
KARIN, KARIN, KARIN... EVERYONE KNOWS YOU WANT SASUKE ALL TO YOURSELF.
WHAH... HEY! YOU WATCH YOUR MOUTH!
...
WHAT'S WITH THE SQUABBLING? I THOUGHT THEY WERE BUDDY-BUDDY, BUT THEY DON'T PLAY WELL TOGETHER?
TOGETHER, WE ARE... TEAM TAKA!
BO—OM
THEY'RE SUPER-FRIENDS!!!

RESTAURANT

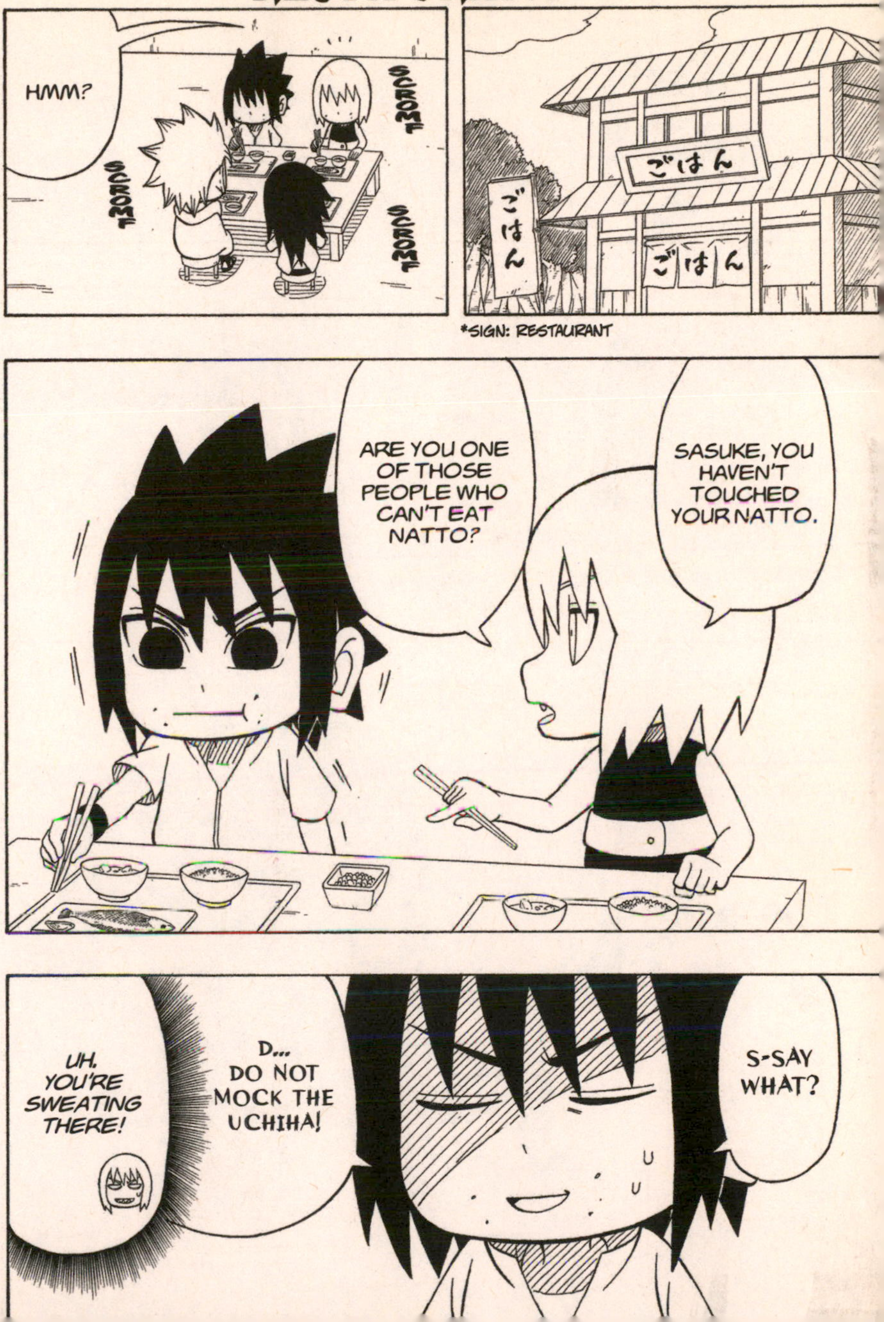
ごはん
ごはん
ごはん
*SIGN: RESTAURANT
HMM?
SCROMF
SCROMF
SCROMF
SASUKE, YOU HAVEN'T TOUCHED YOUR NATTO.
ARE YOU ONE OF THOSE PEOPLE WHO CAN'T EAT NATTO?
S-SAY WHAT?
D... DO NOT MOCK THE UCHIHA!
UH. YOU'RE SWEATING THERE!

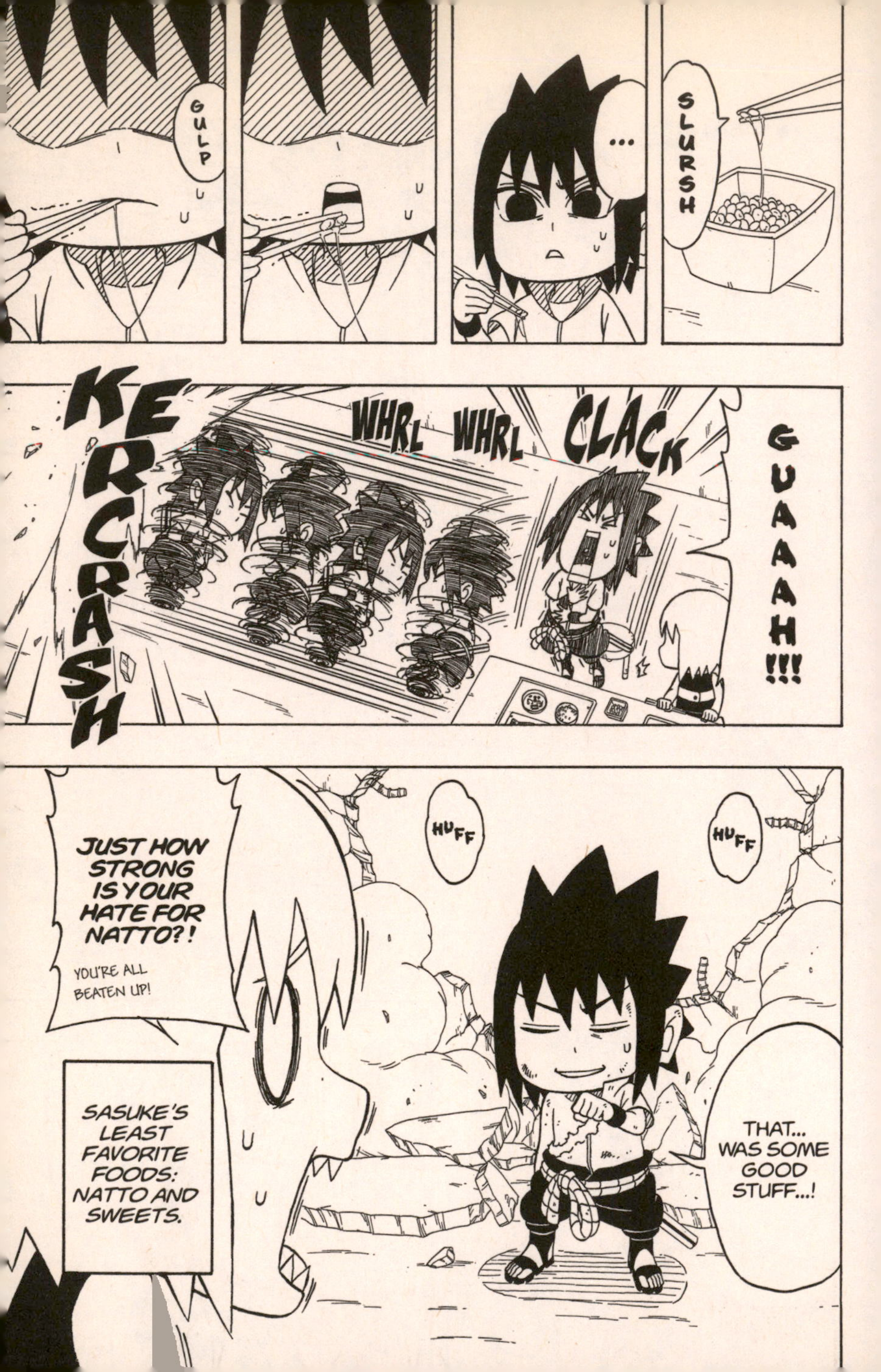
SLURSH
...
GULP
GUAAAAH!!!
CLACK
WHRL WHRL
KERCRASH
THAT... WAS SOME GOOD STUFF...!
HUFF
HUFF
JUST HOW STRONG IS YOUR HATE FOR NATTO?!
YOU'RE ALL BEATEN UP!
SASUKE'S LEAST FAVORITE FOODS: NATTO AND SWEETS.

FIGHT?!

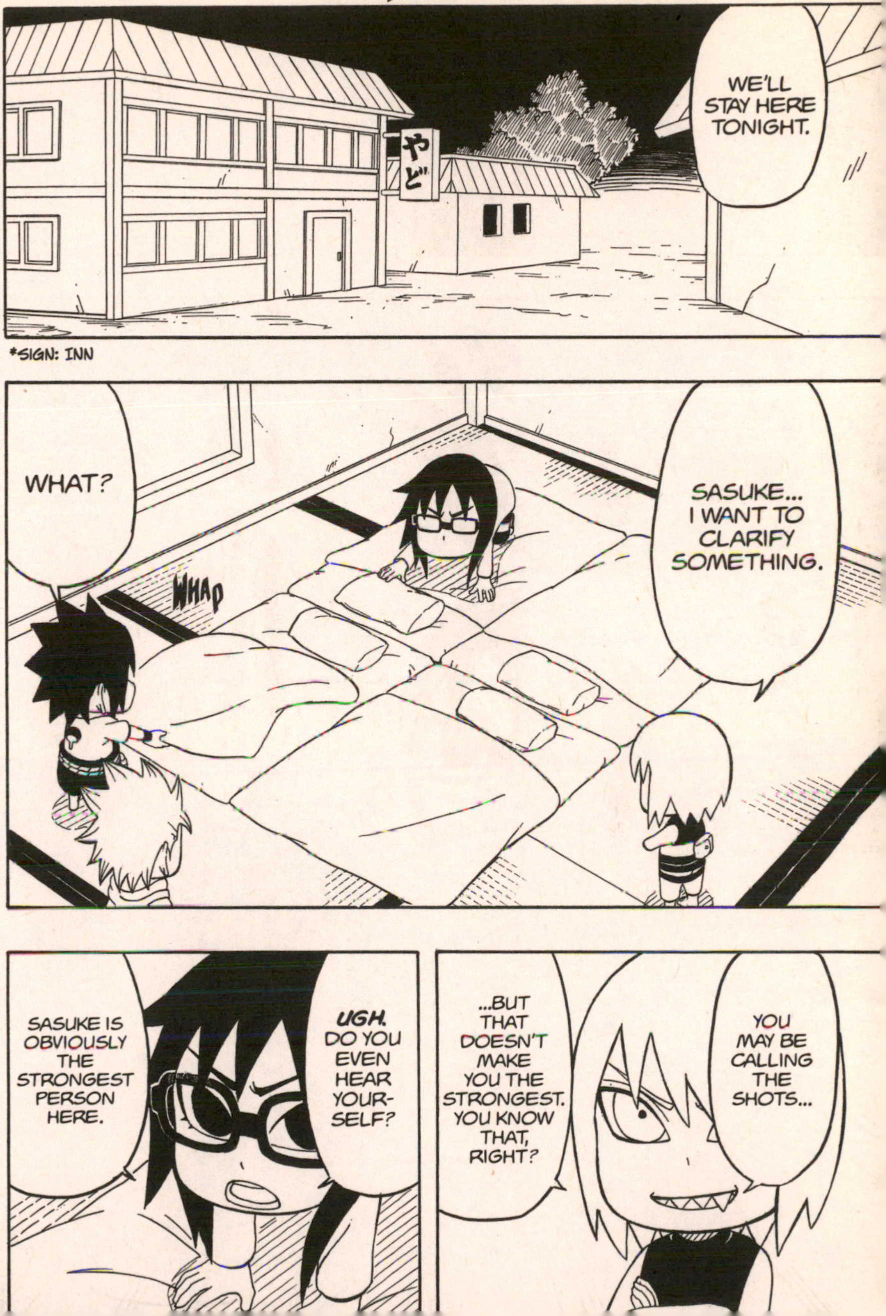
WE'LL STAY HERE TONIGHT.
やど
*SIGN: INN
SASUKE... I WANT TO CLARIFY SOMETHING.
WHAT?
WHAP
YOU MAY BE CALLING THE SHOTS...
...BUT THAT DOESN'T MAKE YOU THE STRONGEST. YOU KNOW THAT, RIGHT?
UGH. DO YOU EVEN HEAR YOUR-SELF?
SASUKE IS OBVIOUSLY THE STRONGEST PERSON HERE.

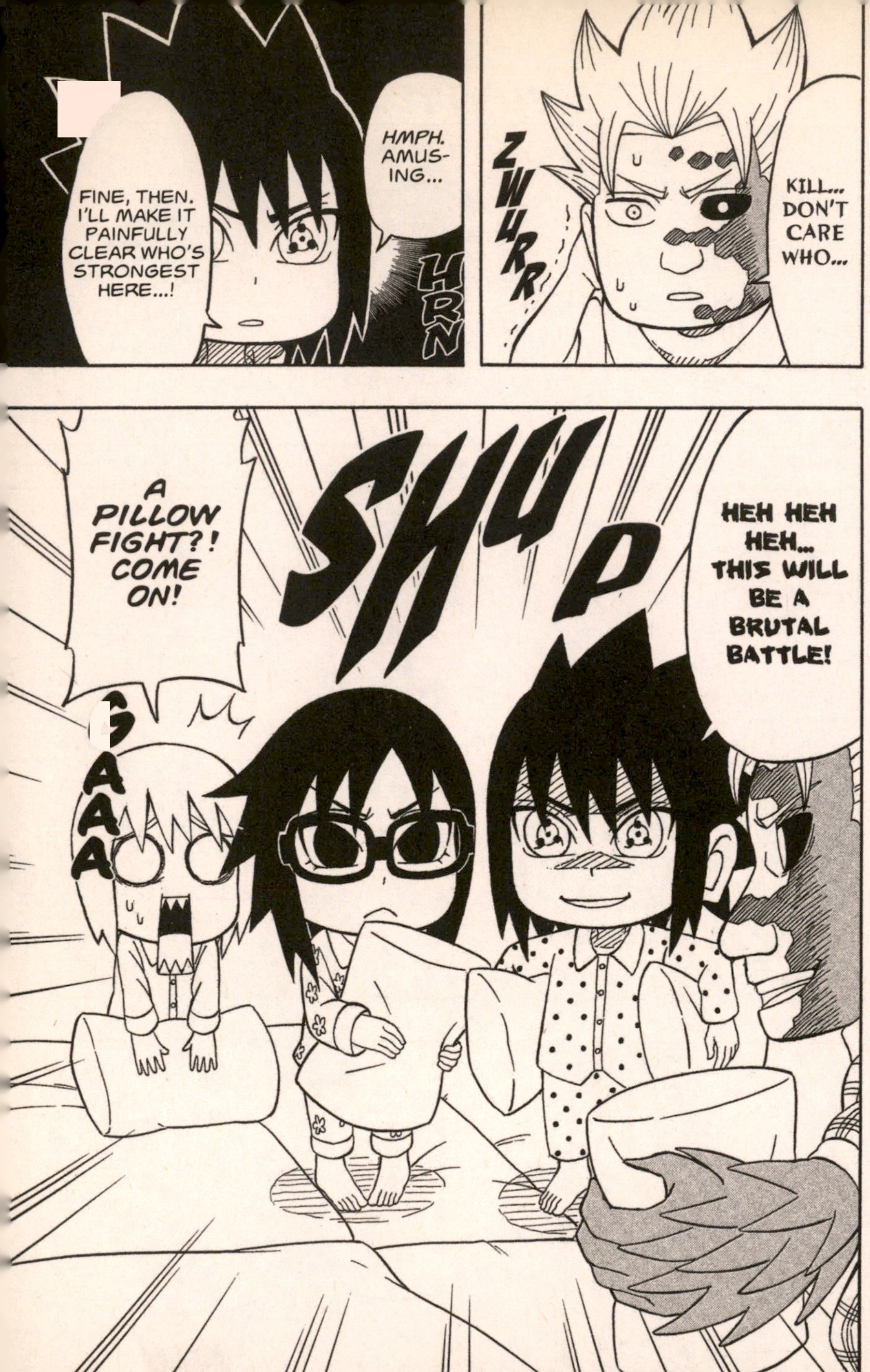
KILL... DON'T CARE WHO...
ZWURR
HMPH. AMUS-ING...
FINE, THEN. I'LL MAKE IT PAINFULLY CLEAR WHO'S STRONGEST HERE...!
HRN
HEH HEH HEH... THIS WILL BE A BRUTAL BATTLE!
SHUD
A PILLOW FIGHT?! COME ON!
GAAAA

PILLOW FIGHT!!

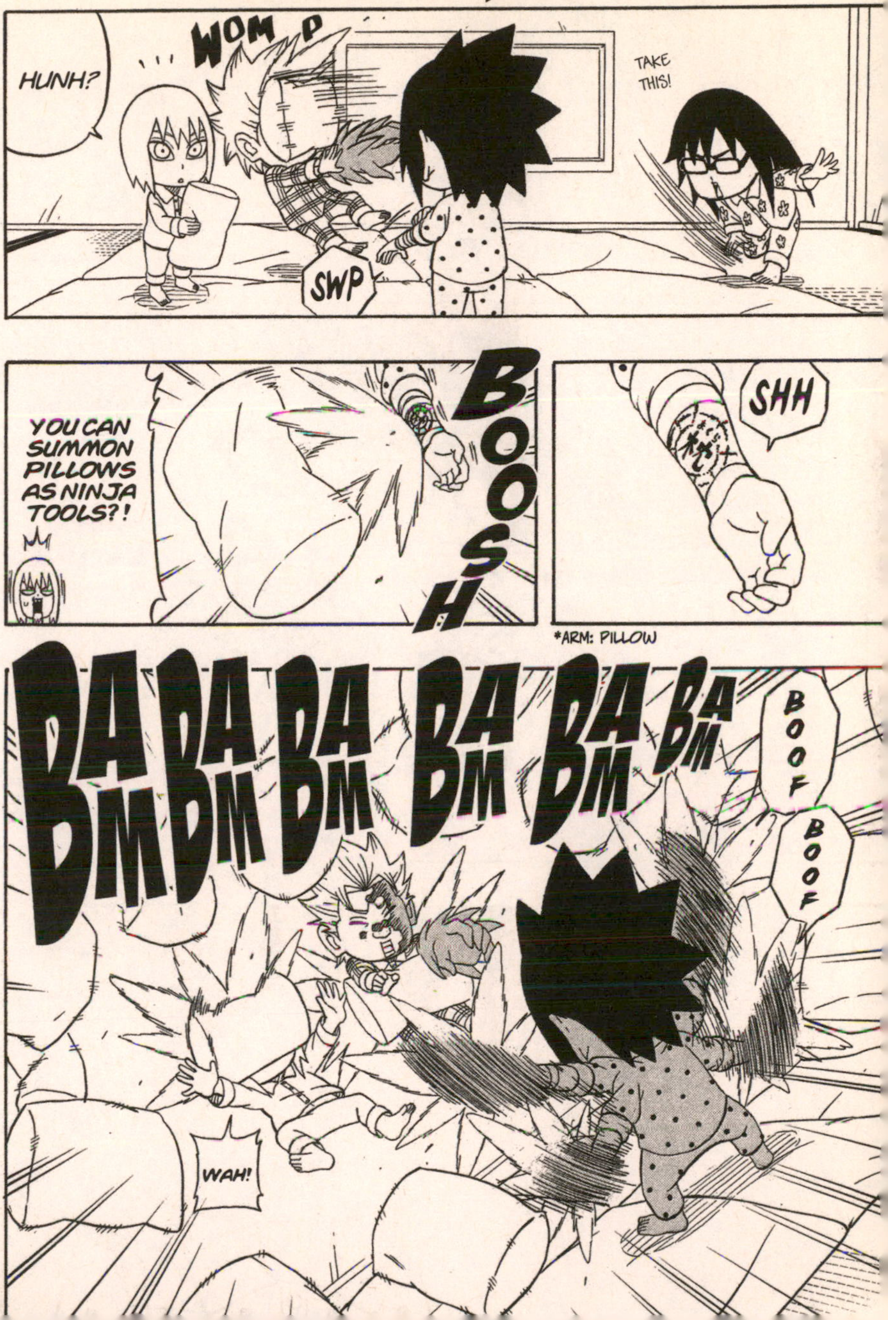
TAKE THIS!
WOMP
SWP
...
HUNH?
SHH
*ARM: PILLOW
BOOOSH
YOU CAN SUMMON PILLOWS AS NINJA TOOLS?!
BOOF
BOOF
BABAM BABAM BABAM BABAM BABAM BABAM
WAH!

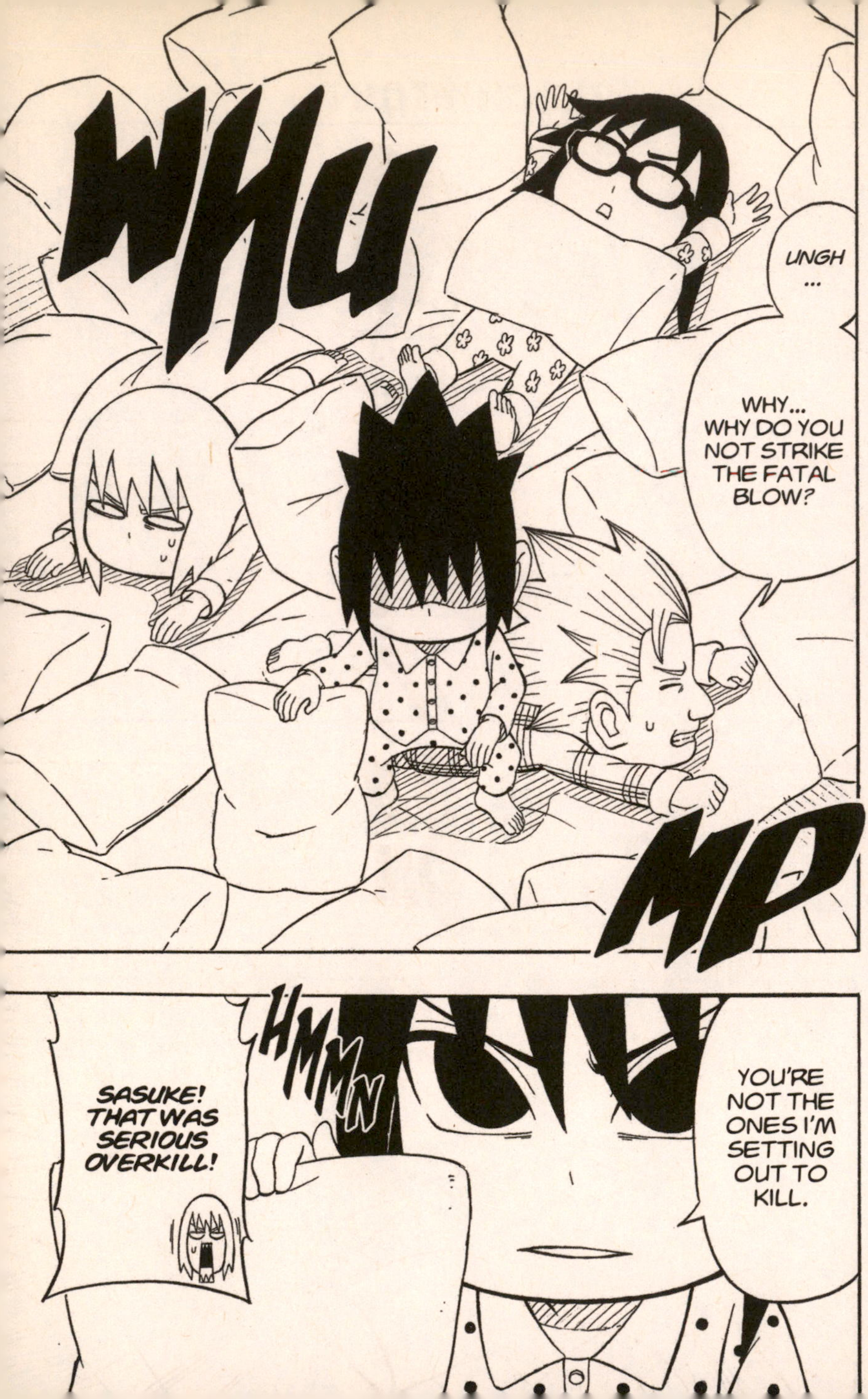
UNGH ...
WHY... WHY DO YOU NOT STRIKE THE FATAL BLOW?
WHU
MP
YOU'RE NOT THE ONES I'M SETTING OUT TO KILL.
HMMMN
SASUKE! THAT WAS SERIOUS OVERKILL!

FORMATION

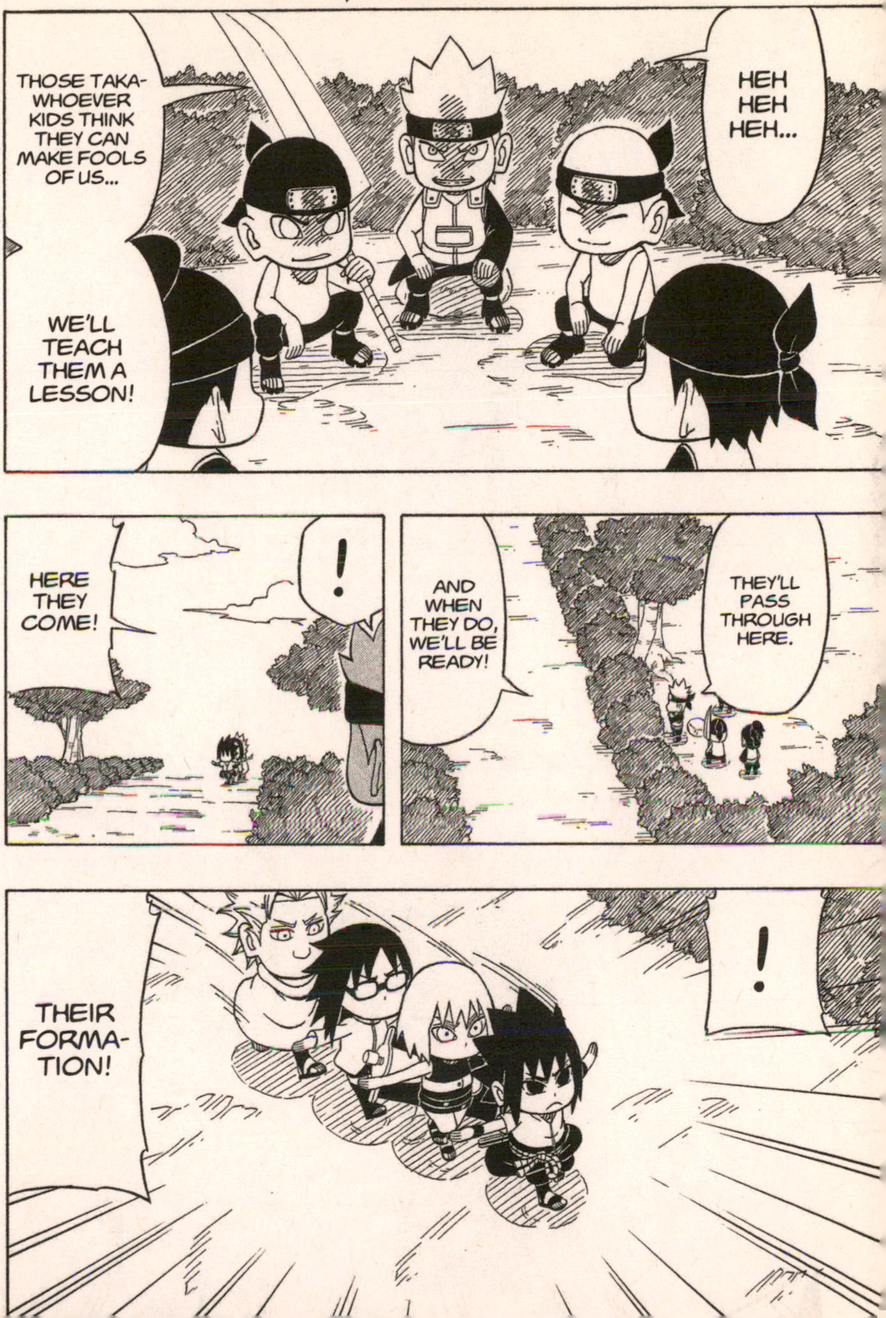
HEH HEH HEH...
THOSE TAKA-WHOEVER KIDS THINK THEY CAN MAKE FOOLS OF US...
WE'LL TEACH THEM A LESSON!
THEY'LL PASS THROUGH HERE.
AND WHEN THEY DO, WE'LL BE READY!
!
HERE THEY COME!
!
THEIR FORMATION!

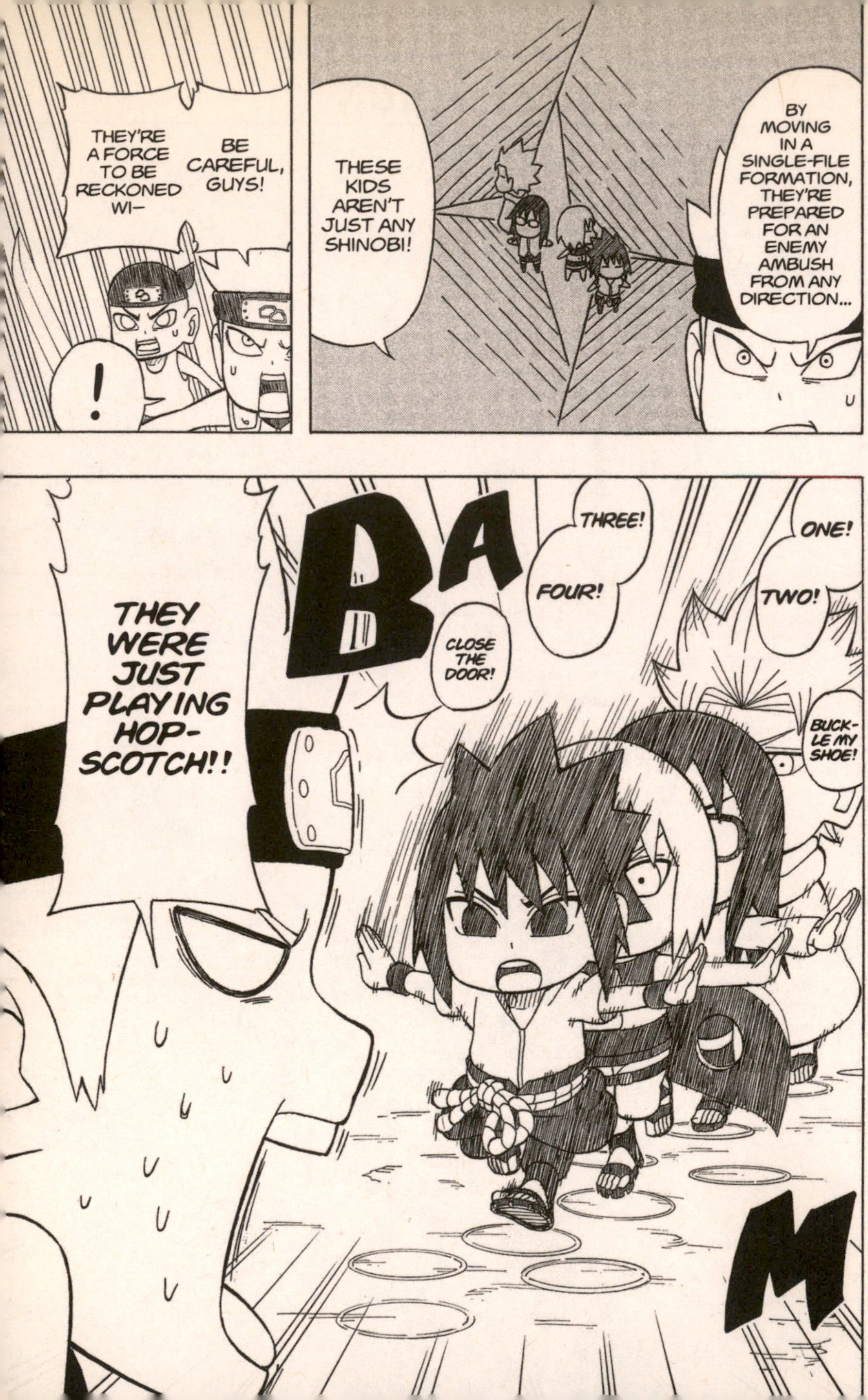
BY MOVING IN A SINGLE-FILE FORMATION, THEY'RE PREPARED FOR AN ENEMY AMBUSH FROM ANY DIRECTION...
THESE KIDS AREN'T JUST ANY SHINOBI!
BE CAREFUL, GUYS!
THEY'RE A FORCE TO BE RECKONED WI–
!
ONE!
TWO!
THREE!
FOUR!
BUCK-LE MY SHOE!
CLOSE THE DOOR!
BA
M
THEY WERE JUST PLAYING HOP-SCOTCH!!

SHARINGAN

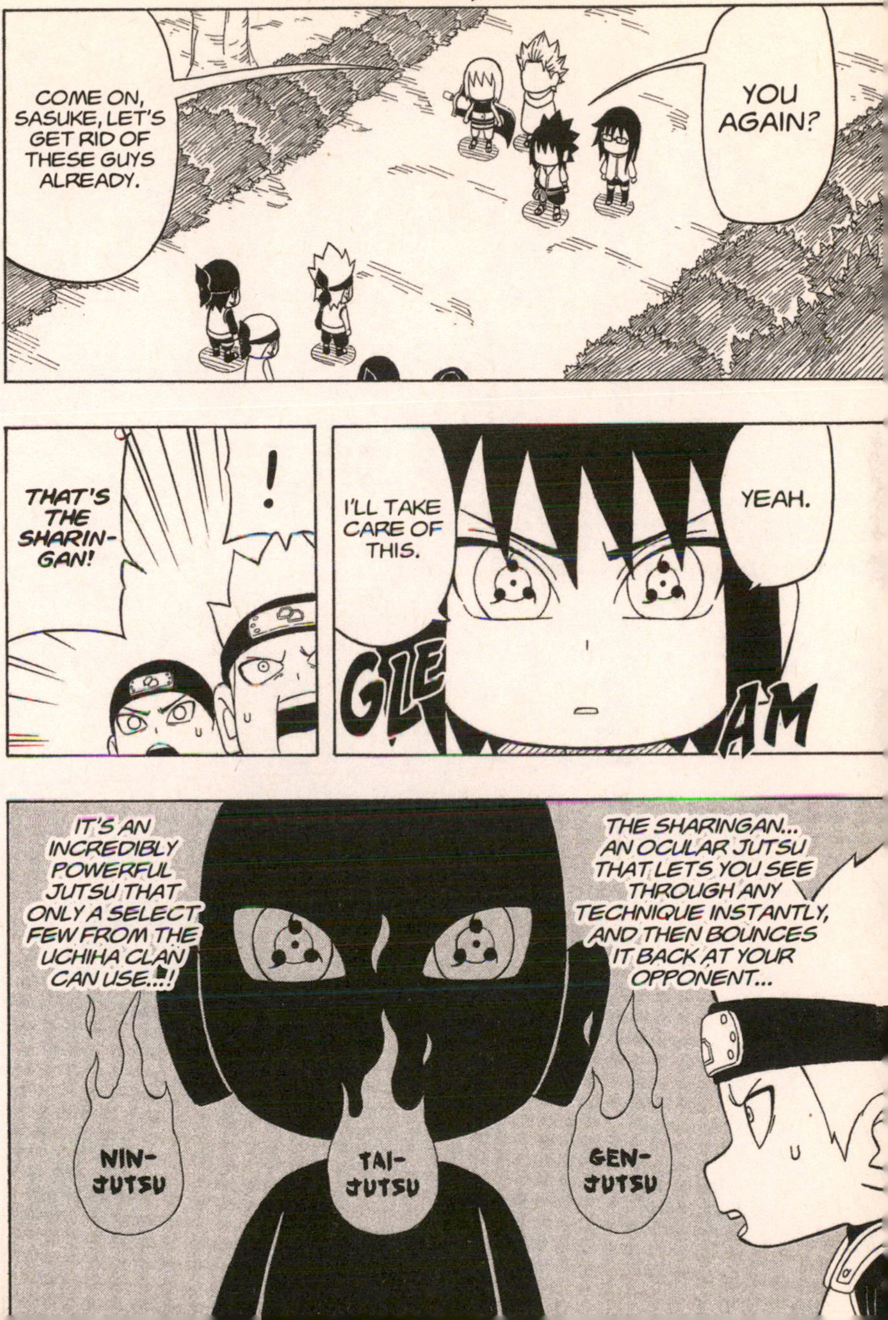
YOU AGAIN?
COME ON, SASUKE, LET'S GET RID OF THESE GUYS ALREADY.
YEAH.
I'LL TAKE CARE OF THIS.
GLEAM
!
THAT'S THE SHARIN-GAN!
THE SHARINGAN... AN OCULAR JUTSU THAT LETS YOU SEE THROUGH ANY TECHNIQUE INSTANTLY, AND THEN BOUNCES IT BACK AT YOUR OPPONENT...
IT'S AN INCREDIBLY POWERFUL JUTSU THAT ONLY A SELECT FEW FROM THE UCHIHA CLAN CAN USE...!
GEN-JUTSU
TAI-JUTSU
NIN-JUTSU

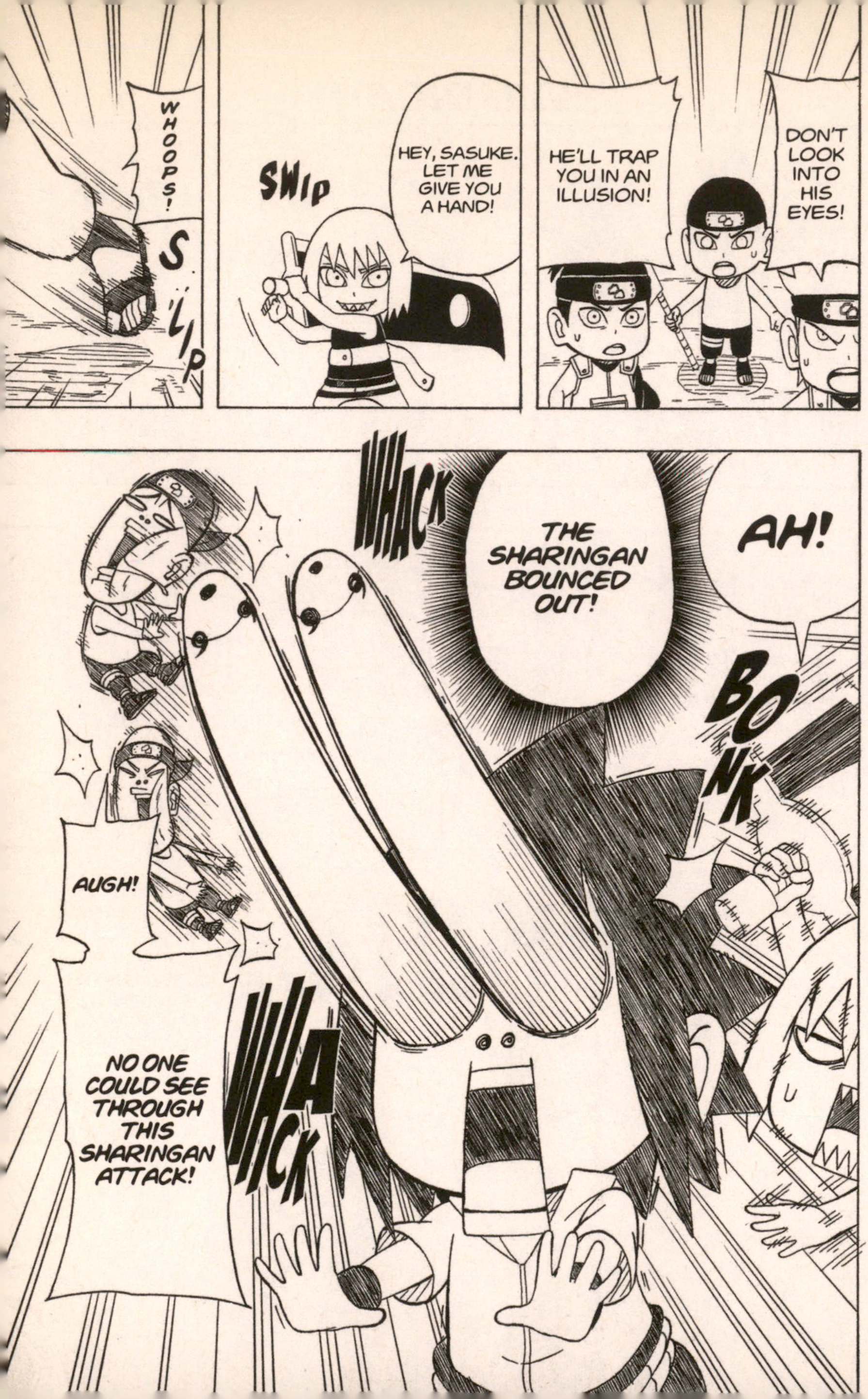
DON'T LOOK INTO HIS EYES!
HE'LL TRAP YOU IN AN ILLUSION!
HEY, SASUKE. LET ME GIVE YOU A HAND!
SWIP
WHOOPS!
SLIP
AH!
BONK
THE SHARINGAN BOUNCED OUT!
WHACK
AUGH!
NO ONE COULD SEE THROUGH THIS SHARINGAN ATTACK!
WHACK

MIRRORING

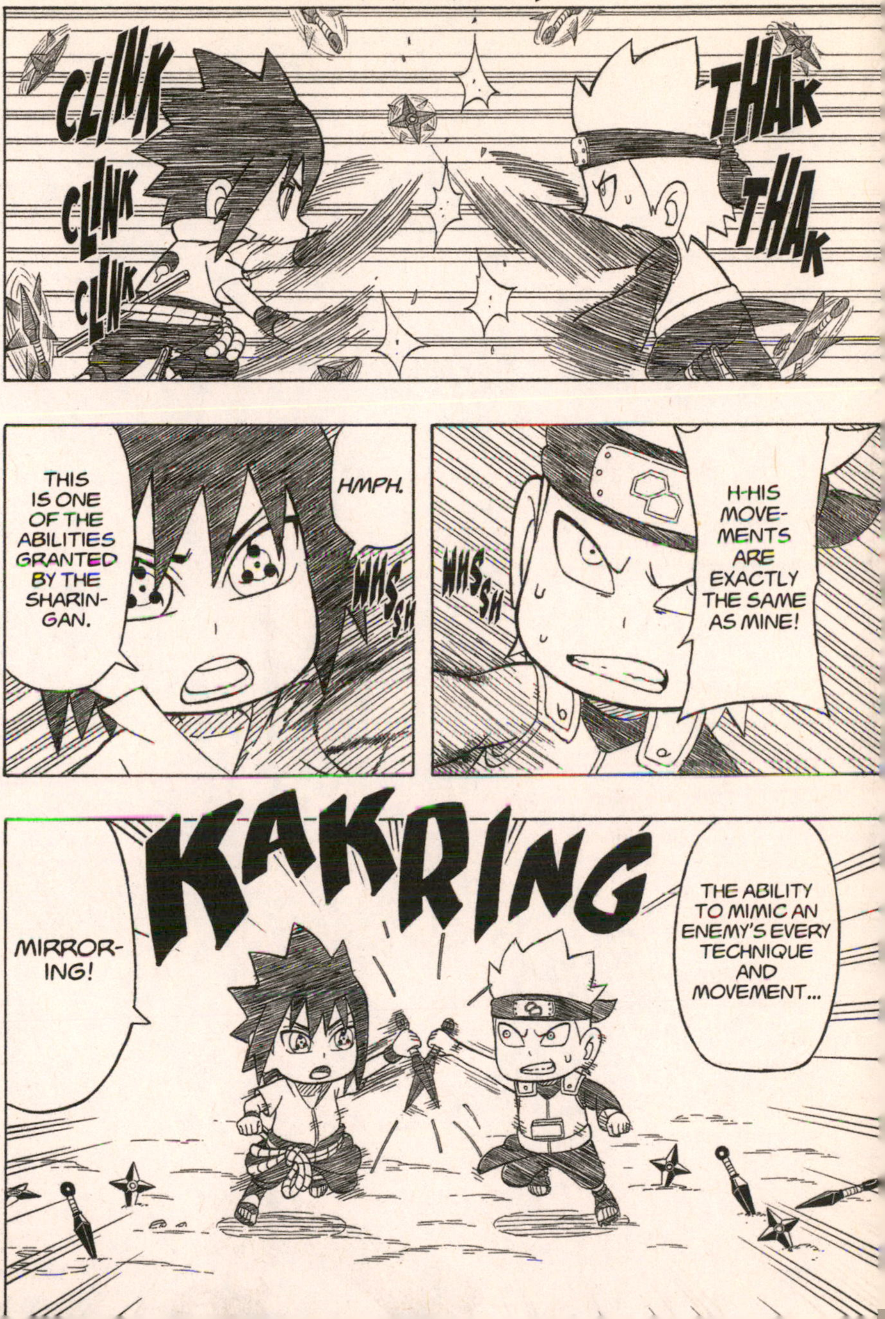
THAK THAK
CLINK CLINK CLINK
WHSSH
H-HIS MOVEMENTS ARE EXACTLY THE SAME AS MINE!
HMPH.
THIS IS ONE OF THE ABILITIES GRANTED BY THE SHARINGAN.
WHSSH
THE ABILITY TO MIMIC AN ENEMY'S EVERY TECHNIQUE AND MOVEMENT...
KAKRING
MIRRORING!

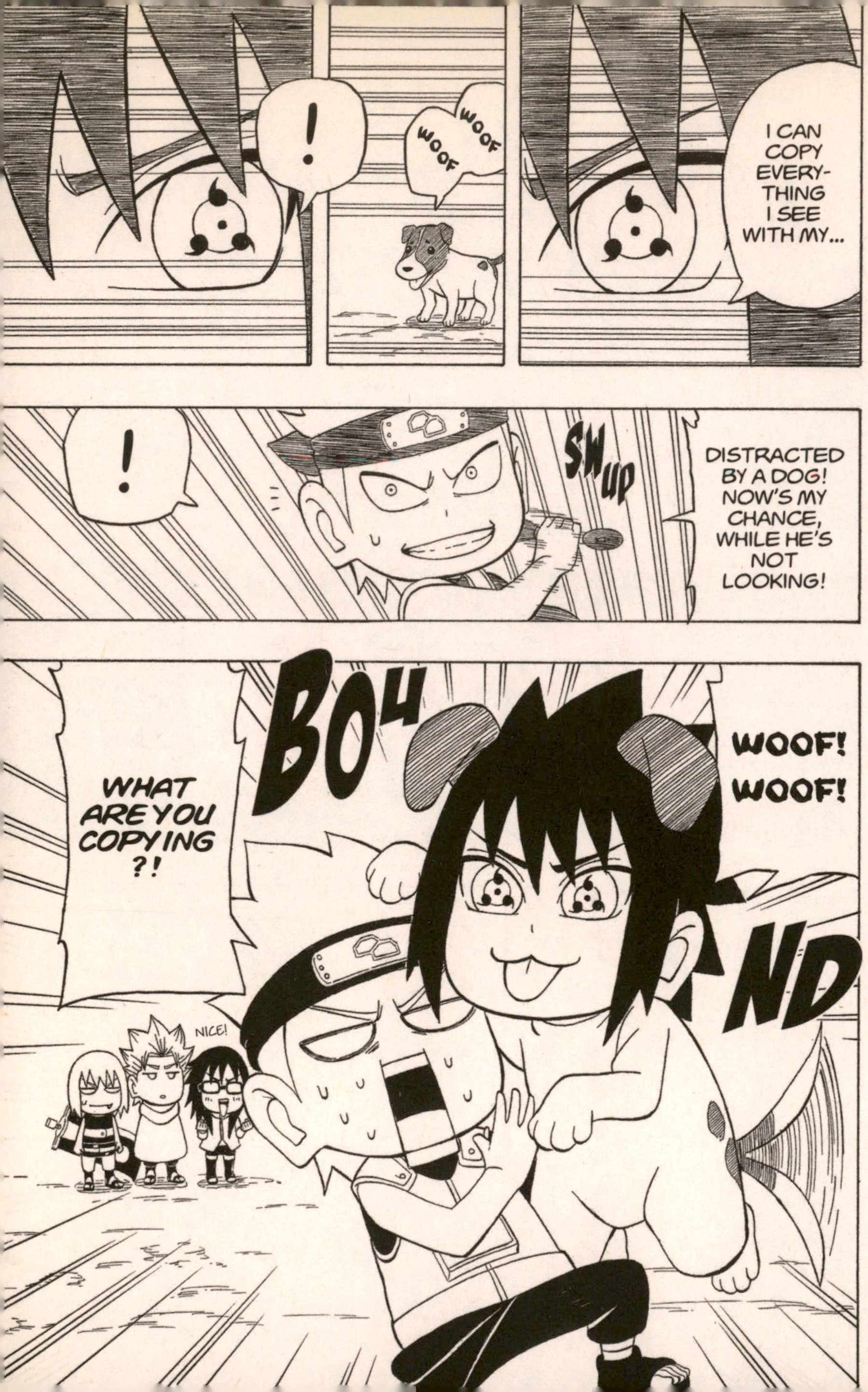
I CAN COPY EVERY-THING I SEE WITH MY...
WOOF WOOF
!
DISTRACTED BY A DOG! NOW'S MY CHANCE, WHILE HE'S NOT LOOKING!
SWUP
!
WOOF! WOOF!
BOUND
WHAT ARE YOU COPYING?!
NICE!

GENJUTSU

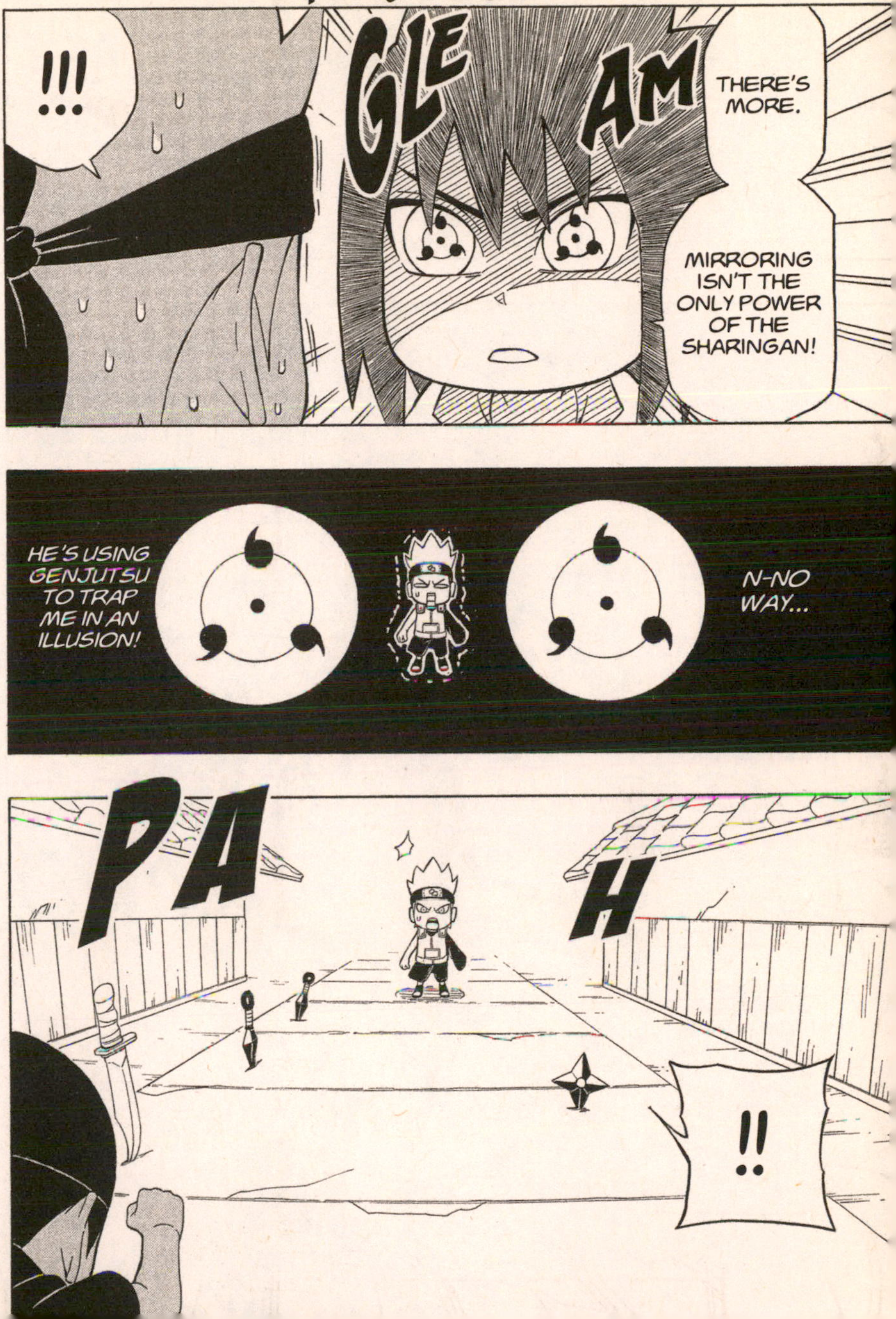
THERE'S MORE.
MIRRORING ISN'T THE ONLY POWER OF THE SHARINGAN!
GLEAM
!!!...
N-NO WAY...
HE'S USING GENJUTSU TO TRAP ME IN AN ILLUSION!
PAH
!!..

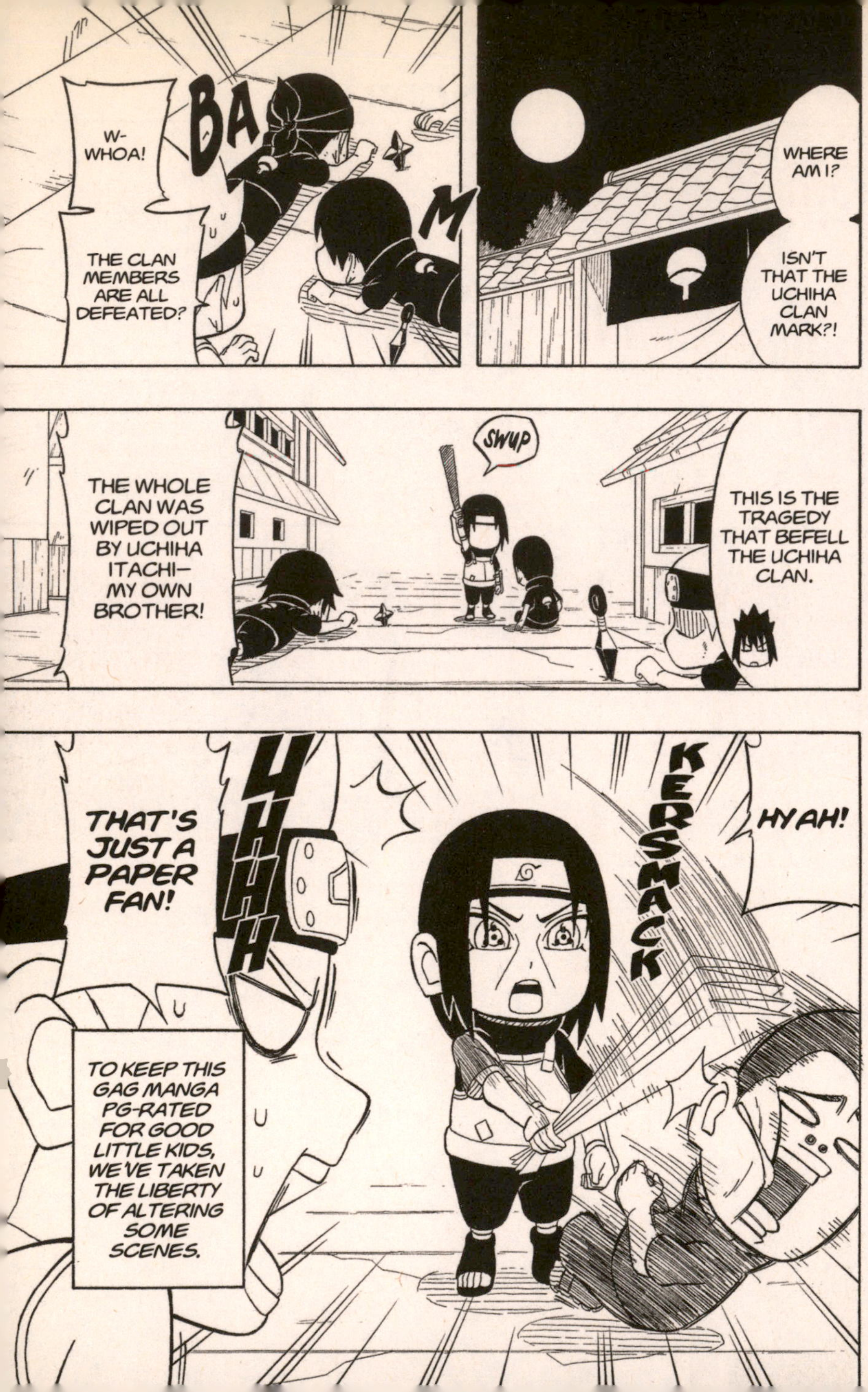
WHERE AM I?
ISN'T THAT THE UCHIHA CLAN MARK?!
BAM
W-WHOA!
THE CLAN MEMBERS ARE ALL DEFEATED?
THIS IS THE TRAGEDY THAT BEFELL THE UCHIHA CLAN.
SWUP
THE WHOLE CLAN WAS WIPED OUT BY UCHIHA ITACHI—MY OWN BROTHER!
HYAH!
KERSMACK
THAT'S JUST A PAPER FAN!
UHHHH
TO KEEP THIS GAG MANGA PG-RATED FOR GOOD LITTLE KIDS, WE'VE TAKEN THE LIBERTY OF ALTERING SOME SCENES.

AVENGER

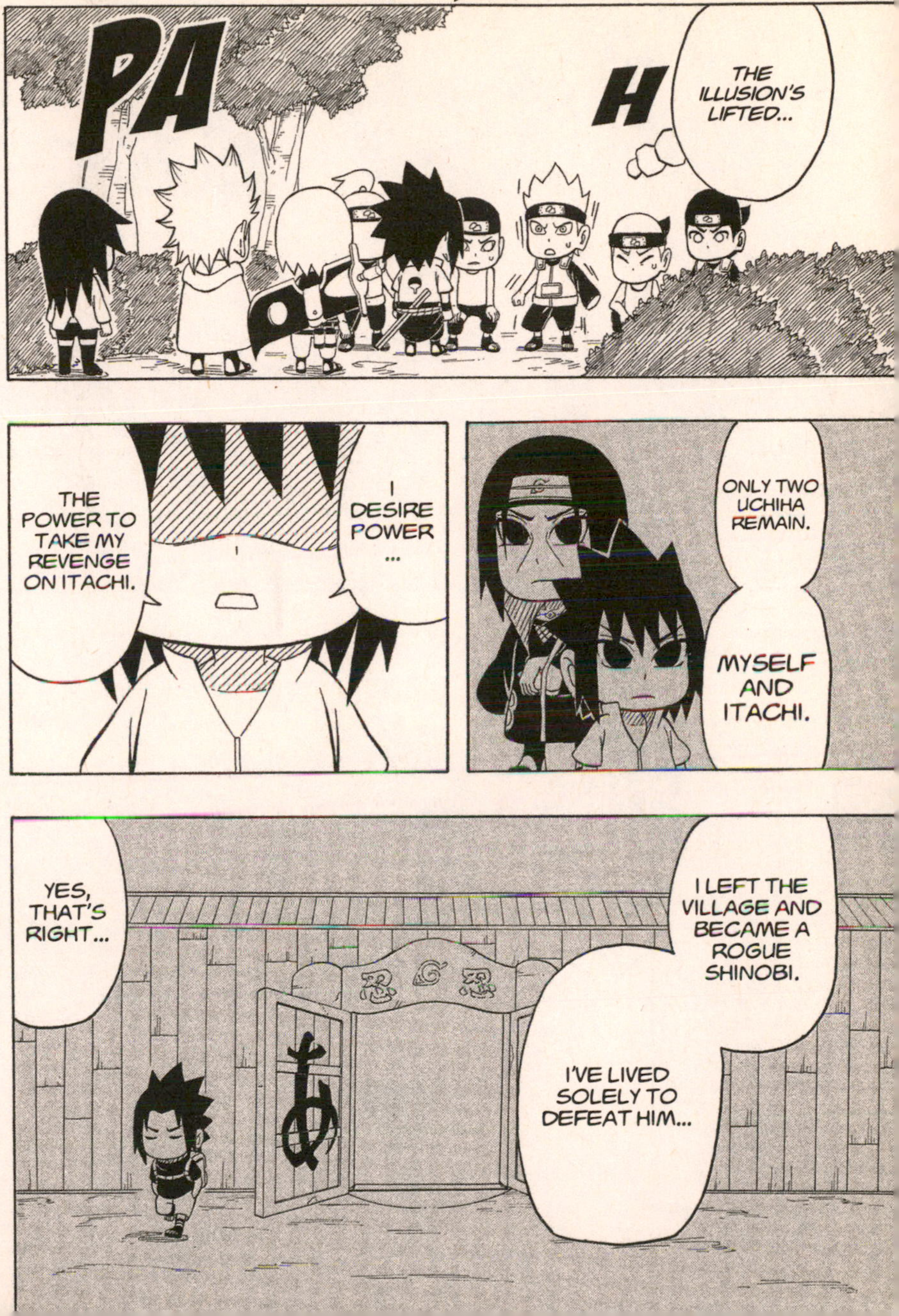
THE ILLUSION'S LIFTED...
PAH
ONLY TWO UCHIHA REMAIN.
MYSELF AND ITACHI.
I DESIRE POWER...
THE POWER TO TAKE MY REVENGE ON ITACHI.
I LEFT THE VILLAGE AND BECAME A ROGUE SHINOBI.
I'VE LIVED SOLELY TO DEFEAT HIM...
YES, THAT'S RIGHT...

I AM AN AVENGER!

CHIRP CHIRP

FIZZ FIZZ FIZZ

WE'VE GOT NOTHIN' TO DO WITH ITACHI!

PLEASE! LET US GO!

!!

H... H-H-H-HOLD ON!

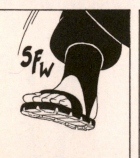

SFW

IT SEEMS YOU REALLY DON'T KNOW ANYTHING ABOUT ITACHI...

...

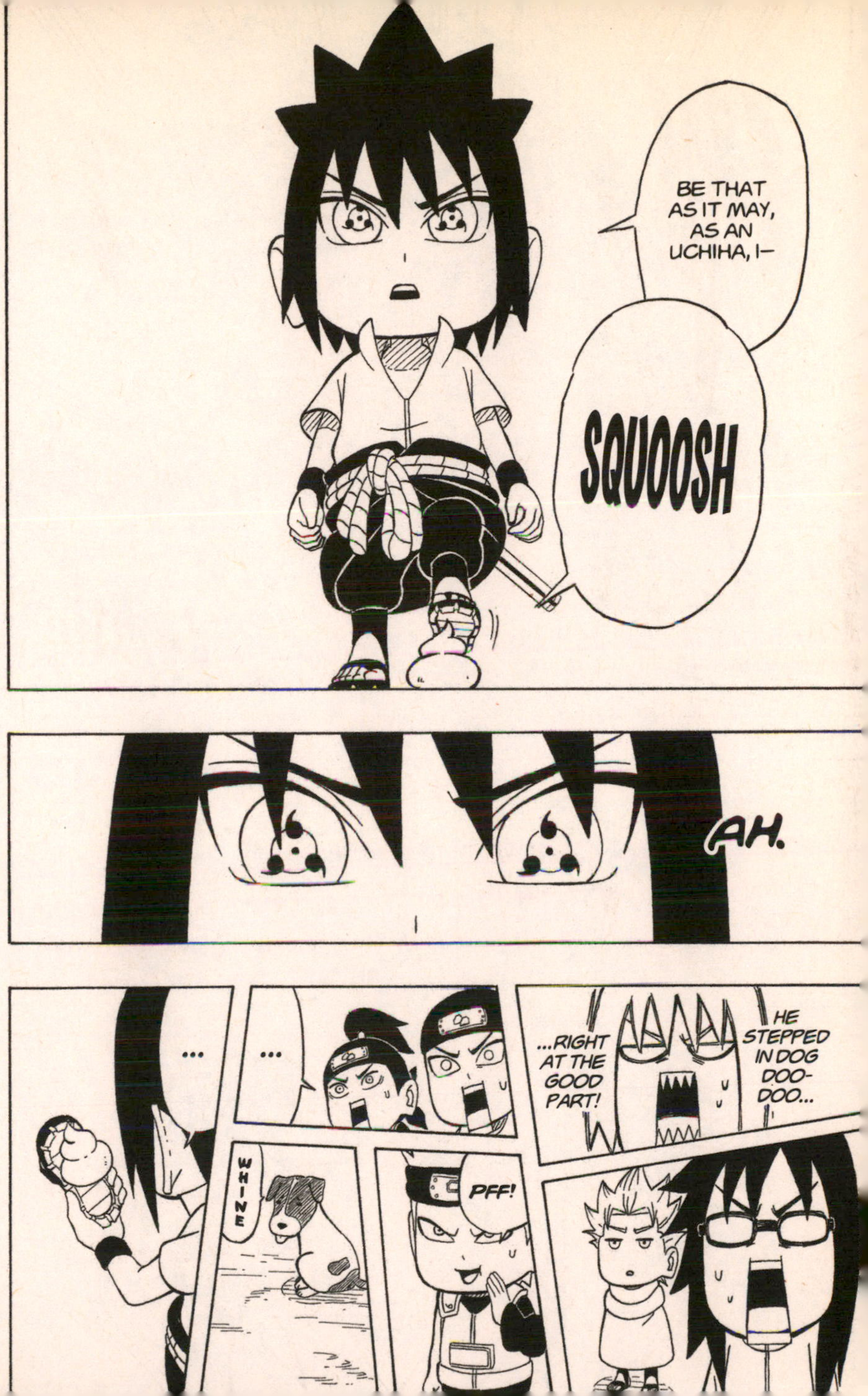
BE THAT AS IT MAY, AS AN UCHIHA, I—
SQUOOSH
AH.
HE STEPPED IN DOG DOO-DOO...
...RIGHT AT THE GOOD PART!
...
PFF!
WHINE
...

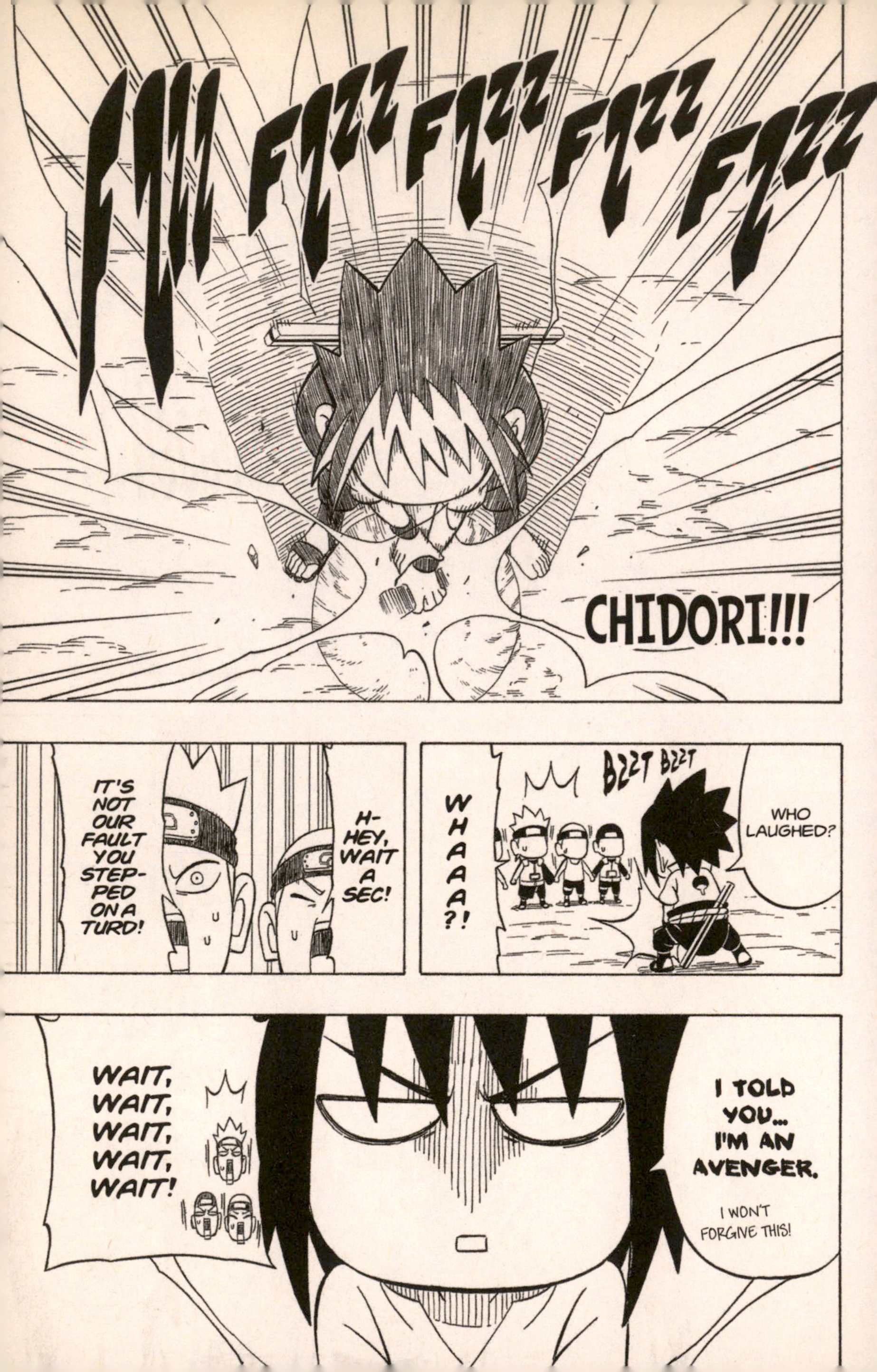
FZZZ FZZZ FZZZ FZZZ FZZZ
CHIDORI!!!
WHO LAUGHED?
BZZT BZZT
WHAAAA?!
H-HEY, WAIT A SEC!
IT'S NOT OUR FAULT YOU STEPPED ON A TURD!
I TOLD YOU... I'M AN AVENGER.
I WON'T FORGIVE THIS!
WAIT, WAIT, WAIT, WAIT, WAIT!

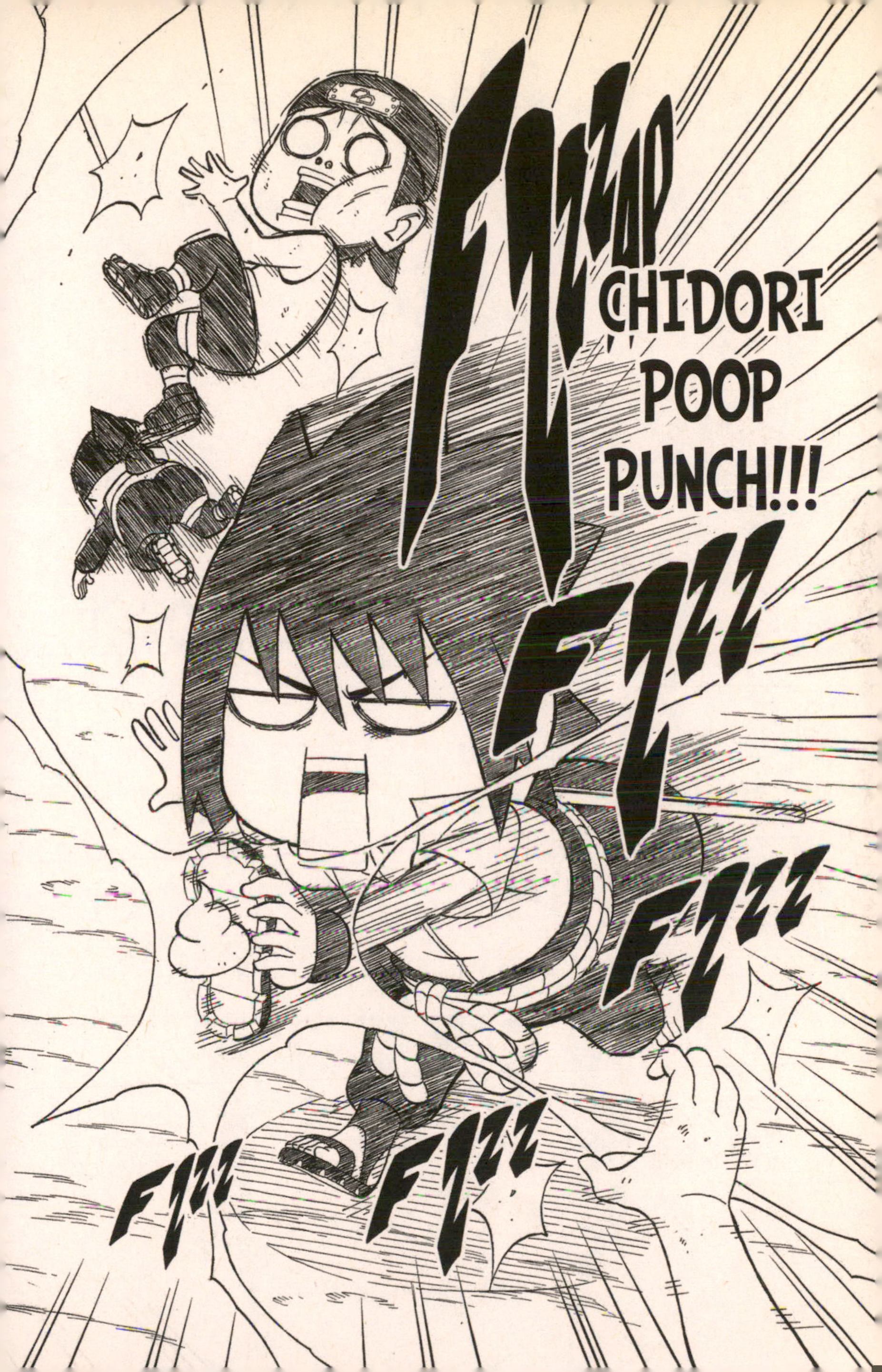
FZZZAP
CHIDORI POOP PUNCH!!!
FZZZ
FZZZ
FZZZ
FZZZ

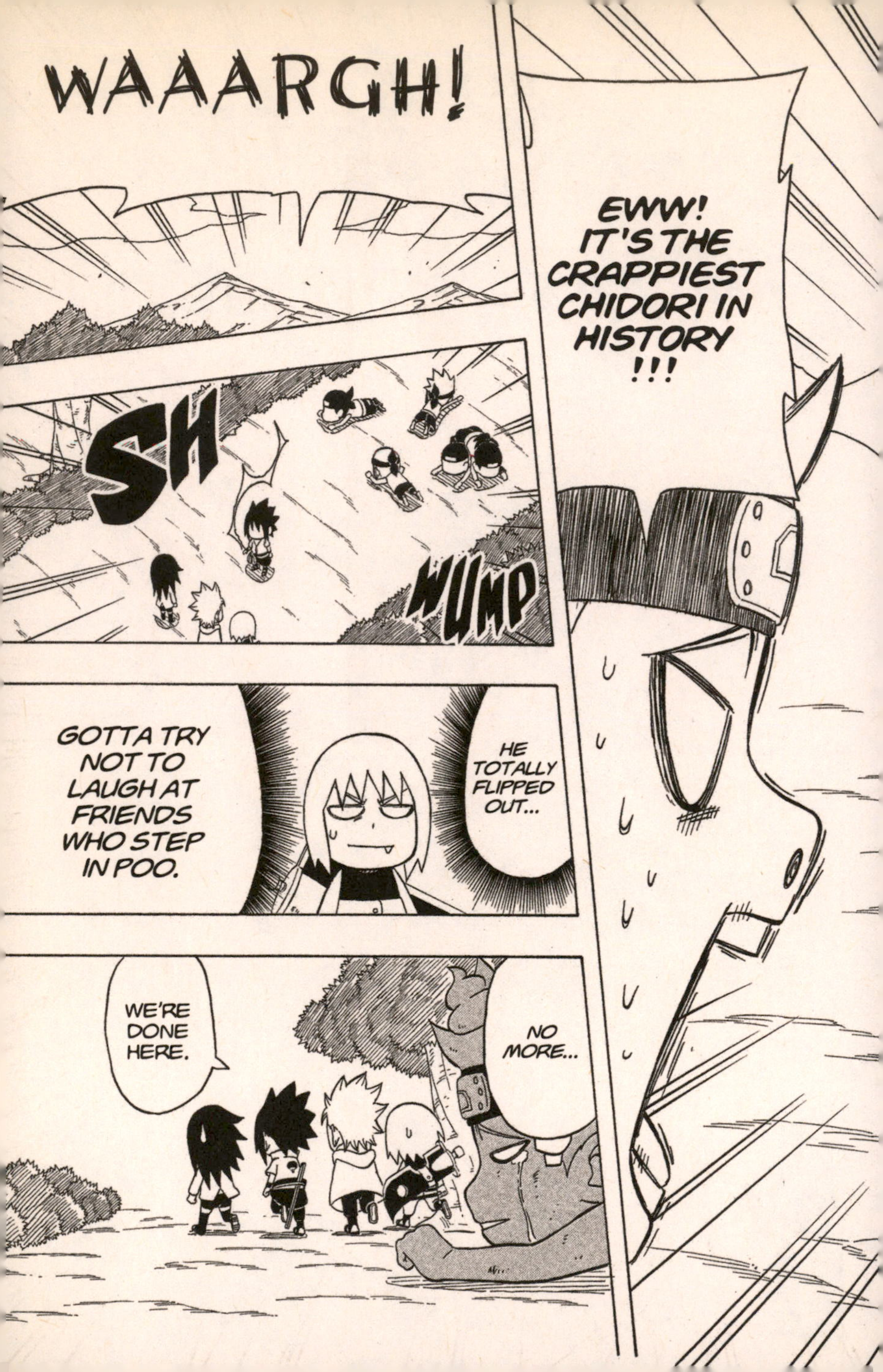

EWW! IT'S THE CRAPPIEST CHIDORI IN HISTORY!!!
WAAARGH!
SH
WUMP
HE TOTALLY FLIPPED OUT...
GOTTA TRY NOT TO LAUGH AT FRIENDS WHO STEP IN POO.
NO MORE...
WE'RE DONE HERE.

HURRY!

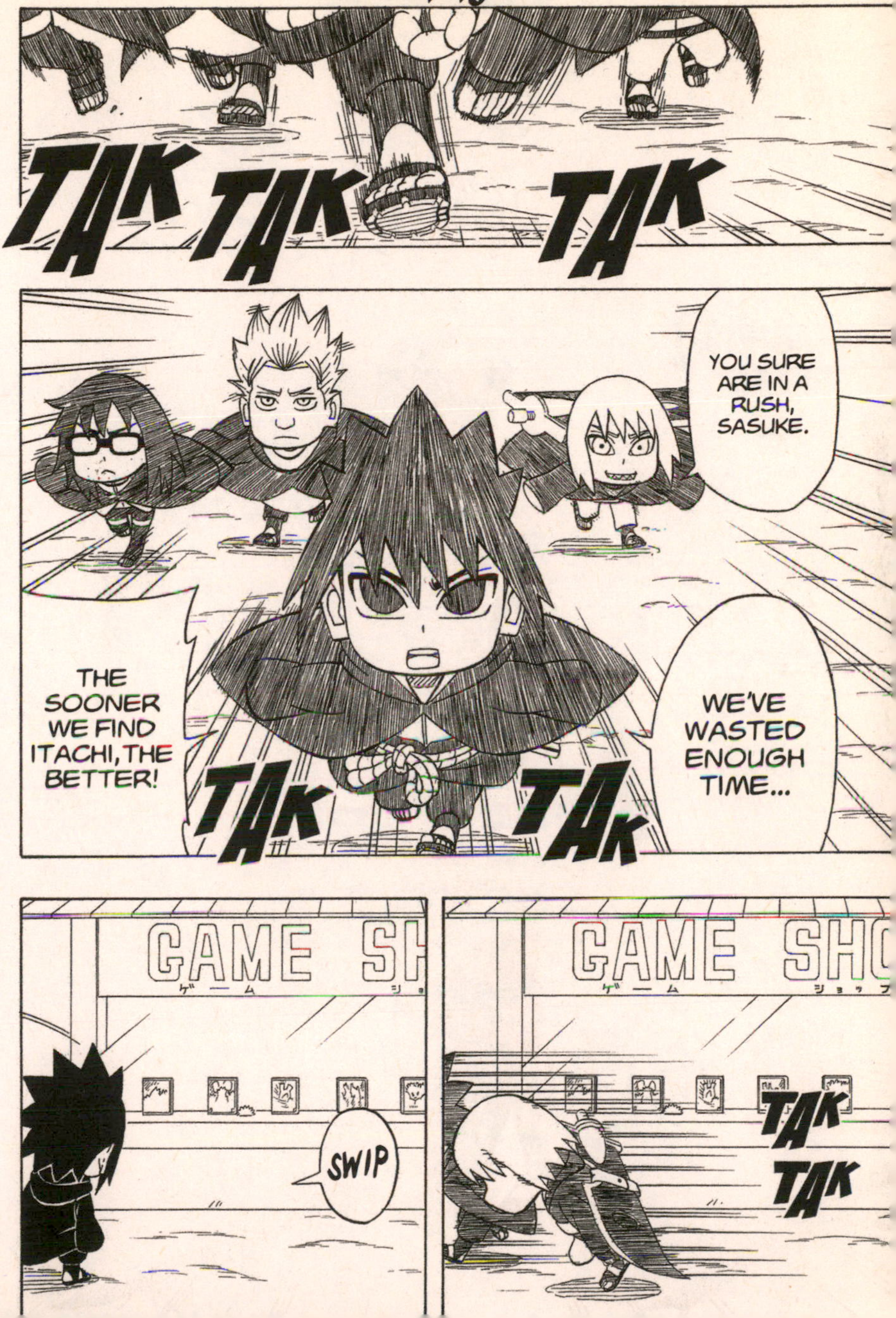
TAK TAK TAK
YOU SURE ARE IN A RUSH, SASUKE.
WE'VE WASTED ENOUGH TIME...
THE SOONER WE FIND ITACHI, THE BETTER!
TAK TAK
GAME SHO
TAK TAK
GAME SH
SWIP

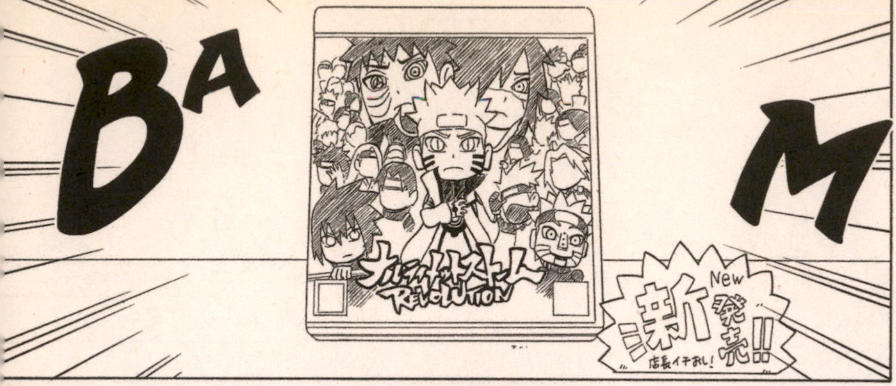
BAM
REVOLUTION
New
新発売!!
店長イチおし!

*GAME: NARUTO SHIPPUDEN: ULTIMATE NINJA STORM REVOLUTION *SIGN: NEW RELEASE! MANAGER'S PICK!

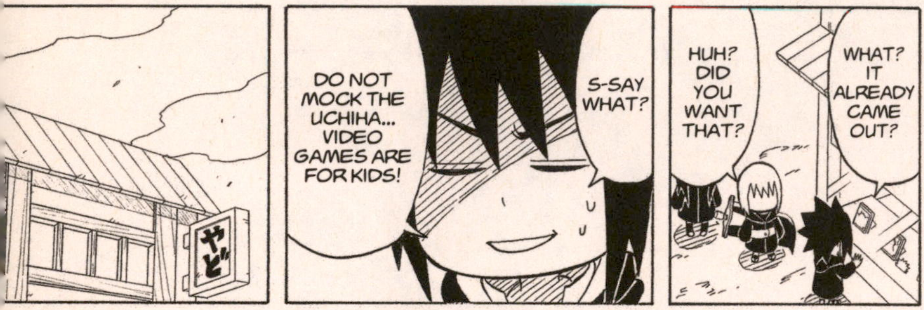
WHAT? IT ALREADY CAME OUT?
HUH? DID YOU WANT THAT?
S-SAY WHAT?
DO NOT MOCK THE UCHIHA... VIDEO GAMES ARE FOR KIDS!
やど

*SIGN: INN

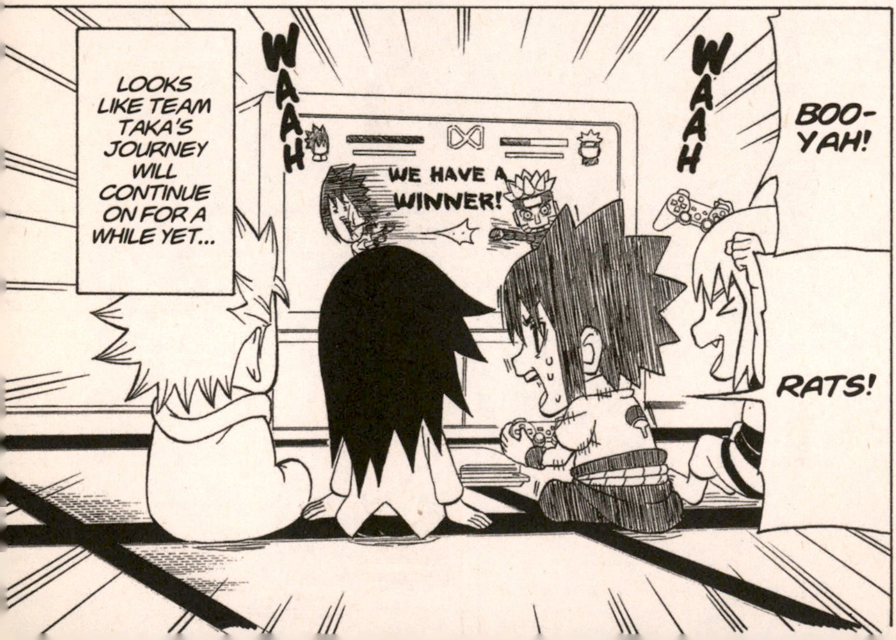
BOO-YAH!
WAAAH
RATS!
WE HAVE A WINNER!
WAAAH
LOOKS LIKE TEAM TAKA'S JOURNEY WILL CONTINUE ON FOR A WHILE YET...

CHAPTER 2:
TAKA...!!

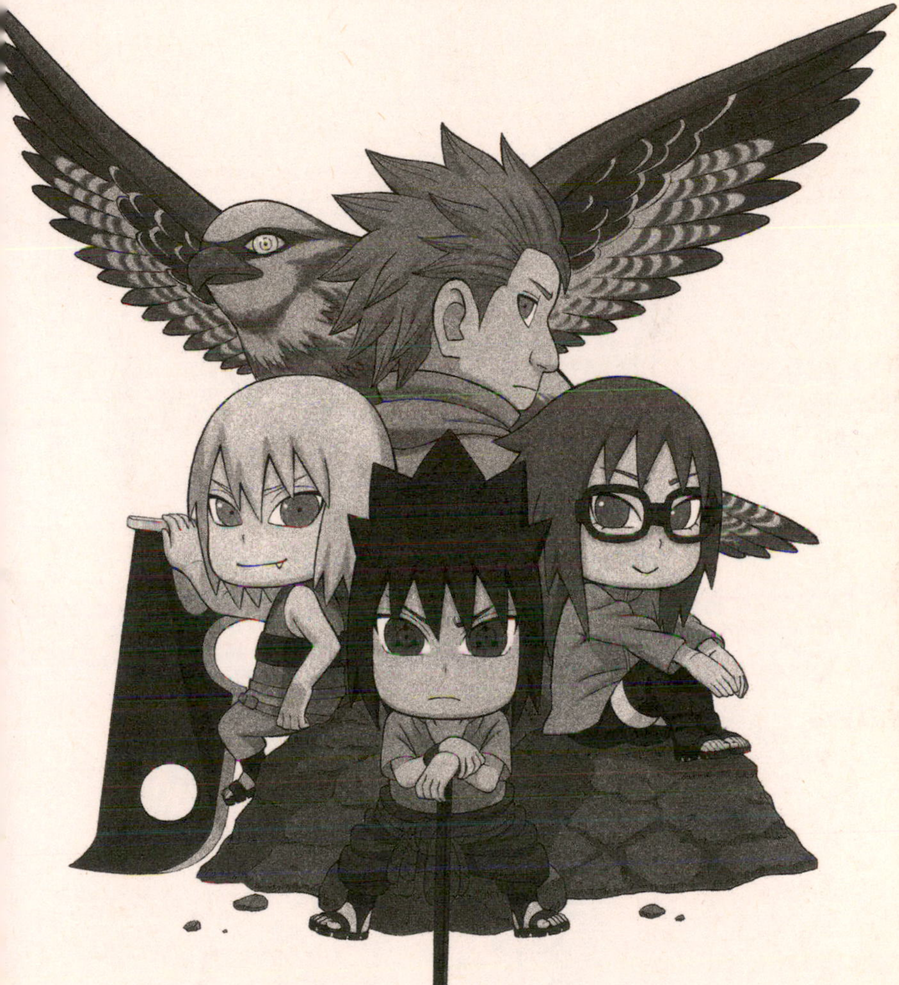

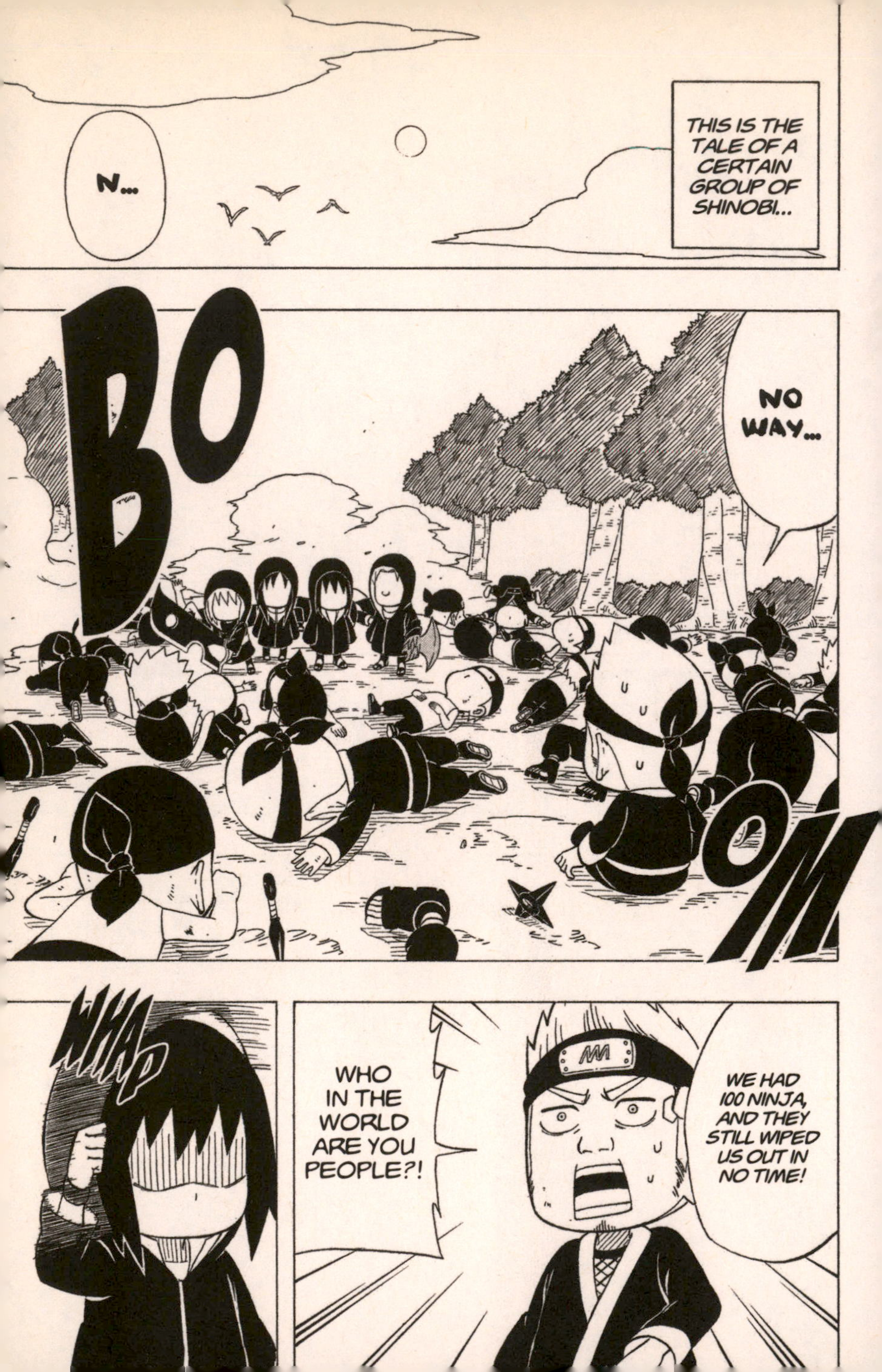
THIS IS THE TALE OF A CERTAIN GROUP OF SHINOBI...
N...
NO WAY...
BOOM
WE HAD 100 NINJA, AND THEY STILL WIPED US OUT IN NO TIME!
WHO IN THE WORLD ARE YOU PEOPLE?!
WHAP

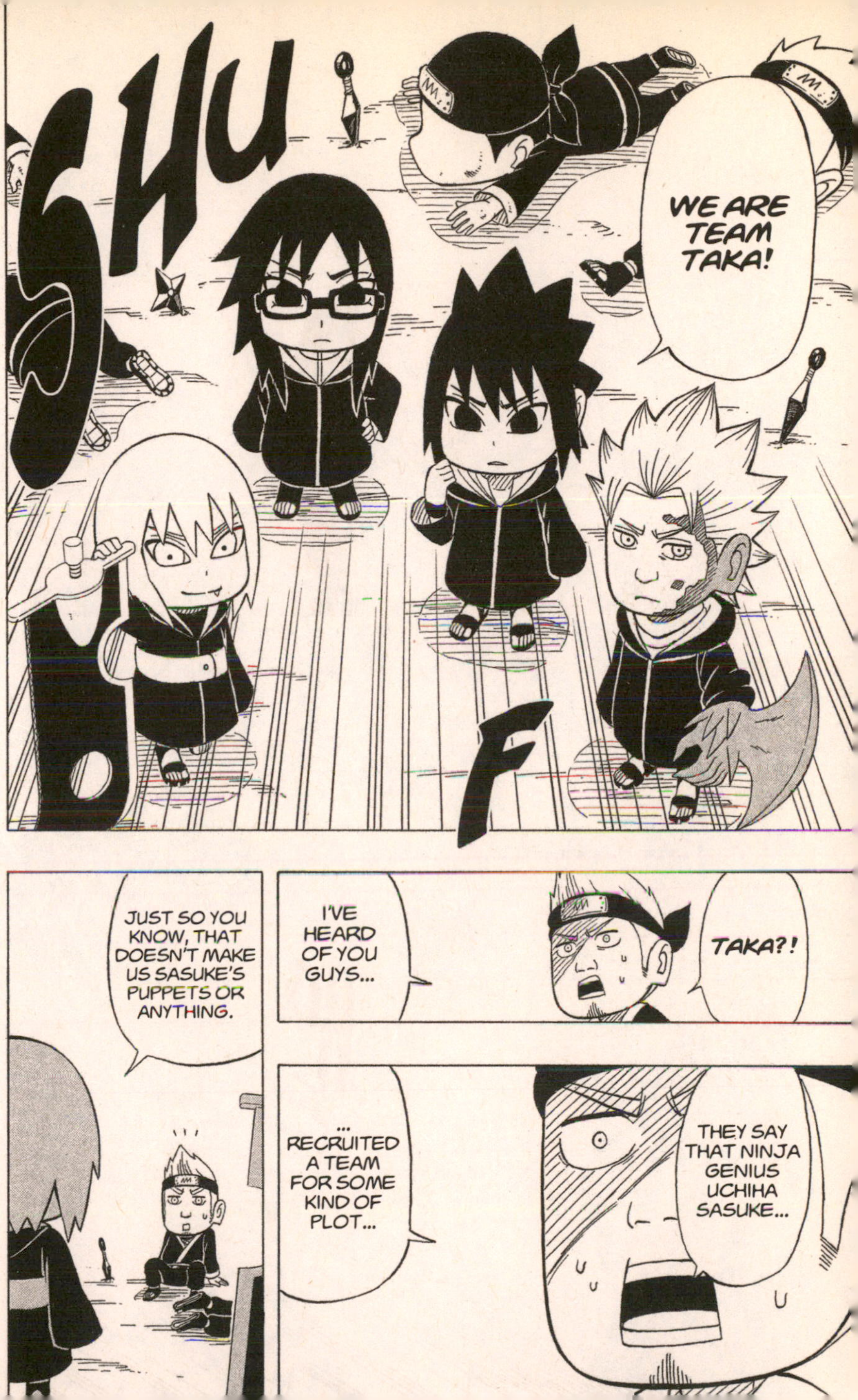
WE ARE TEAM TAKA!
SHU
F
TAKA?!
I'VE HEARD OF YOU GUYS...
THEY SAY THAT NINJA GENIUS UCHIHA SASUKE...
... RECRUITED A TEAM FOR SOME KIND OF PLOT...
JUST SO YOU KNOW, THAT DOESN'T MAKE US SASUKE'S PUPPETS OR ANYTHING.

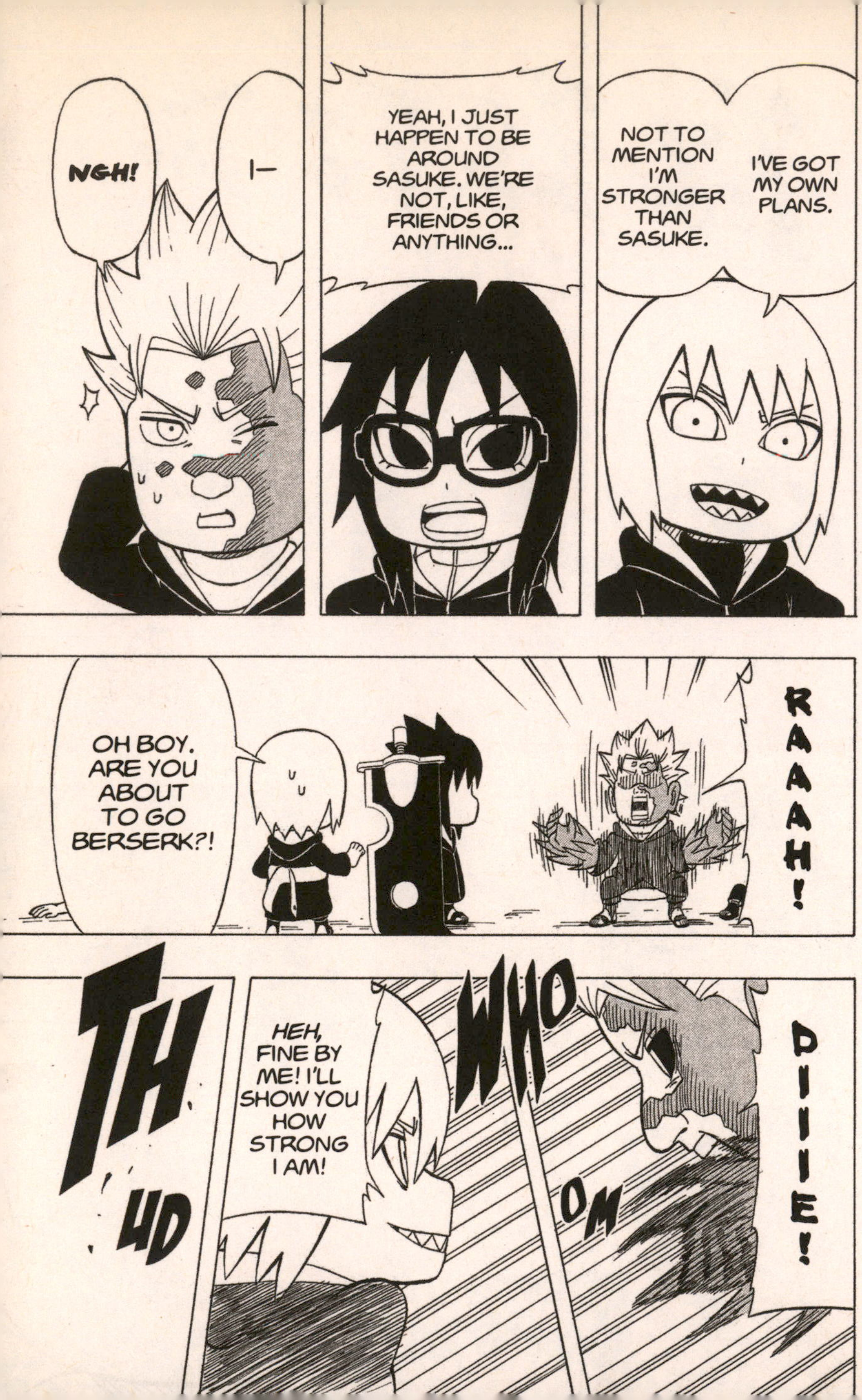
I'VE GOT MY OWN PLANS.
NOT TO MENTION I'M STRONGER THAN SASUKE.
YEAH, I JUST HAPPEN TO BE AROUND SASUKE. WE'RE NOT, LIKE, FRIENDS OR ANYTHING...
I—
NGH!
RAAAAH!
OH BOY. ARE YOU ABOUT TO GO BERSERK?!
DIIIIE!
WHOOM
HEH, FINE BY ME! I'LL SHOW YOU HOW STRONG I AM!
THUD

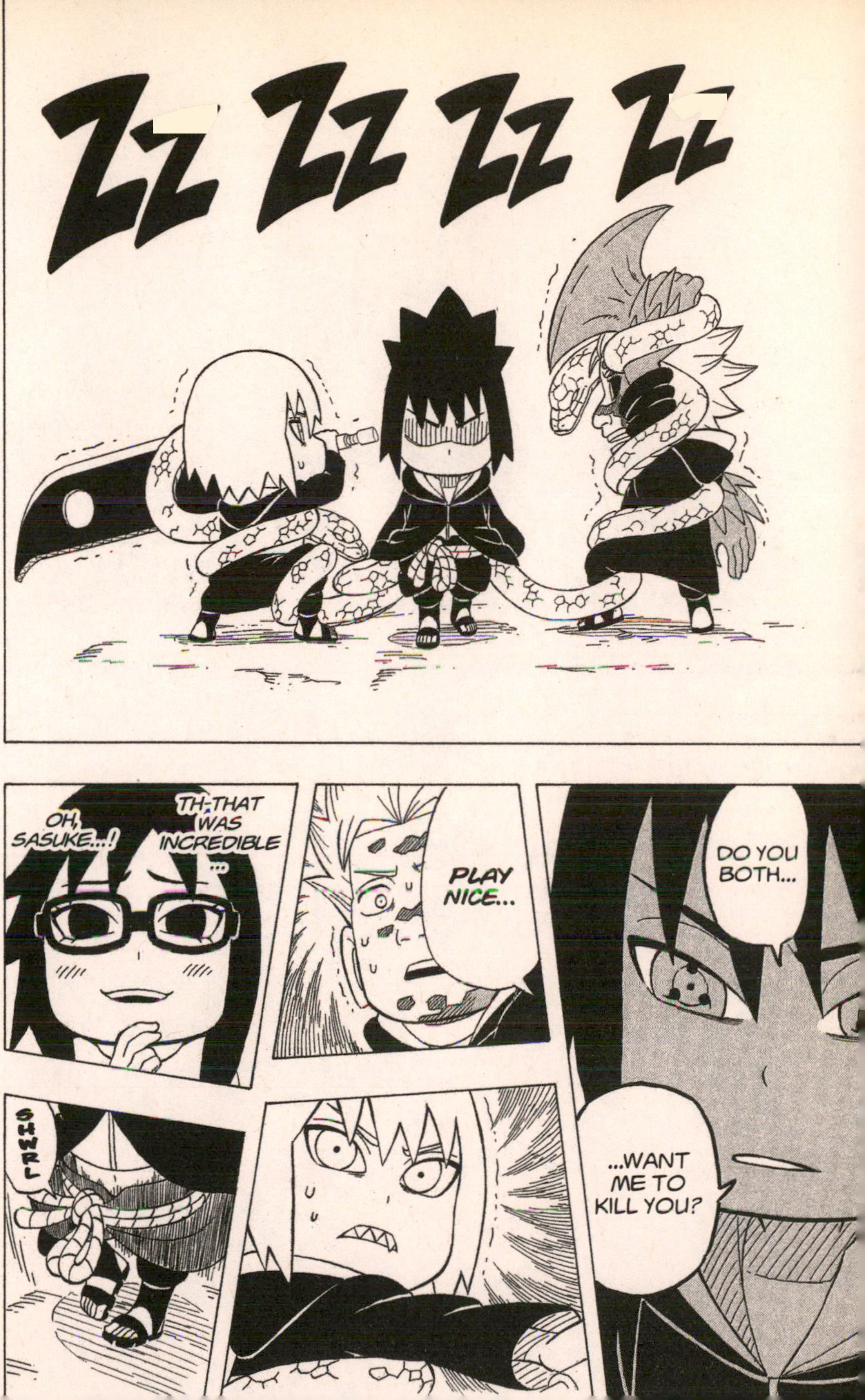
Zz Zz Zz Zz
DO YOU BOTH...
...WANT ME TO KILL YOU?
PLAY NICE...
TH-THAT WAS INCREDIBLE...
OH, SASUKE...!
SHWRL

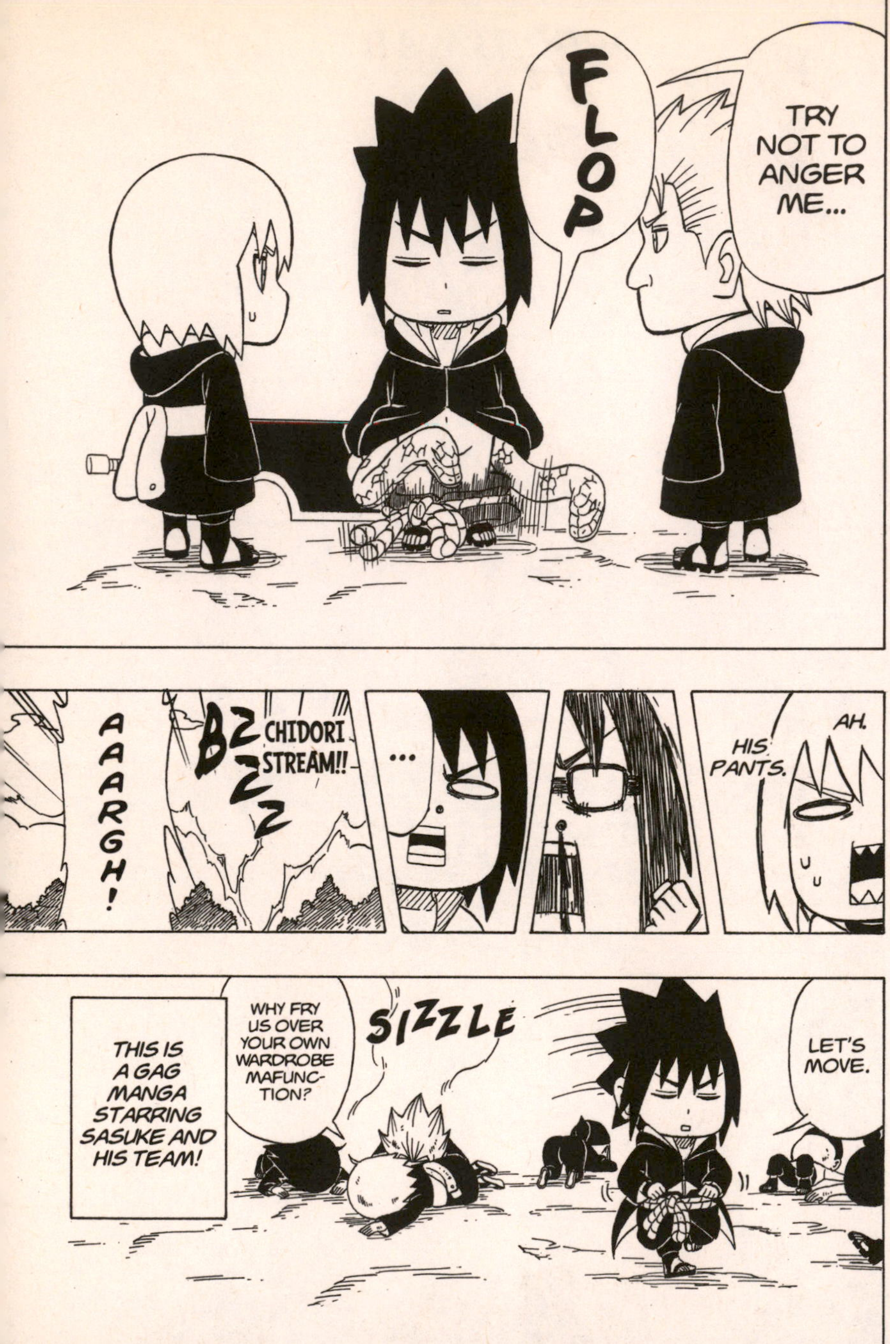
TRY NOT TO ANGER ME...
FLOP
AH.
HIS PANTS.
...
CHIDORI STREAM!!
BZZZ
AAAARGH!
LET'S MOVE.
SIZZLE
WHY FRY US OVER YOUR OWN WARDROBE MAFUNCTION?
THIS IS A GAG MANGA STARRING SASUKE AND HIS TEAM!

OROCHIMARU

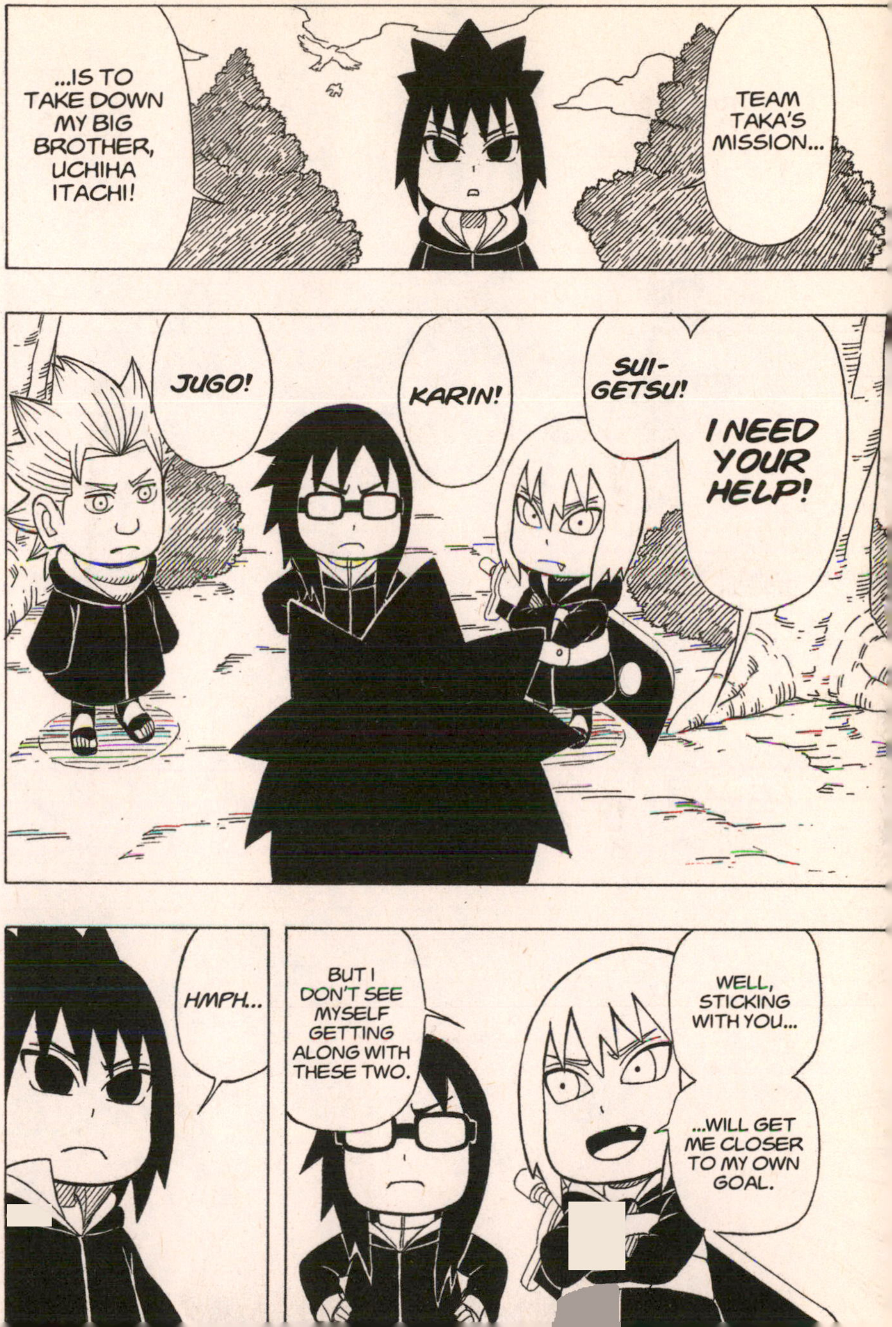
TEAM TAKA'S MISSION...
...IS TO TAKE DOWN MY BIG BROTHER, UCHIHA ITACHI!
SUI-GETSU!
KARIN!
JUGO!
I NEED YOUR HELP!
WELL, STICKING WITH YOU...
...WILL GET ME CLOSER TO MY OWN GOAL.
BUT I DON'T SEE MYSELF GETTING ALONG WITH THESE TWO.
HMPH...

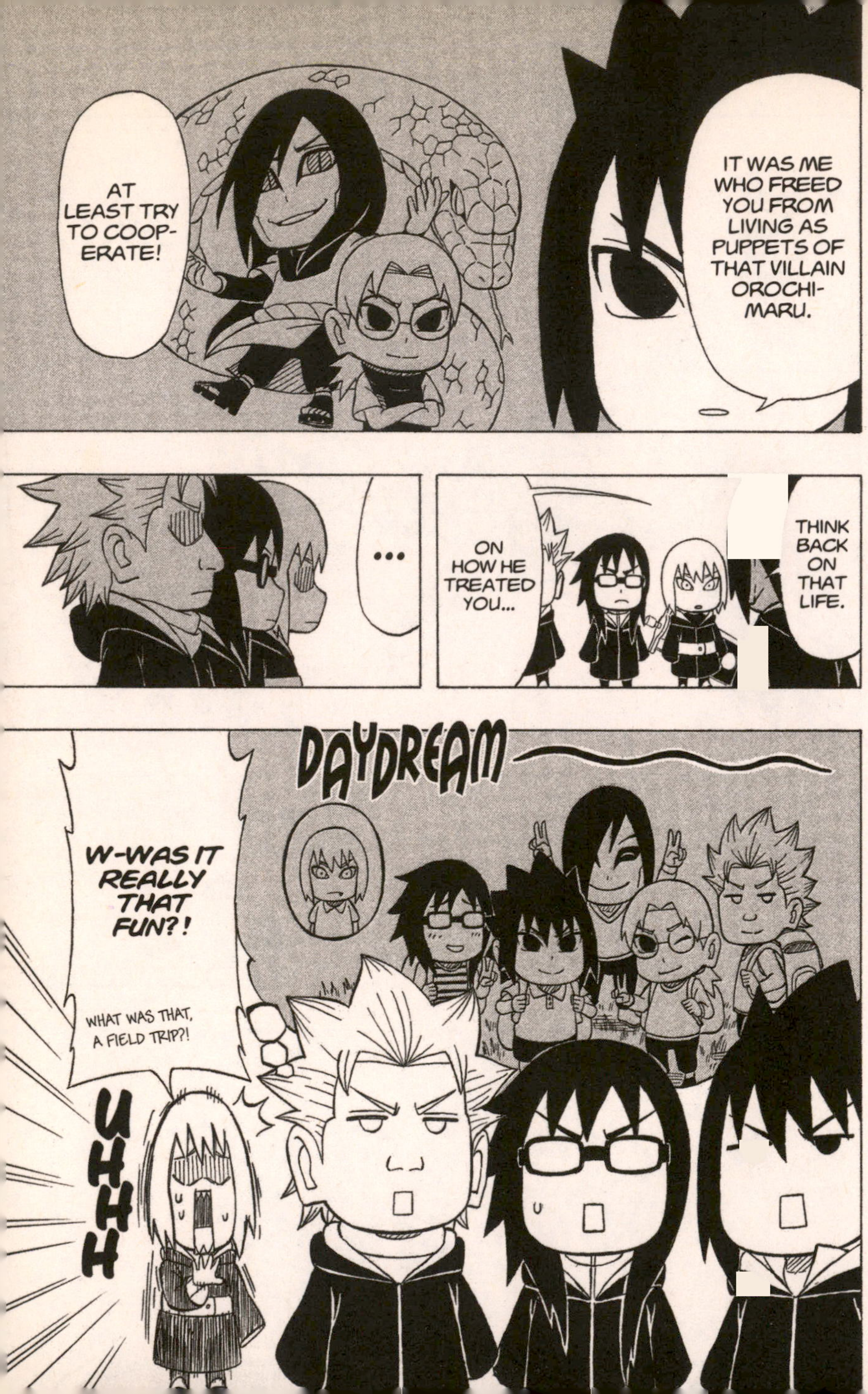
IT WAS ME WHO FREED YOU FROM LIVING AS PUPPETS OF THAT VILLAIN OROCHI-MARU.
AT LEAST TRY TO COOP-ERATE!
THINK BACK ON THAT LIFE.
ON HOW HE TREATED YOU...
...
DAYDREAM
W-WAS IT REALLY THAT FUN?!
WHAT WAS THAT, A FIELD TRIP?!
UHHH

SUIGETSU

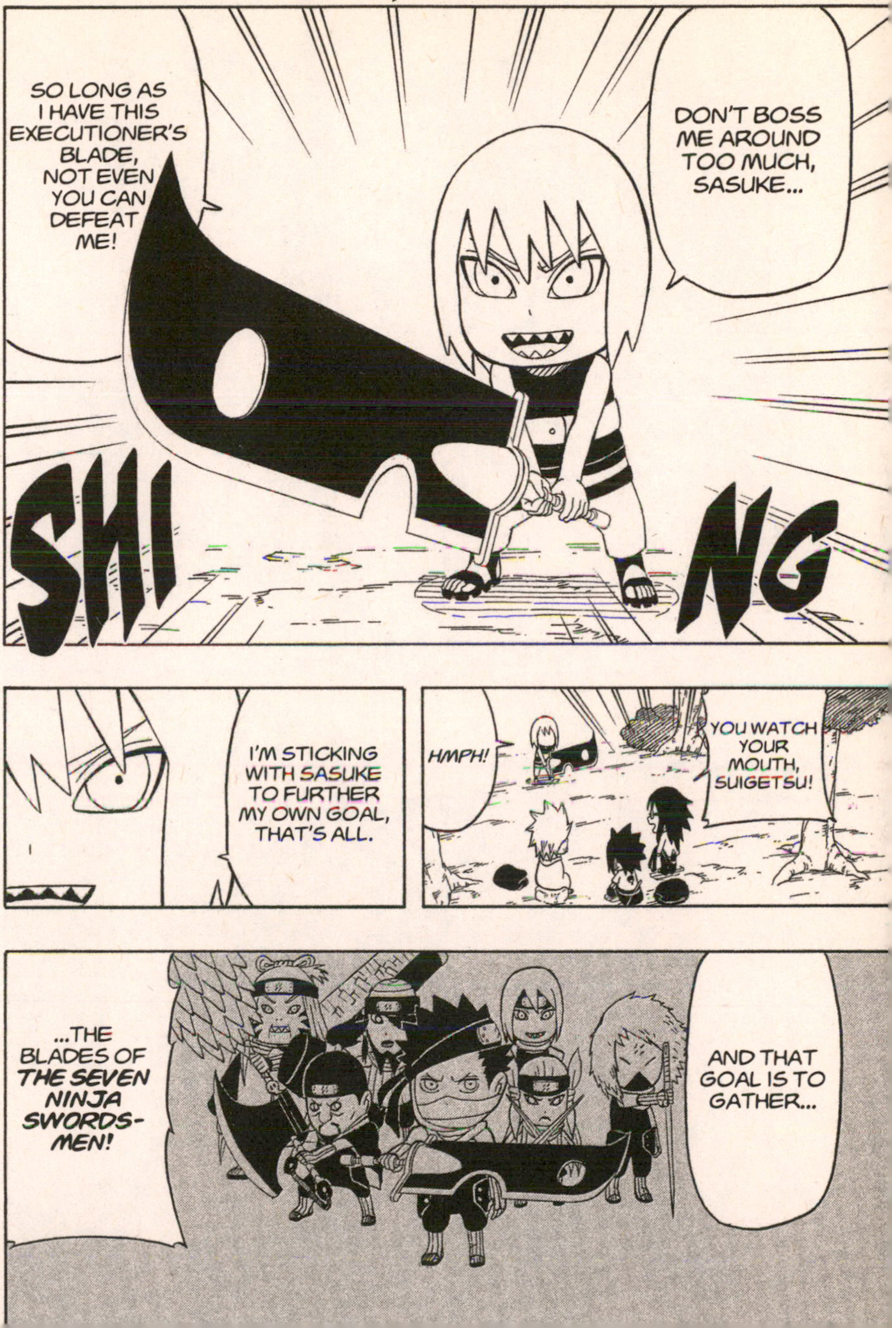
DON'T BOSS ME AROUND TOO MUCH, SASUKE...
SO LONG AS I HAVE THIS EXECUTIONER'S BLADE, NOT EVEN YOU CAN DEFEAT ME!
SHING
YOU WATCH YOUR MOUTH, SUIGETSU!
HMPH!
I'M STICKING WITH SASUKE TO FURTHER MY OWN GOAL, THAT'S ALL.
AND THAT GOAL IS TO GATHER...
...THE BLADES OF THE SEVEN NINJA SWORDSMEN!

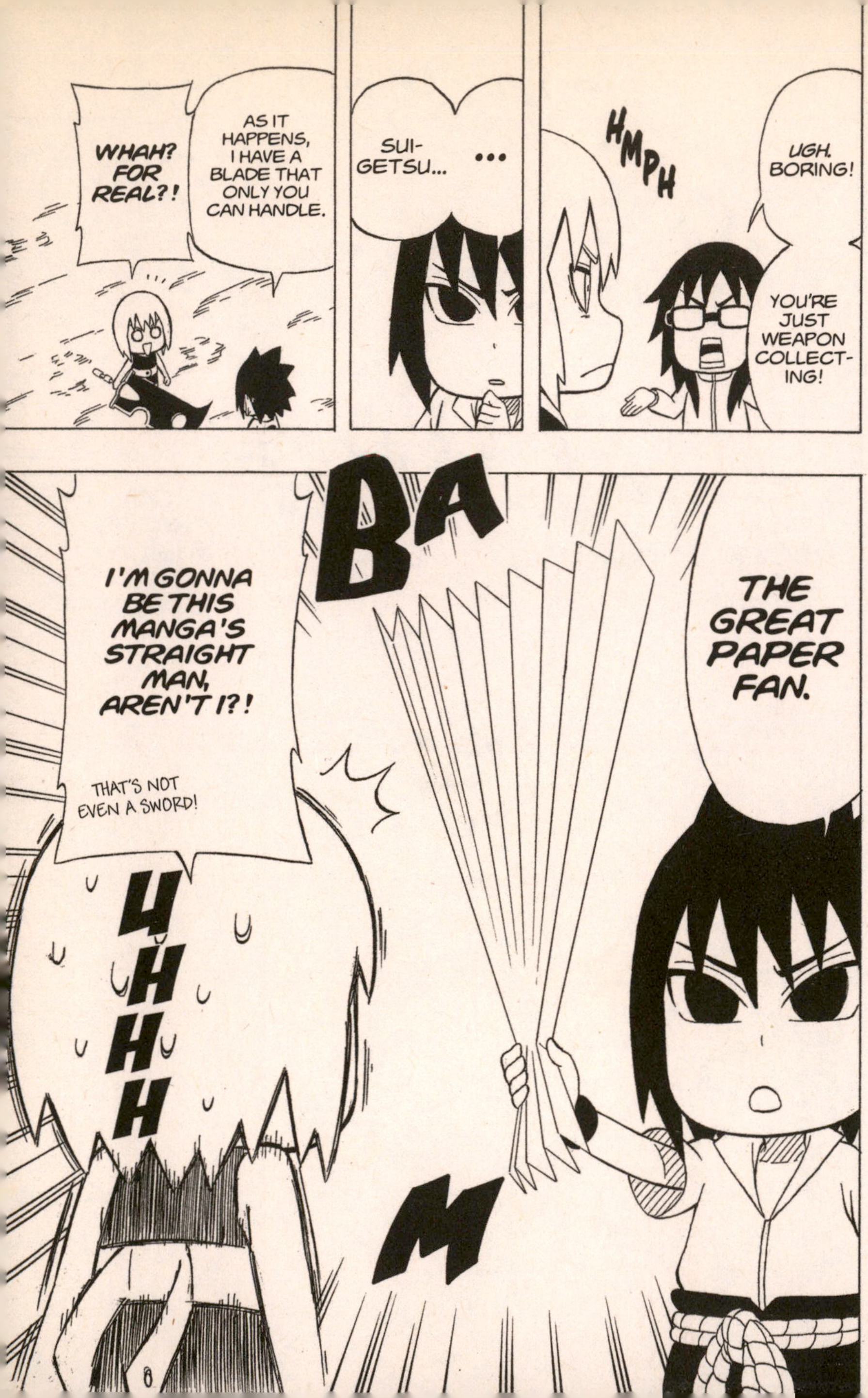
UGH. BORING!
YOU'RE JUST WEAPON COLLECT-ING!
HMPH
SUI-GETSU...
...
AS IT HAPPENS, I HAVE A BLADE THAT ONLY YOU CAN HANDLE.
WHAH? FOR REAL?!
THE GREAT PAPER FAN.
BAM
I'M GONNA BE THIS MANGA'S STRAIGHT MAN, AREN'T I?!
THAT'S NOT EVEN A SWORD!
UHHHH

LIQUEFY JUTSU

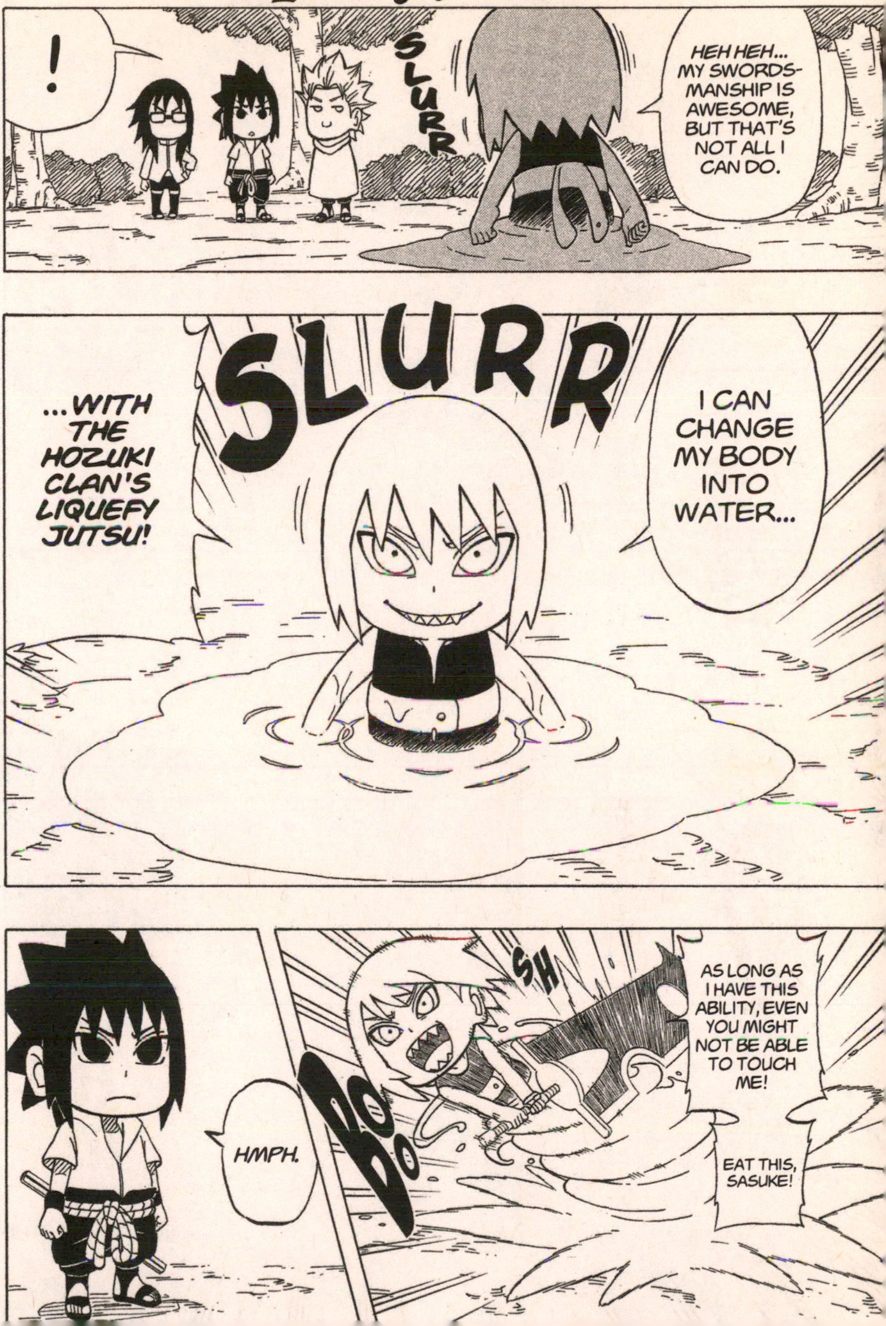
HEH HEH... MY SWORDS-MANSHIP IS AWESOME, BUT THAT'S NOT ALL I CAN DO.
SLURR
!
I CAN CHANGE MY BODY INTO WATER...
SLURR
...WITH THE HOZUKI CLAN'S LIQUEFY JUTSU!
SH
AS LONG AS I HAVE THIS ABILITY, EVEN YOU MIGHT NOT BE ABLE TO TOUCH ME!
EAT THIS, SASUKE!
HMPH.

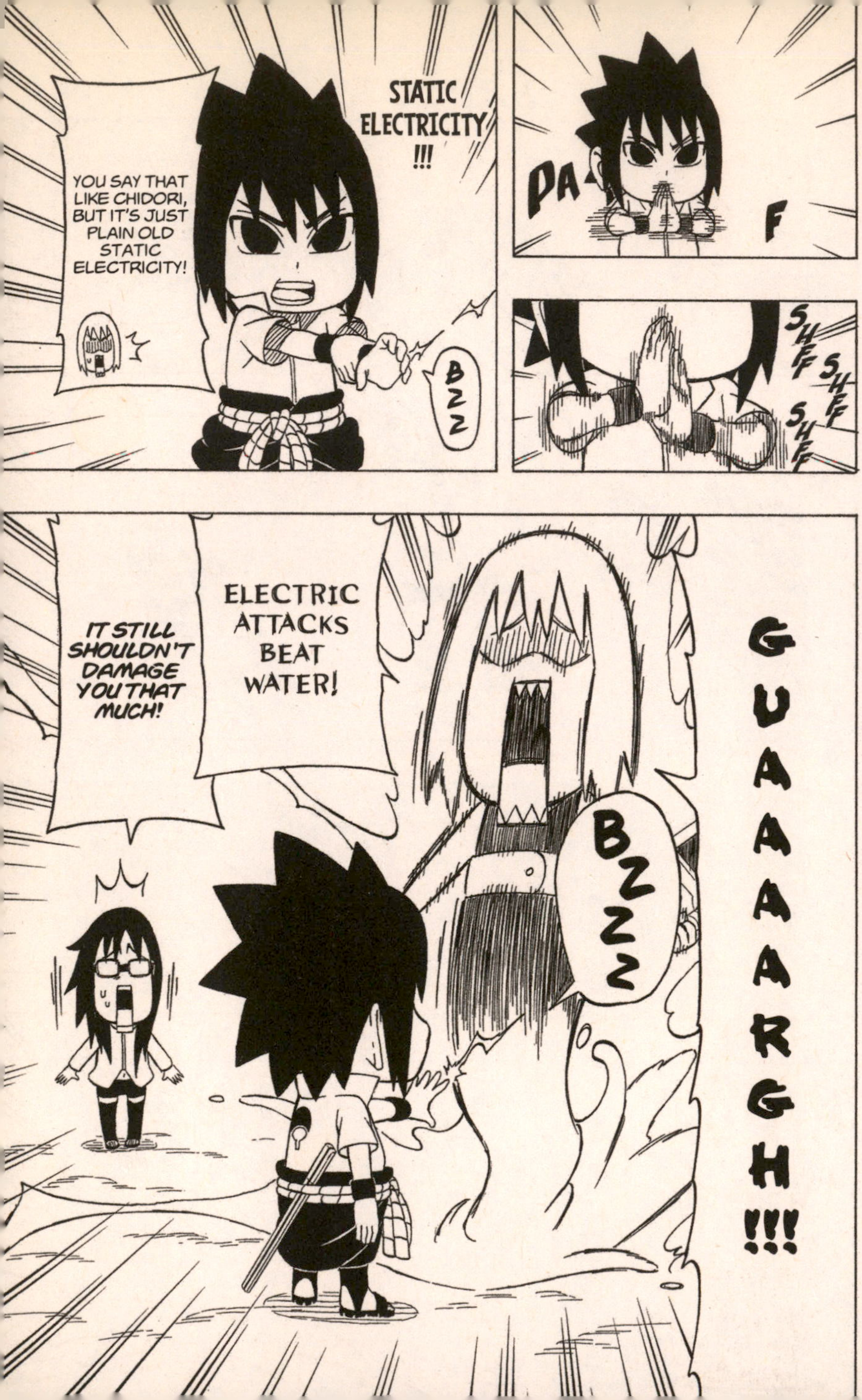
PAF
SHFF SHFF SHFF
STATIC ELECTRICITY!!!
BZZ
YOU SAY THAT LIKE CHIDORI, BUT IT'S JUST PLAIN OLD STATIC ELECTRICITY!
GUAAAARGH!!!
BZZ
ELECTRIC ATTACKS BEAT WATER!
IT STILL SHOULDN'T DAMAGE YOU THAT MUCH!

KARIN

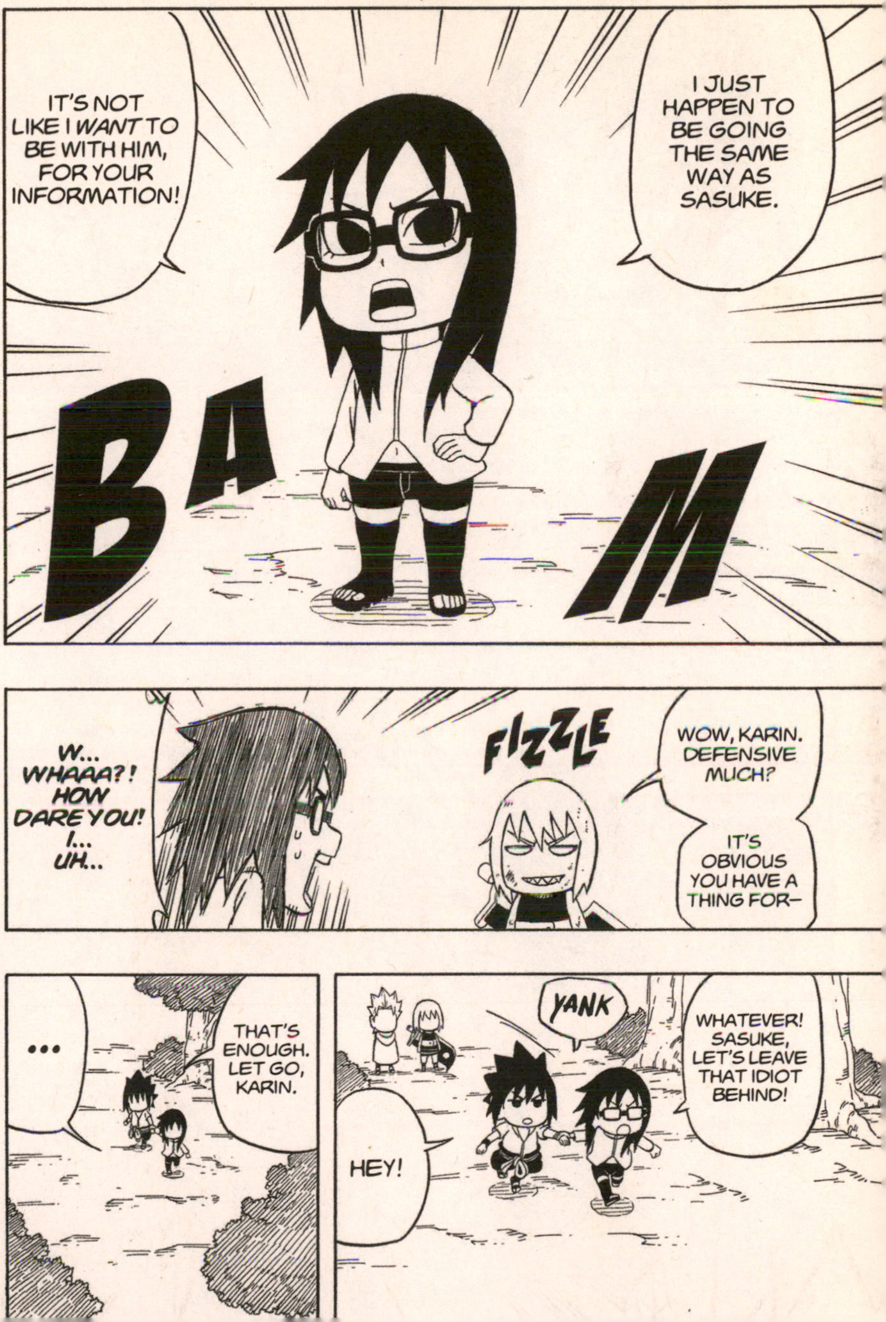
I JUST HAPPEN TO BE GOING THE SAME WAY AS SASUKE.
IT'S NOT LIKE I *WANT* TO BE WITH HIM, FOR YOUR INFORMATION!
BAM
WOW, KARIN. DEFENSIVE MUCH?
IT'S OBVIOUS YOU HAVE A THING FOR—
FIZZLE
W... WHAAA?! HOW DARE YOU! I... UH...
WHATEVER! SASUKE, LET'S LEAVE THAT IDIOT BEHIND!
YANK
HEY!
THAT'S ENOUGH. LET GO, KARIN.
...

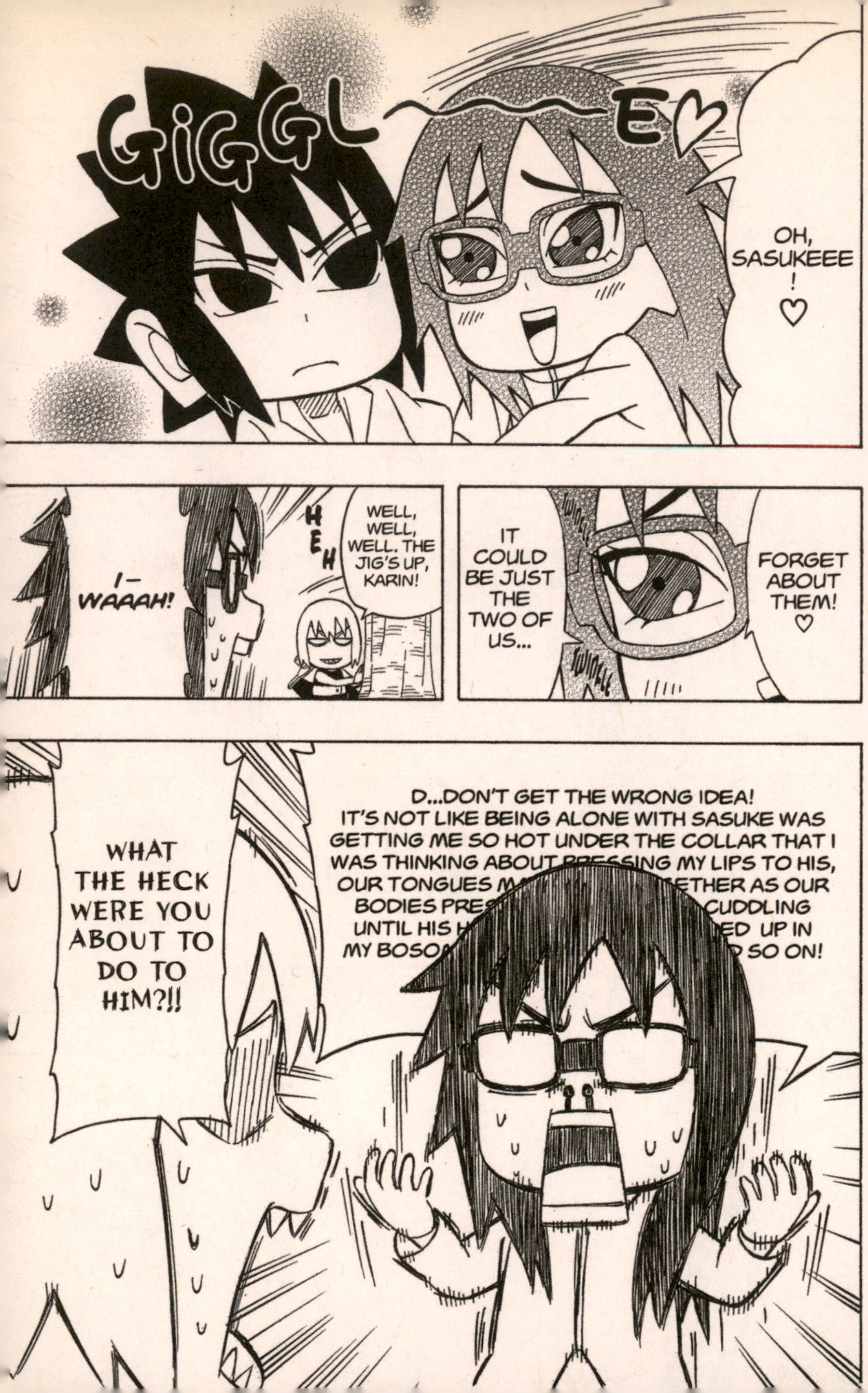
GIGGL~~~E ♡
OH, SASUKEEE! ♡
FORGET ABOUT THEM! ♡
IT COULD BE JUST THE TWO OF US...
WELL, WELL, WELL. THE JIG'S UP, KARIN!
HEH
I—WAAAH!
D...DON'T GET THE WRONG IDEA! IT'S NOT LIKE BEING ALONE WITH SASUKE WAS GETTING ME SO HOT UNDER THE COLLAR THAT I WAS THINKING ABOUT PRESSING MY LIPS TO HIS, OUR TONGUES M ETHER AS OUR BODIES PRES CUDDLING UNTIL HIS H ED UP IN MY BOSO SO ON!
WHAT THE HECK WERE YOU ABOUT TO DO TO HIM?!!

"THAT"

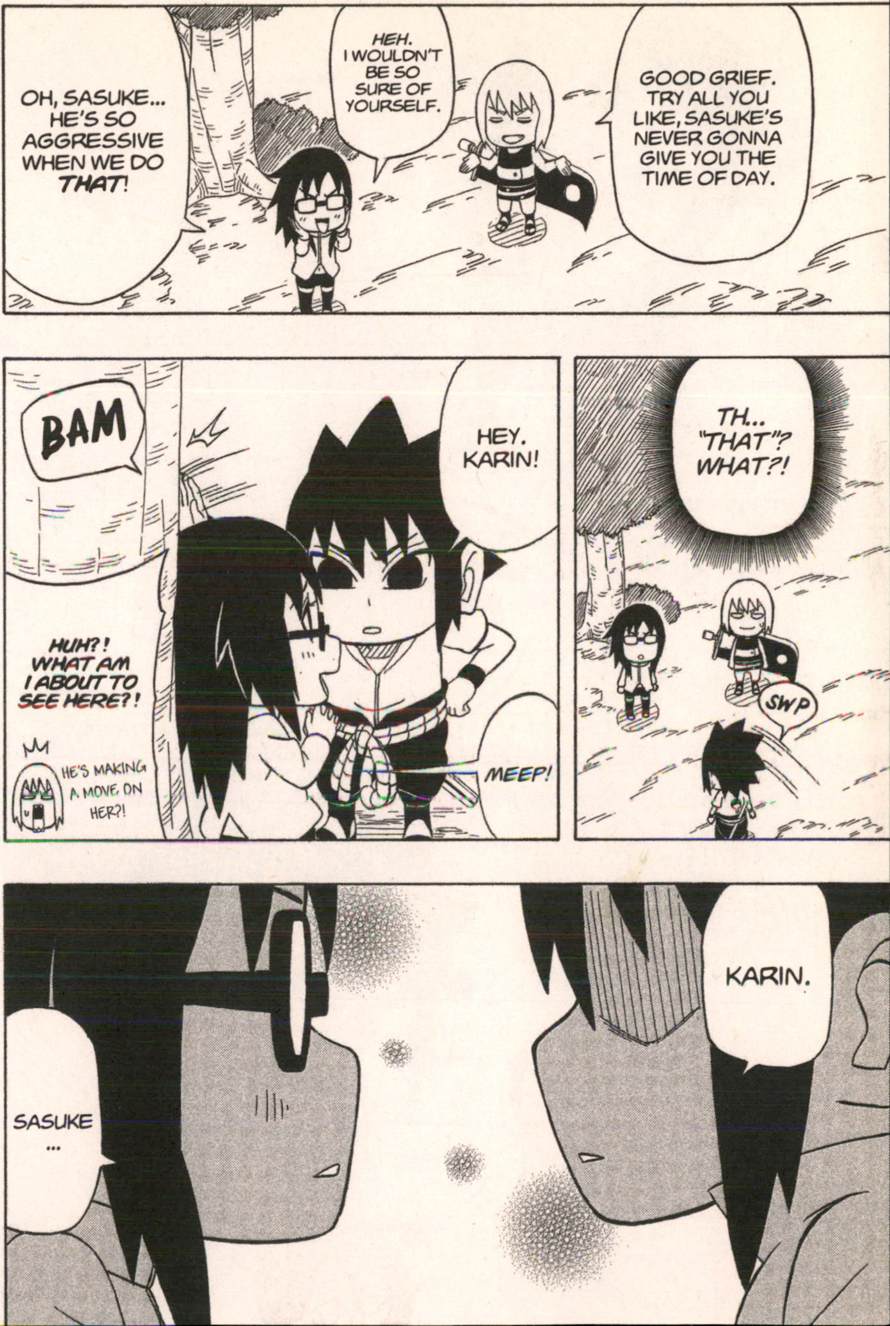
GOOD GRIEF. TRY ALL YOU LIKE, SASUKE'S NEVER GONNA GIVE YOU THE TIME OF DAY.
HEH. I WOULDN'T BE SO SURE OF YOURSELF.
OH, SASUKE... HE'S SO AGGRESSIVE WHEN WE DO *THAT*!
TH... "THAT"? WHAT?!
SWP
HEY. KARIN!
MEEP!
BAM
HUH?! WHAT AM I ABOUT TO SEE HERE?!
HE'S MAKING A MOVE ON HER?!
KARIN.
SASUKE ...

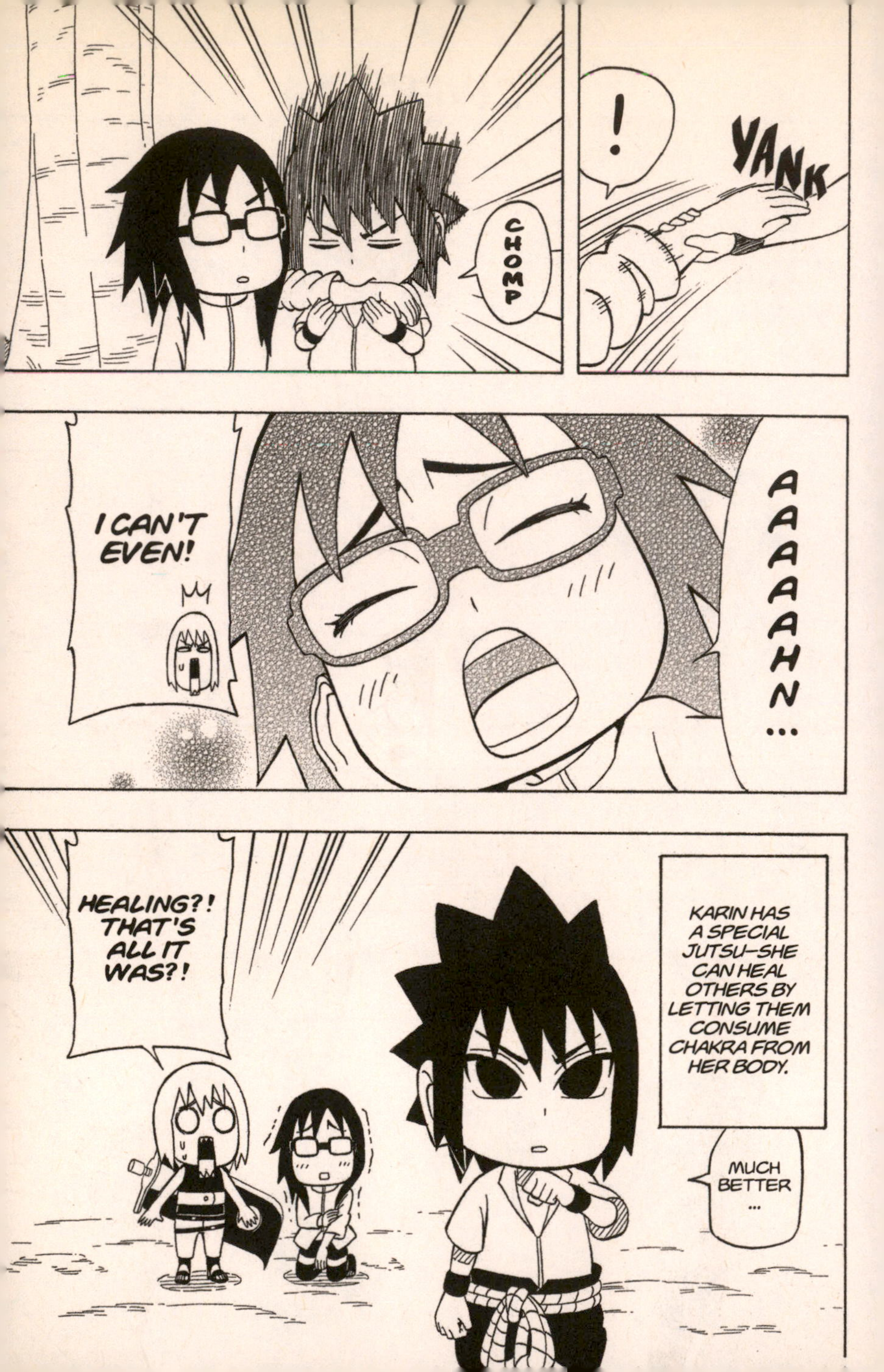
!
YANK
CHOMP
AAAAAAHN...
I CAN'T EVEN!
KARIN HAS A SPECIAL JUTSU—SHE CAN HEAL OTHERS BY LETTING THEM CONSUME CHAKRA FROM HER BODY.
MUCH BETTER ...
HEALING?! THAT'S ALL IT WAS?!

JUGO

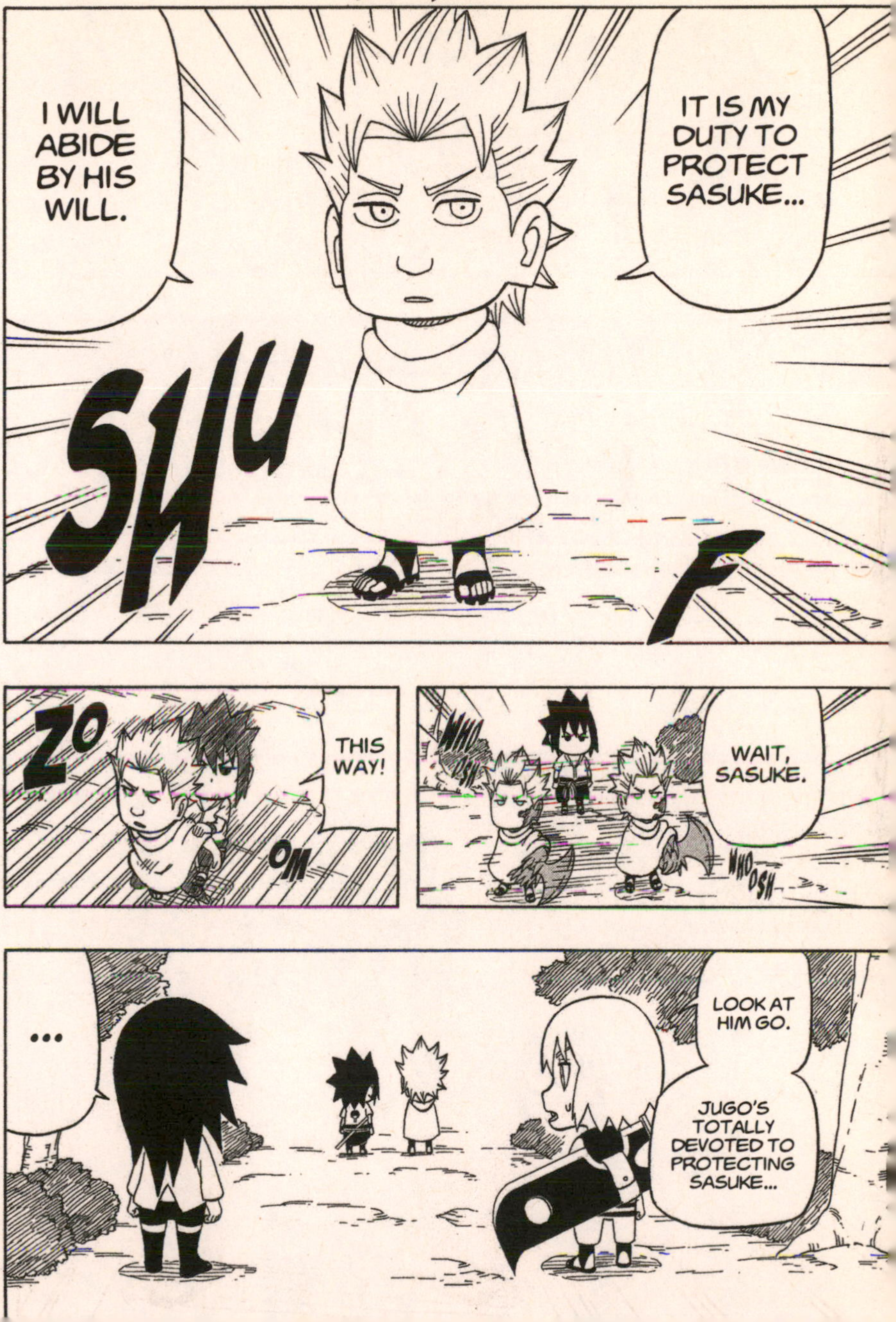
IT IS MY DUTY TO PROTECT SASUKE...
I WILL ABIDE BY HIS WILL.
SHUF
WAIT, SASUKE.
WHOOSH
WHOOSH
THIS WAY!
ZOOM
LOOK AT HIM GO.
JUGO'S TOTALLY DEVOTED TO PROTECTING SASUKE...
...

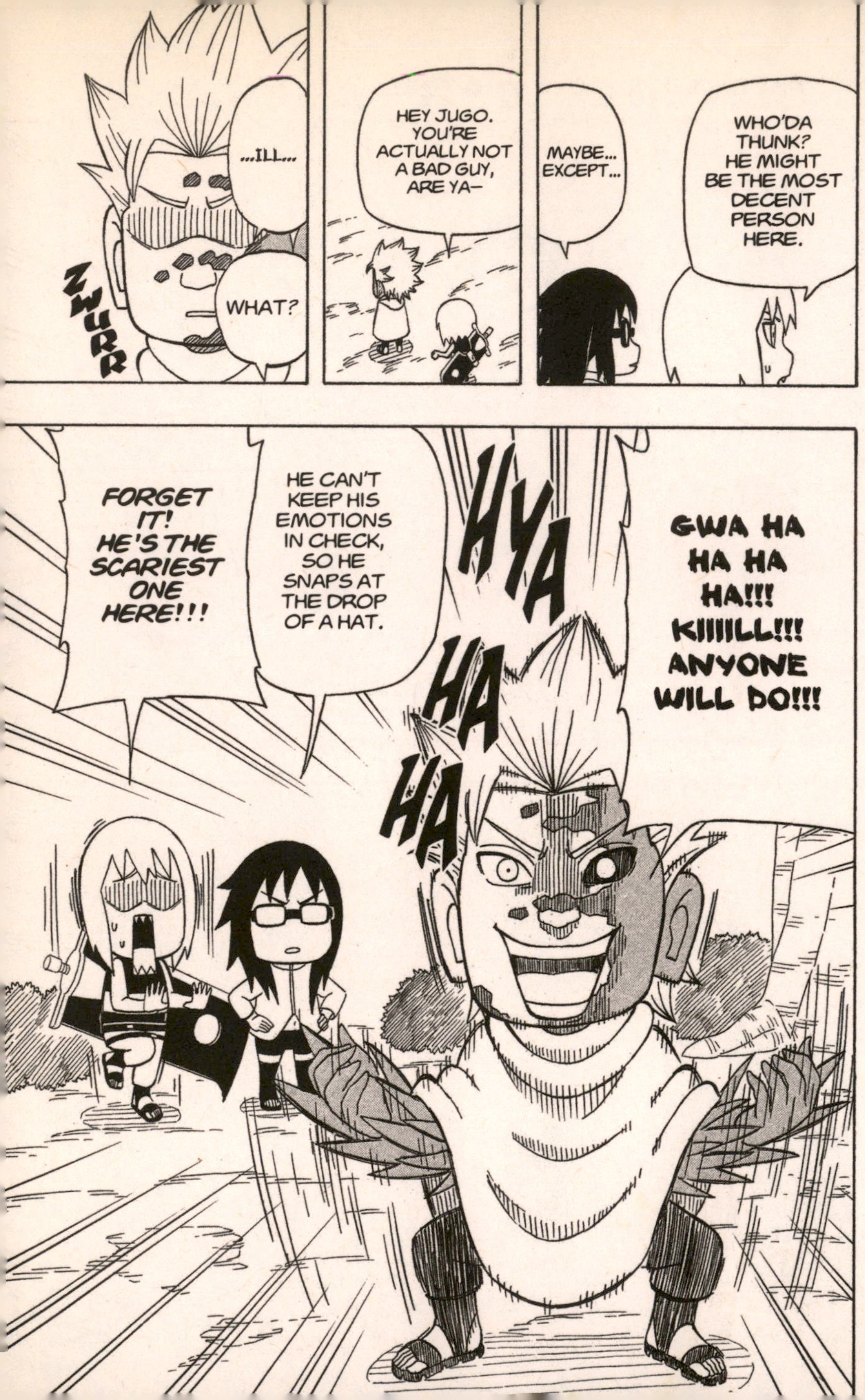

WHO'DA THUNK? HE MIGHT BE THE MOST DECENT PERSON HERE.
MAYBE... EXCEPT...
HEY JUGO. YOU'RE ACTUALLY NOT A BAD GUY, ARE YA—
...ILL...
WHAT?
ZWURR
GWA HA HA HA HA!!! KIIIILL!!! ANYONE WILL DO!!!
HYA HA HA HA
HE CAN'T KEEP HIS EMOTIONS IN CHECK, SO HE SNAPS AT THE DROP OF A HAT.
FORGET IT! HE'S THE SCARIEST ONE HERE!!!

THE POWER TO STOP A RAMPAGE

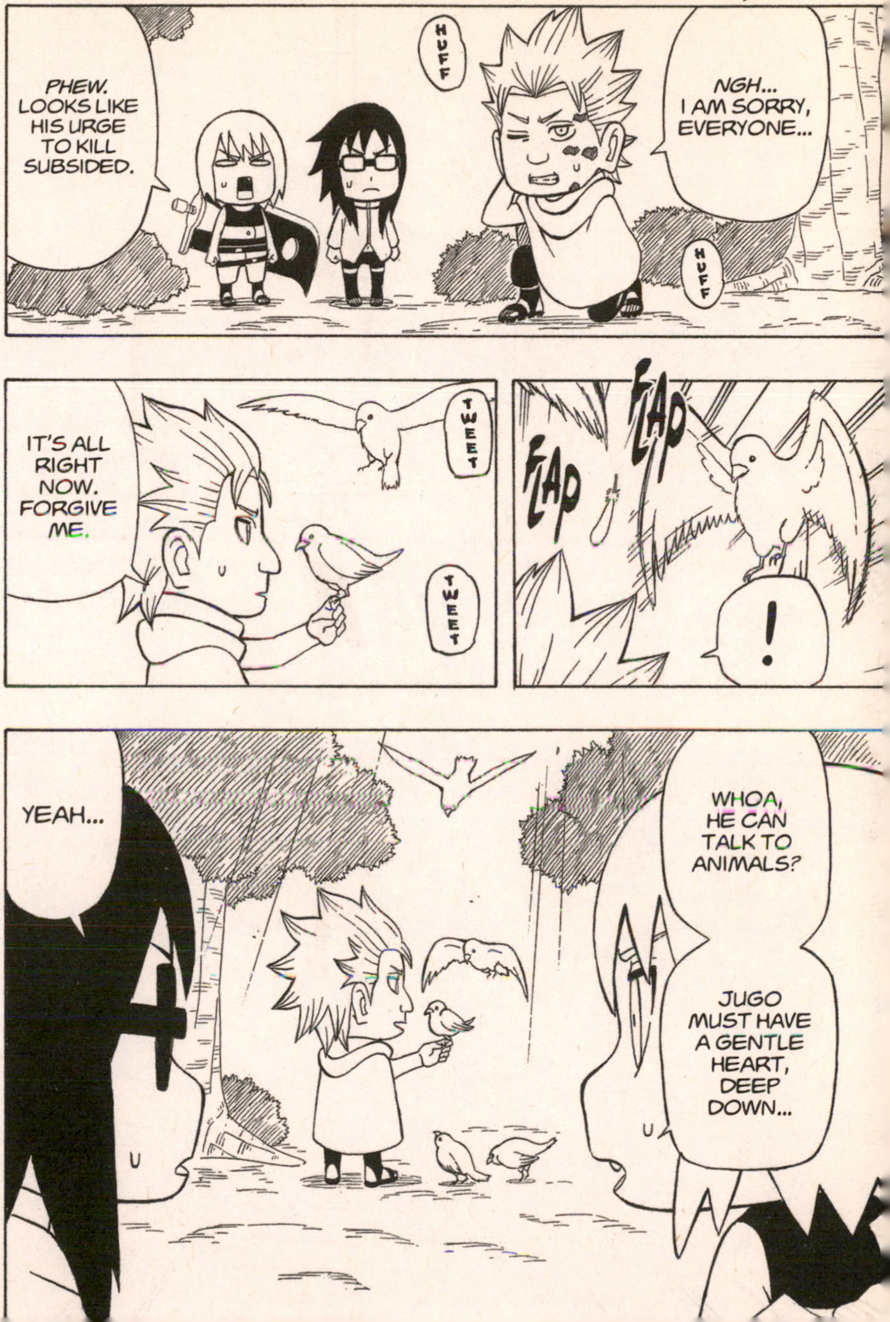
NGH... I AM SORRY, EVERYONE...
HUFF
HUFF
PHEW. LOOKS LIKE HIS URGE TO KILL SUBSIDED.
FLAP
FLAP
!
TWEET
TWEET
IT'S ALL RIGHT NOW. FORGIVE ME.
WHOA, HE CAN TALK TO ANIMALS?
JUGO MUST HAVE A GENTLE HEART, DEEP DOWN...
YEAH...

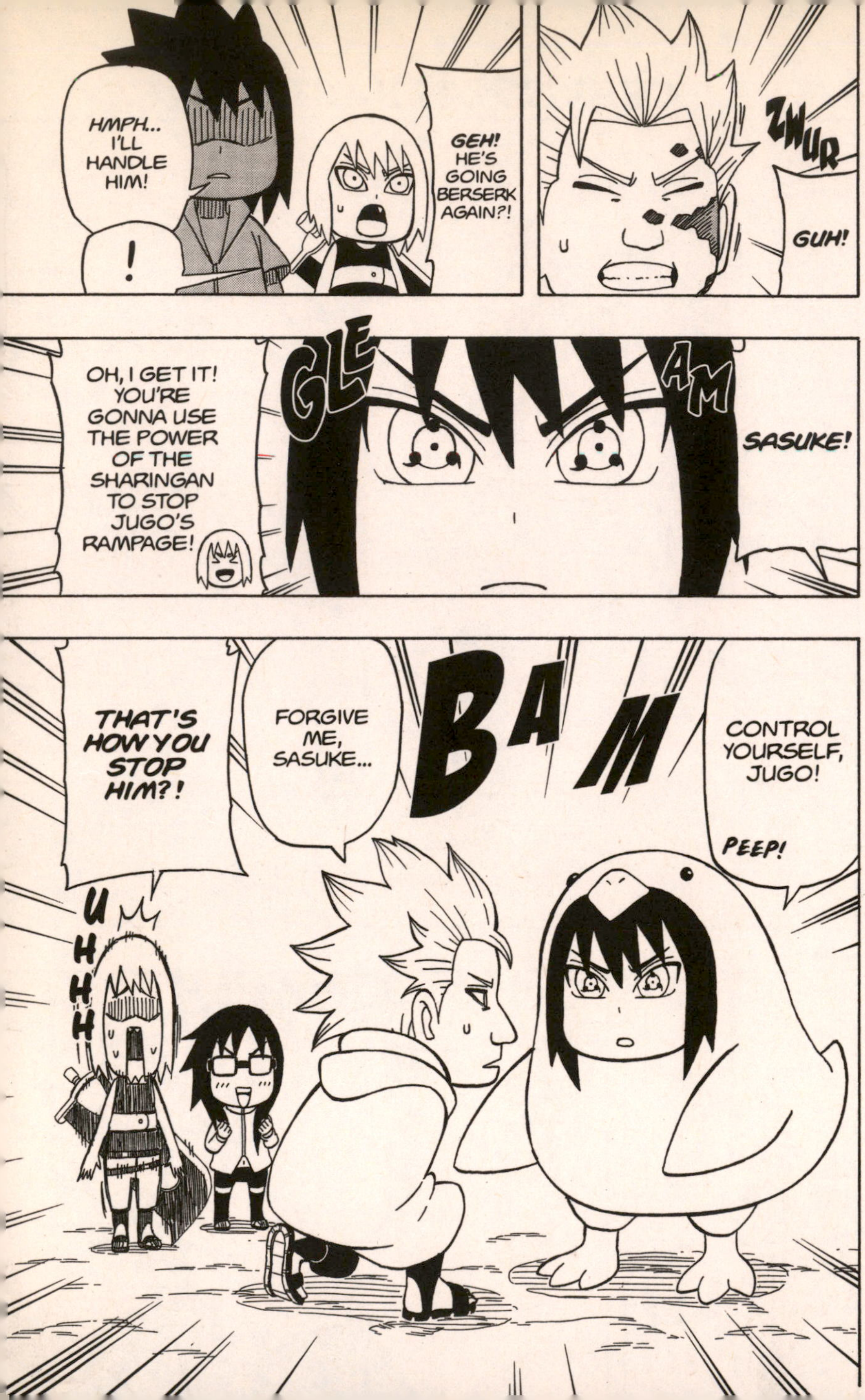
ZWUR
GUH!
GEH! HE'S GOING BERSERK AGAIN?!
HMPH... I'LL HANDLE HIM!
!
SASUKE!
GLEAM
OH, I GET IT! YOU'RE GONNA USE THE POWER OF THE SHARINGAN TO STOP JUGO'S RAMPAGE!
CONTROL YOURSELF, JUGO!
PEEP!
BAM
FORGIVE ME, SASUKE...
THAT'S HOW YOU STOP HIM?!
UHHHH

CHRISTMAS PARTY

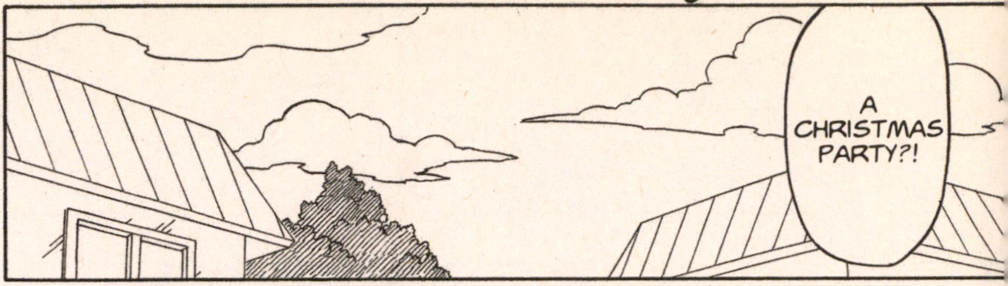
A CHRISTMAS PARTY?!

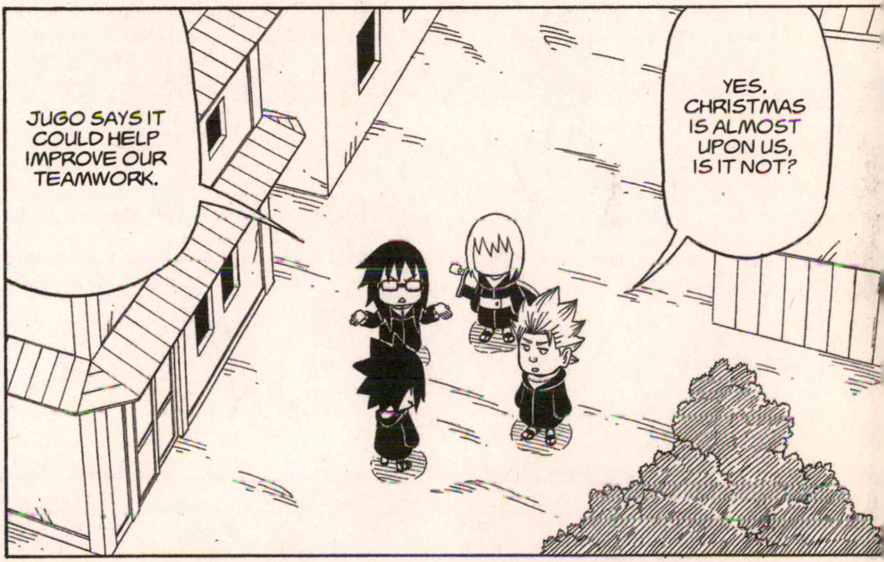
YES. CHRISTMAS IS ALMOST UPON US, IS IT NOT?
JUGO SAYS IT COULD HELP IMPROVE OUR TEAMWORK.

*SIGN: INN

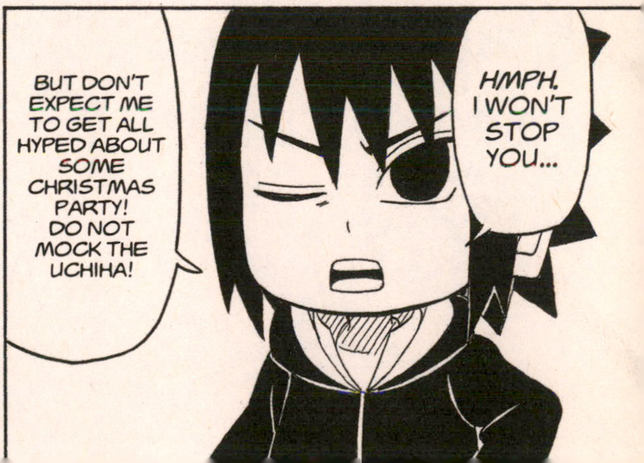
HMPH. I WON'T STOP YOU...
BUT DON'T EXPECT ME TO GET ALL HYPED ABOUT SOME CHRISTMAS PARTY! DO NOT MOCK THE UCHIHA!

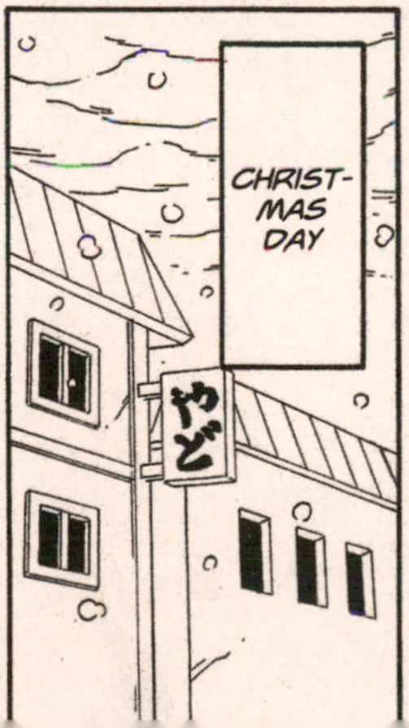
CHRIST-MAS DAY
やど

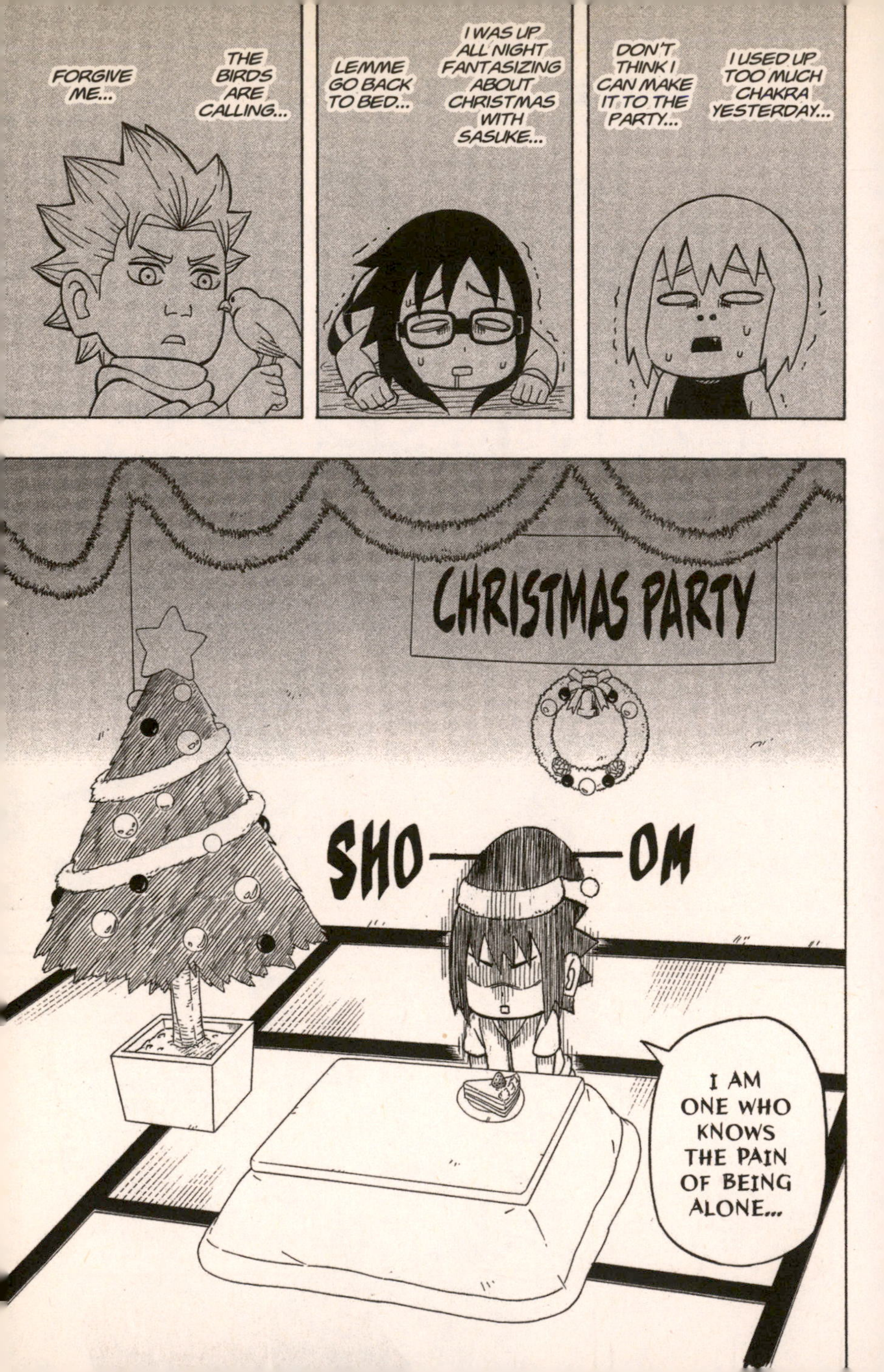

I USED UP TOO MUCH CHAKRA YESTERDAY...
DON'T THINK I CAN MAKE IT TO THE PARTY...
I WAS UP ALL NIGHT FANTASIZING ABOUT CHRISTMAS WITH SASUKE...
LEMME GO BACK TO BED...
THE BIRDS ARE CALLING...
FORGIVE ME...
CHRISTMAS PARTY
SHO—OM
I AM ONE WHO KNOWS THE PAIN OF BEING ALONE...

GIFT EXCHANGE

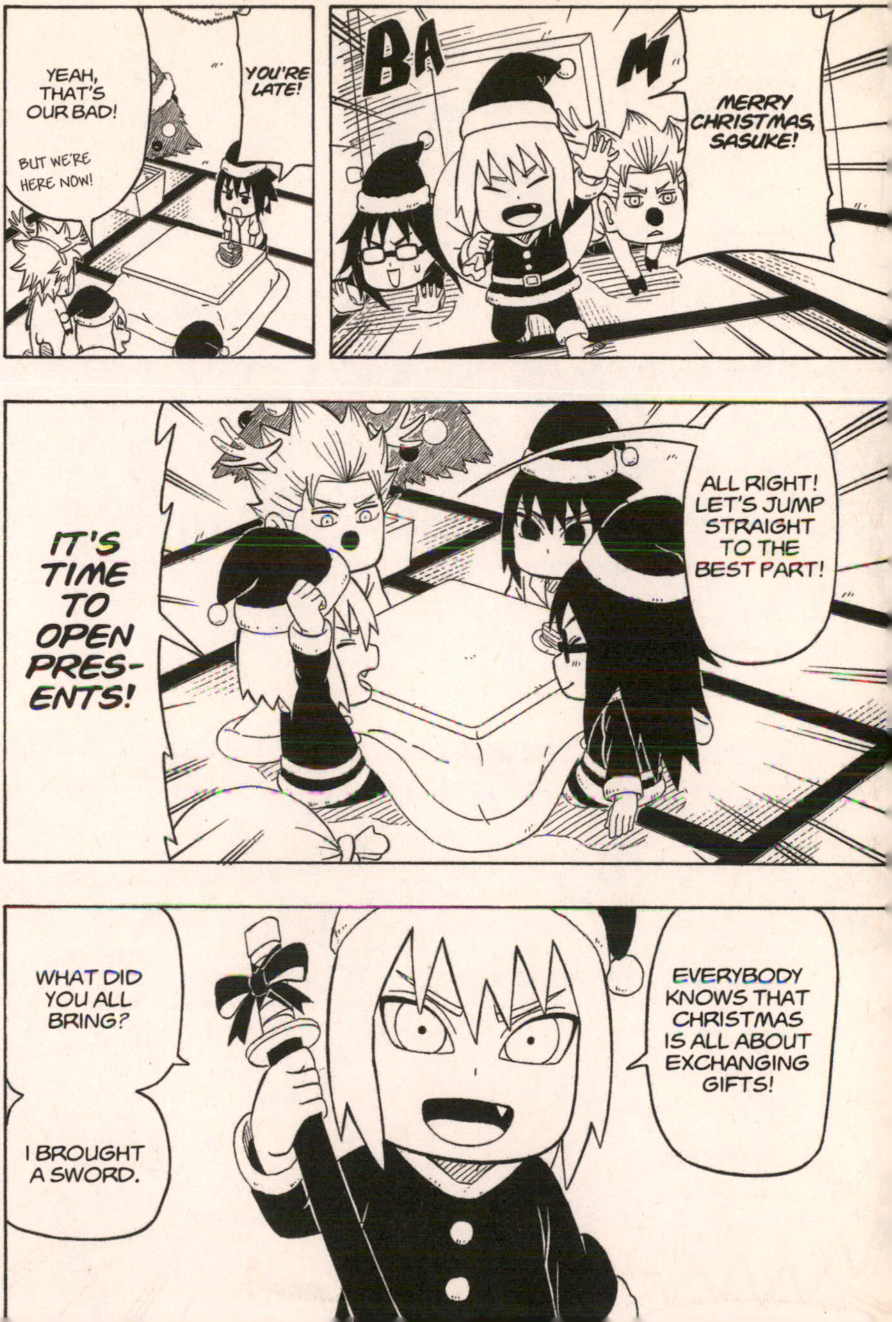
BAM
MERRY CHRISTMAS, SASUKE!
YOU'RE LATE!
YEAH, THAT'S OUR BAD!
BUT WE'RE HERE NOW!
ALL RIGHT! LET'S JUMP STRAIGHT TO THE BEST PART!
IT'S TIME TO OPEN PRES-ENTS!
EVERYBODY KNOWS THAT CHRISTMAS IS ALL ABOUT EXCHANGING GIFTS!
WHAT DID YOU ALL BRING?
I BROUGHT A SWORD.

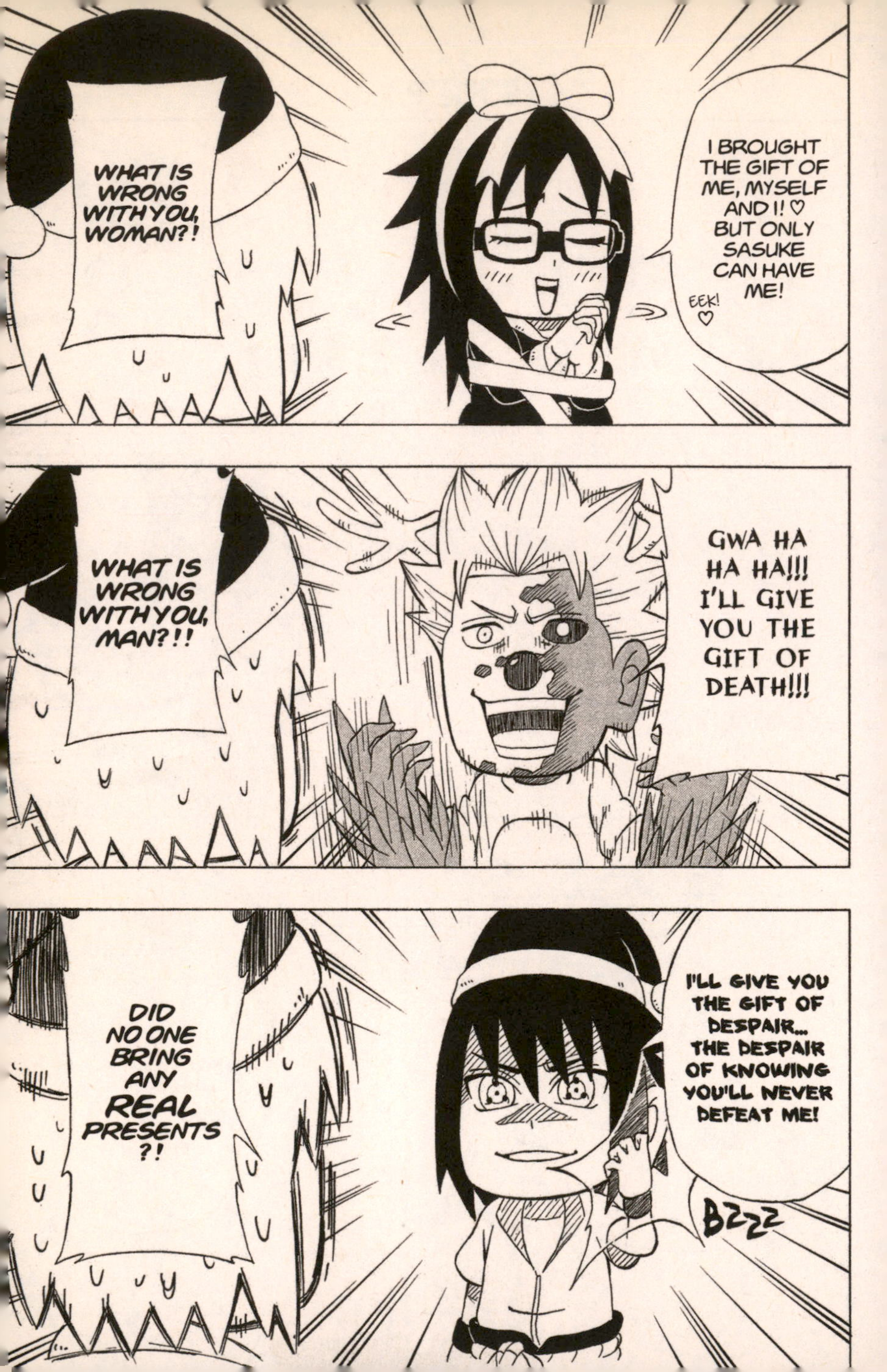
I BROUGHT THE GIFT OF ME, MYSELF AND I! ♡ BUT ONLY SASUKE CAN HAVE ME!
EEK! ♡
WHAT IS WRONG WITH YOU, WOMAN?!
GWA HA HA HA!!! I'LL GIVE YOU THE GIFT OF DEATH!!!
WHAT IS WRONG WITH YOU, MAN?!!
I'LL GIVE YOU THE GIFT OF DESPAIR... THE DESPAIR OF KNOWING YOU'LL NEVER DEFEAT ME!
BZZZ
DID NO ONE BRING ANY REAL PRESENTS?!

TRAP

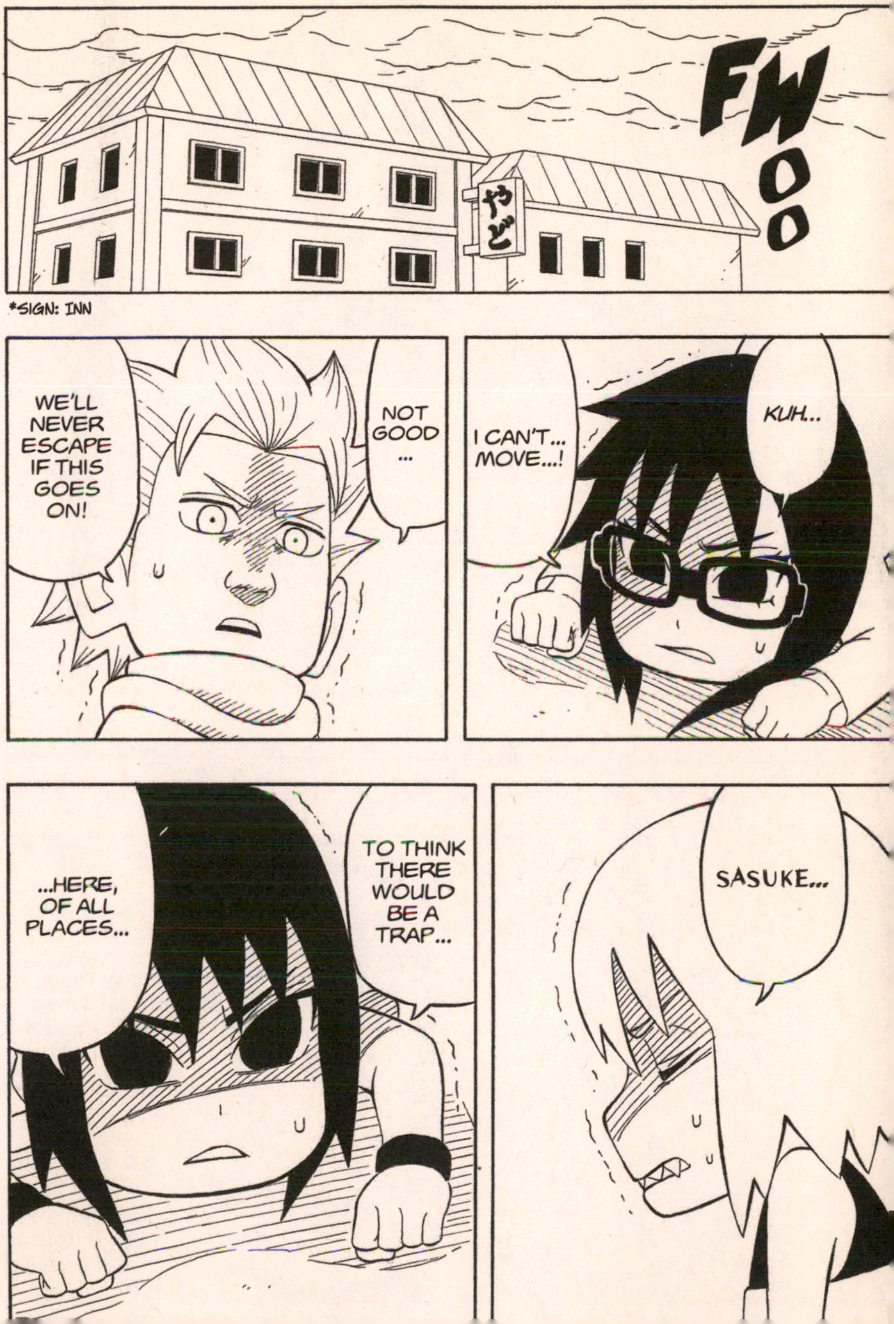
FWOO
やど
*SIGN: INN
KUH...
I CAN'T... MOVE...!
NOT GOOD...
WE'LL NEVER ESCAPE IF THIS GOES ON!
SASUKE...
TO THINK THERE WOULD BE A TRAP...
...HERE, OF ALL PLACES...

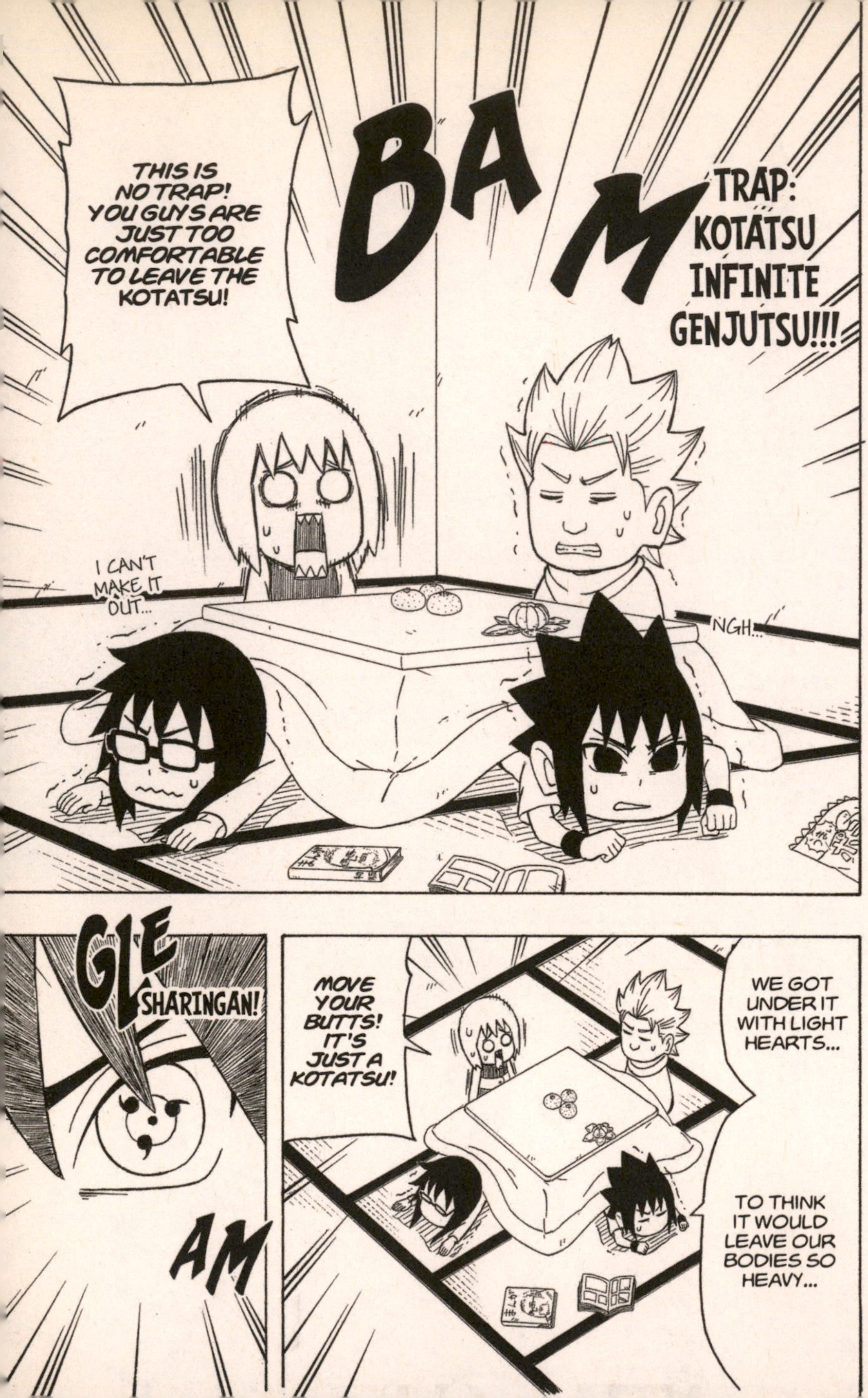
BAM
TRAP: KOTATSU INFINITE GENJUTSU!!!
THIS IS NO TRAP! YOU GUYS ARE JUST TOO COMFORTABLE TO LEAVE THE KOTATSU!
NGH...
I CAN'T MAKE IT OUT...
WE GOT UNDER IT WITH LIGHT HEARTS...
TO THINK IT WOULD LEAVE OUR BODIES SO HEAVY...
MOVE YOUR BUTTS! IT'S JUST A KOTATSU!
GLE
SHARINGAN!
AM

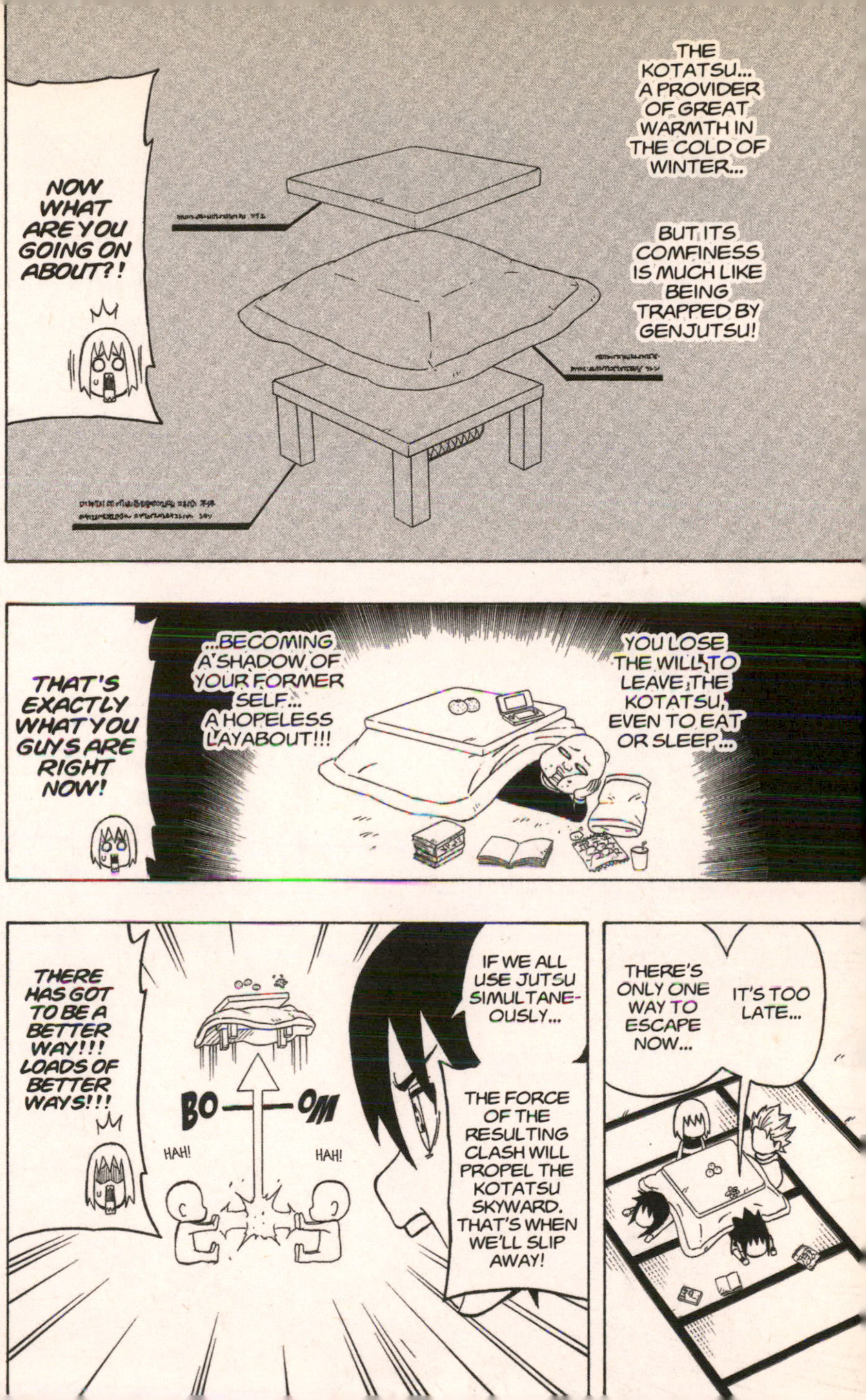
THE KOTATSU... A PROVIDER OF GREAT WARMTH IN THE COLD OF WINTER...
BUT ITS COMFINESS IS MUCH LIKE BEING TRAPPED BY GENJUTSU!
NOW WHAT ARE YOU GOING ON ABOUT?!
YOU LOSE THE WILL TO LEAVE THE KOTATSU, EVEN TO EAT OR SLEEP...
...BECOMING A SHADOW OF YOUR FORMER SELF... A HOPELESS LAYABOUT!!!
THAT'S EXACTLY WHAT YOU GUYS ARE RIGHT NOW!
IT'S TOO LATE...
THERE'S ONLY ONE WAY TO ESCAPE NOW...
IF WE ALL USE JUTSU SIMULTANE-OUSLY...
THE FORCE OF THE RESULTING CLASH WILL PROPEL THE KOTATSU SKYWARD. THAT'S WHEN WE'LL SLIP AWAY!
HAH!
HAH!
BO—OM
THERE HAS GOT TO BE A BETTER WAY!!! LOADS OF BETTER WAYS!!!

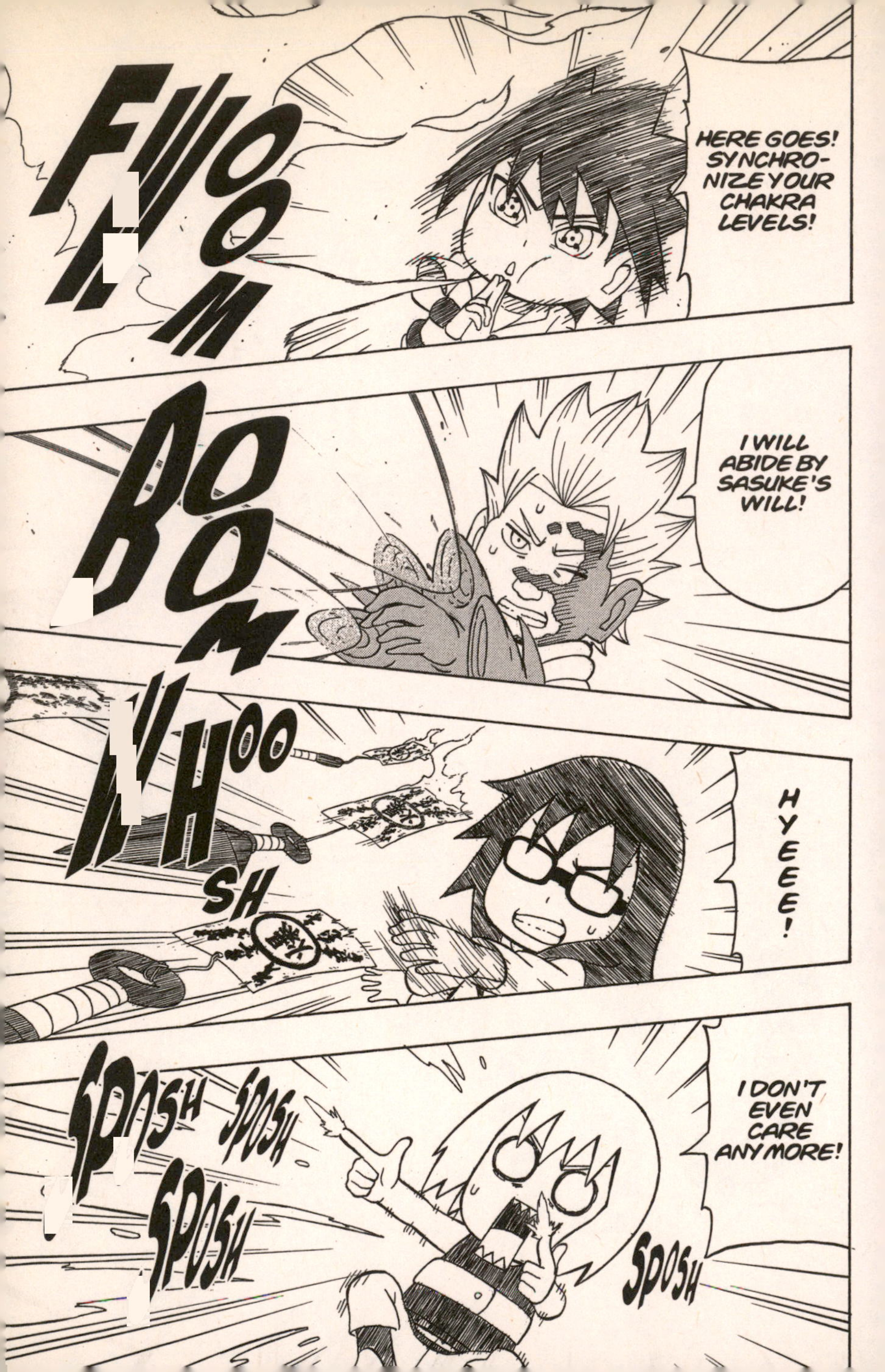
HERE GOES! SYNCHRO-NIZE YOUR CHAKRA LEVELS!
FWOOM
I WILL ABIDE BY SASUKE'S WILL!
BOOM
HYEEEE!
WHOOSH
I DON'T EVEN CARE ANYMORE!
SPOSH
SPOSH
SPOSH
SPOSH

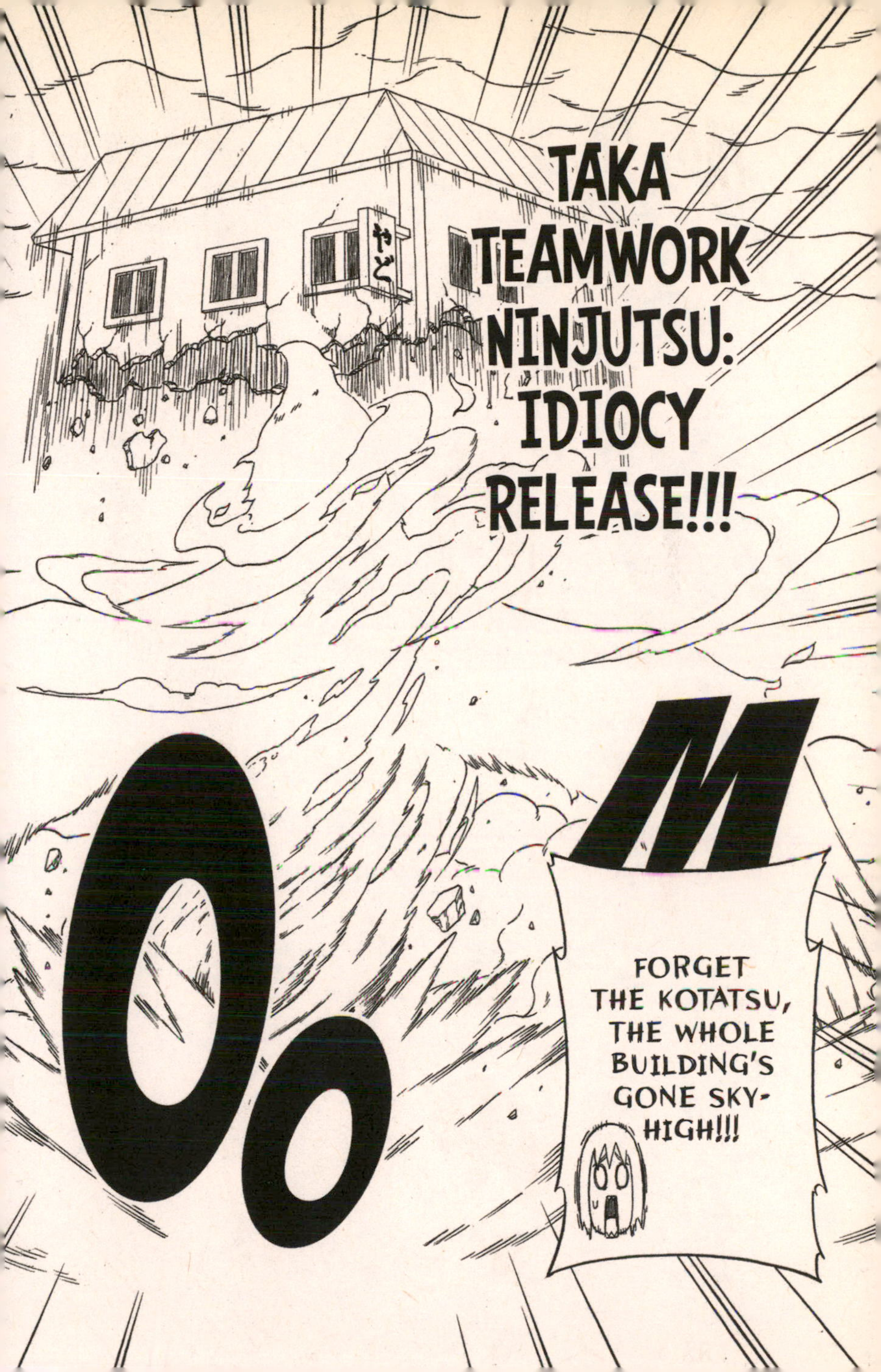
やど
TAKA TEAMWORK NINJUTSU: IDIOCY RELEASE!!!
OOM
FORGET THE KOTATSU, THE WHOLE BUILDING'S GONE SKY-HIGH!!!

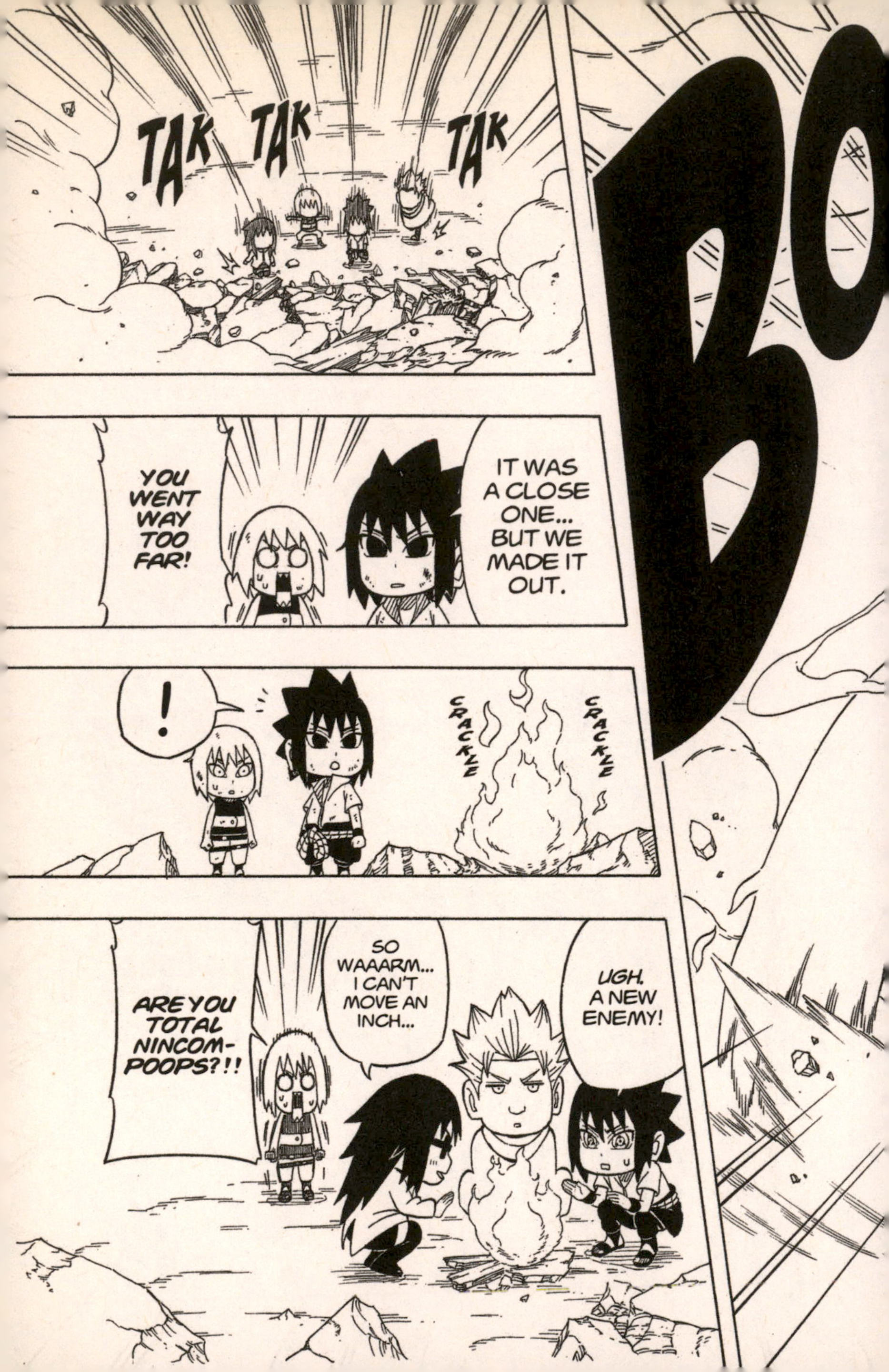
BO
TAK TAK TAK
IT WAS A CLOSE ONE... BUT WE MADE IT OUT.
YOU WENT WAY TOO FAR!
CRACKLE
CRACKLE
!
UGH. A NEW ENEMY!
SO WAAARM... I CAN'T MOVE AN INCH...
ARE YOU TOTAL NINCOM-POOPS?!!

MOVIE

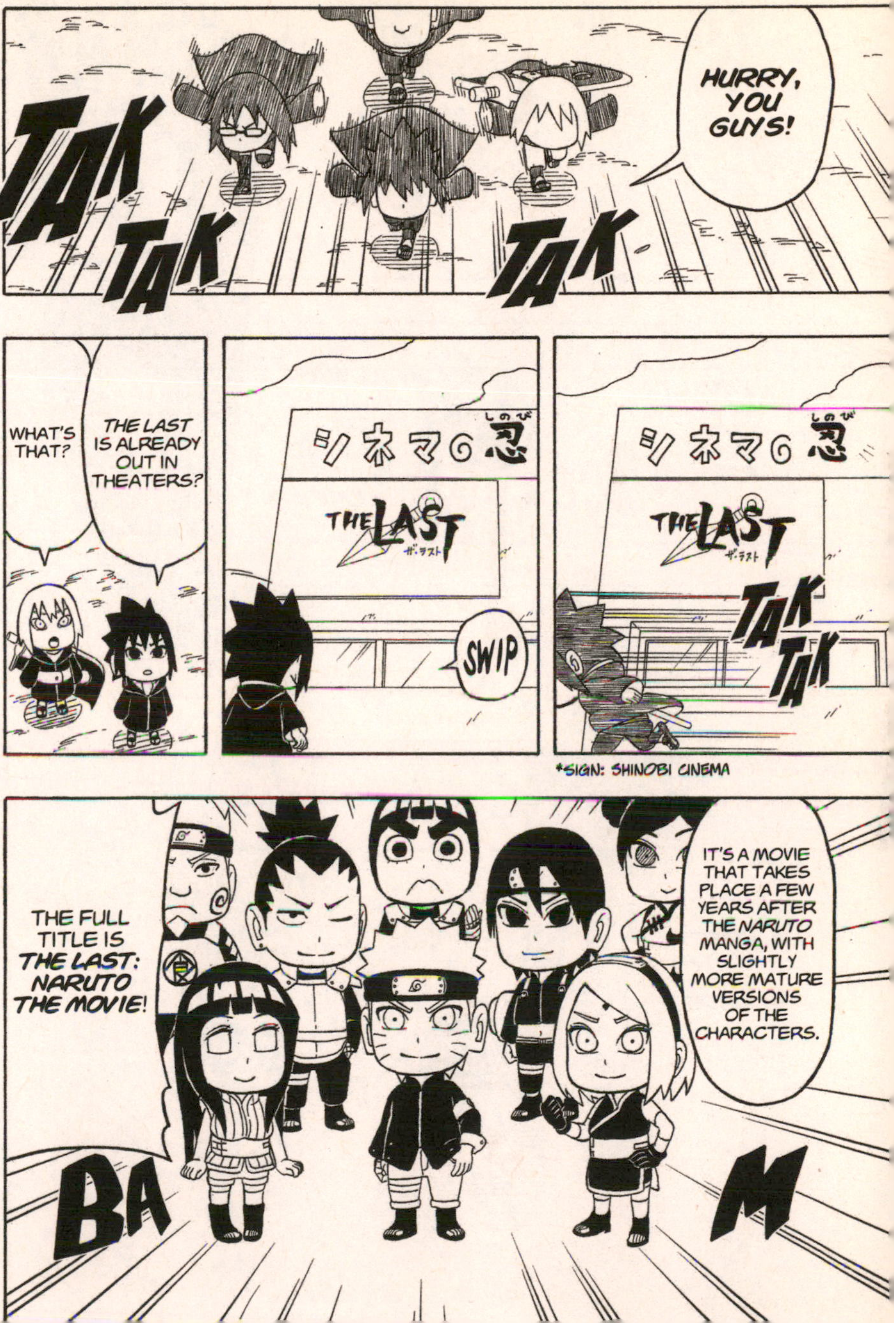
HURRY, YOU GUYS!
TAK
TAK
TAK
TAK
TAK
シネマ忍
THE LAST
ザ・ラスト
SWIP
シネマ忍
THE LAST
ザ・ラスト
THE LAST IS ALREADY OUT IN THEATERS?
WHAT'S THAT?
IT'S A MOVIE THAT TAKES PLACE A FEW YEARS AFTER THE NARUTO MANGA, WITH SLIGHTLY MORE MATURE VERSIONS OF THE CHARACTERS.
THE FULL TITLE IS THE LAST: NARUTO THE MOVIE!
BAM

*SIGN: SHINOBI CINEMA

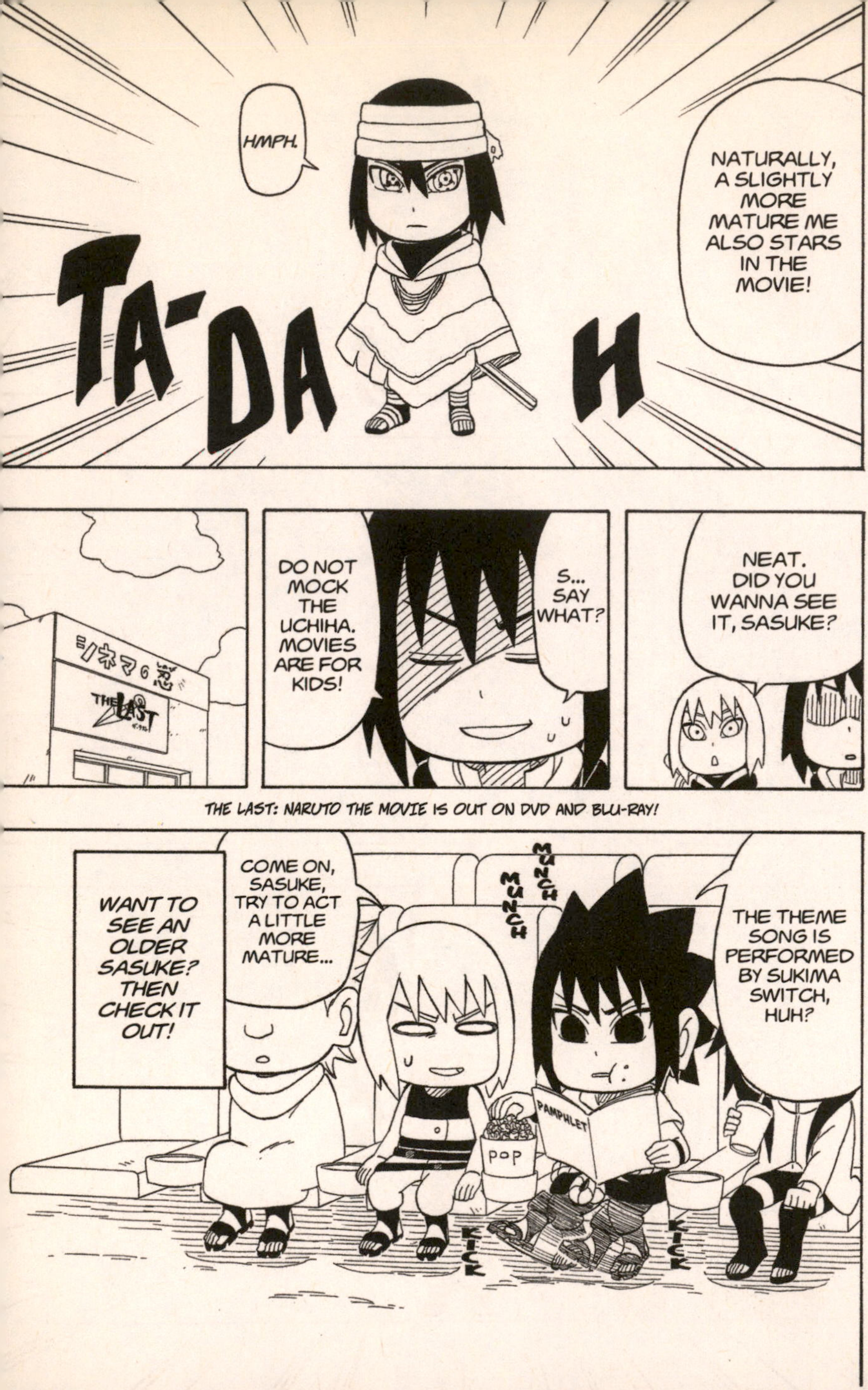
NATURALLY, A SLIGHTLY MORE MATURE ME ALSO STARS IN THE MOVIE!
HMPH.
TA-DAH
NEAT. DID YOU WANNA SEE IT, SASUKE?
S... SAY WHAT?
DO NOT MOCK THE UCHIHA. MOVIES ARE FOR KIDS!
THE LAST
THE LAST: NARUTO THE MOVIE IS OUT ON DVD AND BLU-RAY!
THE THEME SONG IS PERFORMED BY SUKIMA SWITCH, HUH?
MUNCH
MUNCH
COME ON, SASUKE, TRY TO ACT A LITTLE MORE MATURE...
WANT TO SEE AN OLDER SASUKE? THEN CHECK IT OUT!
PAMPHLET
POP
KICK
KICK

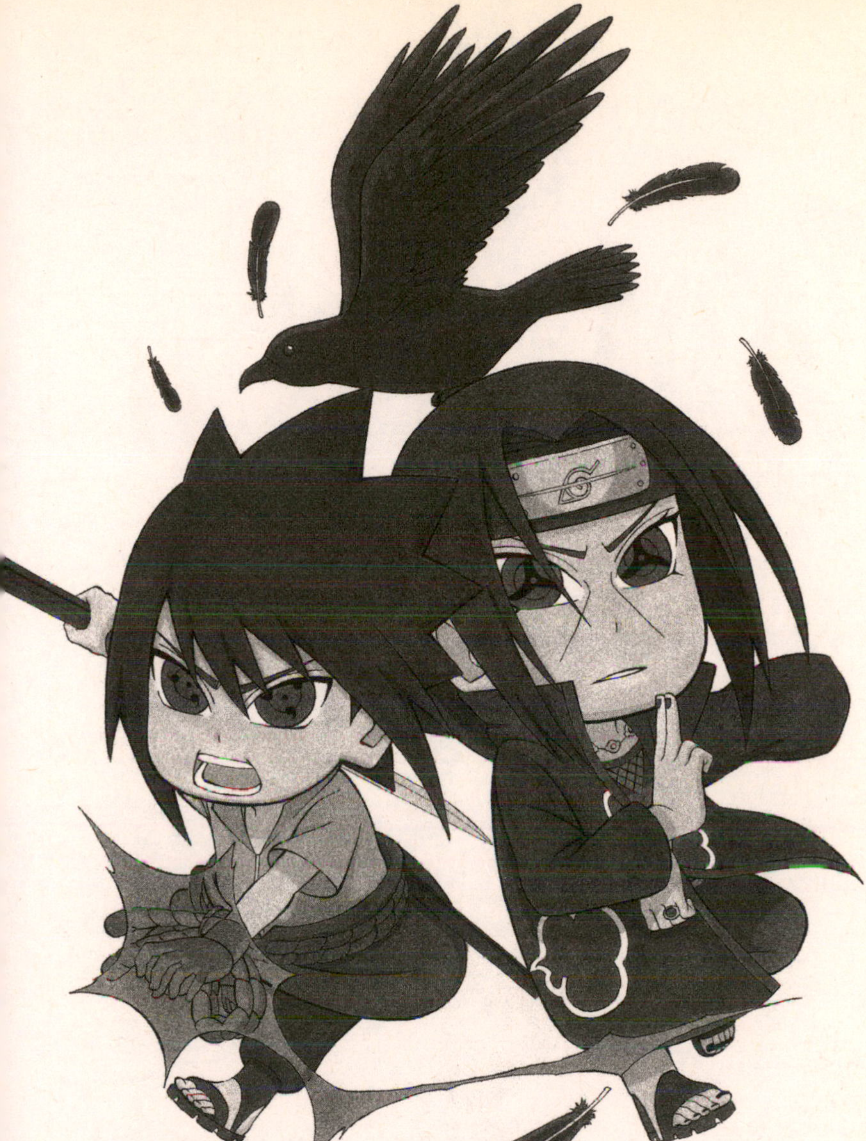

CHAPTER 3: UCHIHA ITACHI!!

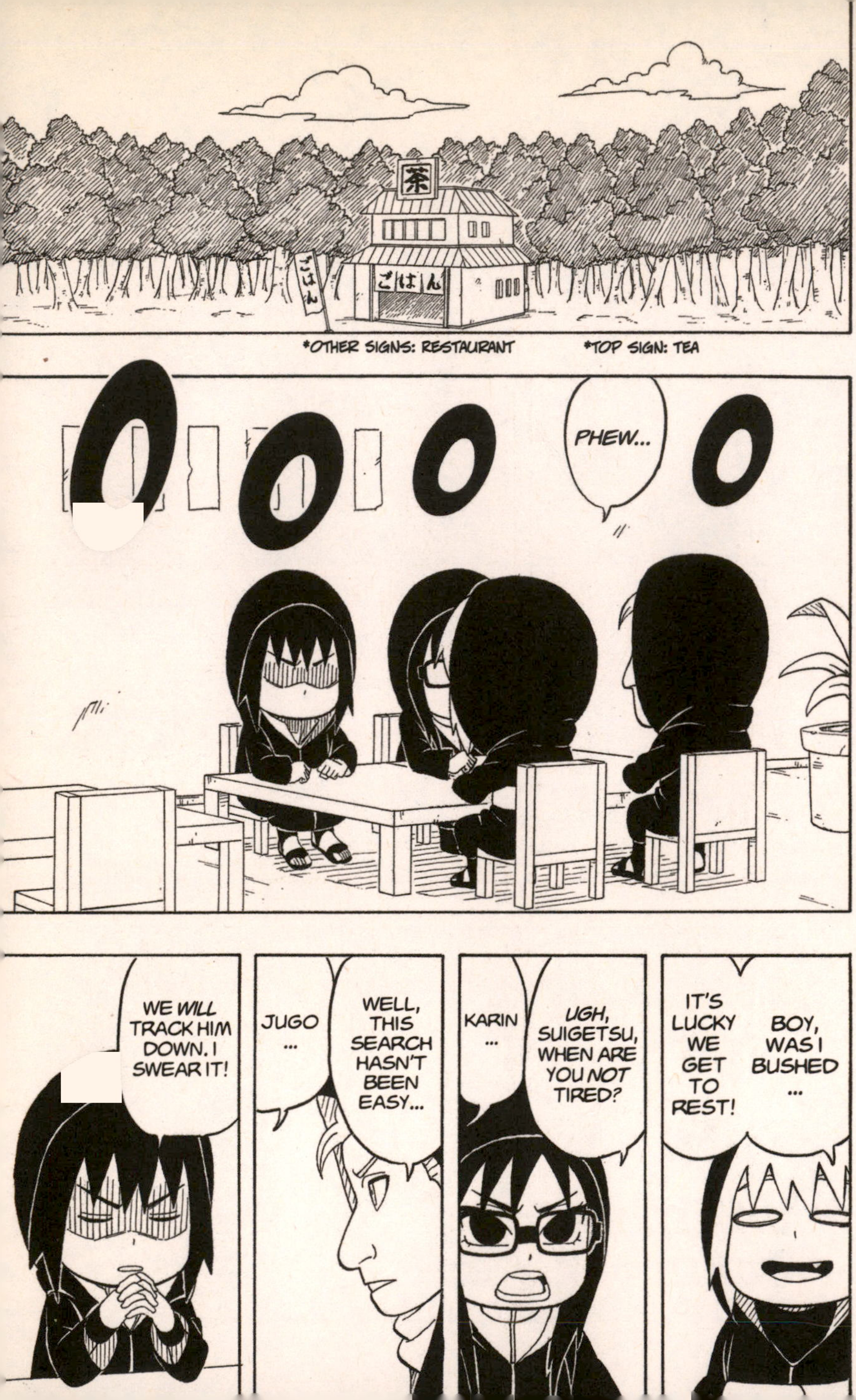
茶
ごはん
ごはん
*OTHER SIGNS: RESTAURANT
*TOP SIGN: TEA
PHEW...
BOY, WAS I BUSHED ...
IT'S LUCKY WE GET TO REST!
UGH, SUIGETSU, WHEN ARE YOU NOT TIRED?
KARIN ...
WELL, THIS SEARCH HASN'T BEEN EASY...
JUGO ...
WE WILL TRACK HIM DOWN. I SWEAR IT!

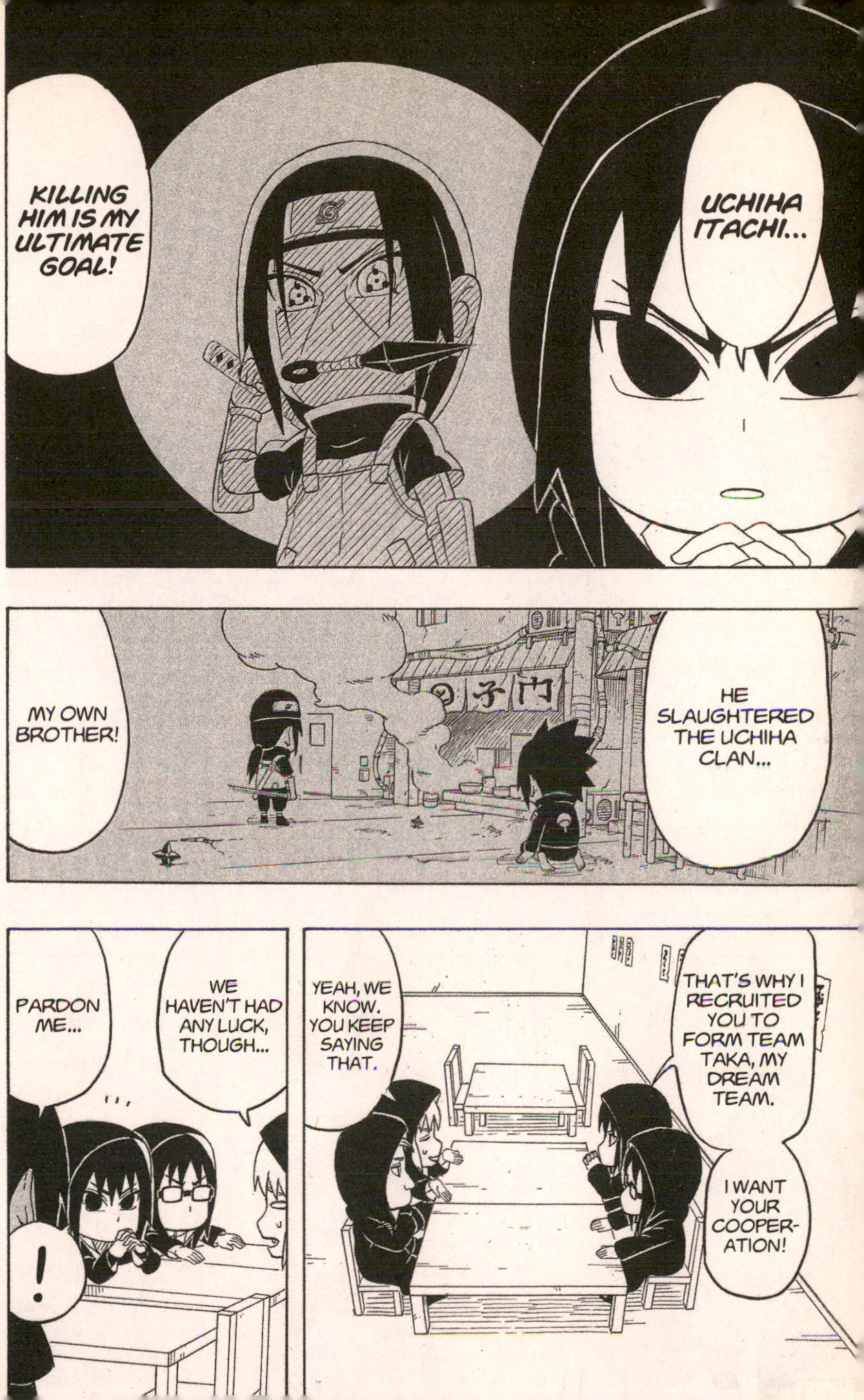
UCHIHA ITACHI...
KILLING HIM IS MY ULTIMATE GOAL!
HE SLAUGHTERED THE UCHIHA CLAN...
MY OWN BROTHER!
THAT'S WHY I RECRUITED YOU TO FORM TEAM TAKA, MY DREAM TEAM.
I WANT YOUR COOPER-ATION!
YEAH, WE KNOW. YOU KEEP SAYING THAT.
WE HAVEN'T HAD ANY LUCK, THOUGH...
PARDON ME...
!

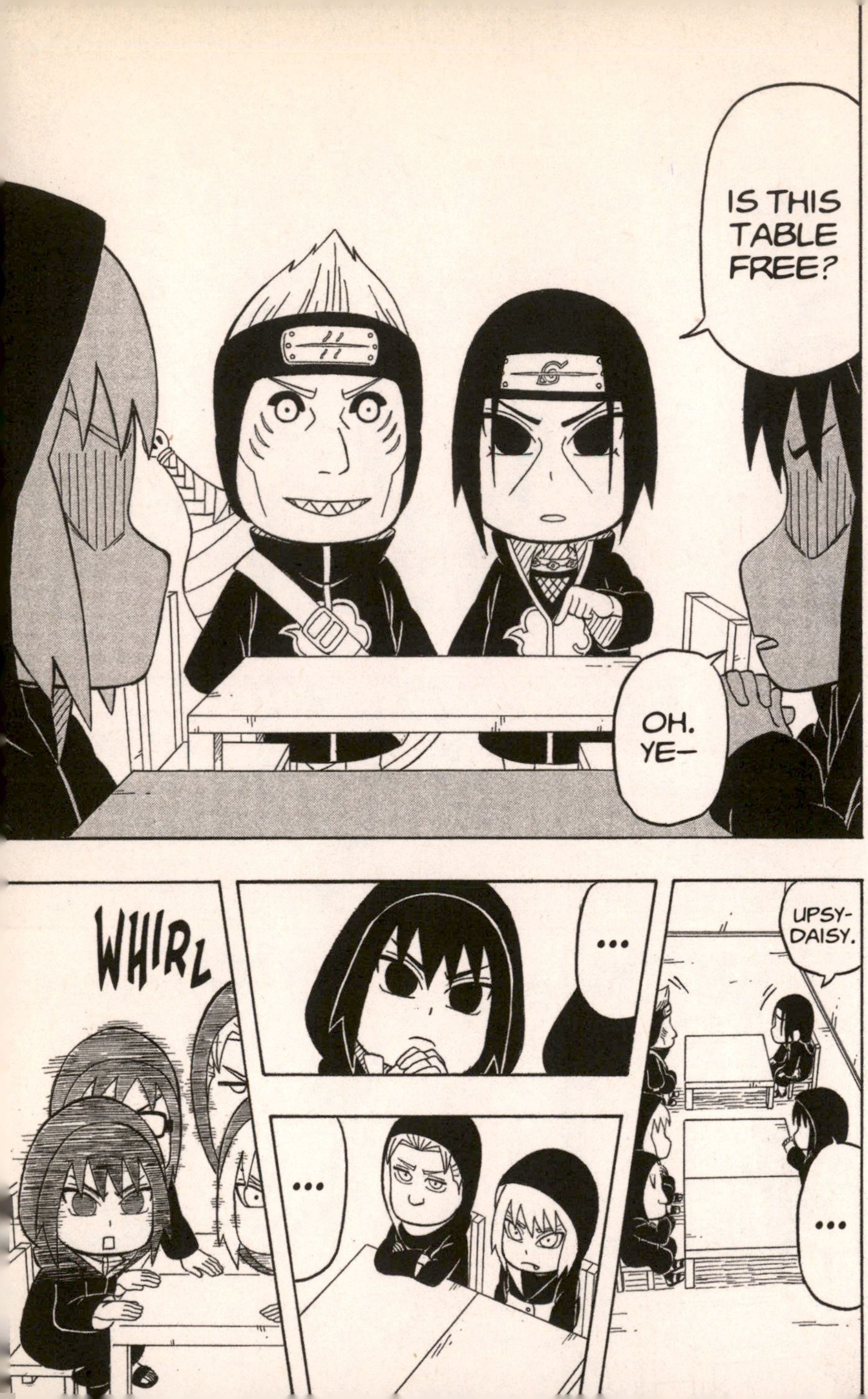
IS THIS TABLE FREE?
OH. YE—
UPSY-DAISY.
...
...
...
WHIRL

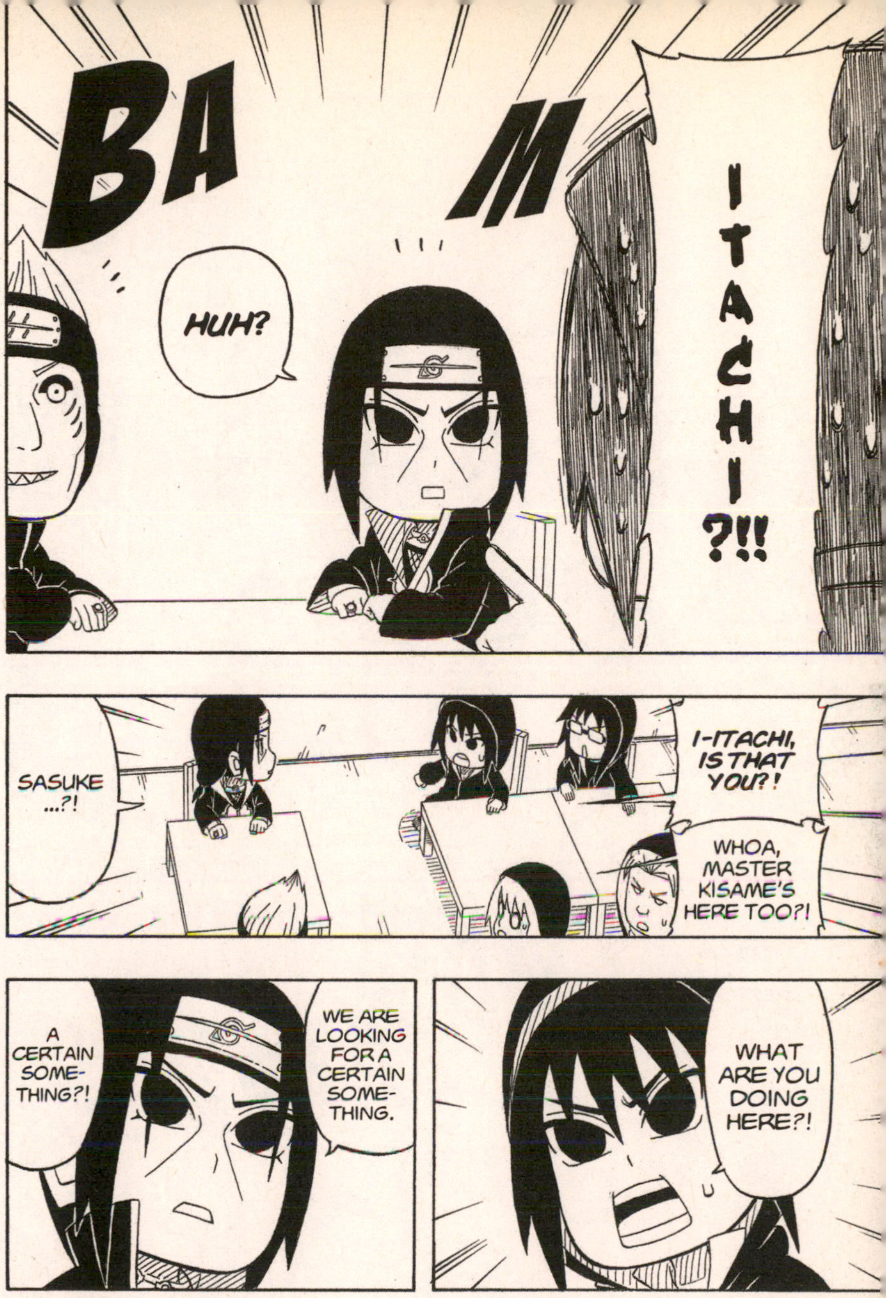
ITACHI?!!
BAM
HUH?
I-ITACHI, IS THAT YOU?!
WHOA, MASTER KISAME'S HERE TOO?!
SASUKE ...?!
WHAT ARE YOU DOING HERE?!
WE ARE LOOKING FOR A CERTAIN SOME-THING.
A CERTAIN SOME-THING?!

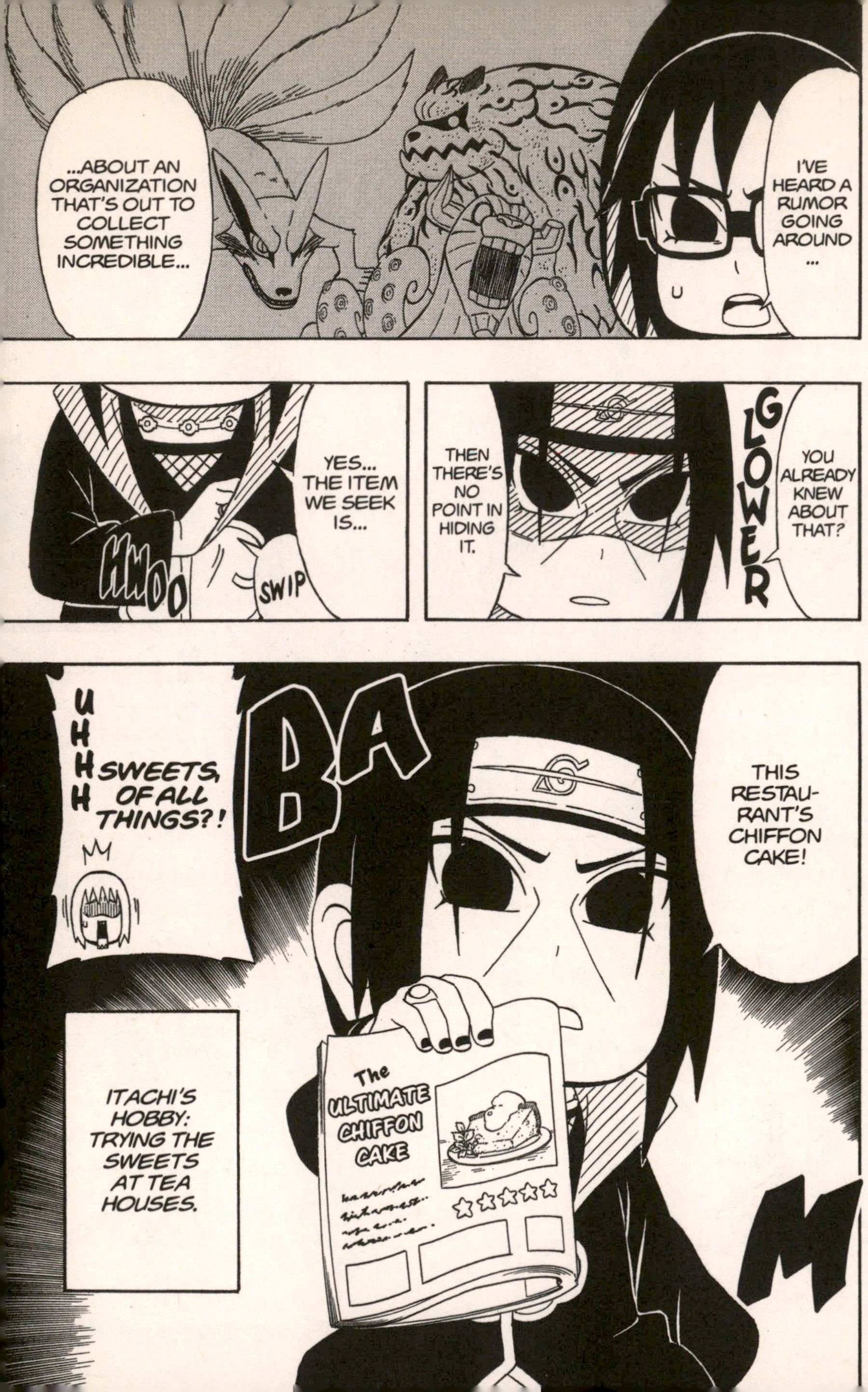
I'VE HEARD A RUMOR GOING AROUND ...
...ABOUT AN ORGANIZATION THAT'S OUT TO COLLECT SOMETHING INCREDIBLE...
YOU ALREADY KNEW ABOUT THAT?
GLOWER
THEN THERE'S NO POINT IN HIDING IT.
YES... THE ITEM WE SEEK IS...
SWIP
HWOO
THIS RESTAU-RANT'S CHIFFON CAKE!
BAM
The ULTIMATE CHIFFON CAKE
UHHH SWEETS, OF ALL THINGS?!
ITACHI'S HOBBY: TRYING THE SWEETS AT TEA HOUSES.

THE TRAGEDY OF THE UCHIHA

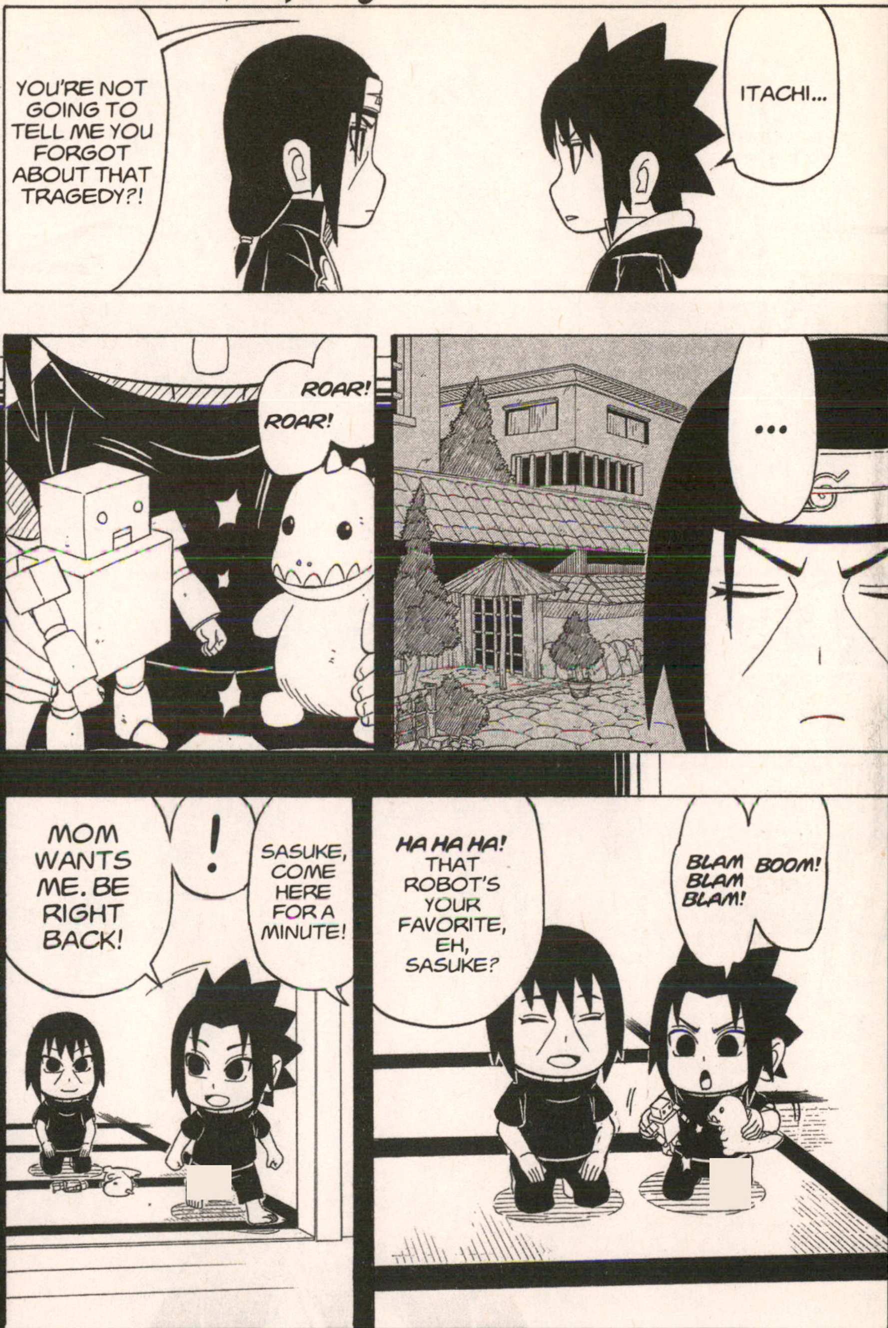
ITACHI...
YOU'RE NOT GOING TO TELL ME YOU FORGOT ABOUT THAT TRAGEDY?!
...
ROAR! ROAR!
BLAM BLAM BLAM! BOOM!
HA HA HA! THAT ROBOT'S YOUR FAVORITE, EH, SASUKE?
SASUKE, COME HERE FOR A MINUTE!
!
MOM WANTS ME. BE RIGHT BACK!

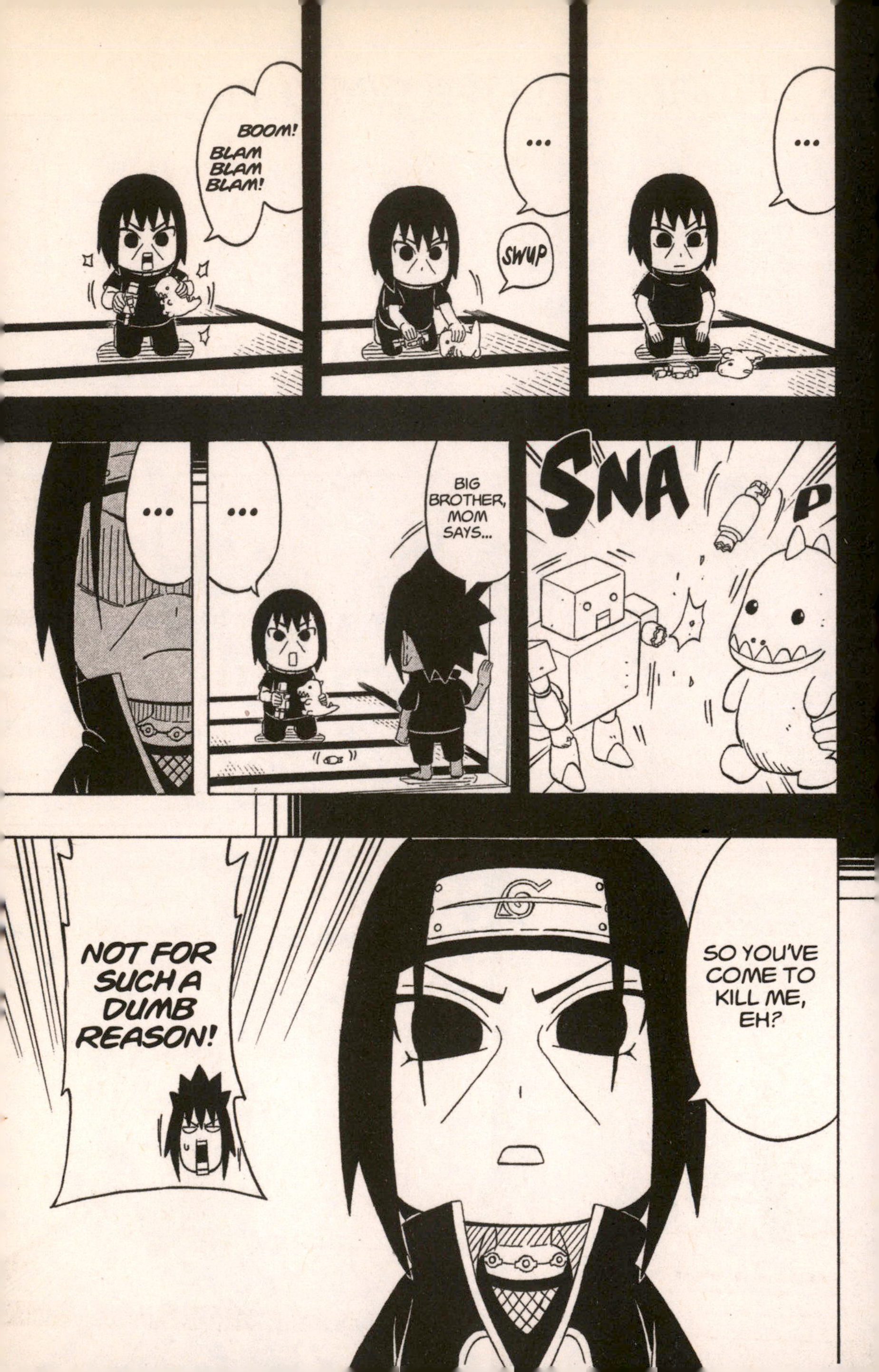
...
...
SWUP
BOOM! BLAM BLAM BLAM!
SNAP
BIG BROTHER, MOM SAYS...
...
...
SO YOU'VE COME TO KILL ME, EH?
NOT FOR SUCH A DUMB REASON!

BROTHER VS. BROTHER

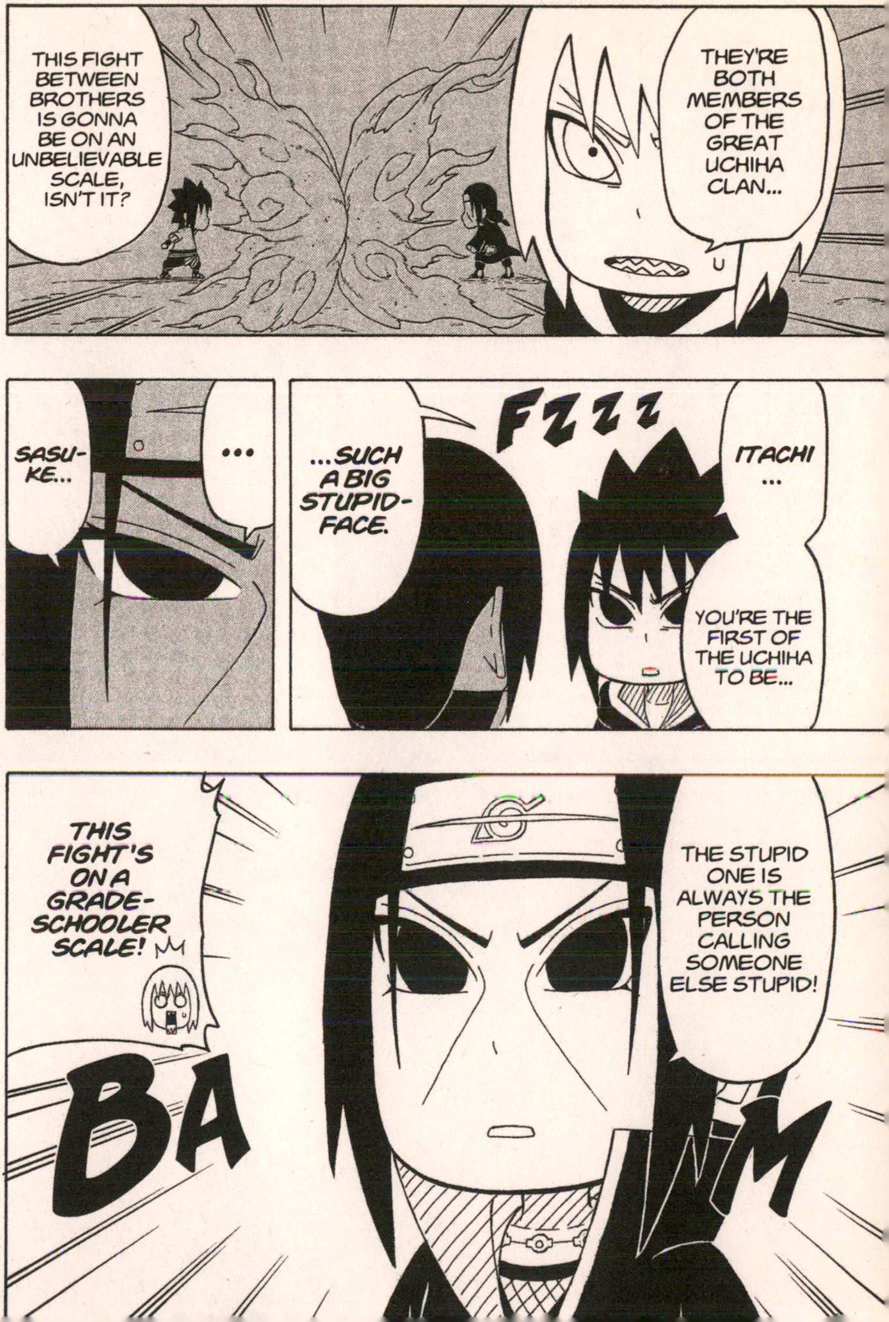
THEY'RE BOTH MEMBERS OF THE GREAT UCHIHA CLAN...
THIS FIGHT BETWEEN BROTHERS IS GONNA BE ON AN UNBELIEVABLE SCALE, ISN'T IT?
ITACHI ...
YOU'RE THE FIRST OF THE UCHIHA TO BE...
FZZZ
...SUCH A BIG STUPID-FACE.
...
SASUKE...
THE STUPID ONE IS ALWAYS THE PERSON CALLING SOMEONE ELSE STUPID!
THIS FIGHT'S ON A GRADE-SCHOOLER SCALE!
BAM

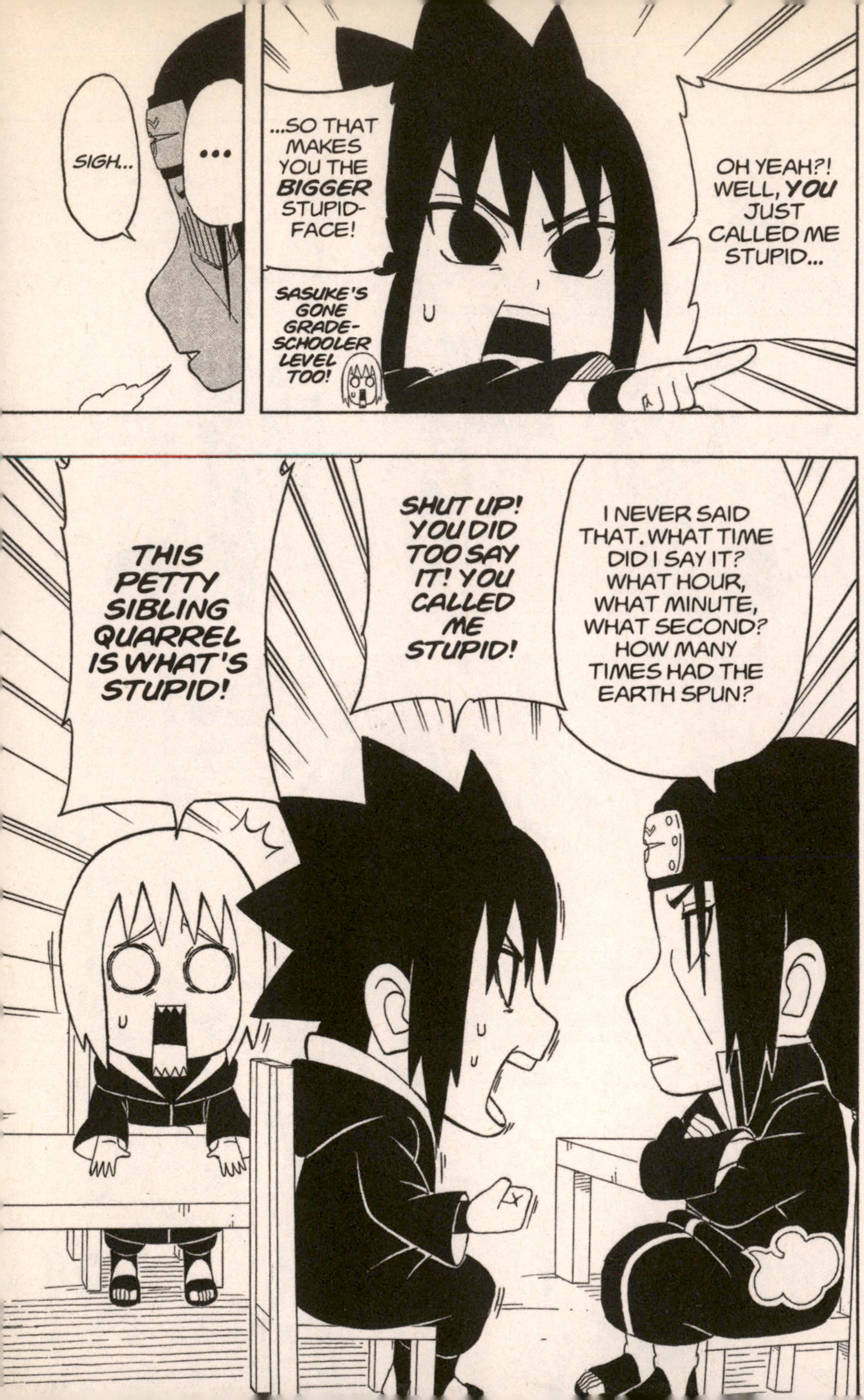
OH YEAH?! WELL, YOU JUST CALLED ME STUPID...
...SO THAT MAKES YOU THE BIGGER STUPID-FACE!
SASUKE'S GONE GRADE-SCHOOLER LEVEL TOO!
...
SIGH...
I NEVER SAID THAT. WHAT TIME DID I SAY IT? WHAT HOUR, WHAT MINUTE, WHAT SECOND? HOW MANY TIMES HAD THE EARTH SPUN?
SHUT UP! YOU DID TOO SAY IT! YOU CALLED ME STUPID!
THIS PETTY SIBLING QUARREL IS WHAT'S STUPID!

BATTLE?!

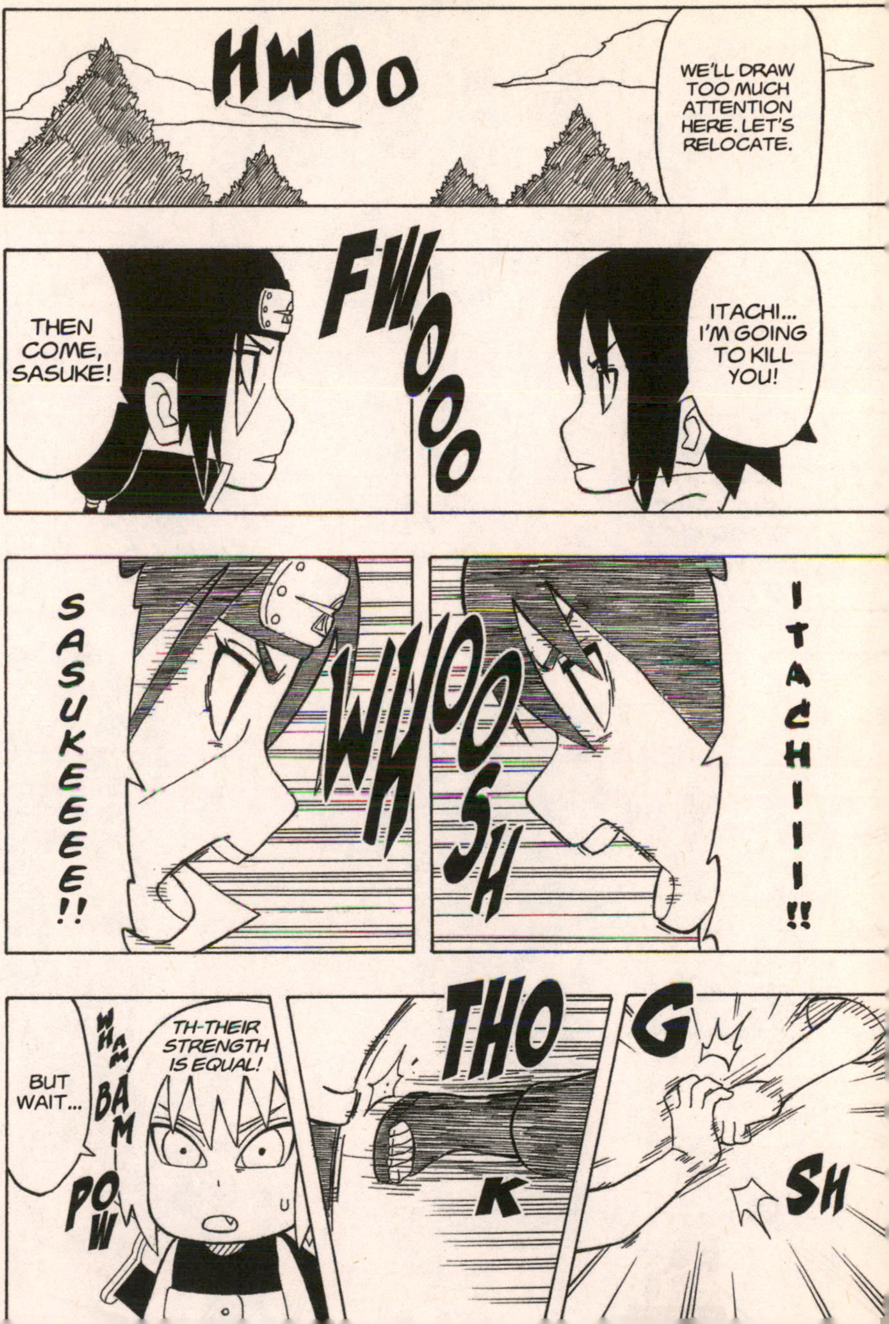
WE'LL DRAW TOO MUCH ATTENTION HERE. LET'S RELOCATE.
HWOO
ITACHI... I'M GOING TO KILL YOU!
FWOOOO
THEN COME, SASUKE!
ITACHIIII!!
WHOOSH
SASUKEEEEE!!
G
SH
THO
K
TH-THEIR STRENGTH IS EQUAL!
WHAM
BAM
POW
BUT WAIT...

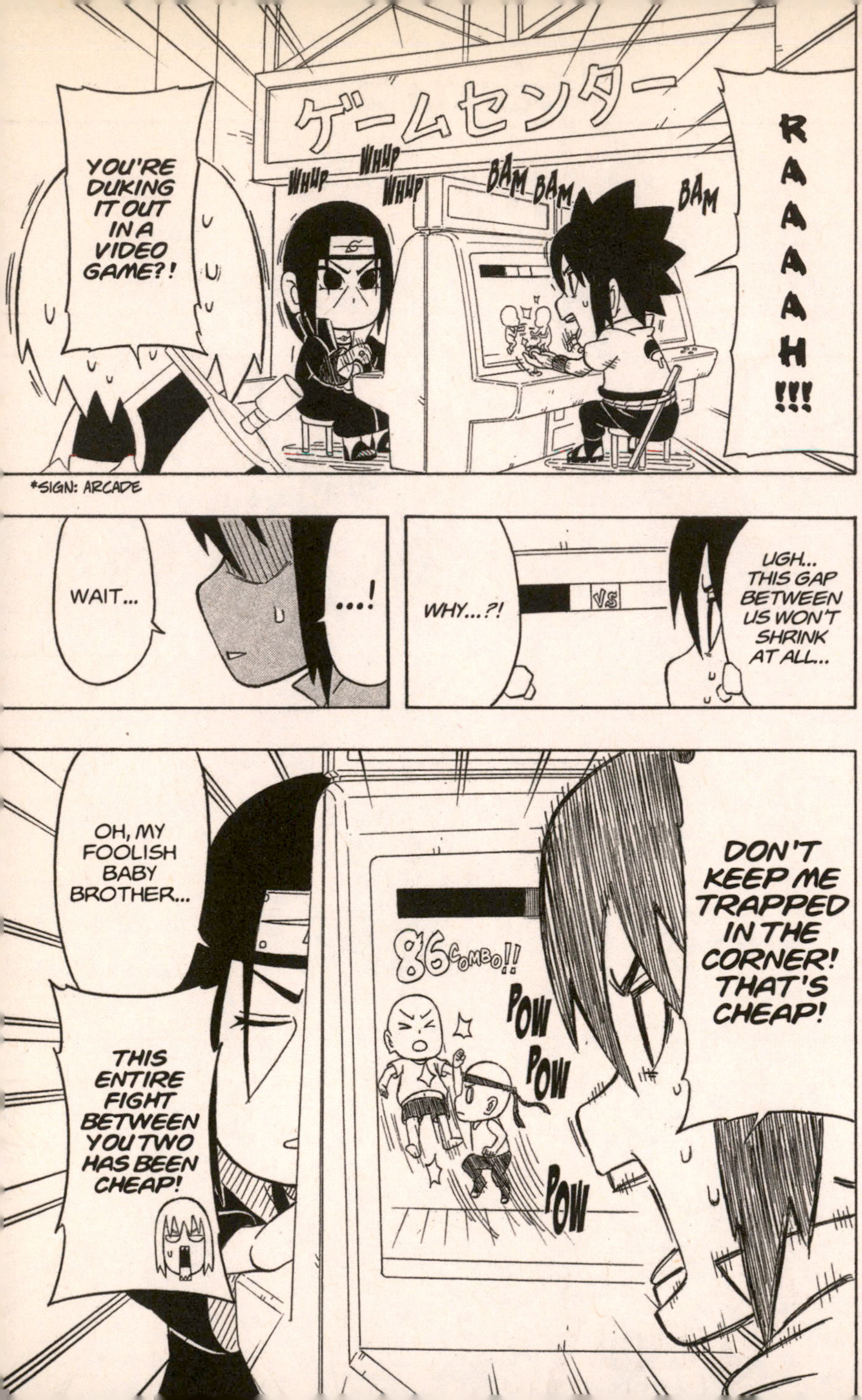
RAAAAAH!!!
ゲームセンター
BAM BAM BAM
WHUP WHUP WHUP
YOU'RE DUKING IT OUT IN A VIDEO GAME?!
*SIGN: ARCADE
UGH... THIS GAP BETWEEN US WON'T SHRINK AT ALL...
VS
WHY...?!
...!
WAIT...
DON'T KEEP ME TRAPPED IN THE CORNER! THAT'S CHEAP!
86 COMBO!!
POW POW POW
OH, MY FOOLISH BABY BROTHER...
THIS ENTIRE FIGHT BETWEEN YOU TWO HAS BEEN CHEAP!

KISAME

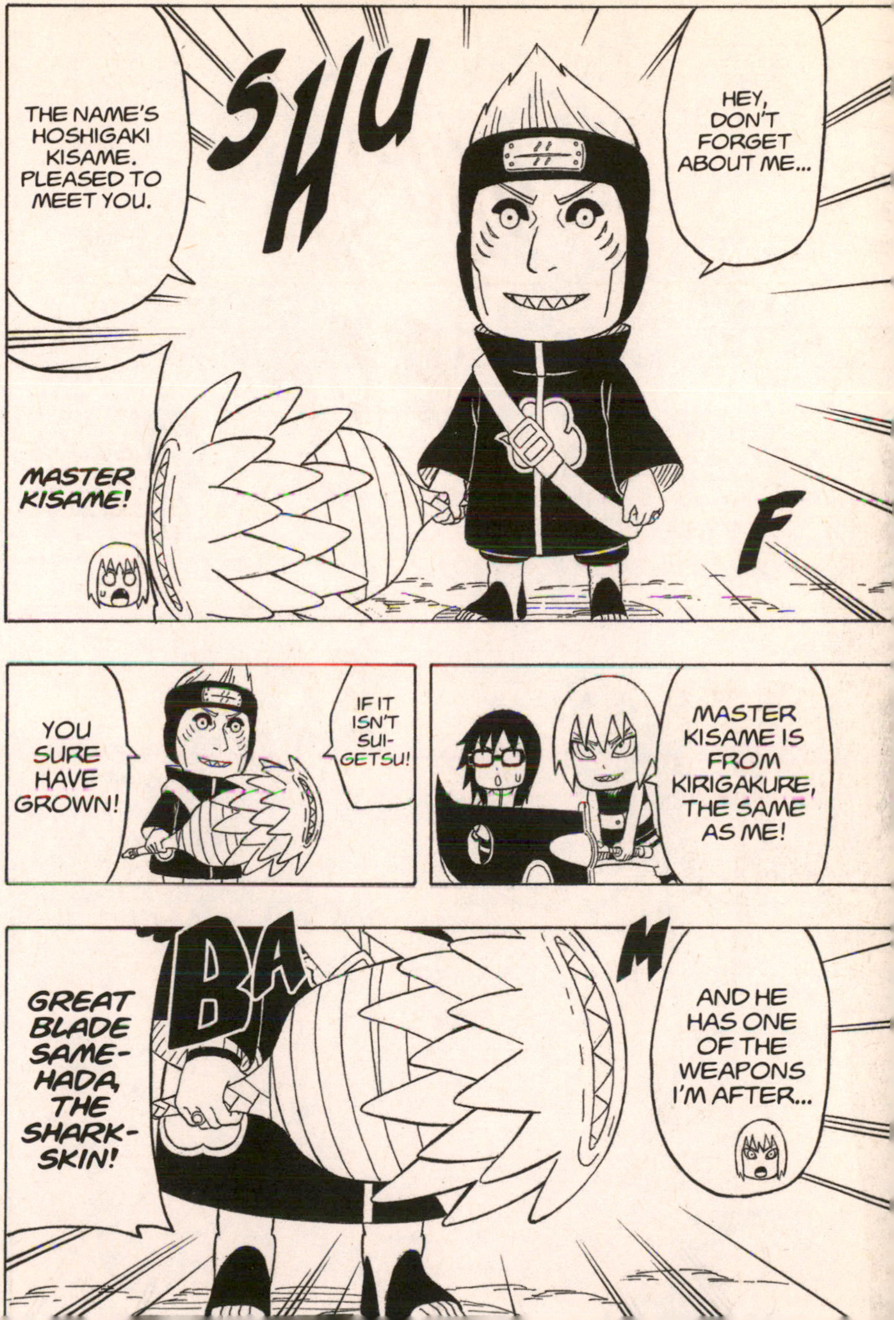
HEY, DON'T FORGET ABOUT ME...
SHU
THE NAME'S HOSHIGAKI KISAME. PLEASED TO MEET YOU.
F
MASTER KISAME!
MASTER KISAME IS FROM KIRIGAKURE, THE SAME AS ME!
IF IT ISN'T SUI-GETSU!
YOU SURE HAVE GROWN!
AND HE HAS ONE OF THE WEAPONS I'M AFTER...
BAM
GREAT BLADE SAME-HADA, THE SHARK-SKIN!

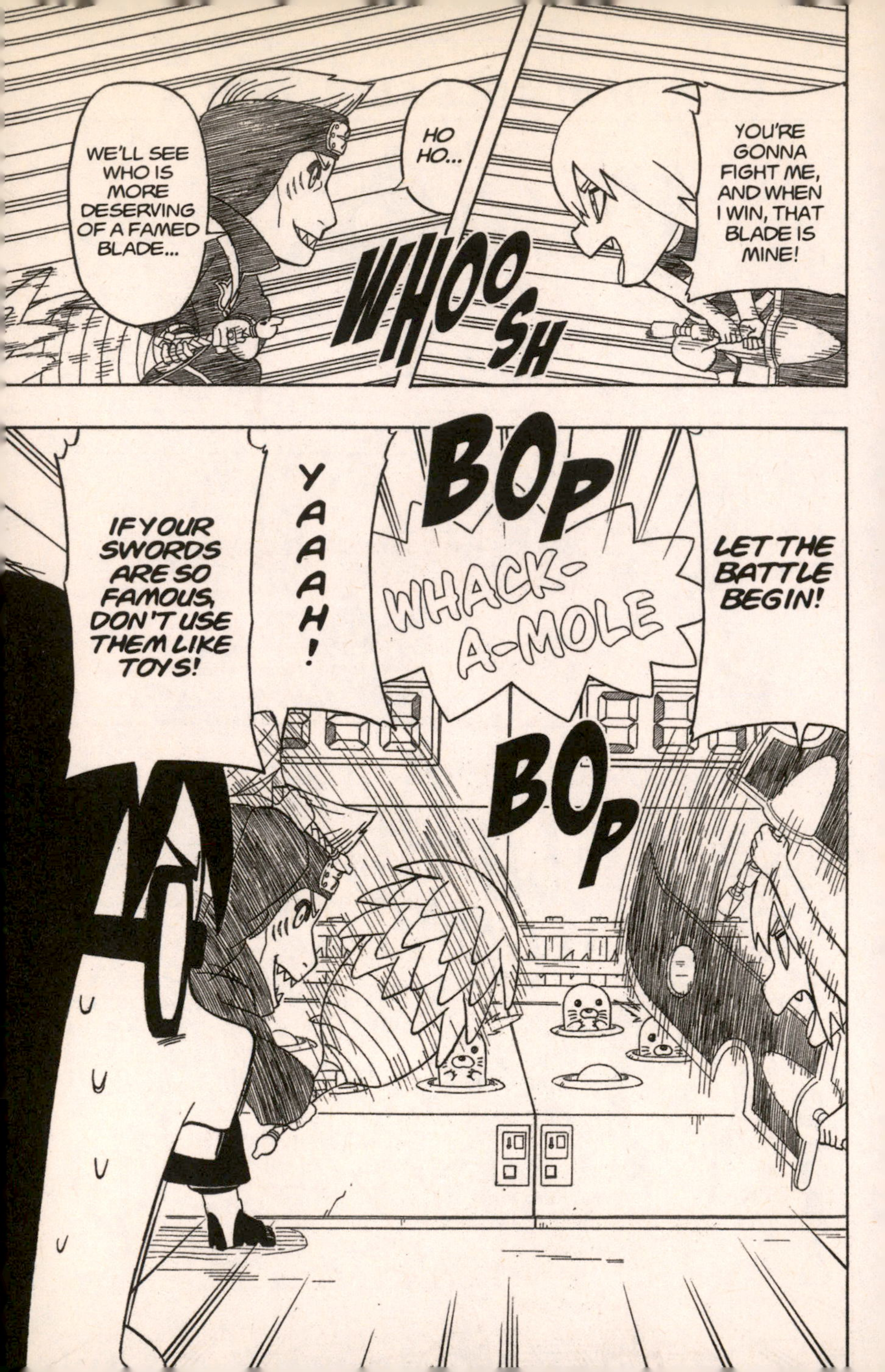
YOU'RE GONNA FIGHT ME, AND WHEN I WIN, THAT BLADE IS MINE!
HO HO...
WE'LL SEE WHO IS MORE DESERVING OF A FAMED BLADE...
WHOOSH
LET THE BATTLE BEGIN!
BOP
WHACK-A-MOLE
YAAAAH!
IF YOUR SWORDS ARE SO FAMOUS, DON'T USE THEM LIKE TOYS!
BOP

FAMED BLADES SHOWDOWN

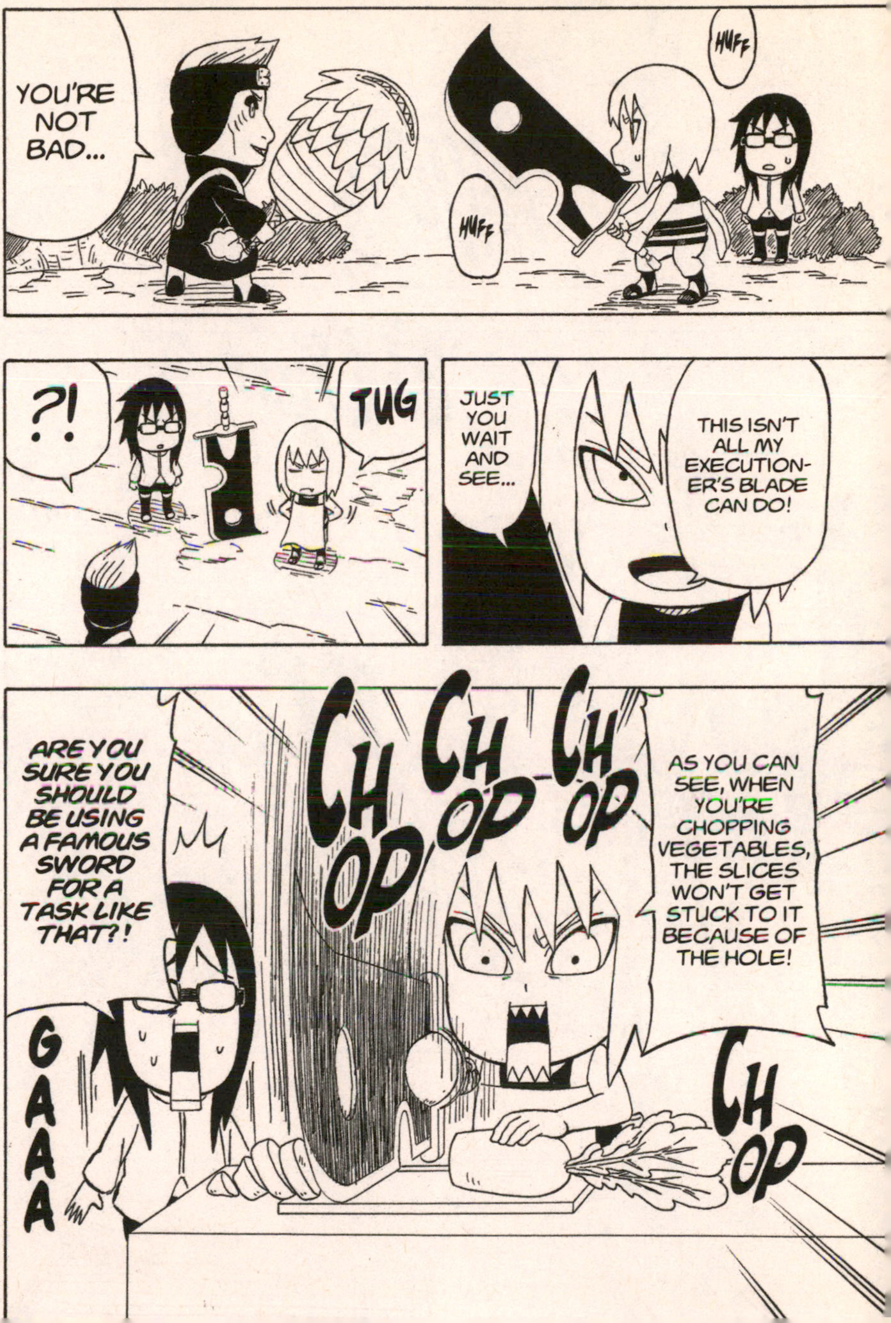
HUFF
YOU'RE NOT BAD...
HUFF
THIS ISN'T ALL MY EXECUTIONER'S BLADE CAN DO!
JUST YOU WAIT AND SEE...
TUG
?!
AS YOU CAN SEE, WHEN YOU'RE CHOPPING VEGETABLES, THE SLICES WON'T GET STUCK TO IT BECAUSE OF THE HOLE!
CHOP
CHOP
CHOP
CHOP
ARE YOU SURE YOU SHOULD BE USING A FAMOUS SWORD FOR A TASK LIKE THAT?!
GAAAA

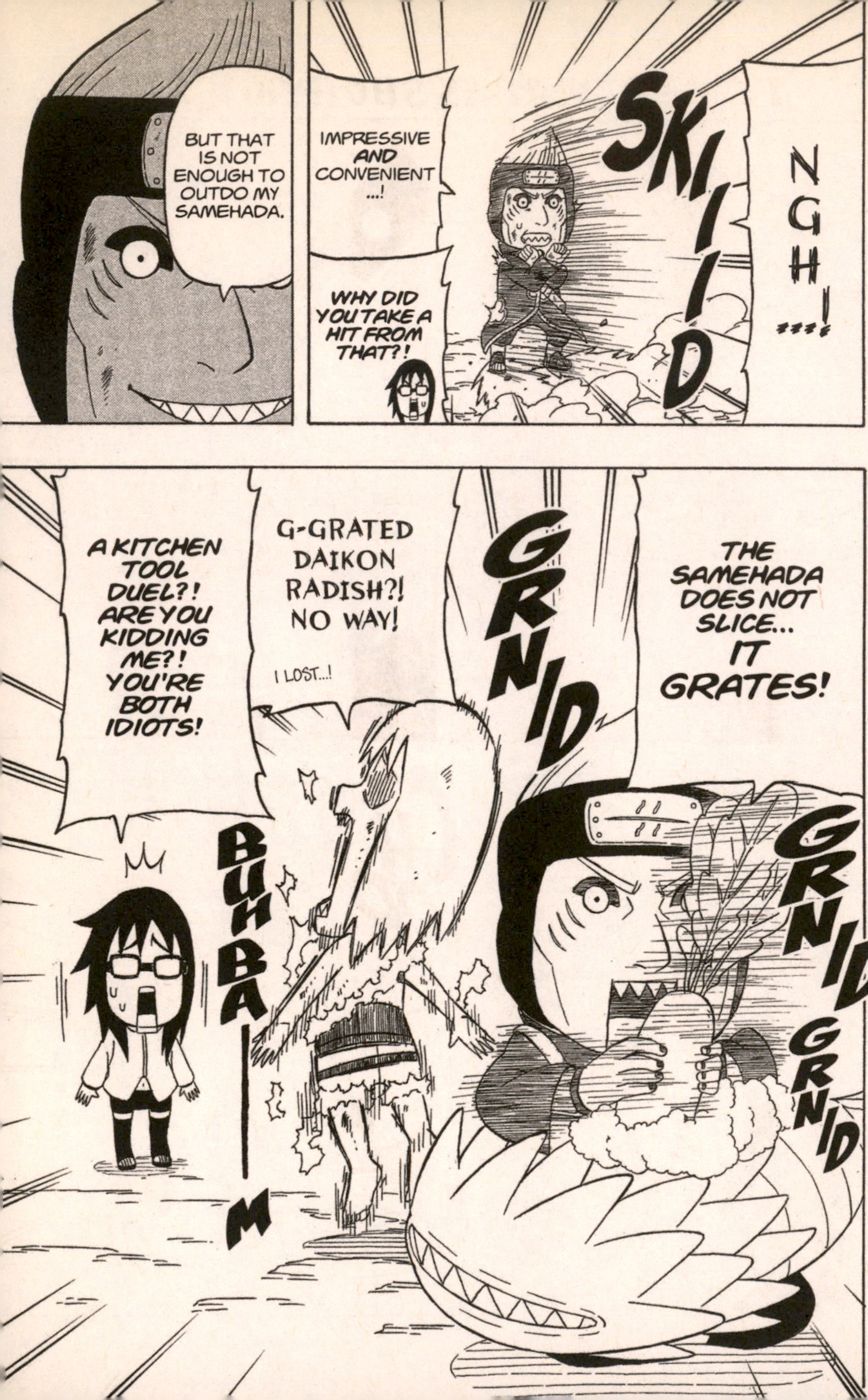
NGH...!
SKIIID
IMPRESSIVE AND CONVENIENT...!
WHY DID YOU TAKE A HIT FROM THAT?!
BUT THAT IS NOT ENOUGH TO OUTDO MY SAMEHADA.
THE SAMEHADA DOES NOT SLICE... IT GRATES!
GRNID
GRNID GRNID GRNID
G-GRATED DAIKON RADISH?! NO WAY!
I LOST...!
A KITCHEN TOOL DUEL?! ARE YOU KIDDING ME?! YOU'RE BOTH IDIOTS!
BUHBA—M

BEAN THROWING

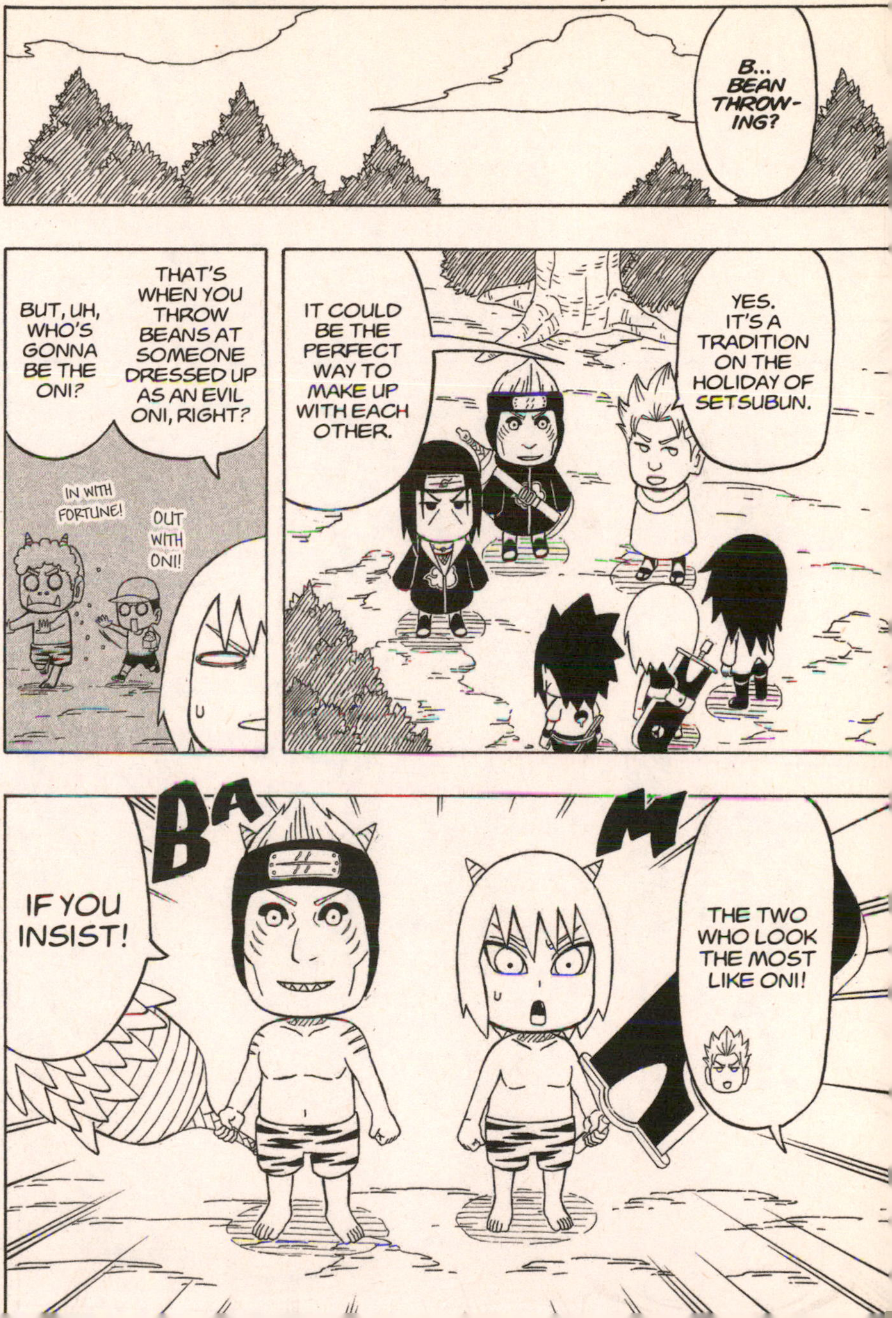
B... BEAN THROWING?
YES. IT'S A TRADITION ON THE HOLIDAY OF SETSUBUN.
IT COULD BE THE PERFECT WAY TO MAKE UP WITH EACH OTHER.
THAT'S WHEN YOU THROW BEANS AT SOMEONE DRESSED UP AS AN EVIL ONI, RIGHT?
BUT, UH, WHO'S GONNA BE THE ONI?
OUT WITH ONI!
IN WITH FORTUNE!
THE TWO WHO LOOK THE MOST LIKE ONI!
BAM
IF YOU INSIST!

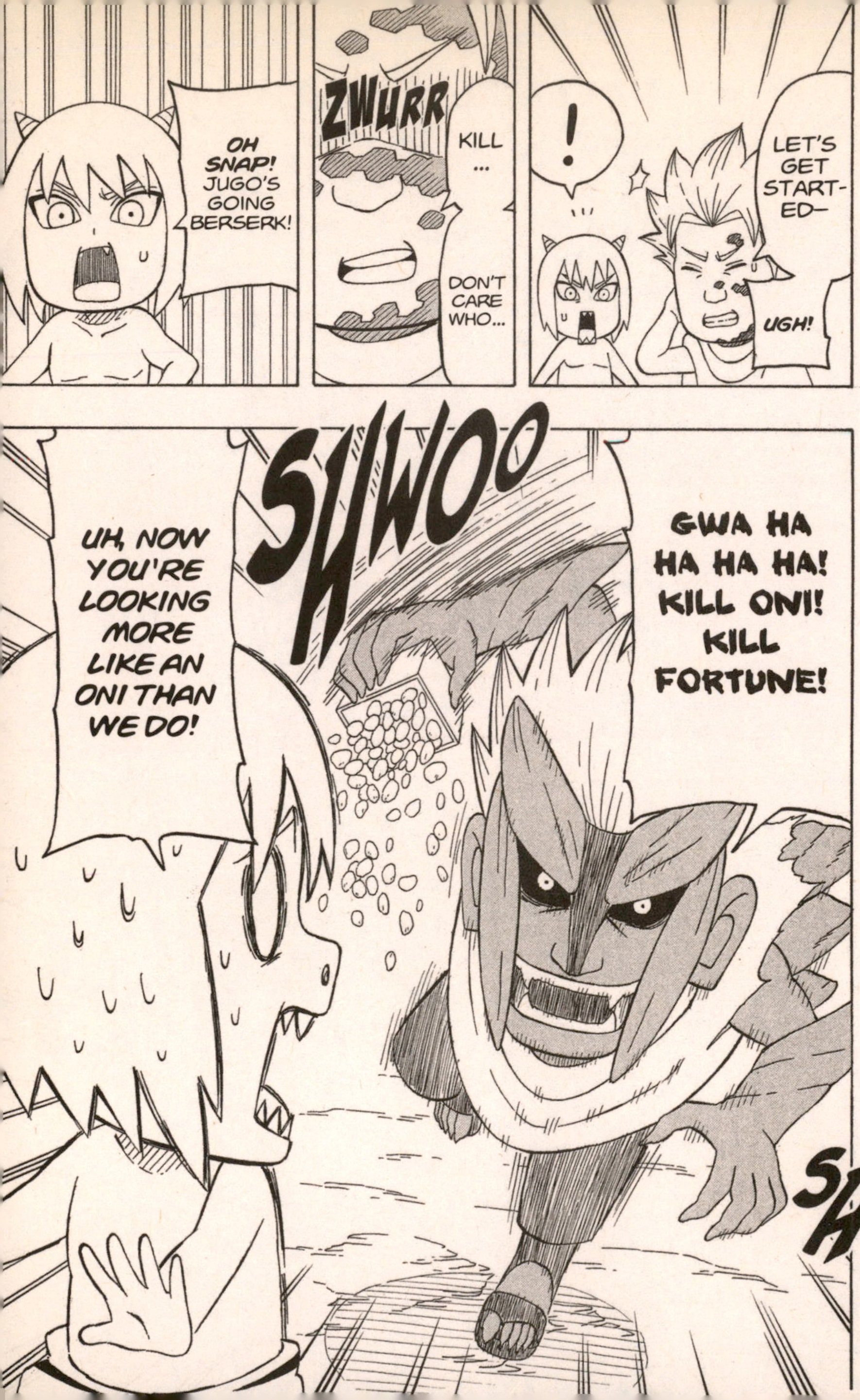

LET'S GET START-ED—
!
UGH!
ZWURR
KILL ...
DON'T CARE WHO...
OH SNAP! JUGO'S GOING BERSERK!
GWA HA HA HA HA! KILL ONI! KILL FORTUNE!
SHWOO
UH, NOW YOU'RE LOOKING MORE LIKE AN ONI THAN WE DO!
SH

VALENTINE'S DAY

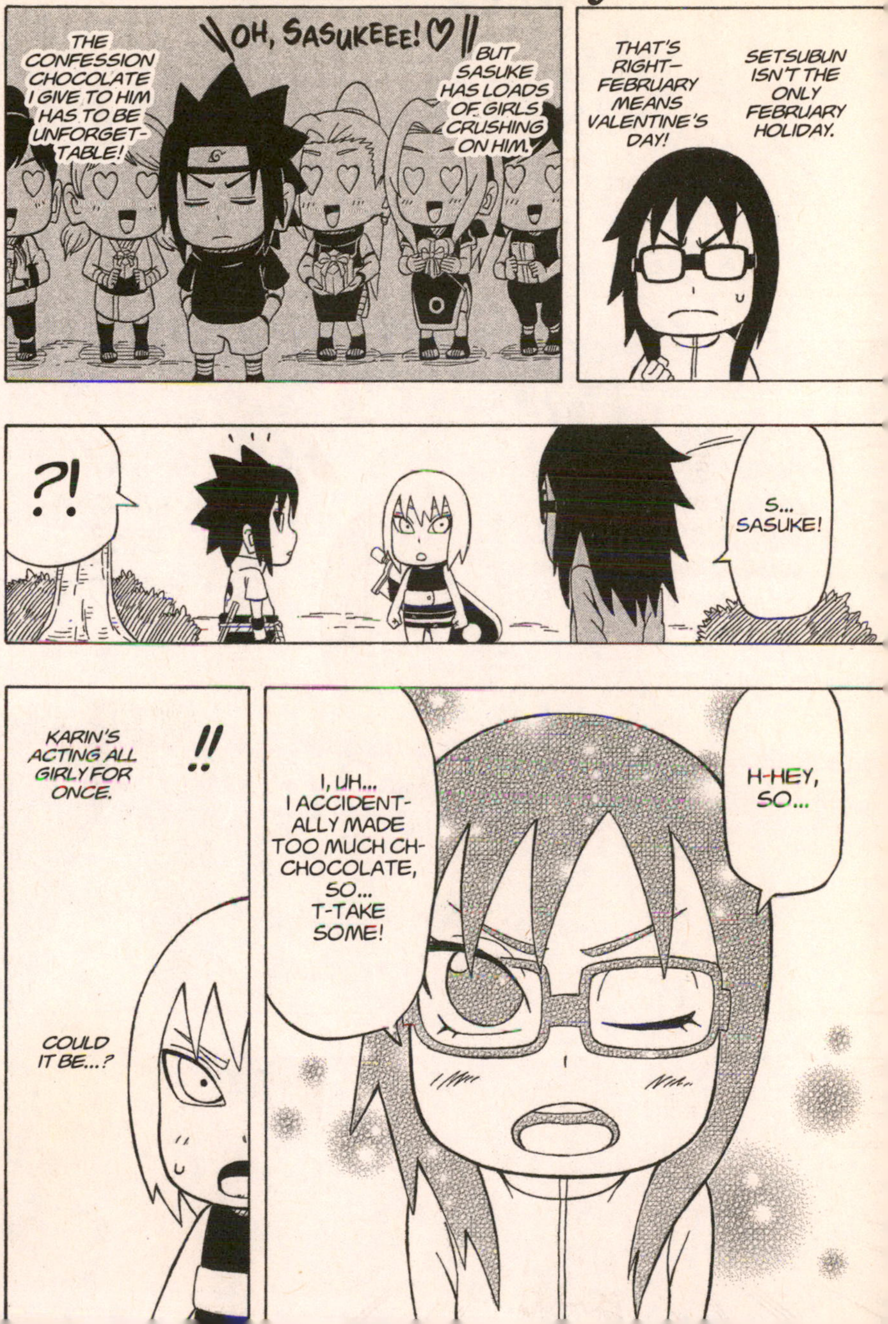

SETSUBUN ISN'T THE ONLY FEBRUARY HOLIDAY.
THAT'S RIGHT—FEBRUARY MEANS VALENTINE'S DAY!
OH, SASUKEEE! ♡
BUT SASUKE HAS LOADS OF GIRLS CRUSHING ON HIM.
THE CONFESSION CHOCOLATE I GIVE TO HIM HAS TO BE UNFORGET-TABLE!
S... SASUKE!
?!
H-HEY, SO...
I, UH... I ACCIDENT-ALLY MADE TOO MUCH CH-CHOCOLATE, SO... T-TAKE SOME!
!!
KARIN'S ACTING ALL GIRLY FOR ONCE.
COULD IT BE...?

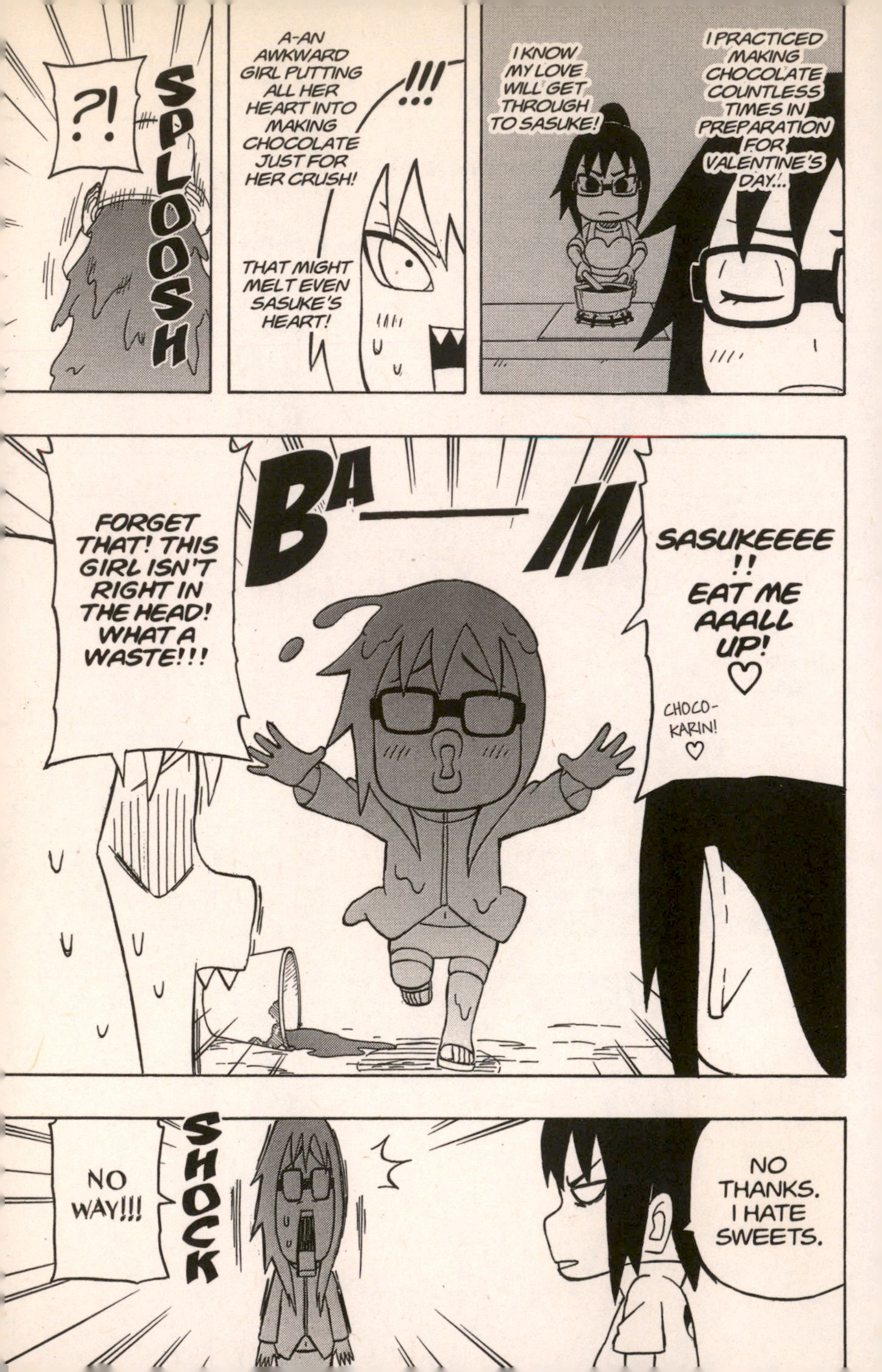
I PRACTICED MAKING CHOCOLATE COUNTLESS TIMES IN PREPARATION FOR VALENTINE'S DAY...
I KNOW MY LOVE WILL GET THROUGH TO SASUKE!
!!!...
A-AN AWKWARD GIRL PUTTING ALL HER HEART INTO MAKING CHOCOLATE JUST FOR HER CRUSH!
THAT MIGHT MELT EVEN SASUKE'S HEART!
SPLOOSH
?!
SASUKEEEE!! EAT ME AAALL UP! ♡
CHOCO-KARIN! ♡
BA—M
FORGET THAT! THIS GIRL ISN'T RIGHT IN THE HEAD! WHAT A WASTE!!!
NO THANKS. I HATE SWEETS.
SHOCK
NO WAY!!!

MANGEKYO SHARINGAN

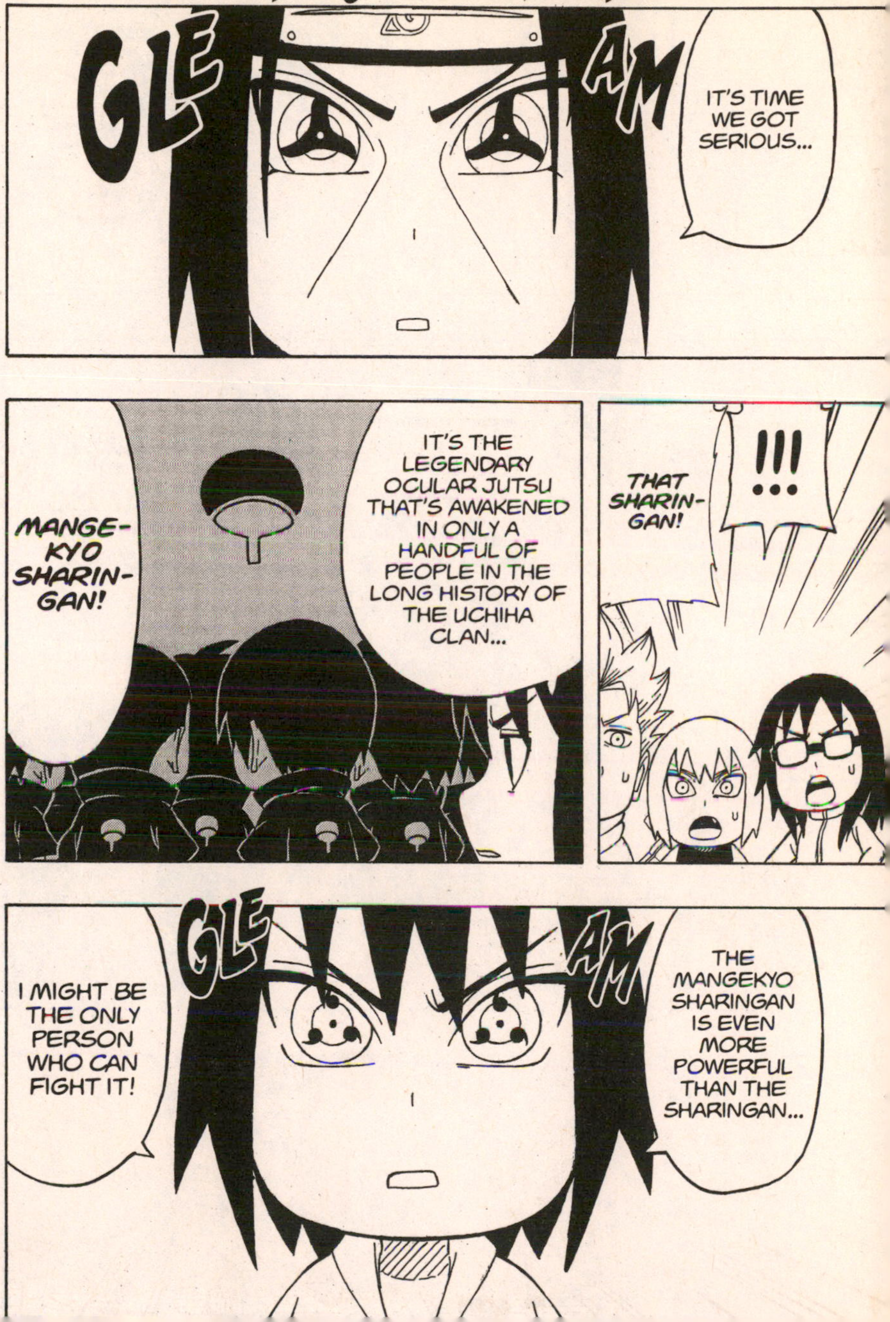
GLEAM
IT'S TIME WE GOT SERIOUS...
!!!...
THAT SHARINGAN!
IT'S THE LEGENDARY OCULAR JUTSU THAT'S AWAKENED IN ONLY A HANDFUL OF PEOPLE IN THE LONG HISTORY OF THE UCHIHA CLAN...
MANGEKYO SHARINGAN!
GLEAM
THE MANGEKYO SHARINGAN IS EVEN MORE POWERFUL THAN THE SHARINGAN...
I MIGHT BE THE ONLY PERSON WHO CAN FIGHT IT!

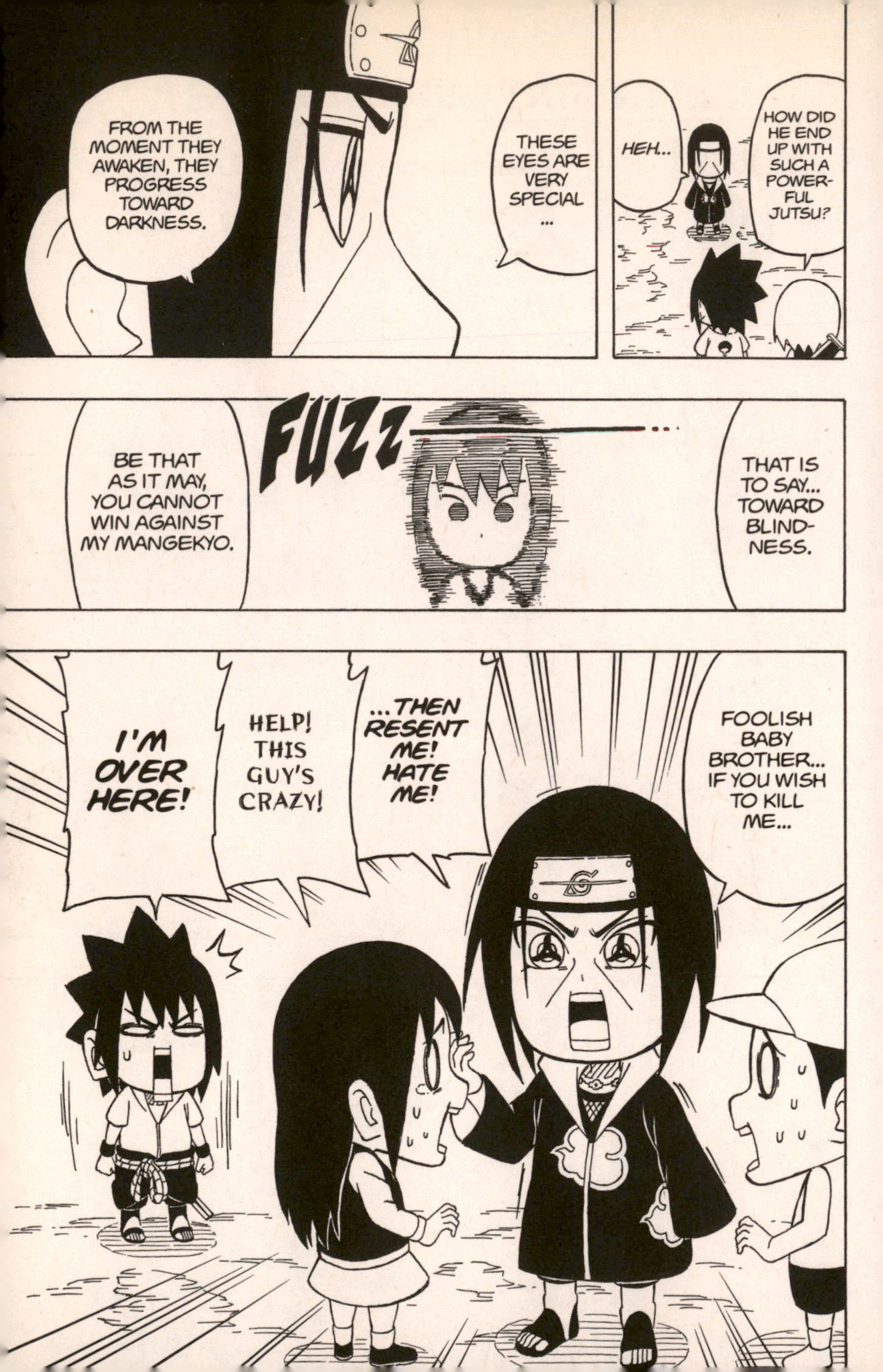
HOW DID HE END UP WITH SUCH A POWERFUL JUTSU?
HEH...
THESE EYES ARE VERY SPECIAL ...
FROM THE MOMENT THEY AWAKEN, THEY PROGRESS TOWARD DARKNESS.
THAT IS TO SAY... TOWARD BLINDNESS.
FUZZ
BE THAT AS IT MAY, YOU CANNOT WIN AGAINST MY MANGEKYO.
FOOLISH BABY BROTHER... IF YOU WISH TO KILL ME...
...THEN RESENT ME! HATE ME!
HELP! THIS GUY'S CRAZY!
I'M OVER HERE!

HEAT-ENDURANCE CONTEST

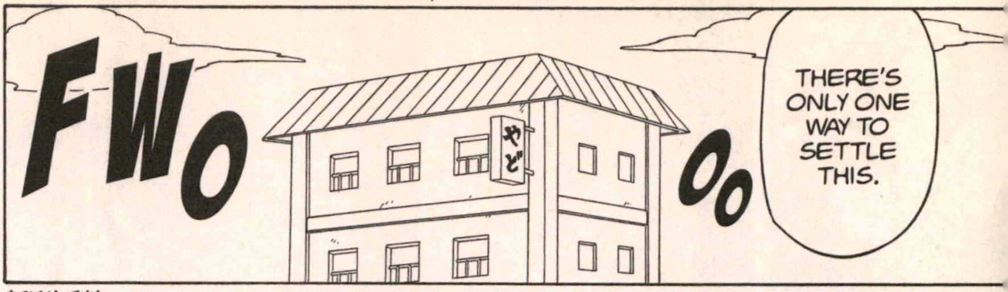
THERE'S ONLY ONE WAY TO SETTLE THIS.
やど
FWOOO

*SIGN: INN

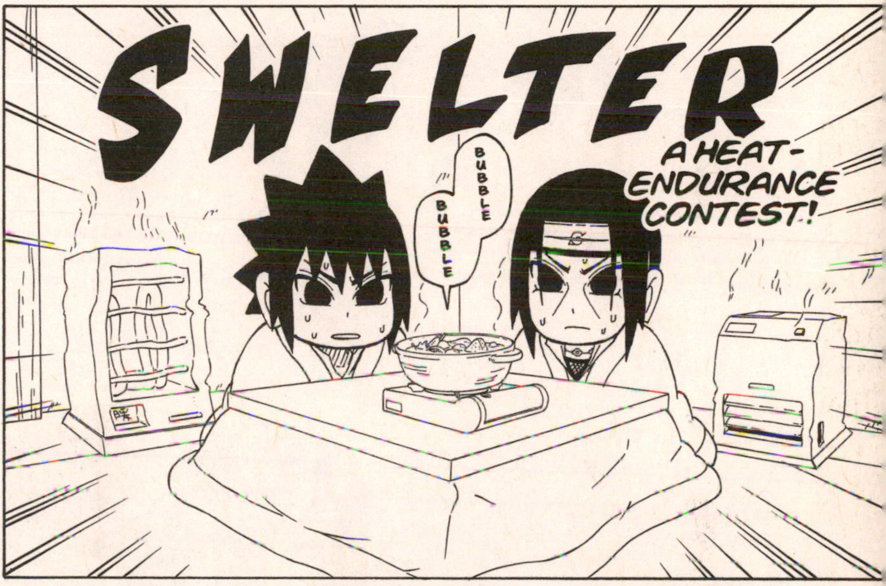
SWELTER
A HEAT-ENDURANCE CONTEST!
BUBBLE
BUBBLE

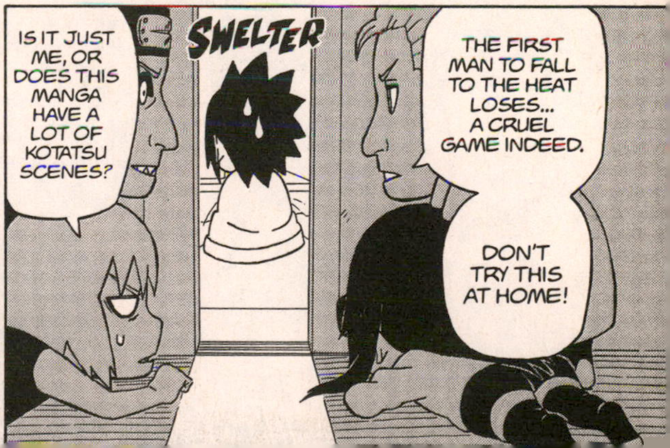
THE FIRST MAN TO FALL TO THE HEAT LOSES... A CRUEL GAME INDEED.
DON'T TRY THIS AT HOME!
SWELTER
IS IT JUST ME, OR DOES THIS MANGA HAVE A LOT OF KOTATSU SCENES?

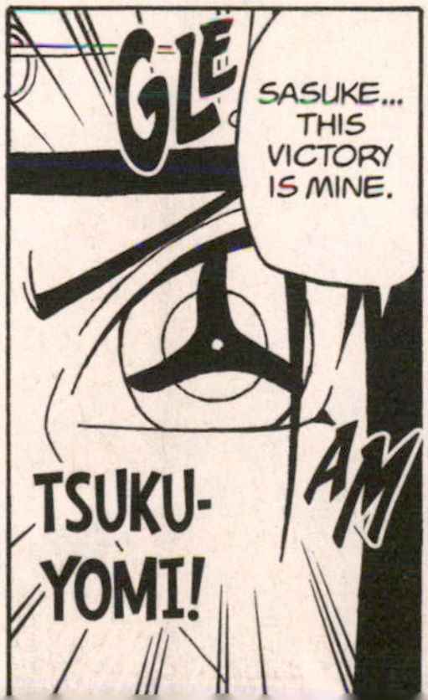
GLE
SASUKE... THIS VICTORY IS MINE.
AM
TSUKU-YOMI!

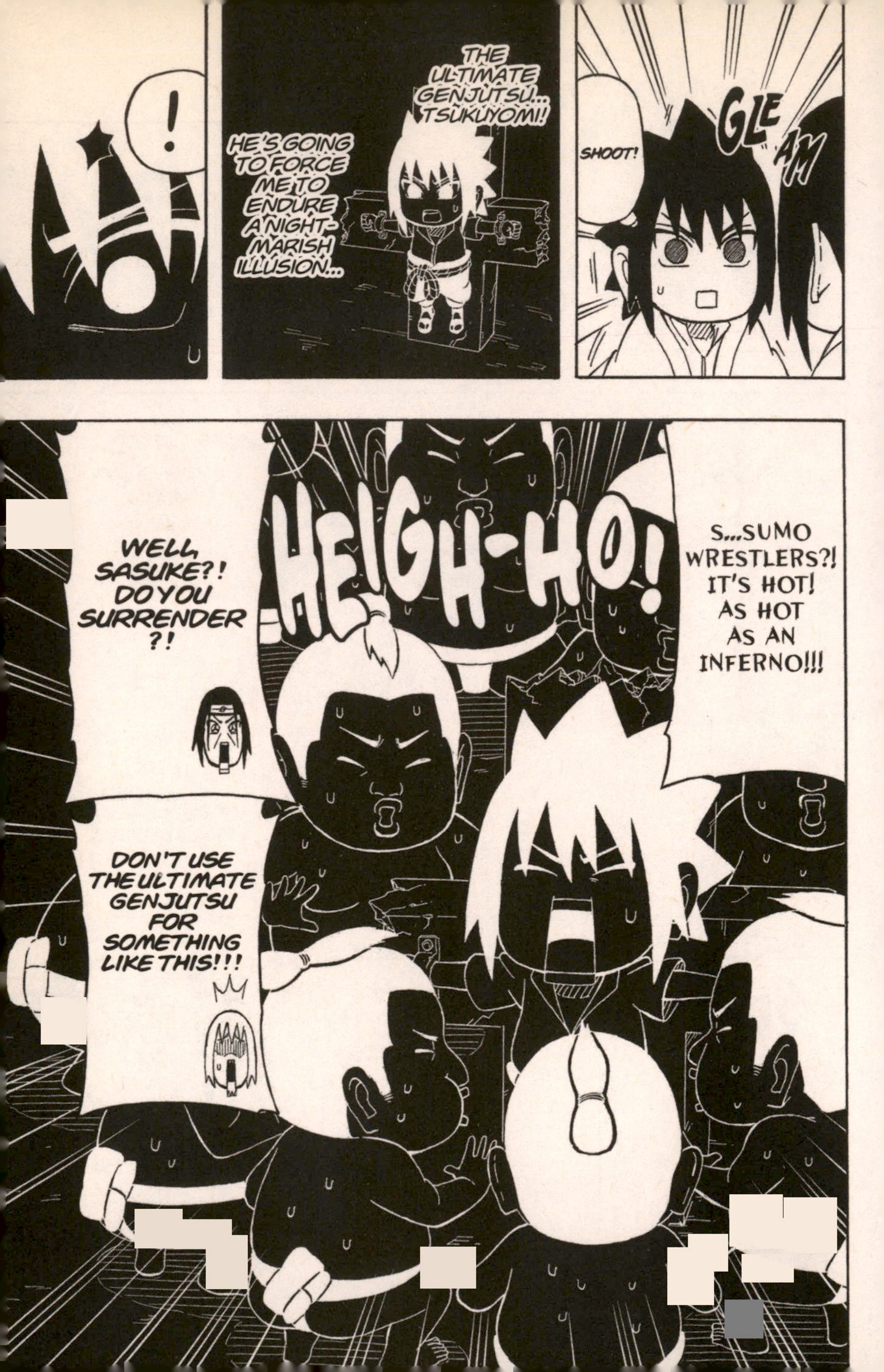
GLEAM
SHOOT!
THE ULTIMATE GENJUTSU... TSUKUYOMI!
HE'S GOING TO FORCE ME TO ENDURE A NIGHT-MARISH ILLUSION...
!
S...SUMO WRESTLERS?! IT'S HOT! AS HOT AS AN INFERNO!!!
HEIGH-HO!
WELL, SASUKE?! DO YOU SURRENDER?!
DON'T USE THE ULTIMATE GENJUTSU FOR SOMETHING LIKE THIS!!!

THE CHANNEL BATTLE

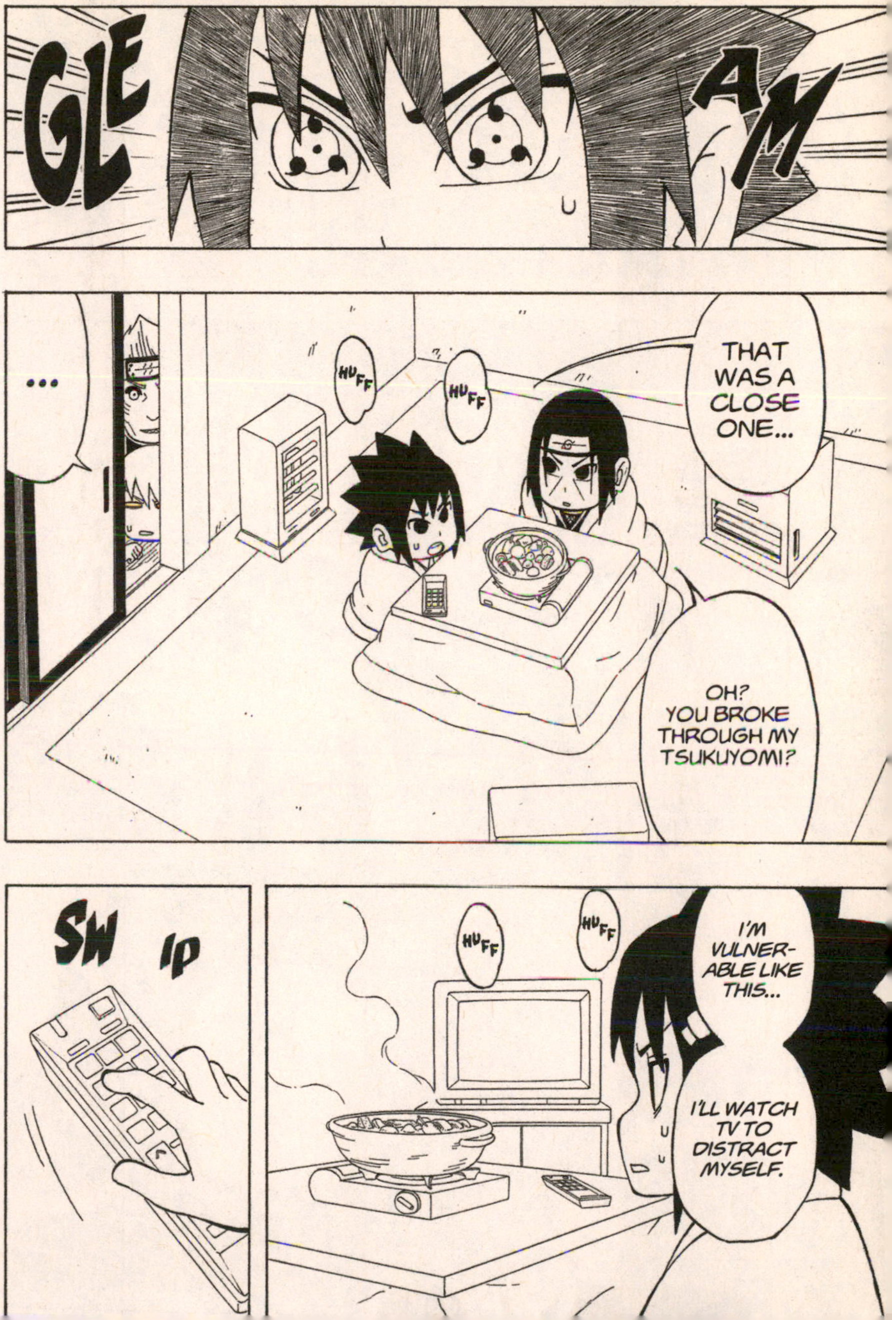
GLEAM
THAT WAS A CLOSE ONE...
OH? YOU BROKE THROUGH MY TSUKUYOMI?
HUFF
HUFF
...
I'M VULNERABLE LIKE THIS...
I'LL WATCH TV TO DISTRACT MYSELF.
HUFF
HUFF
SWIP

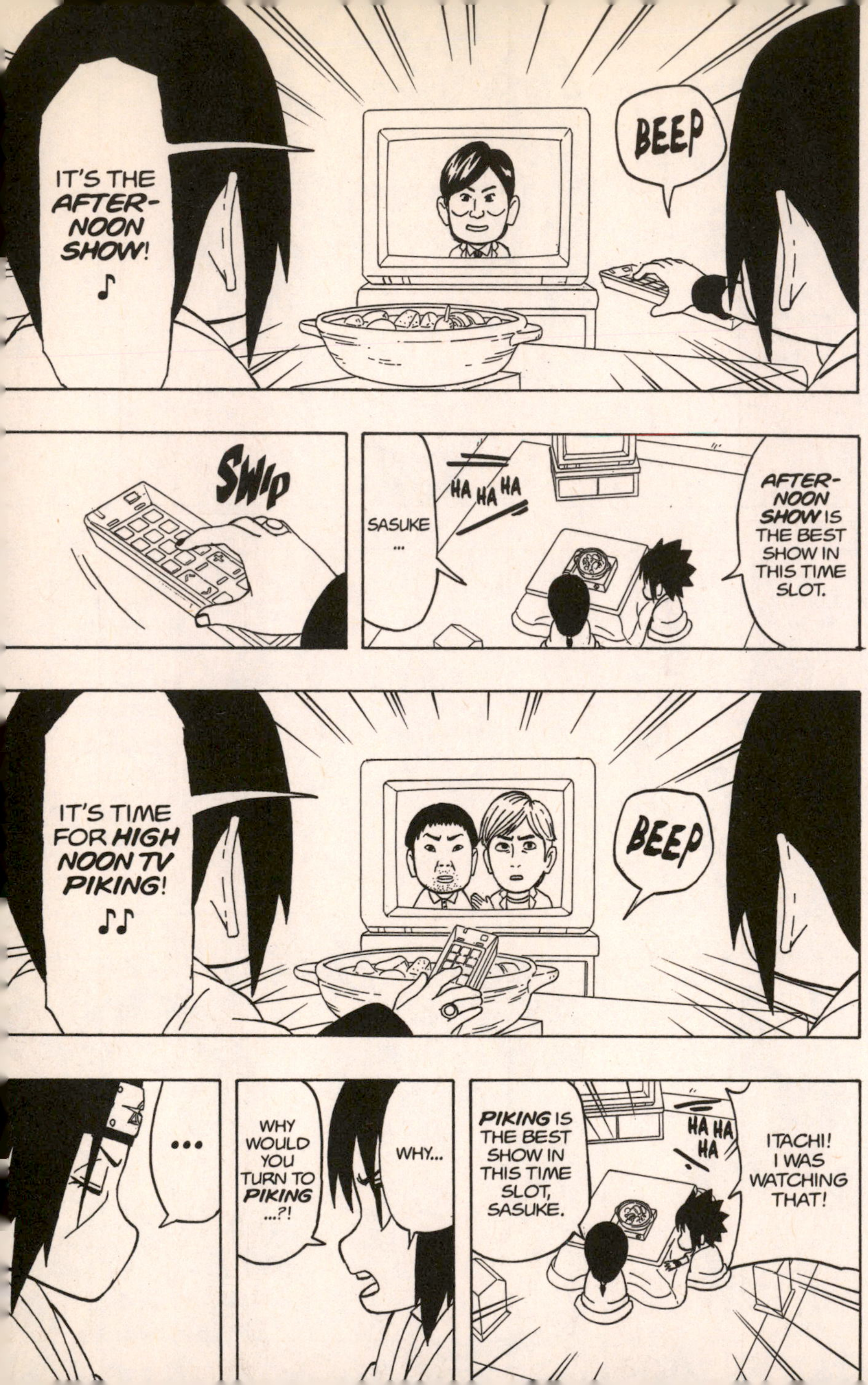

BEEP
IT'S THE AFTERNOON SHOW! ♪
AFTERNOON SHOW IS THE BEST SHOW IN THIS TIME SLOT.
HA HA HA
SASUKE...
SWIP
BEEP
IT'S TIME FOR HIGH NOON TV PIKING! ♪♪
ITACHI! I WAS WATCHING THAT!
HA HA HA
PIKING IS THE BEST SHOW IN THIS TIME SLOT, SASUKE.
WHY...
WHY WOULD YOU TURN TO PIKING ...?!
...

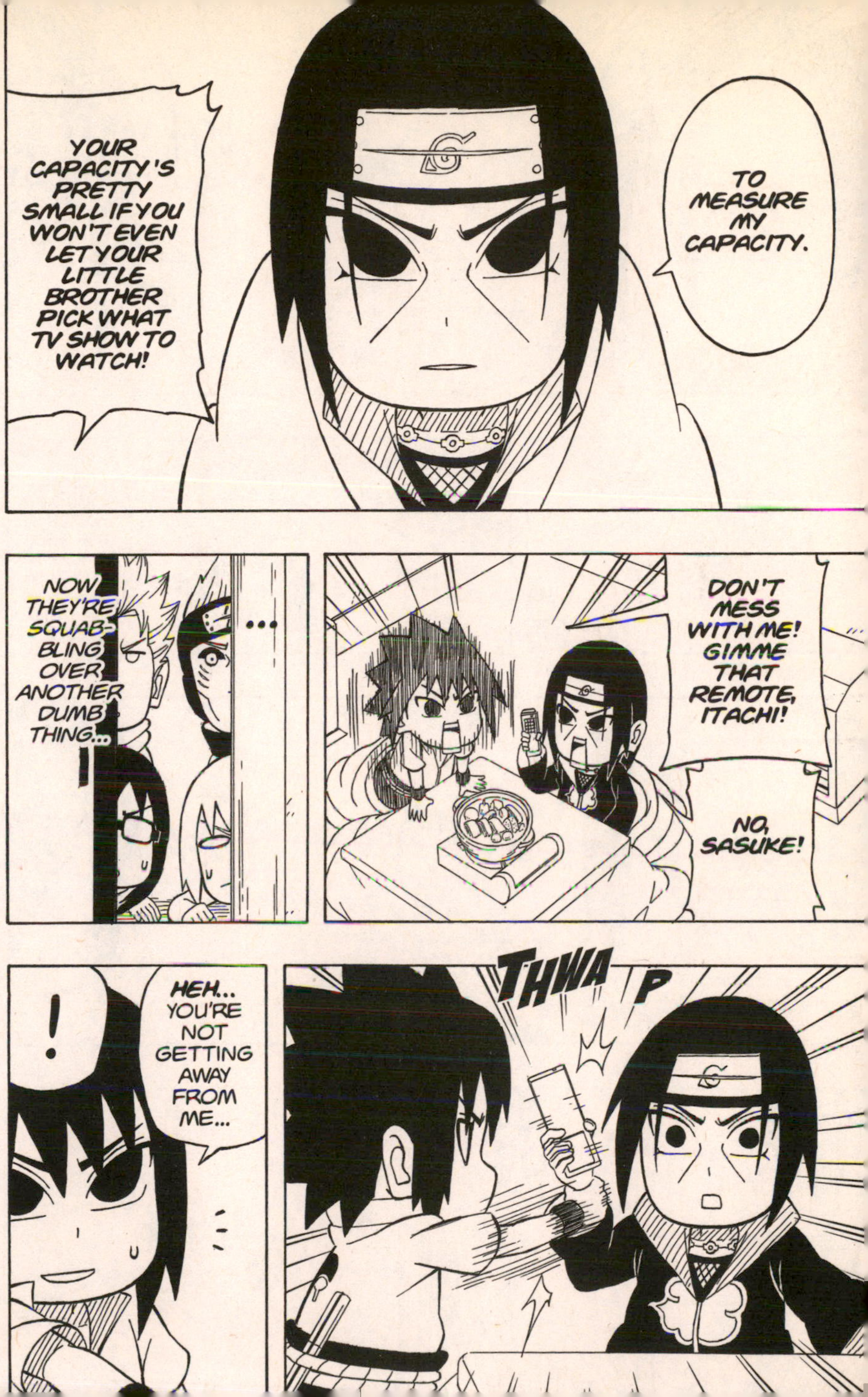
TO MEASURE MY CAPACITY.
YOUR CAPACITY'S PRETTY SMALL IF YOU WON'T EVEN LET YOUR LITTLE BROTHER PICK WHAT TV SHOW TO WATCH!
DON'T MESS WITH ME! GIMME THAT REMOTE, ITACHI!
NO, SASUKE!
...
NOW THEY'RE SQUAB-BLING OVER ANOTHER DUMB THING...
THWAP
HEH... YOU'RE NOT GETTING AWAY FROM ME...
!

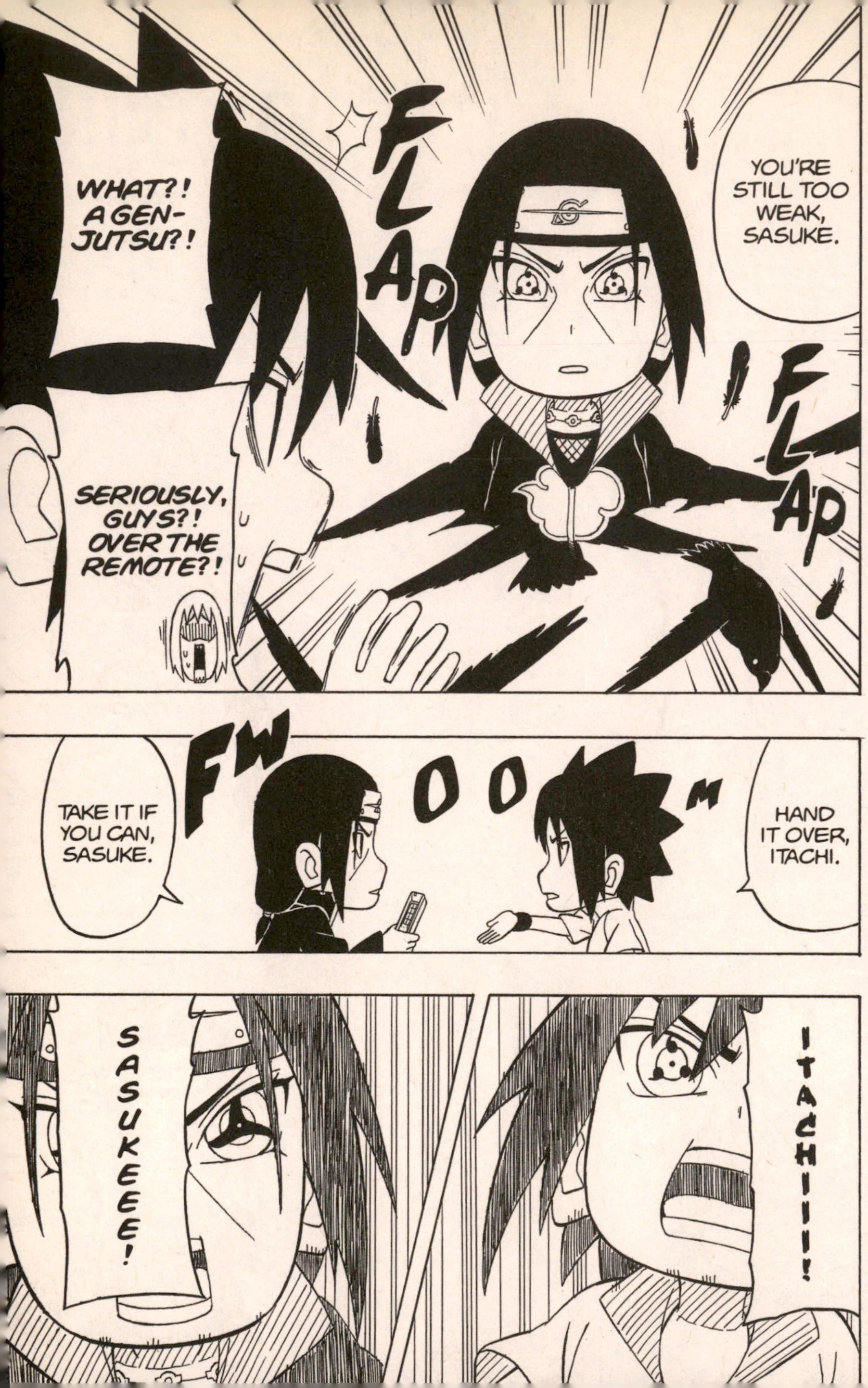
YOU'RE STILL TOO WEAK, SASUKE.
FLAP
FLAP
WHAT?! A GEN-JUTSU?!
SERIOUSLY, GUYS?! OVER THE REMOTE?!
HAND IT OVER, ITACHI.
FWOOM
TAKE IT IF YOU CAN, SASUKE.
ITACHIIII!
SASUKEEE!

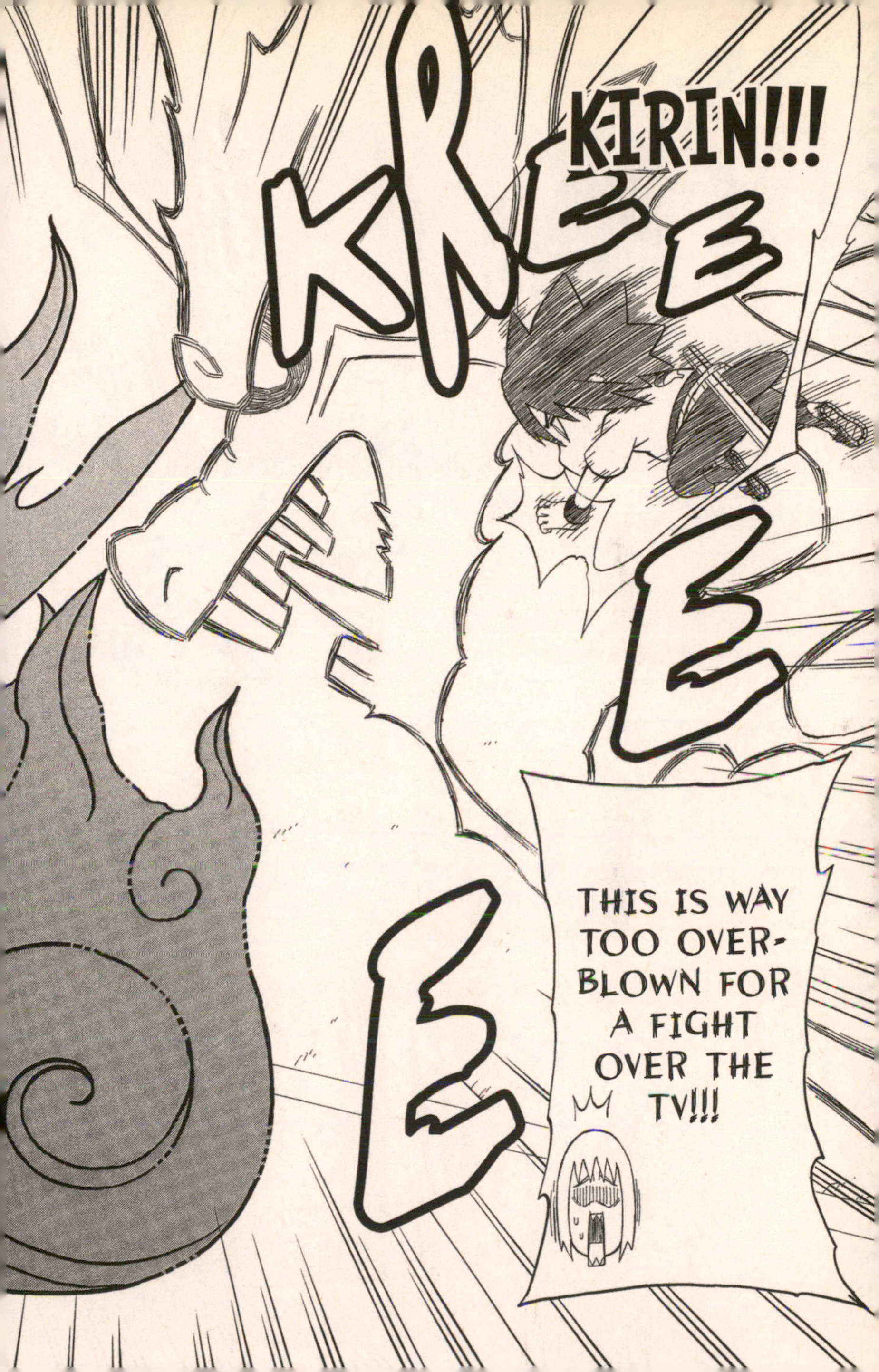

KIRIN!!!
KRGEEEE
THIS IS WAY TOO OVER-BLOWN FOR A FIGHT OVER THE TV!!!

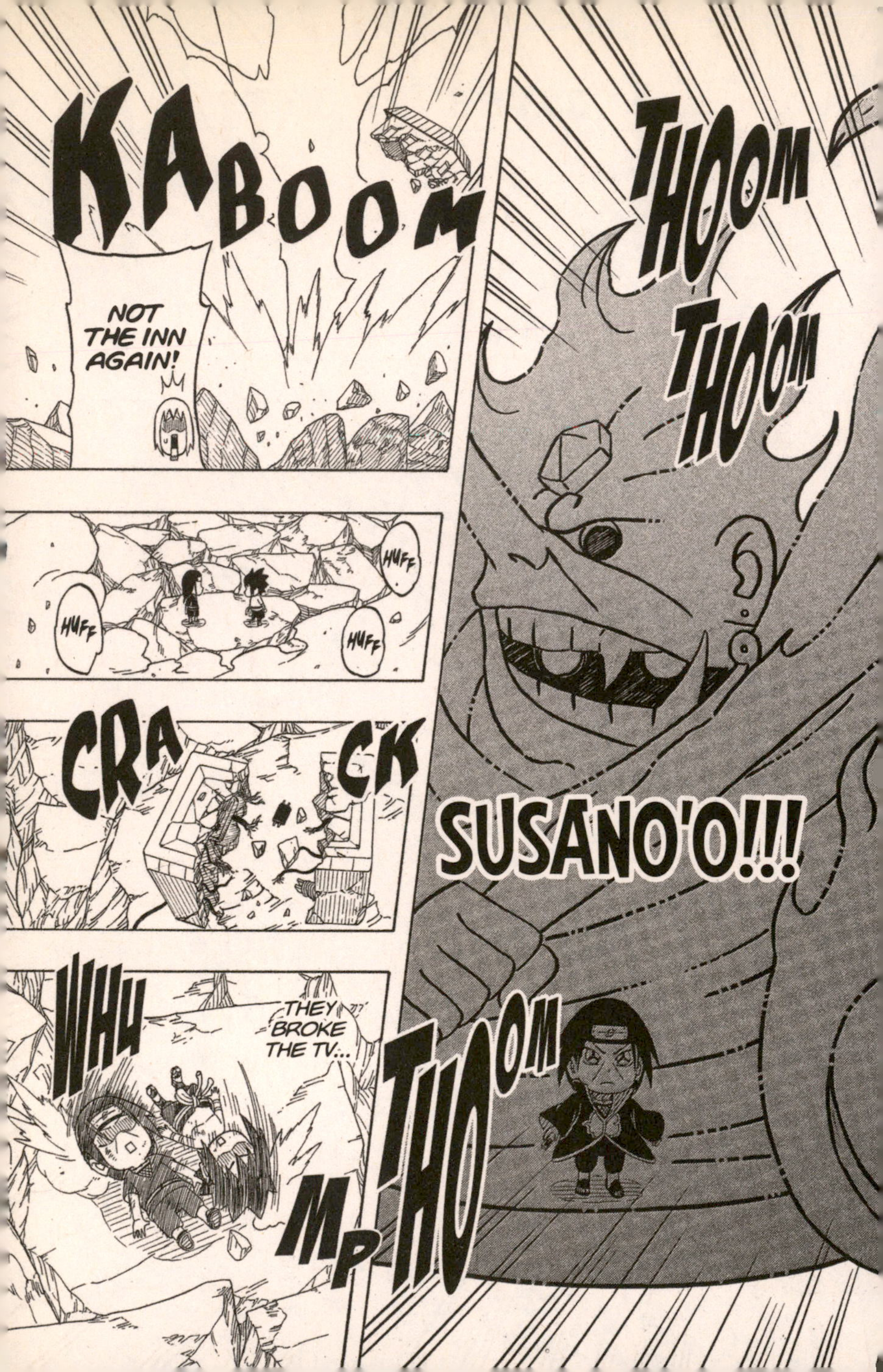

THOOM
THOOM
SUSANO'O!!!
THOOM
THOMP
KABOOM
NOT THE INN AGAIN!
HUFF
HUFF
HUFF
CRACK
WHU
THEY BROKE THE TV...

A BROTHER'S LOVE?

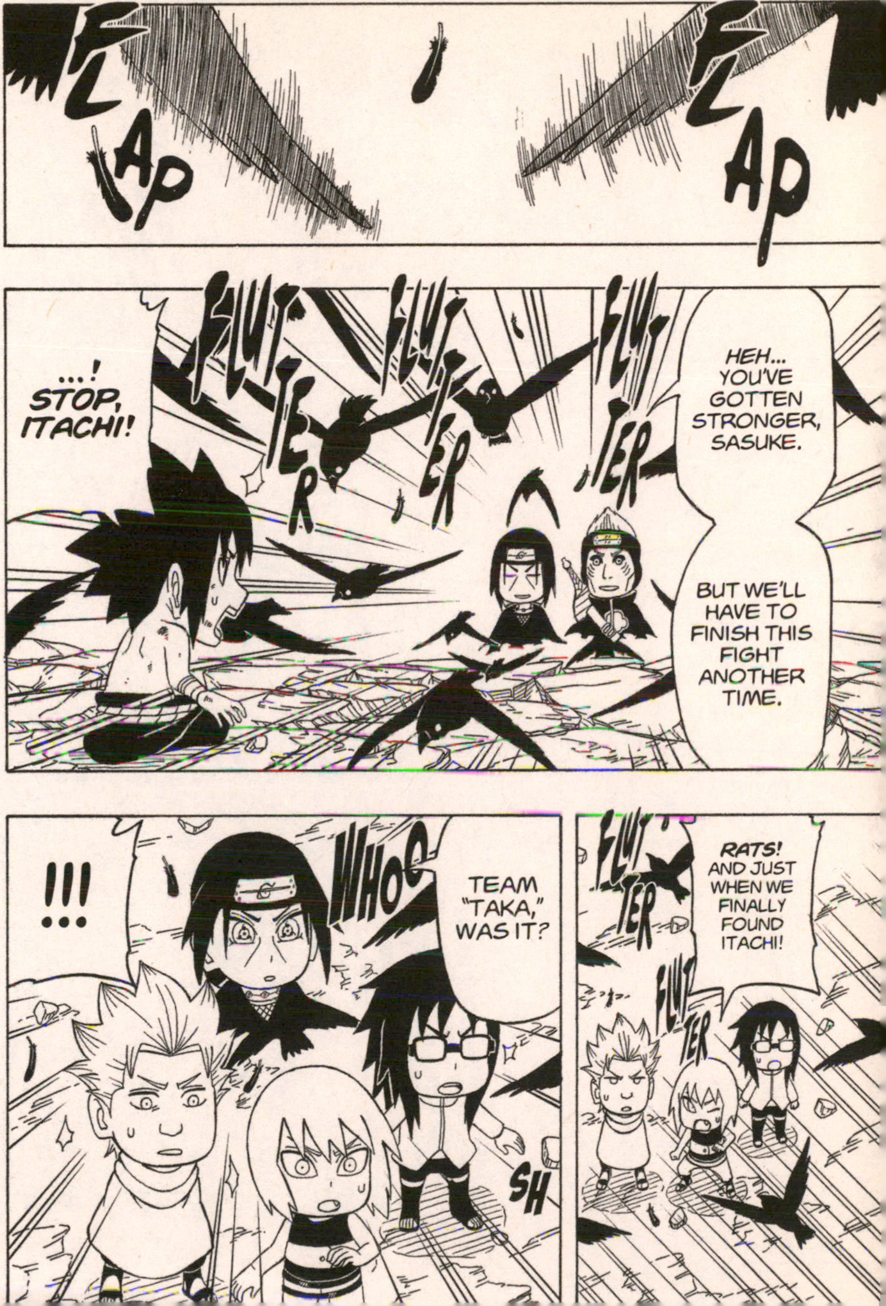
FLAP
FLAP
HEH... YOU'VE GOTTEN STRONGER, SASUKE.
BUT WE'LL HAVE TO FINISH THIS FIGHT ANOTHER TIME.
FLUTTER
FLUTTER
FLUTTER
...! STOP, ITACHI!
RATS! AND JUST WHEN WE FINALLY FOUND ITACHI!
FLUTTER
FLUTTER
TEAM "TAKA," WAS IT?
WHOO
!!!
SH

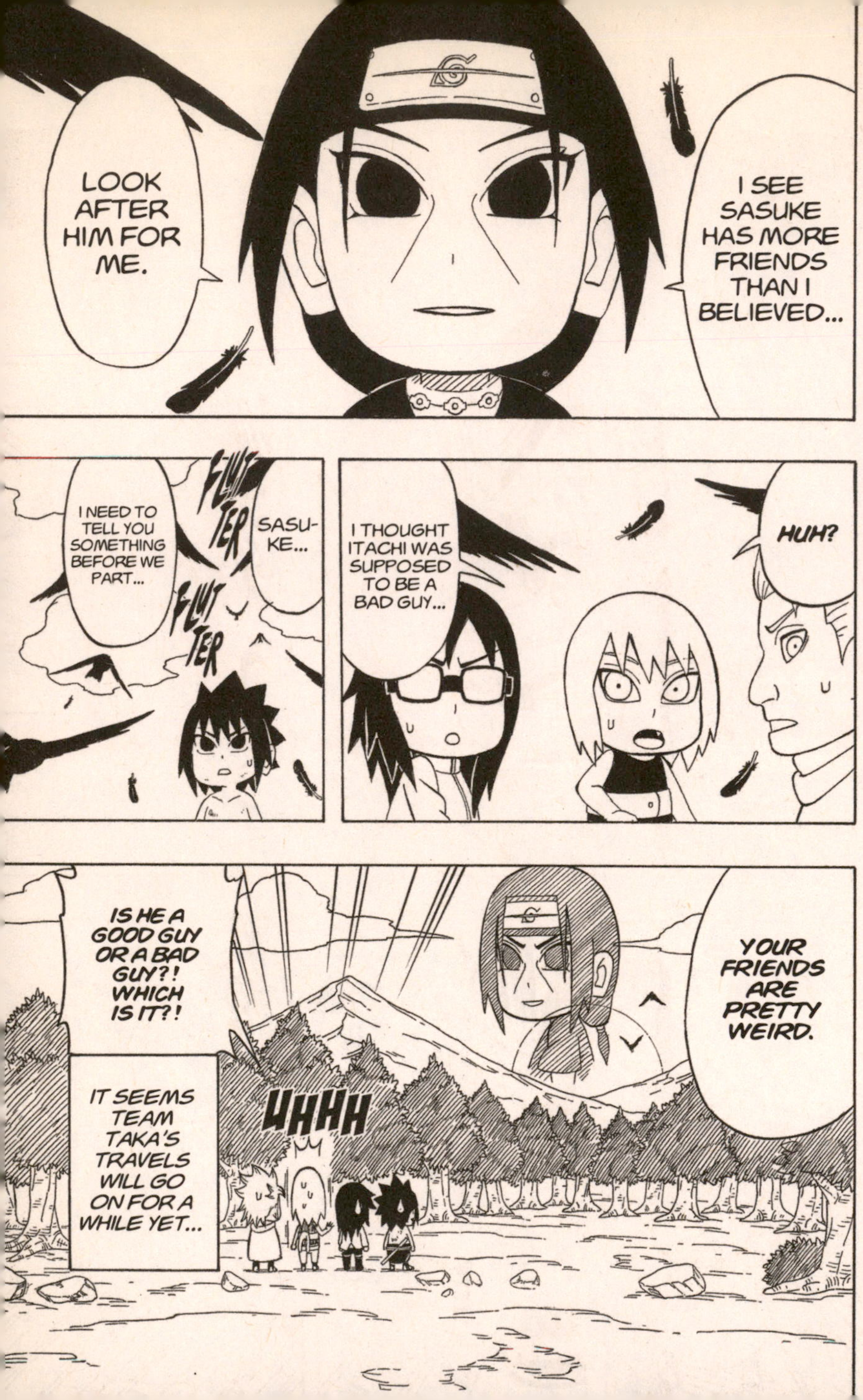
I SEE SASUKE HAS MORE FRIENDS THAN I BELIEVED...
LOOK AFTER HIM FOR ME.
HUH?
I THOUGHT ITACHI WAS SUPPOSED TO BE A BAD GUY...
FLUTTER
SASU-KE...
FLUTTER
I NEED TO TELL YOU SOMETHING BEFORE WE PART...
YOUR FRIENDS ARE PRETTY WEIRD.
IS HE A GOOD GUY OR A BAD GUY?! WHICH IS IT?!
UHHH
IT SEEMS TEAM TAKA'S TRAVELS WILL GO ON FOR A WHILE YET...

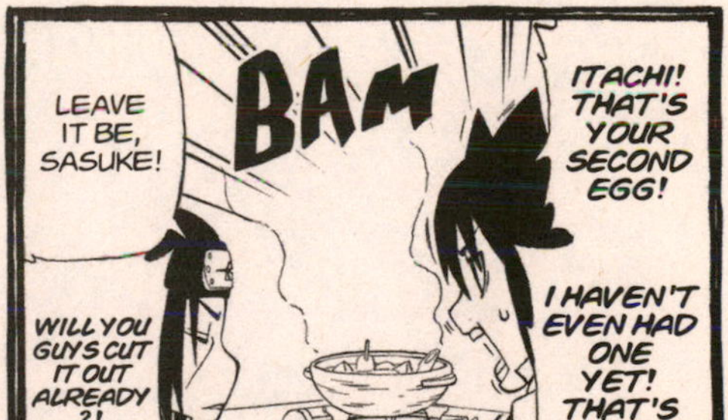
ITACHI! THAT'S YOUR SECOND EGG!
BAM
LEAVE IT BE, SASUKE!
I HAVEN'T EVEN HAD ONE YET! THAT'S MINE!
WILL YOU GUYS CUT IT OUT ALREADY ?!

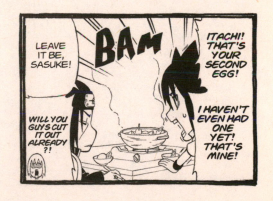

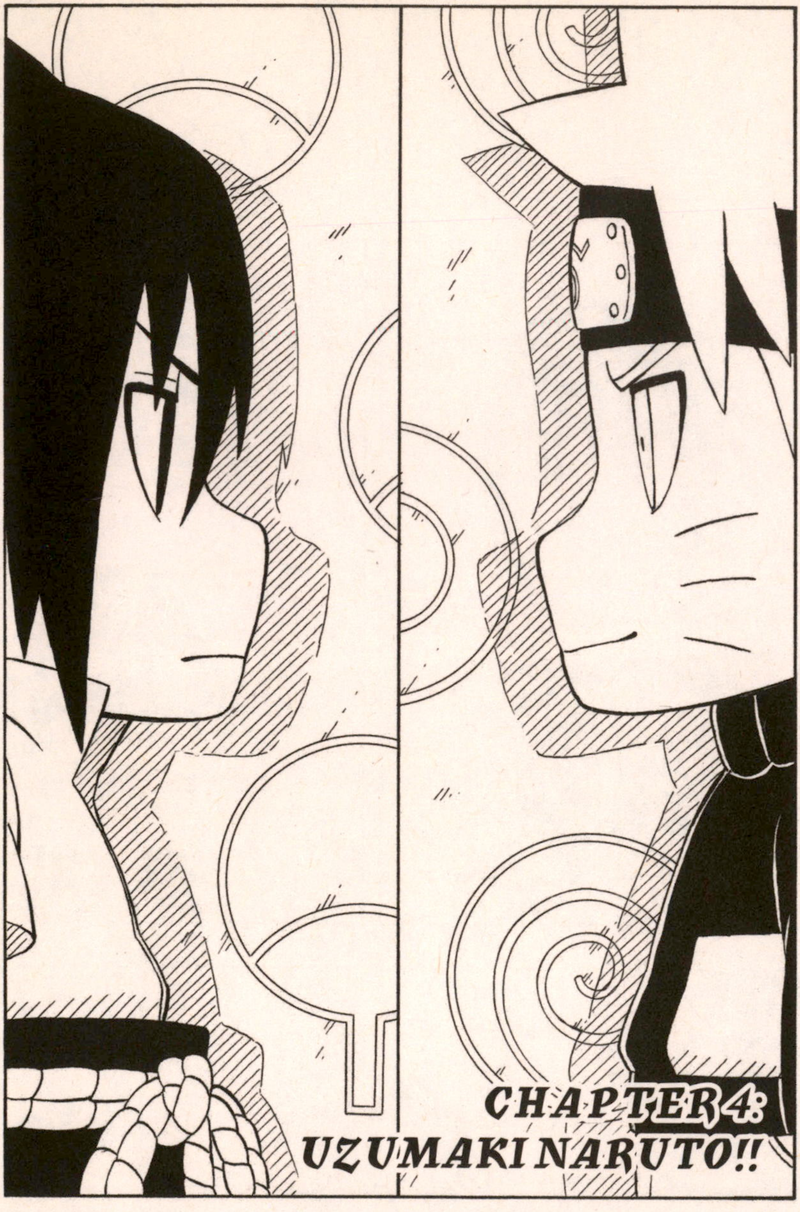
CHAPTER 4:
UZUMAKI NARUTO!!

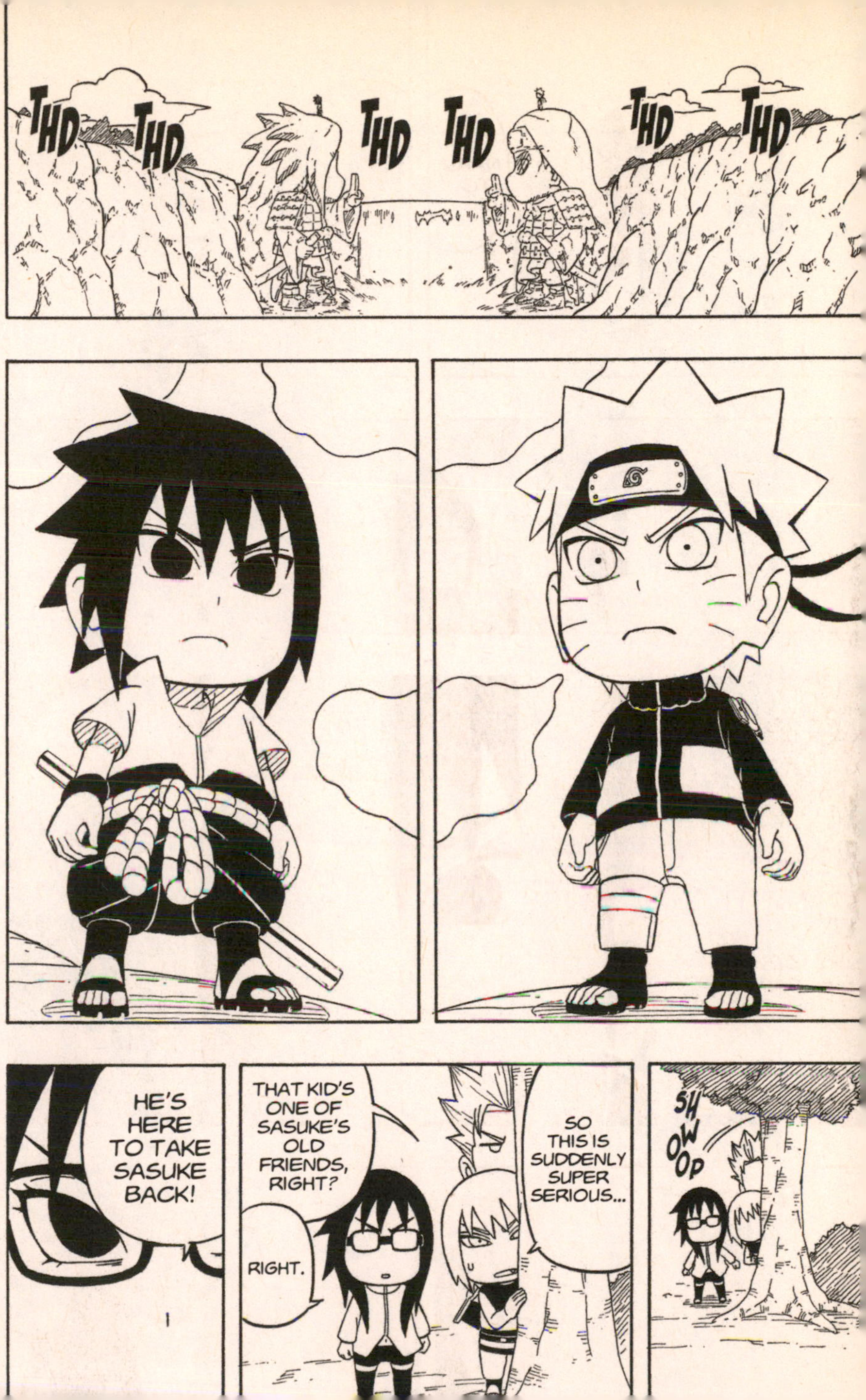
THD
THD
THD
THD
THD
THD
SHWOOOP
SO THIS IS SUDDENLY SUPER SERIOUS...
THAT KID'S ONE OF SASUKE'S OLD FRIENDS, RIGHT?
RIGHT.
HE'S HERE TO TAKE SASUKE BACK!

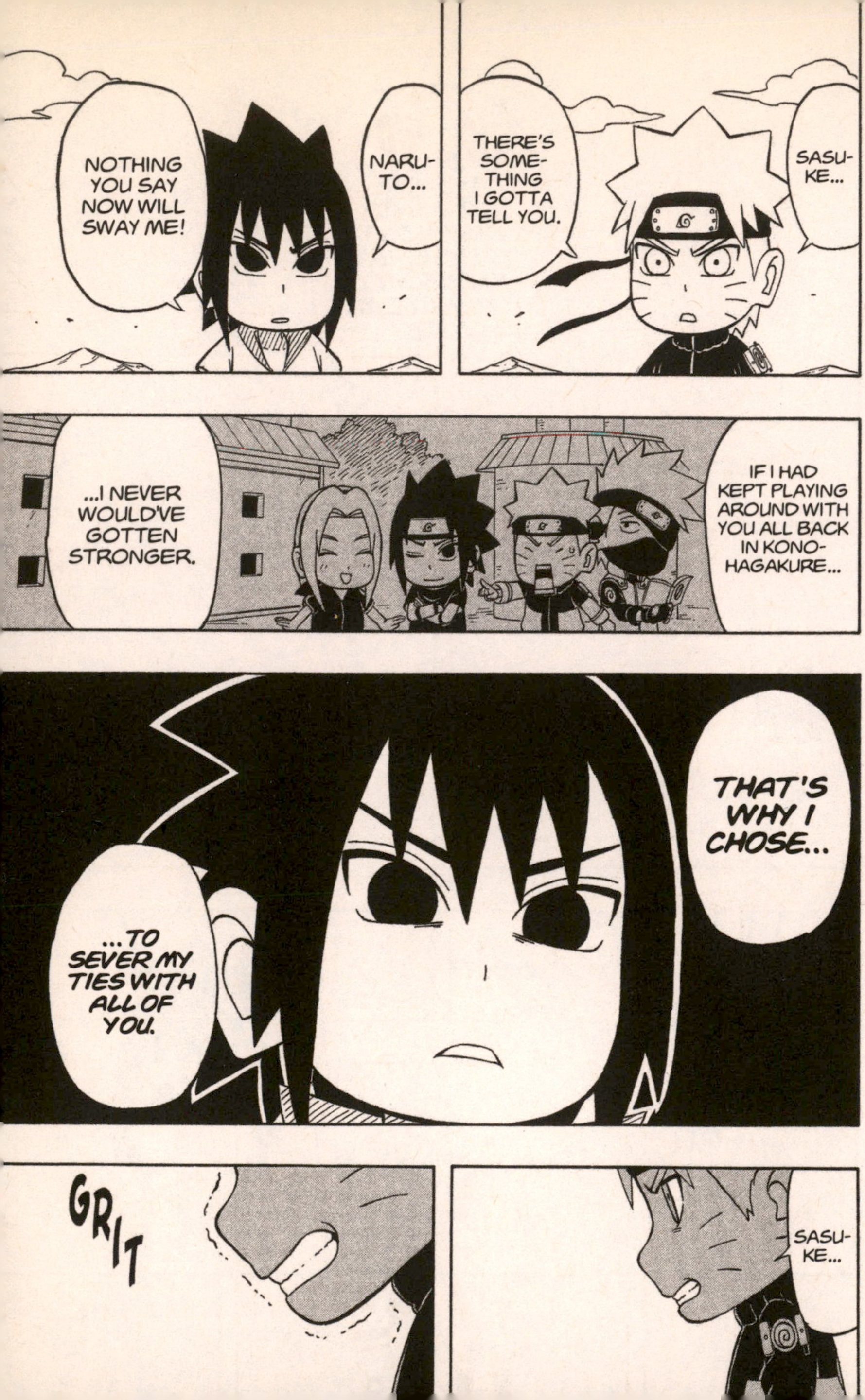
SASU-KE...
THERE'S SOME-THING I GOTTA TELL YOU.
NARU-TO...
NOTHING YOU SAY NOW WILL SWAY ME!
IF I HAD KEPT PLAYING AROUND WITH YOU ALL BACK IN KONO-HAGAKURE...
...I NEVER WOULD'VE GOTTEN STRONGER.
THAT'S WHY I CHOSE...
...TO SEVER MY TIES WITH ALL OF YOU.
SASU-KE...
GRIT

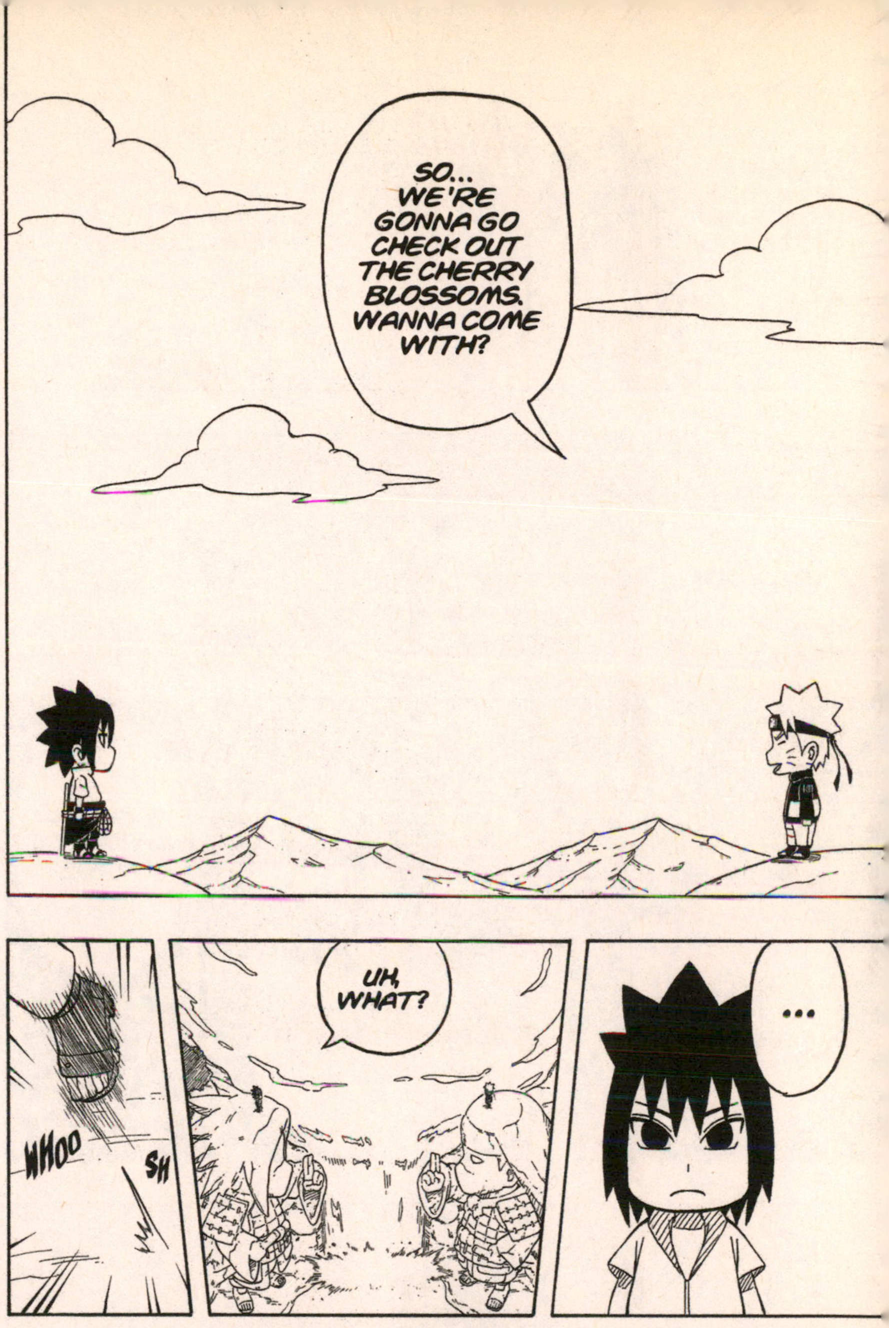
SO... WE'RE GONNA GO CHECK OUT THE CHERRY BLOSSOMS. WANNA COME WITH?
...
UH, WHAT?
WHOOSH

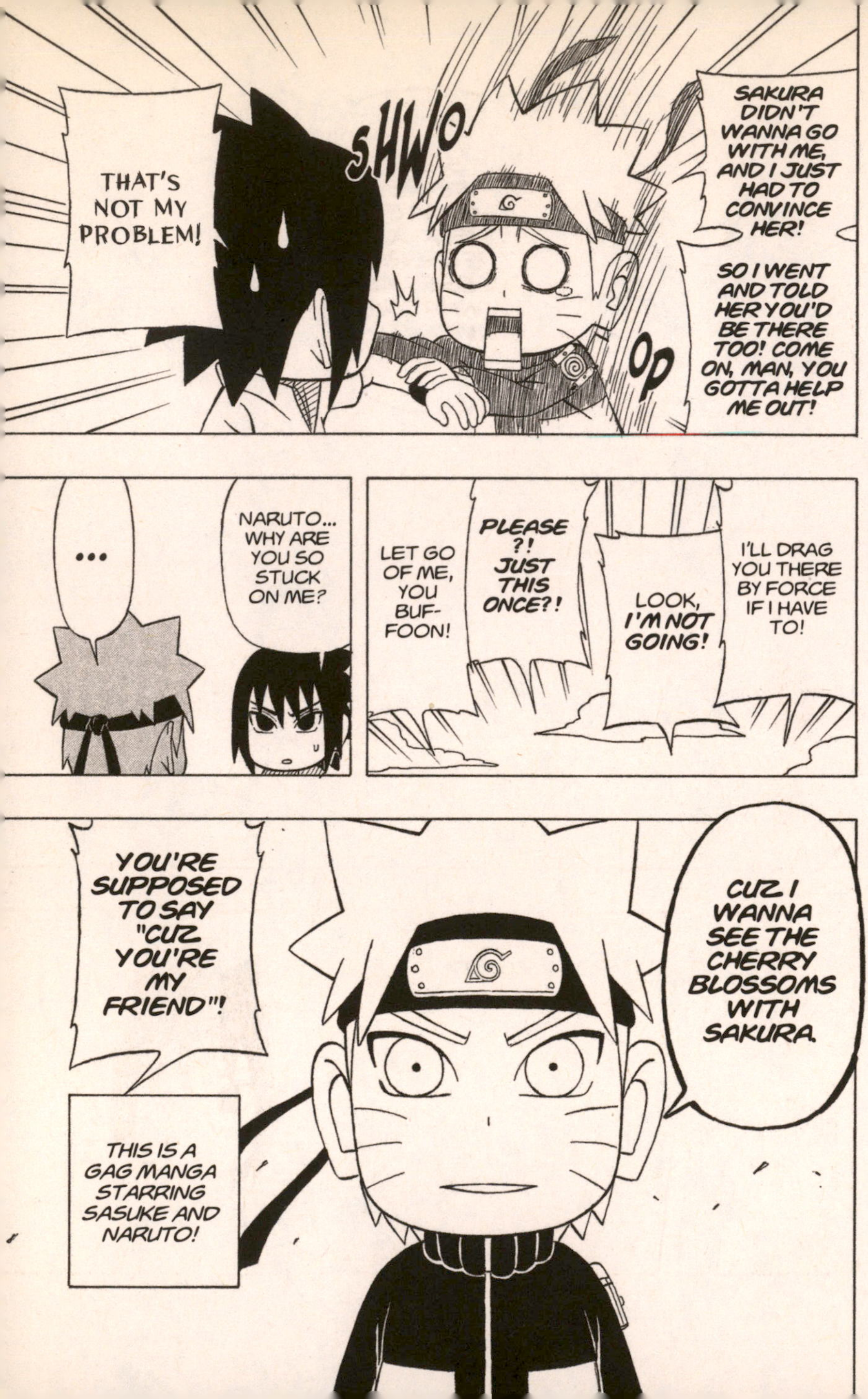
SAKURA DIDN'T WANNA GO WITH ME, AND I JUST HAD TO CONVINCE HER!
SO I WENT AND TOLD HER YOU'D BE THERE TOO! COME ON, MAN, YOU GOTTA HELP ME OUT!
SHWO
OP
THAT'S NOT MY PROBLEM!
I'LL DRAG YOU THERE BY FORCE IF I HAVE TO!
LOOK, I'M NOT GOING!
PLEASE?! JUST THIS ONCE?!
LET GO OF ME, YOU BUF-FOON!
NARUTO... WHY ARE YOU SO STUCK ON ME?
...
CUZ I WANNA SEE THE CHERRY BLOSSOMS WITH SAKURA.
YOU'RE SUPPOSED TO SAY "CUZ YOU'RE MY FRIEND"!
THIS IS A GAG MANGA STARRING SASUKE AND NARUTO!

CHERRY BLOSSOMS!

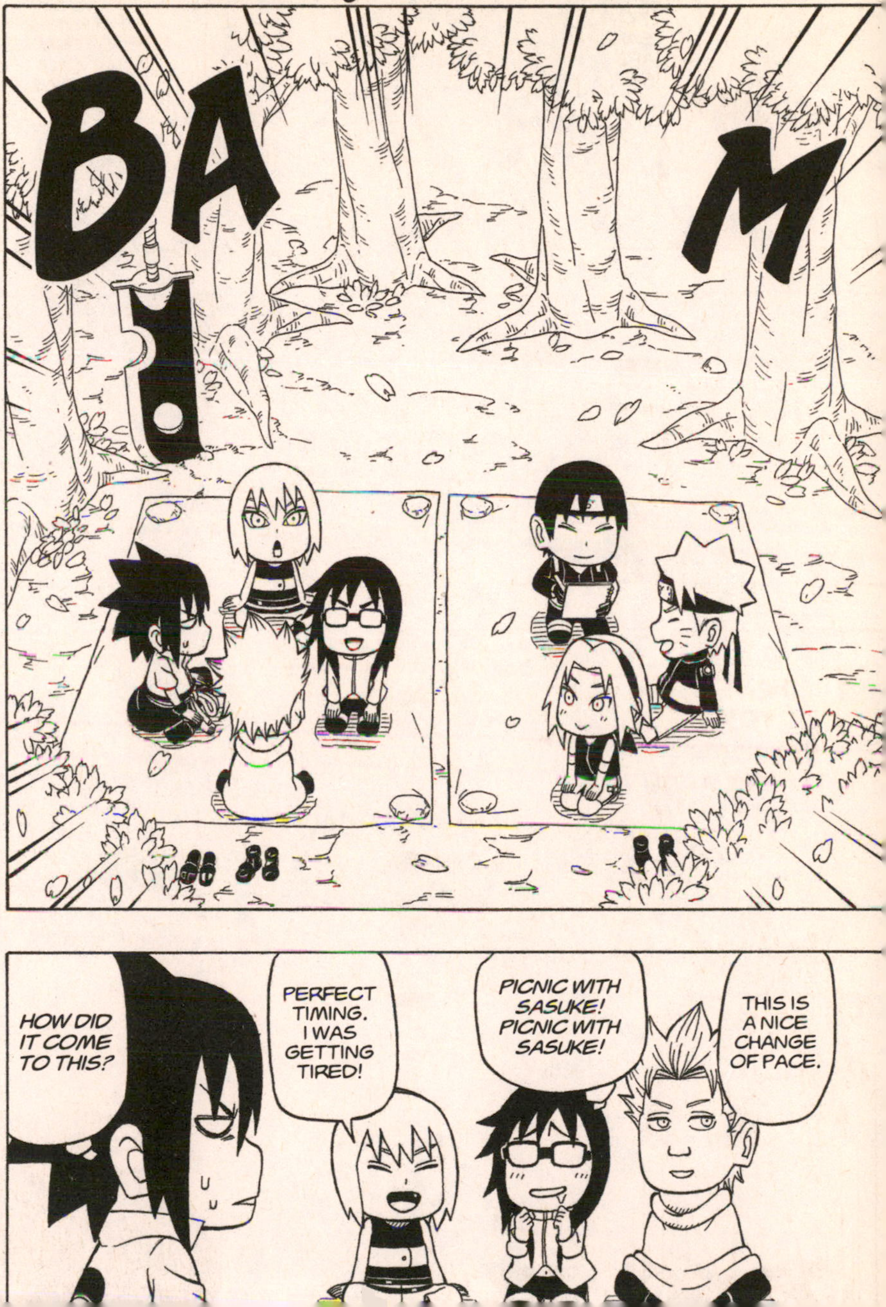
BAM
THIS IS A NICE CHANGE OF PACE.
PICNIC WITH SASUKE! PICNIC WITH SASUKE!
PERFECT TIMING. I WAS GETTING TIRED!
HOW DID IT COME TO THIS?

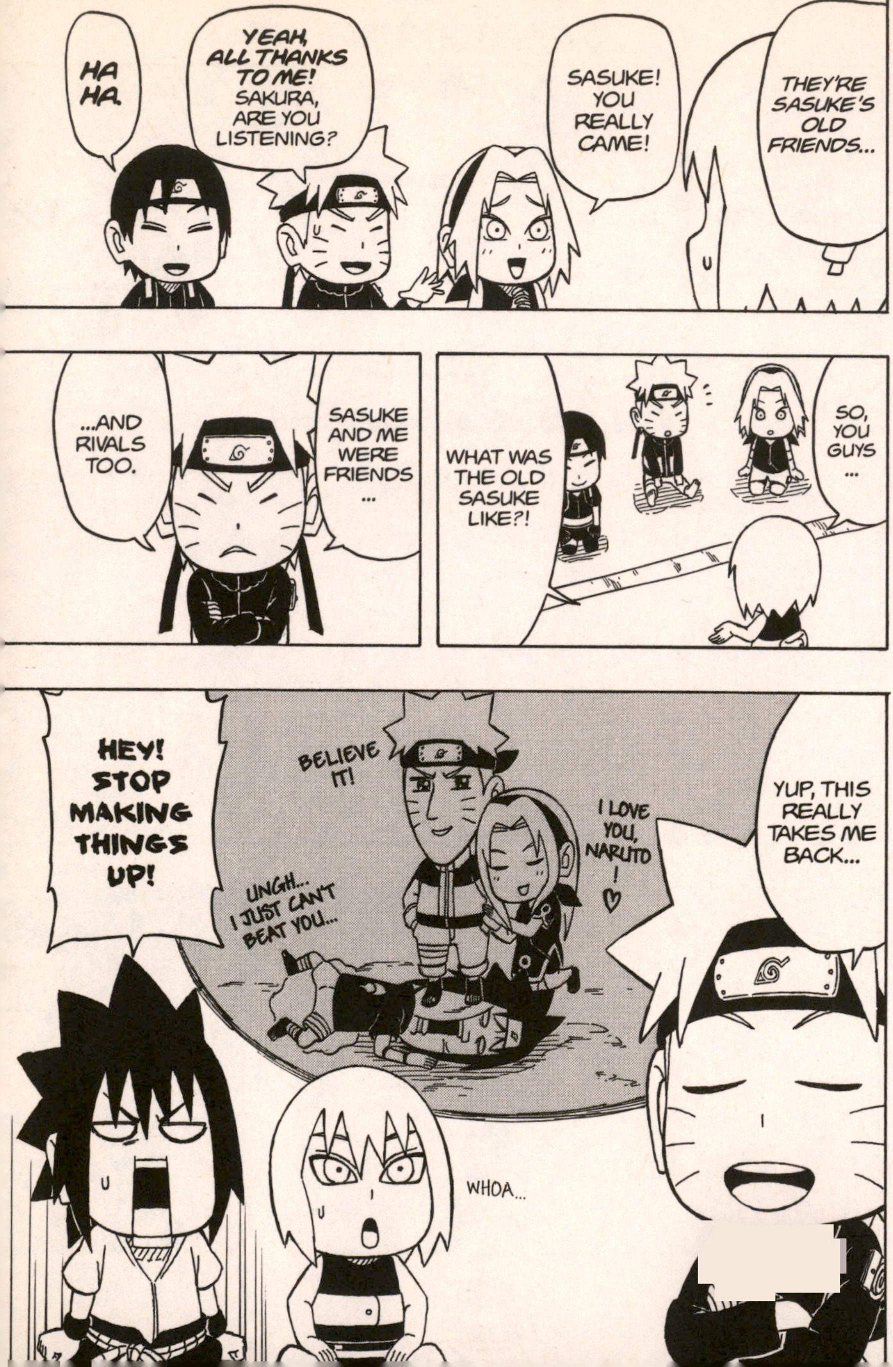
THEY'RE SASUKE'S OLD FRIENDS...
SASUKE! YOU REALLY CAME!
YEAH, ALL THANKS TO ME! SAKURA, ARE YOU LISTENING?
HA HA.
SO, YOU GUYS ...
WHAT WAS THE OLD SASUKE LIKE?!
SASUKE AND ME WERE FRIENDS ...
...AND RIVALS TOO.
YUP, THIS REALLY TAKES ME BACK...
I LOVE YOU, NARUTO ! ♡
BELIEVE IT!
UNGH... I JUST CAN'T BEAT YOU...
HEY! STOP MAKING THINGS UP!
WHOA...

CELL SEVEN

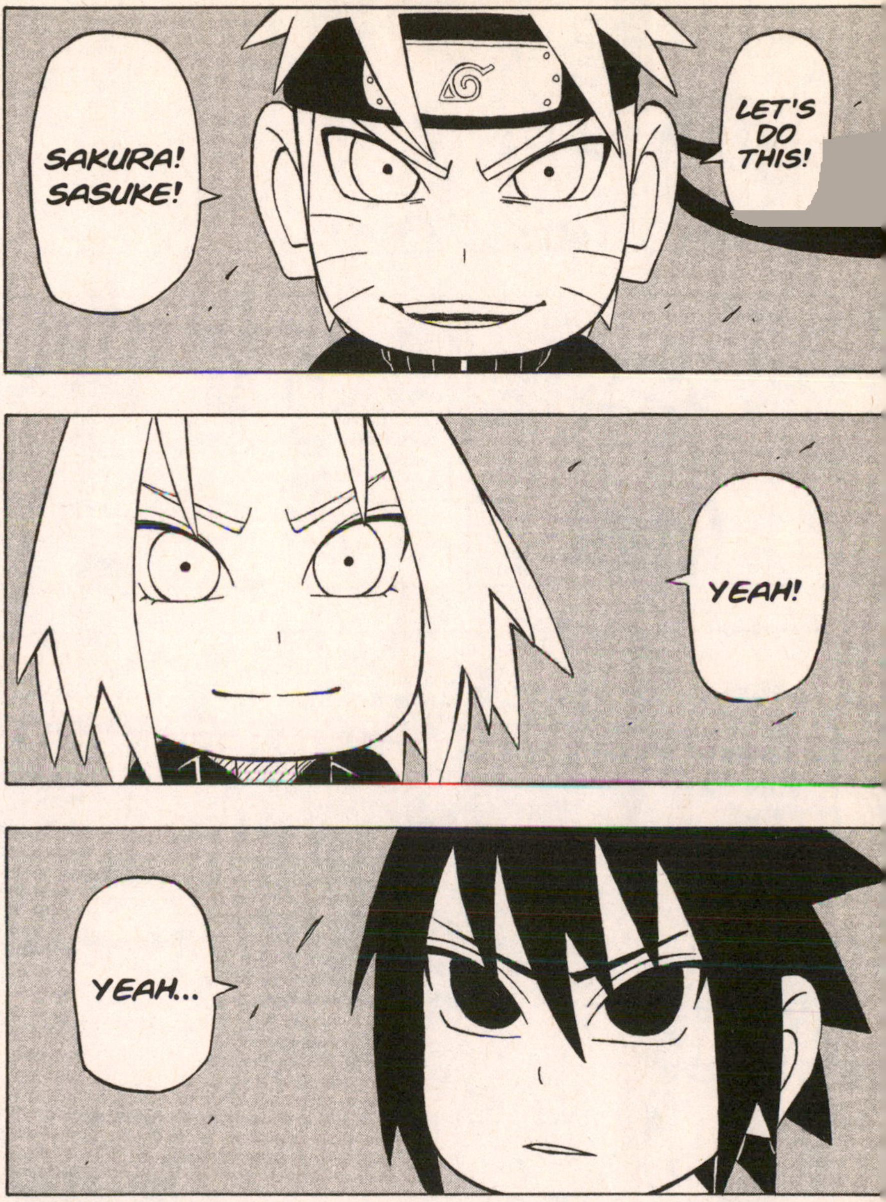
LET'S DO THIS!
SAKURA! SASUKE!
YEAH!
YEAH...

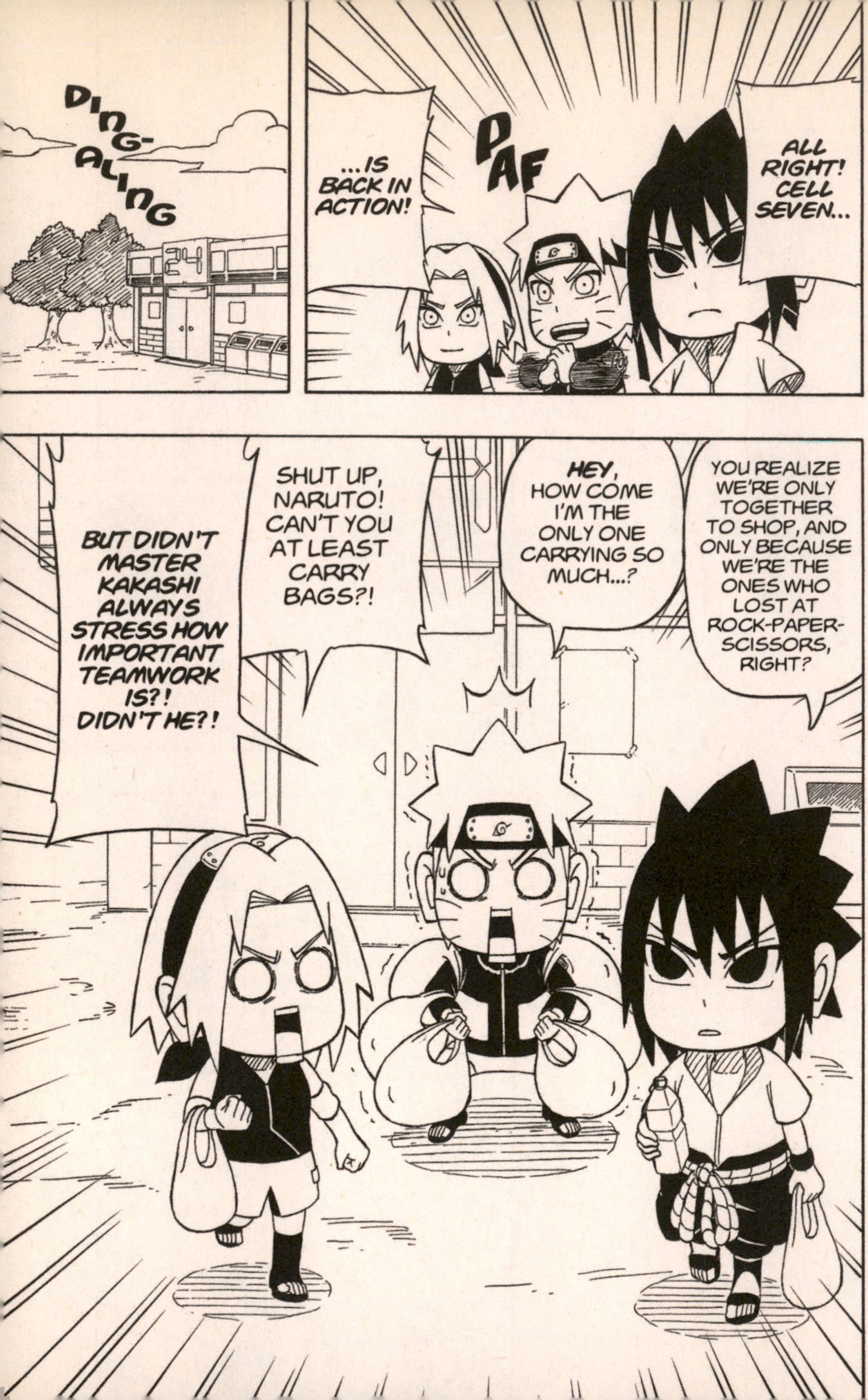
ALL RIGHT! CELL SEVEN...
PAF
...IS BACK IN ACTION!
DING-ALING
YOU REALIZE WE'RE ONLY TOGETHER TO SHOP, AND ONLY BECAUSE WE'RE THE ONES WHO LOST AT ROCK-PAPER-SCISSORS, RIGHT?
HEY, HOW COME I'M THE ONLY ONE CARRYING SO MUCH...?
SHUT UP, NARUTO! CAN'T YOU AT LEAST CARRY BAGS?!
BUT DIDN'T MASTER KAKASHI ALWAYS STRESS HOW IMPORTANT TEAMWORK IS?! DIDN'T HE?!

SAI

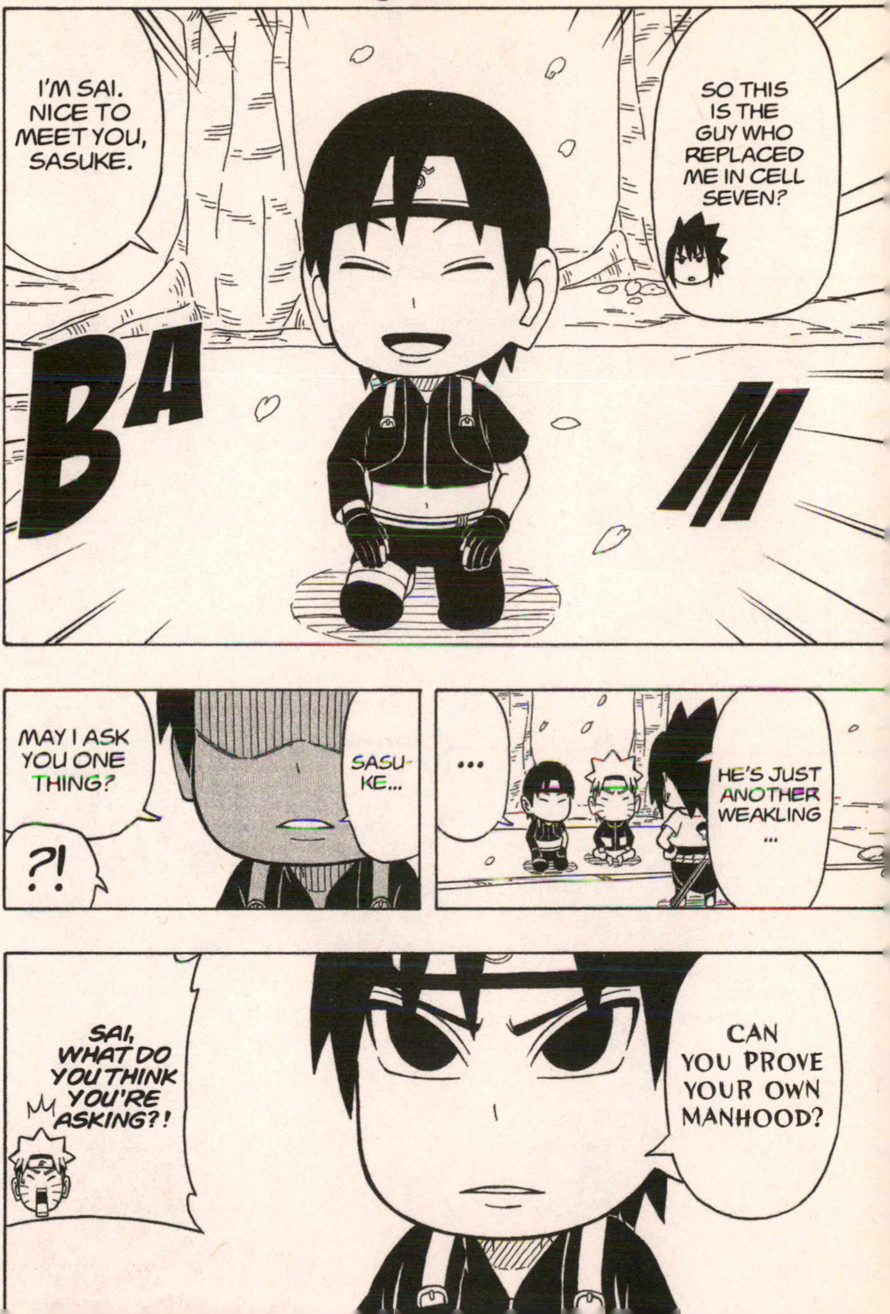

SO THIS IS THE GUY WHO REPLACED ME IN CELL SEVEN?
I'M SAI. NICE TO MEET YOU, SASUKE.
BAM
HE'S JUST ANOTHER WEAKLING ...
...
SASU-KE...
MAY I ASK YOU ONE THING?
?!
CAN YOU PROVE YOUR OWN MANHOOD?
SAI, WHAT DO YOU THINK YOU'RE ASKING?!

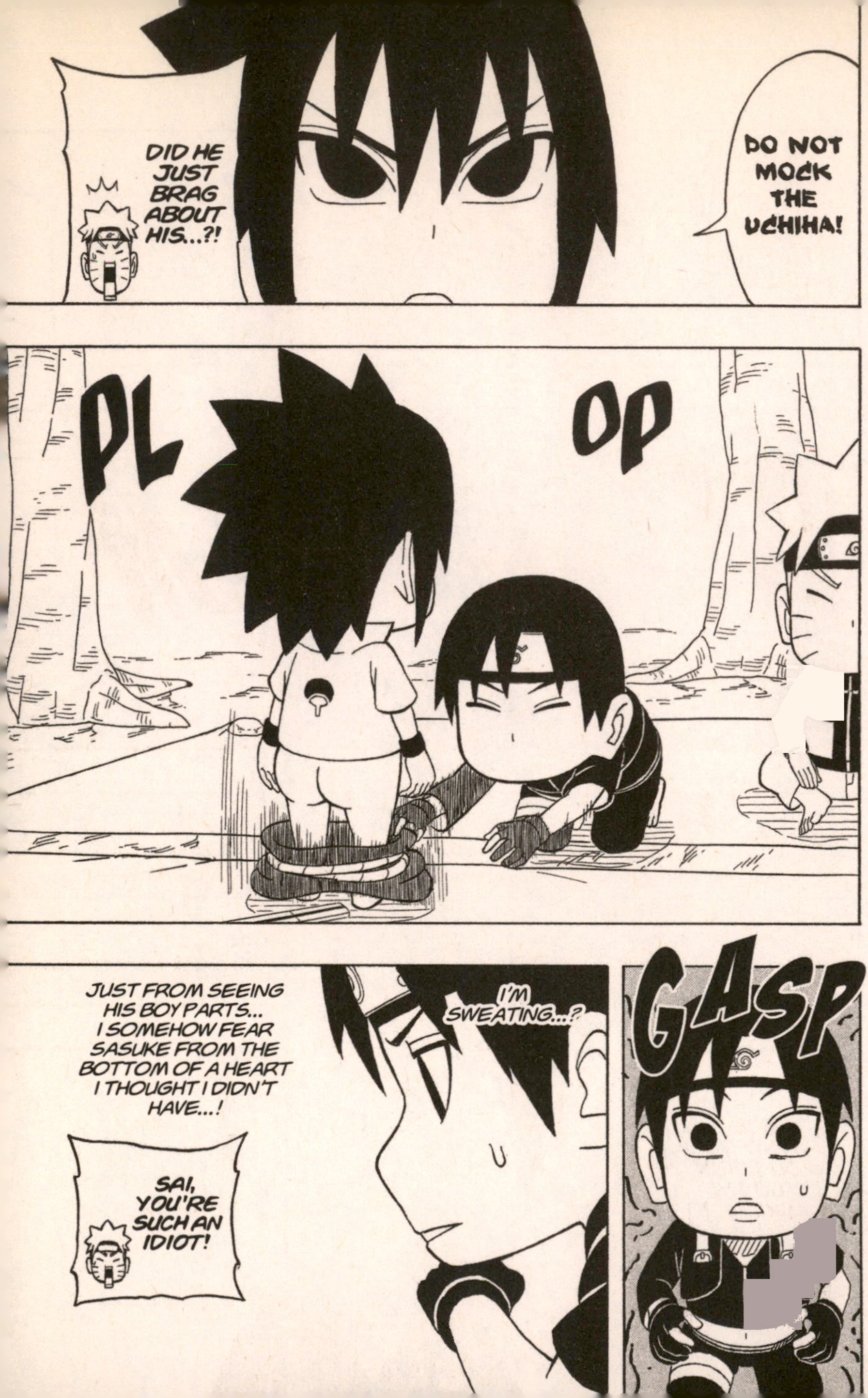
DO NOT MOCK THE UCHIHA!
DID HE JUST BRAG ABOUT HIS...?!
PL OP
GASP
I'M SWEATING...?
JUST FROM SEEING HIS BOY PARTS... I SOMEHOW FEAR SASUKE FROM THE BOTTOM OF A HEART I THOUGHT I DIDN'T HAVE...!
SAI, YOU'RE SUCH AN IDIOT!

KARIN VS. SAKURA

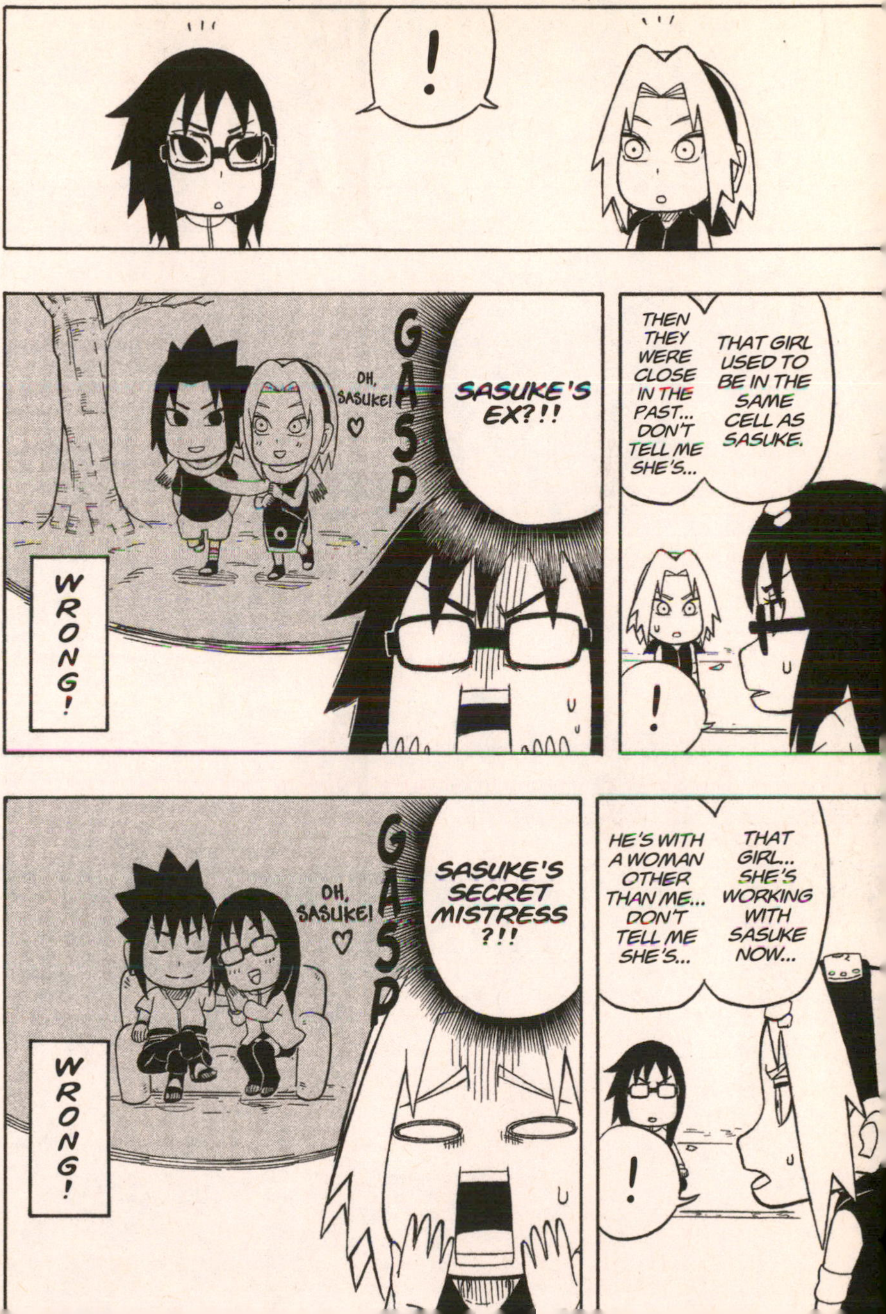
!
THAT GIRL USED TO BE IN THE SAME CELL AS SASUKE.
THEN THEY WERE CLOSE IN THE PAST... DON'T TELL ME SHE'S...
!
SASUKE'S EX?!!
GASP
OH, SASUKE! ♡
WRONG!
THAT GIRL... SHE'S WORKING WITH SASUKE NOW...
HE'S WITH A WOMAN OTHER THAN ME... DON'T TELL ME SHE'S...
!
SASUKE'S SECRET MISTRESS?!!
GASP
OH, SASUKE! ♡
WRONG!

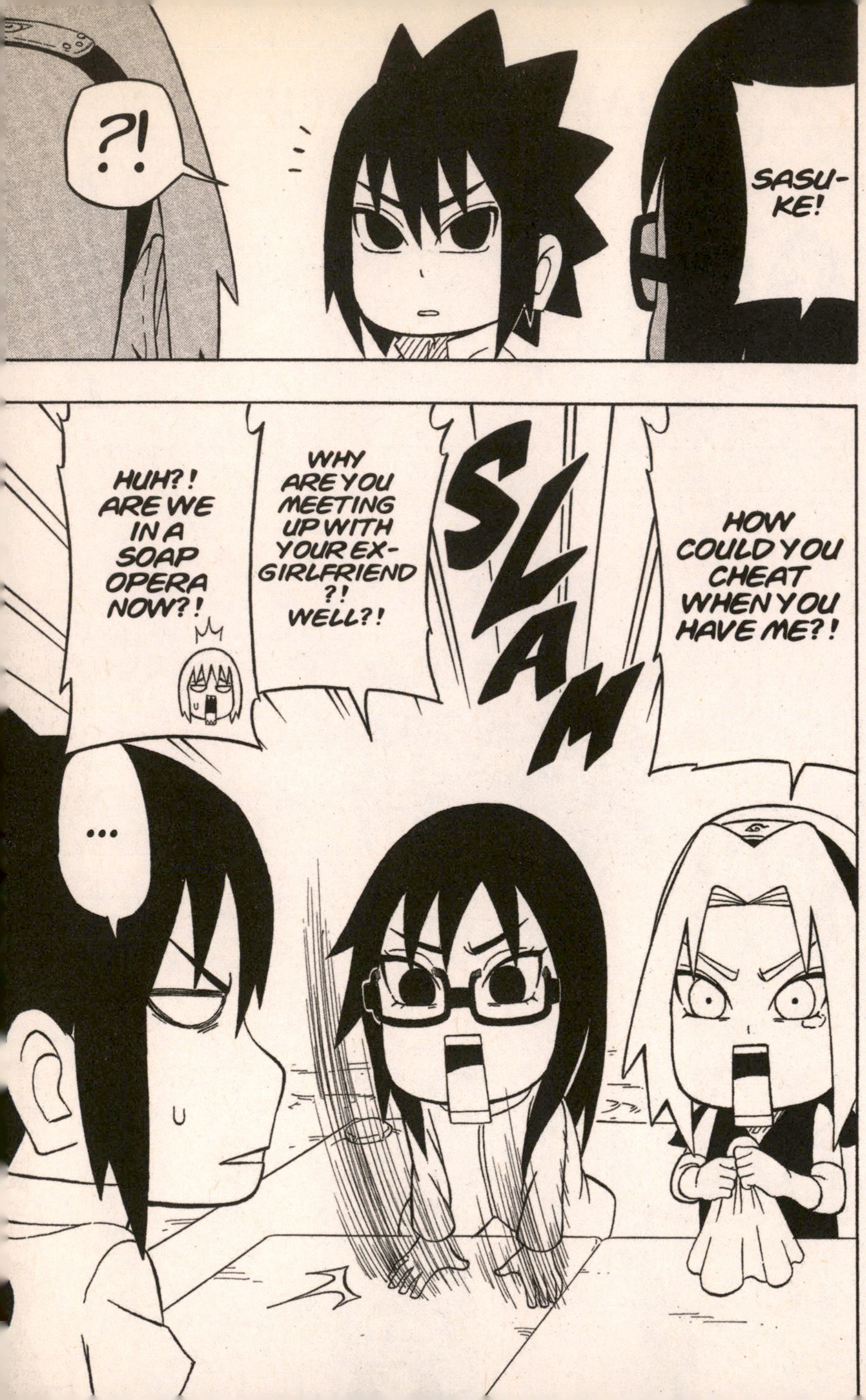
SASU-KE!
?!
HOW COULD YOU CHEAT WHEN YOU HAVE ME?!
SLAM
WHY ARE YOU MEETING UP WITH YOUR EX-GIRLFRIEND?! WELL?!
HUH?! ARE WE IN A SOAP OPERA NOW?!
...

FEMININE CHARM SHOWDOWN

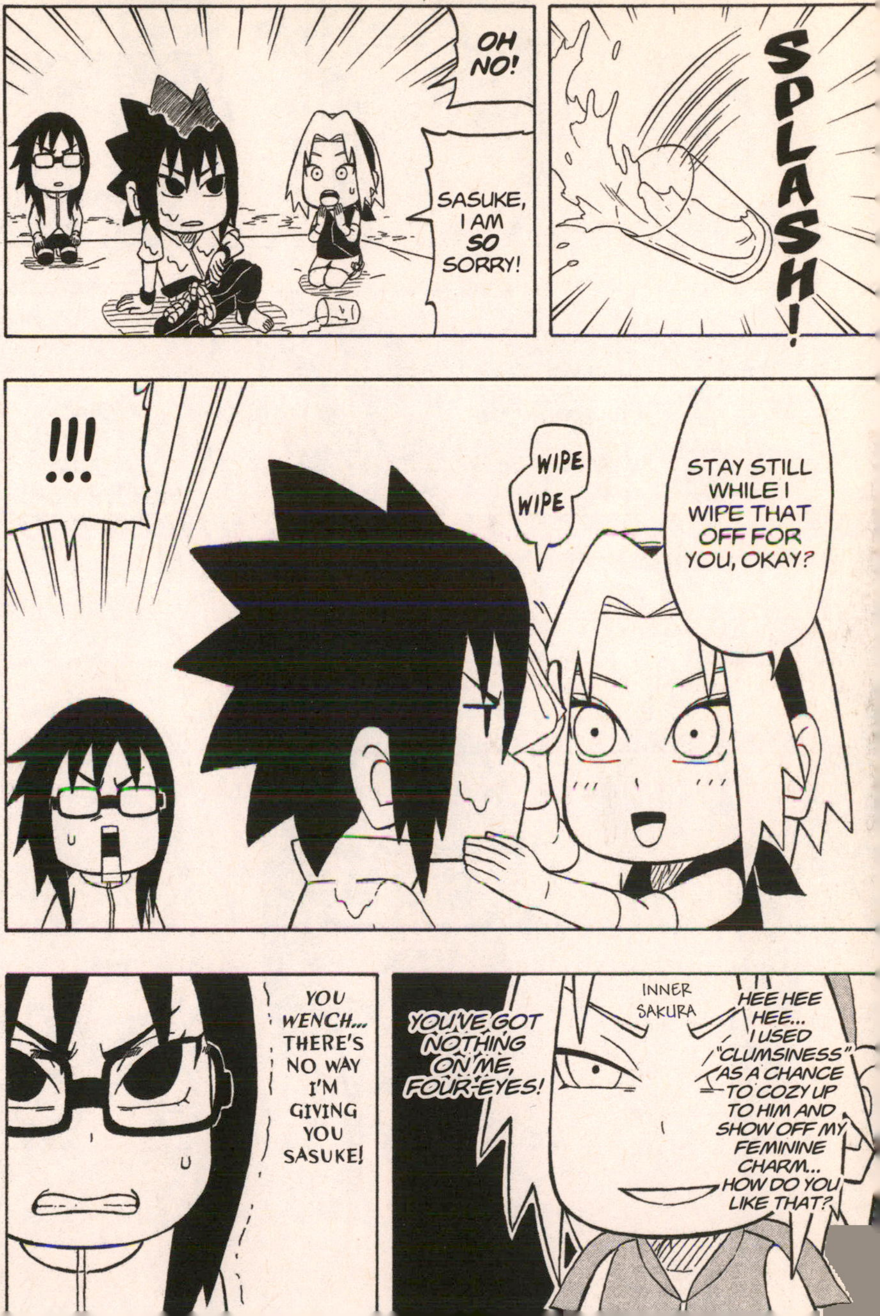
SPLASH!
OH NO!
SASUKE, I AM SO SORRY!
STAY STILL WHILE I WIPE THAT OFF FOR YOU, OKAY?
WIPE WIPE
!!!
...
INNER SAKURA
HEE HEE HEE... I USED "CLUMSINESS" AS A CHANCE TO COZY UP TO HIM AND SHOW OFF MY FEMININE CHARM... HOW DO YOU LIKE THAT?
YOU'VE GOT NOTHING ON ME, FOUR-EYES!
YOU WENCH... THERE'S NO WAY I'M GIVING YOU SASUKE!

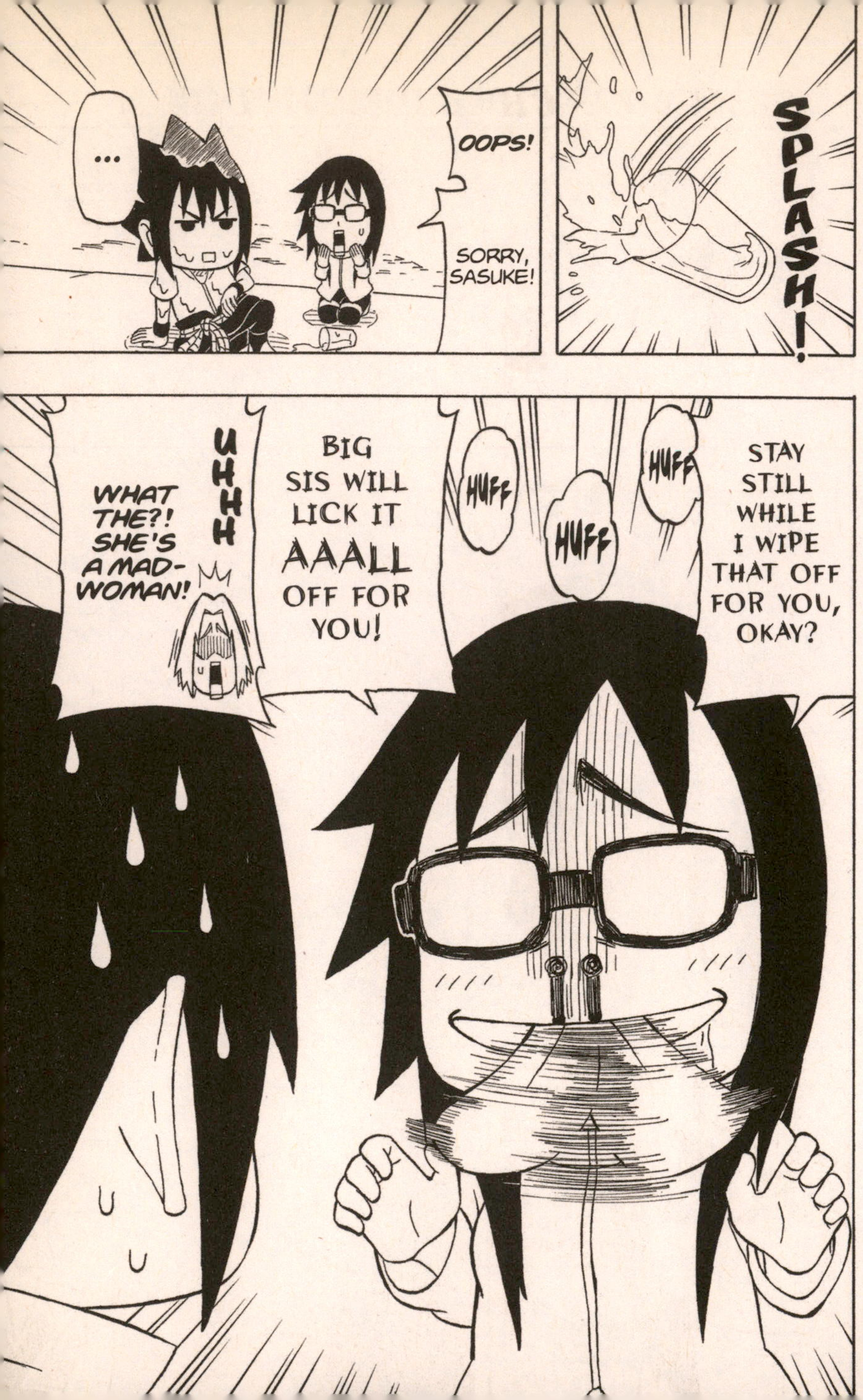
SPLASH!
OOPS!
SORRY, SASUKE!
...
STAY STILL WHILE I WIPE THAT OFF FOR YOU, OKAY?
HUFF
HUFF
HUFF
BIG SIS WILL LICK IT AAALL OFF FOR YOU!
UHHH
WHAT THE?! SHE'S A MAD-WOMAN!

JUGO VS. THE DRUNKARD

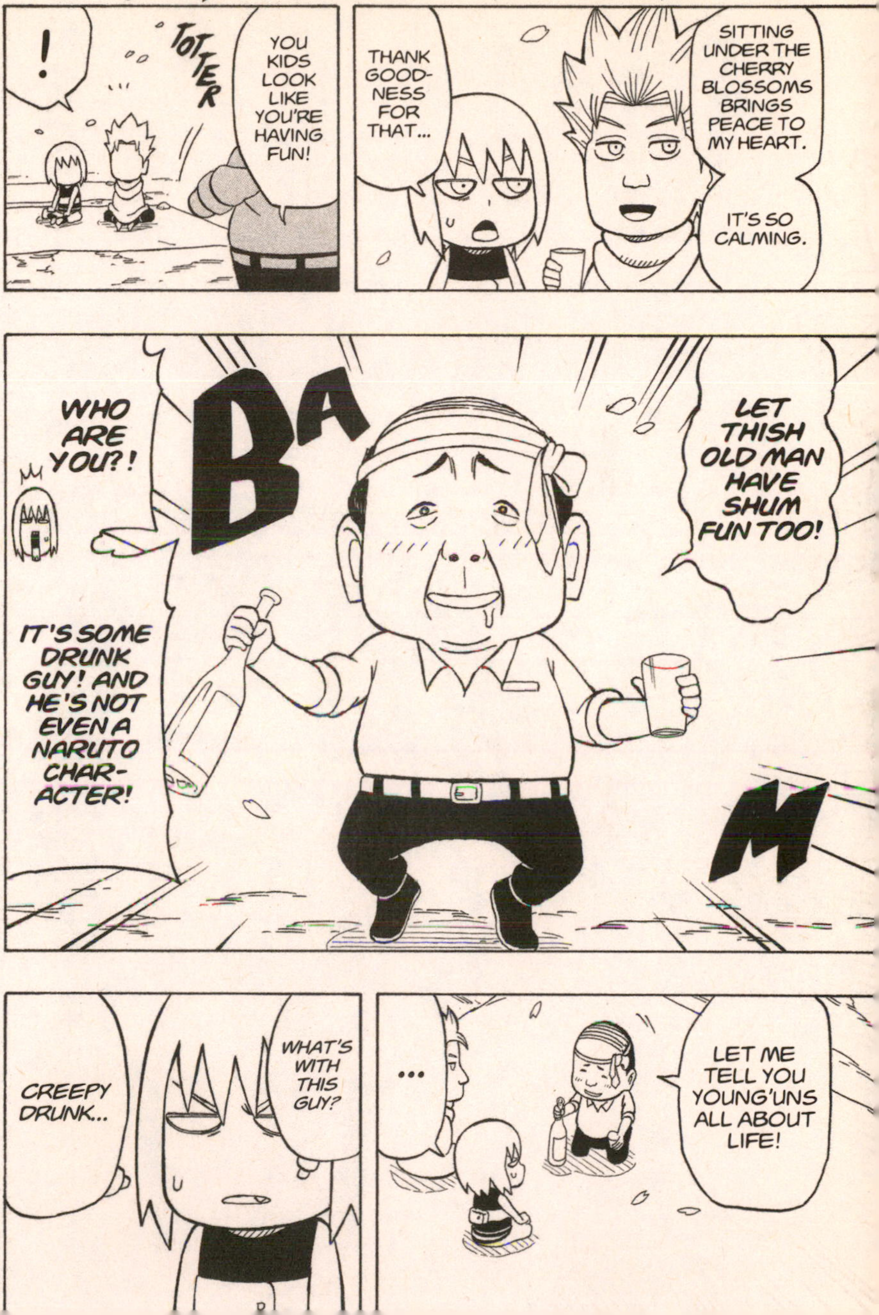
SITTING UNDER THE CHERRY BLOSSOMS BRINGS PEACE TO MY HEART.
IT'S SO CALMING.
THANK GOODNESS FOR THAT...
YOU KIDS LOOK LIKE YOU'RE HAVING FUN!
TOTTER
!
LET THISH OLD MAN HAVE SHUM FUN TOO!
BA
WHO ARE YOU?!
IT'S SOME DRUNK GUY! AND HE'S NOT EVEN A NARUTO CHARACTER!
M
LET ME TELL YOU YOUNG'UNS ALL ABOUT LIFE!
...
WHAT'S WITH THIS GUY?
CREEPY DRUNK...

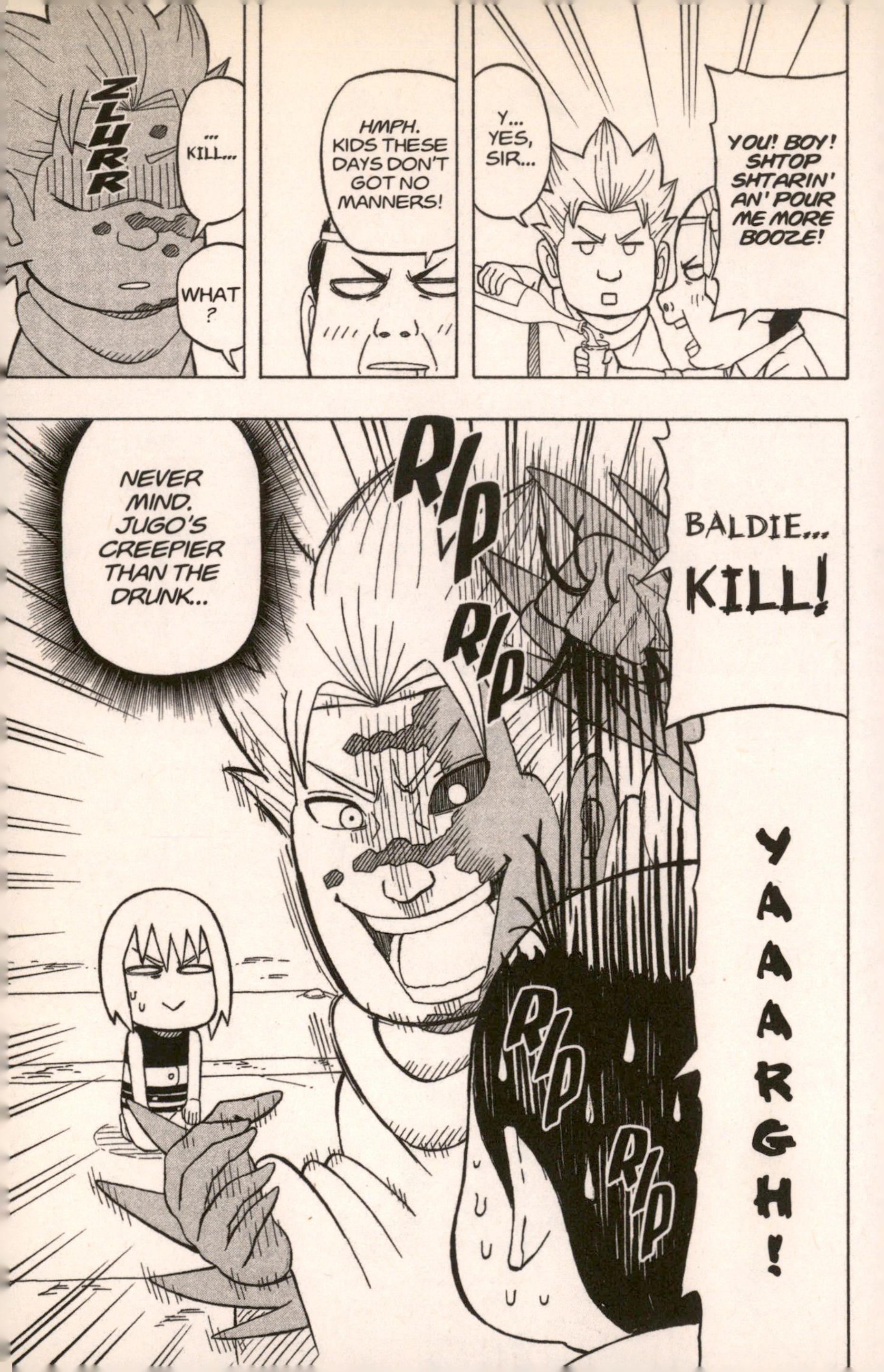
YOU! BOY! SHTOP SHTARIN' AN' POUR ME MORE BOOZE!
Y... YES, SIR...
HMPH. KIDS THESE DAYS DON'T GOT NO MANNERS!
... KILL...
ZLURR
WHAT?
BALDIE... KILL!
RIP RIP
NEVER MIND. JUGO'S CREEPIER THAN THE DRUNK...
YAAAARGH!
RIP RIP

SHARINGAN VS. SAGE MODE

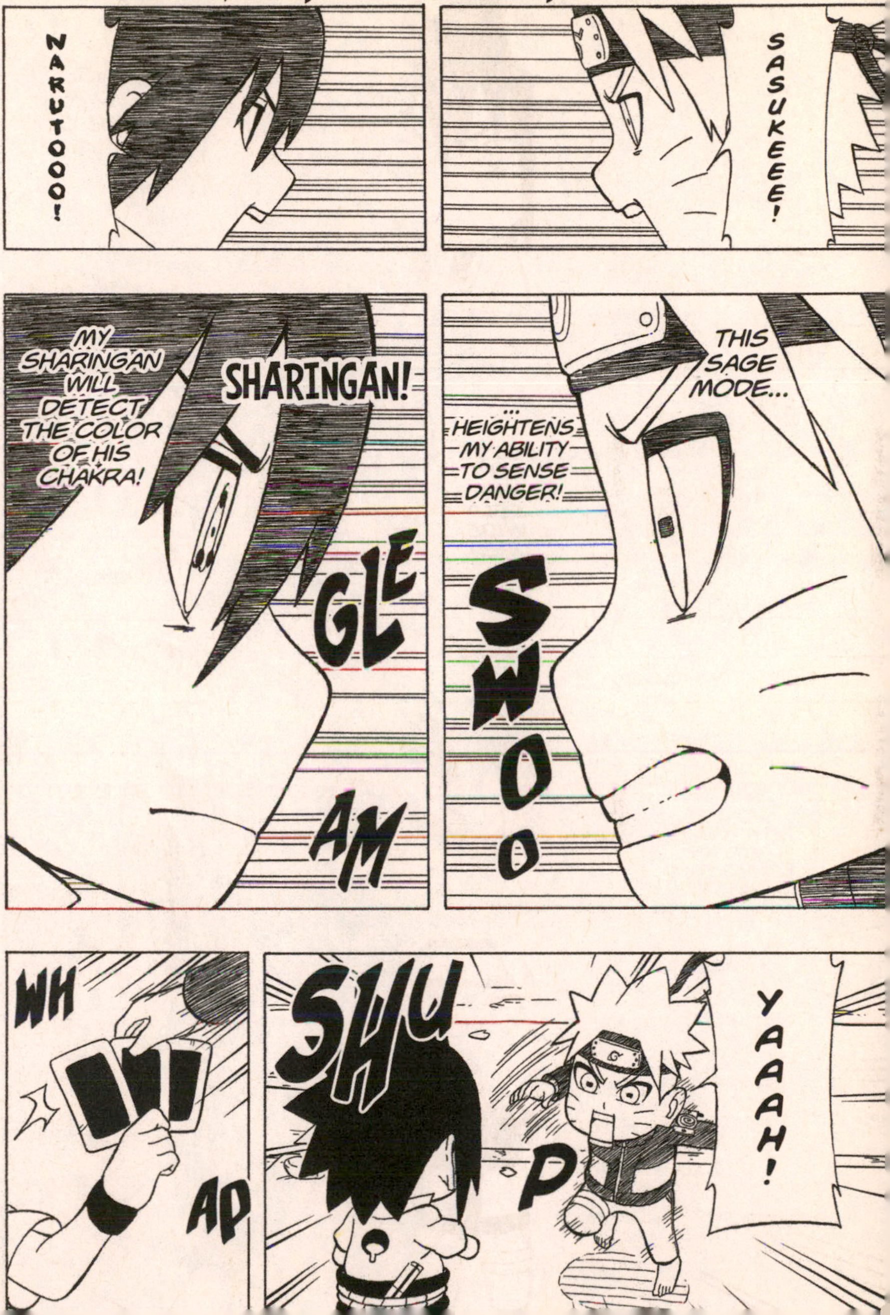
SASUKEEE!
NARUTOOO!
THIS SAGE MODE...
...HEIGHTENS MY ABILITY TO SENSE DANGER!
SWOOO
SHARINGAN!
MY SHARINGAN WILL DETECT THE COLOR OF HIS CHAKRA!
GLEAM
YAAAAH!
SHUP
WHAP

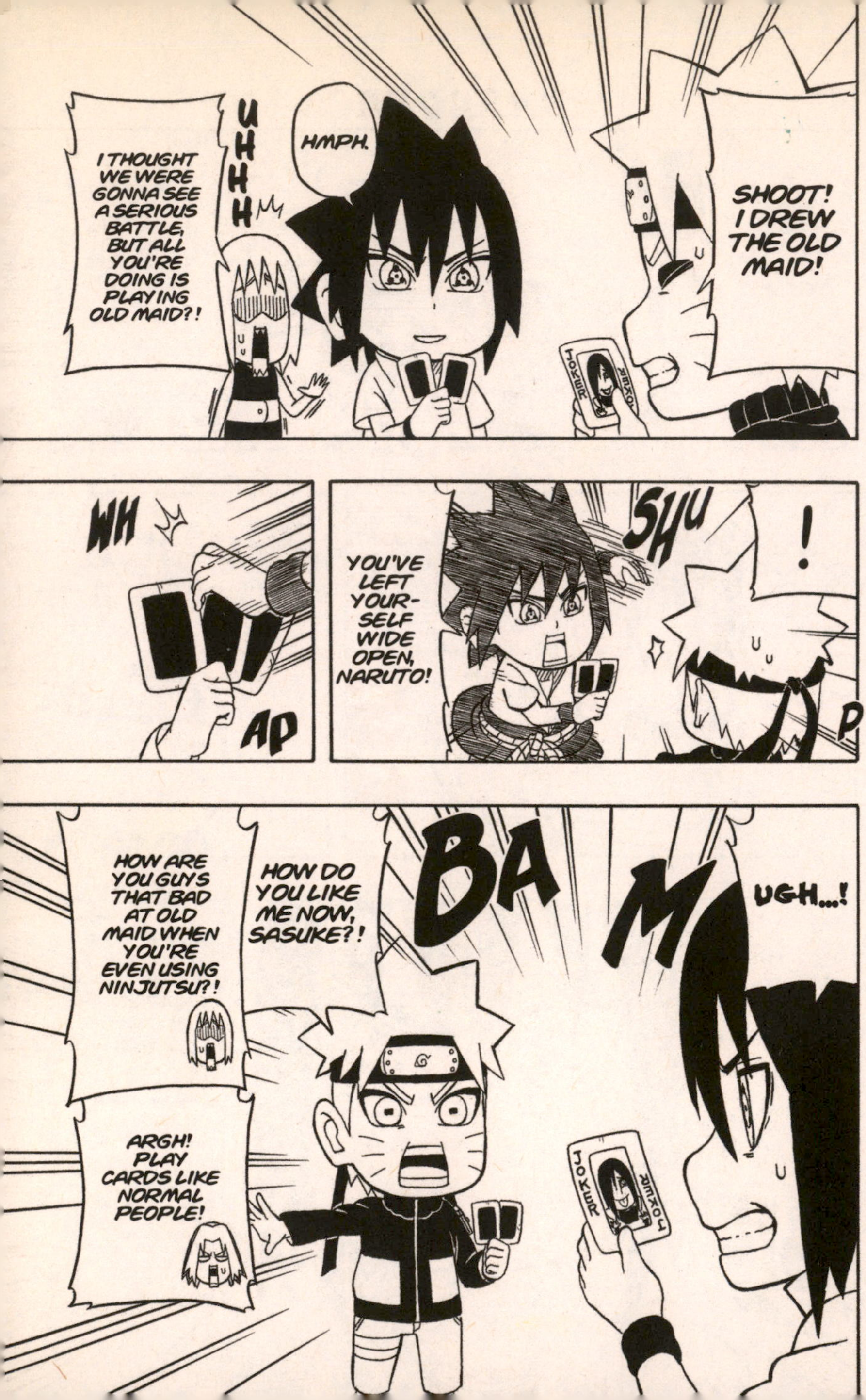
SHOOT! I DREW THE OLD MAID!
JOKER
HMPH.
UHHH
I THOUGHT WE WERE GONNA SEE A SERIOUS BATTLE, BUT ALL YOU'RE DOING IS PLAYING OLD MAID?!
!
SHU
YOU'VE LEFT YOURSELF WIDE OPEN, NARUTO!
P
WH
AP
UGH...!
BAM
JOKER
HOW DO YOU LIKE ME NOW, SASUKE?!
HOW ARE YOU GUYS THAT BAD AT OLD MAID WHEN YOU'RE EVEN USING NINJUTSU?!
ARGH! PLAY CARDS LIKE NORMAL PEOPLE!

KARAOKE

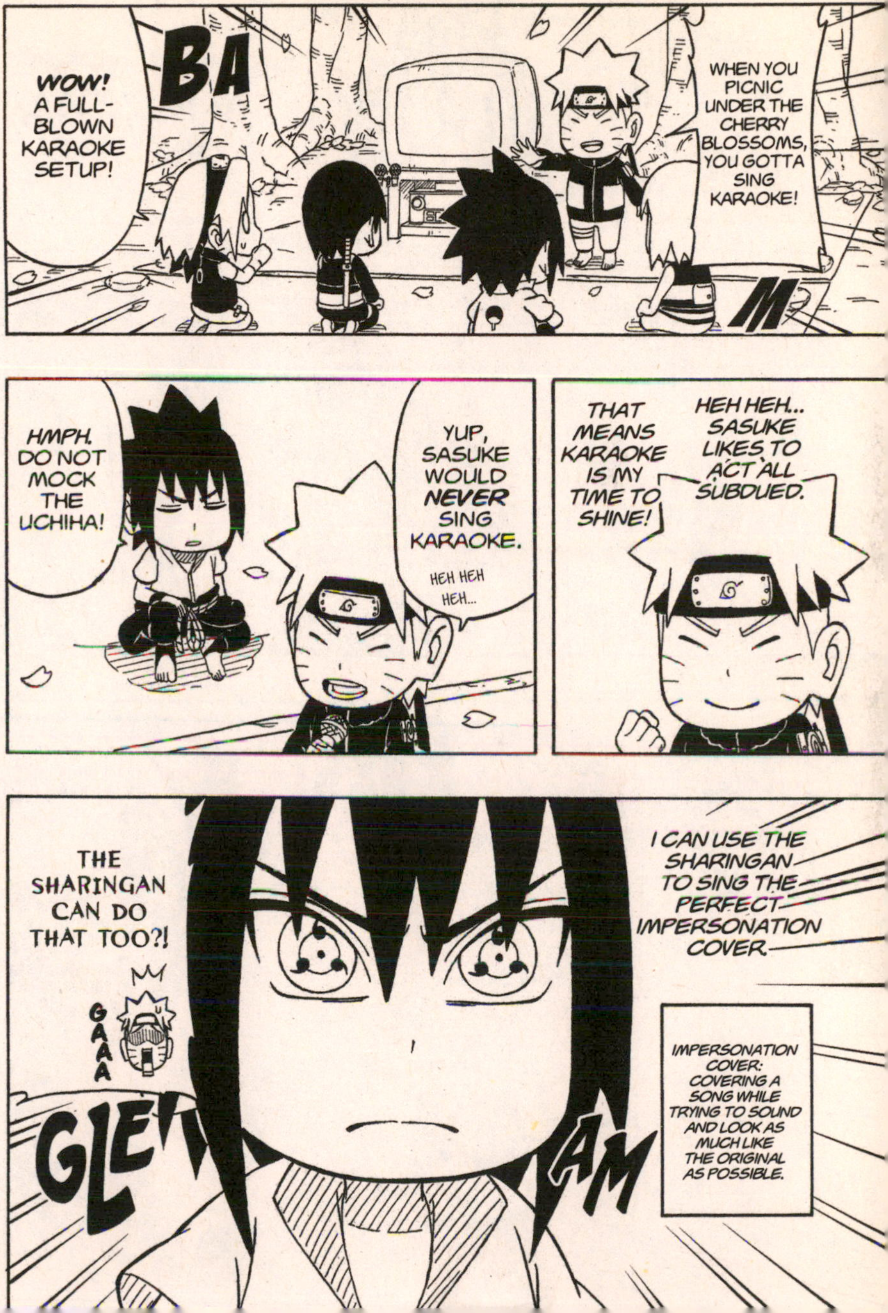
WHEN YOU PICNIC UNDER THE CHERRY BLOSSOMS, YOU GOTTA SING KARAOKE!
WOW! A FULL-BLOWN KARAOKE SETUP!
BA
M
HEH HEH... SASUKE LIKES TO ACT ALL SUBDUED.
THAT MEANS KARAOKE IS MY TIME TO SHINE!
YUP, SASUKE WOULD NEVER SING KARAOKE.
HEH HEH HEH...
HMPH. DO NOT MOCK THE UCHIHA!
I CAN USE THE SHARINGAN TO SING THE PERFECT IMPERSONATION COVER.
IMPERSONATION COVER: COVERING A SONG WHILE TRYING TO SOUND AND LOOK AS MUCH LIKE THE ORIGINAL AS POSSIBLE.
AM
GLE
THE SHARINGAN CAN DO THAT TOO?!
GAAA

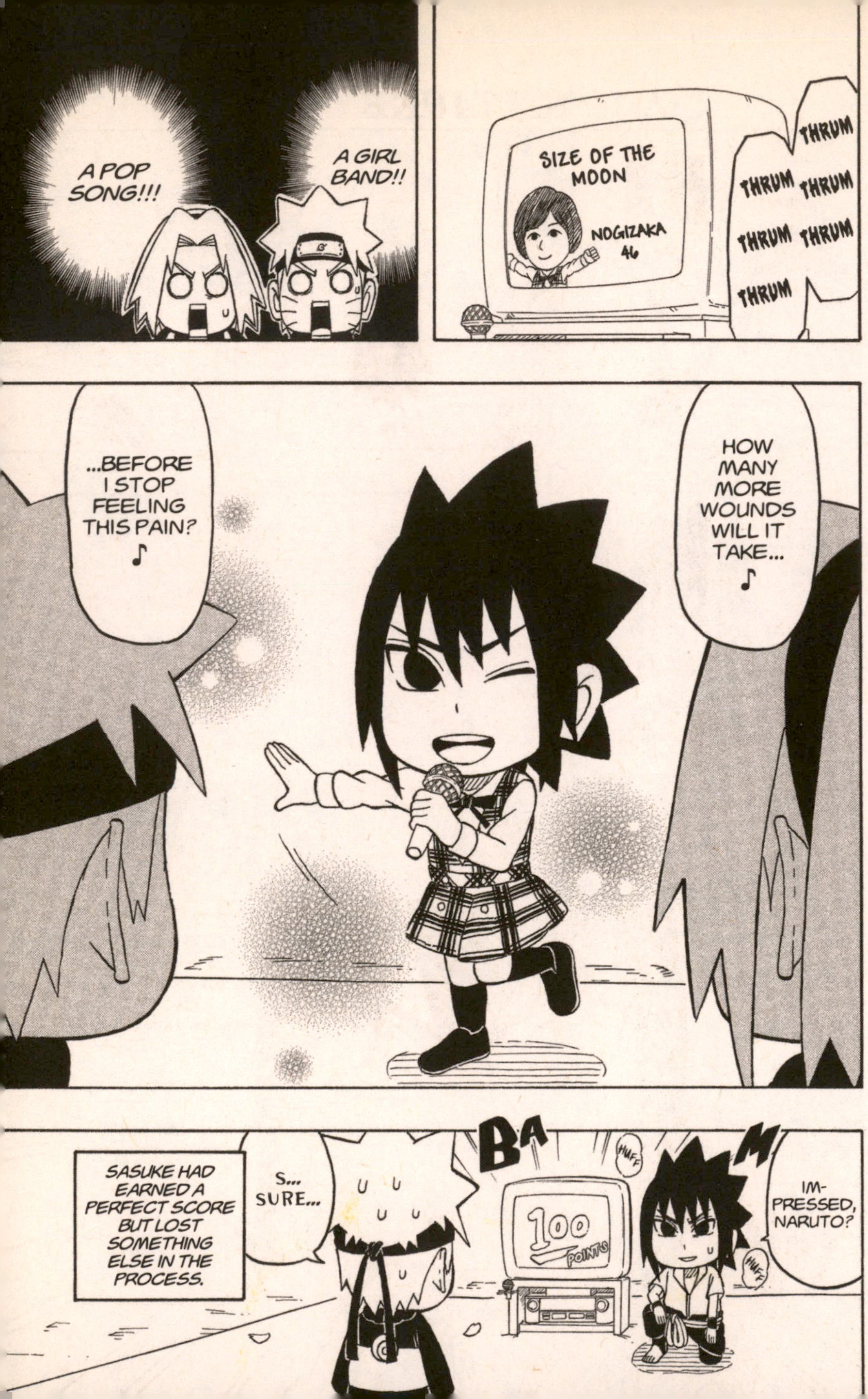
SIZE OF THE MOON
NOGIZAKA 46
THRUM THRUM THRUM THRUM THRUM THRUM THRUM
A GIRL BAND!!
A POP SONG!!!
HOW MANY MORE WOUNDS WILL IT TAKE... ♪
...BEFORE I STOP FEELING THIS PAIN? ♪
BAM
IM-PRESSED, NARUTO?
HUFF
HUFF
100 POINTS
S... SURE...
SASUKE HAD EARNED A PERFECT SCORE BUT LOST SOMETHING ELSE IN THE PROCESS.

COMPETITIVE EATING

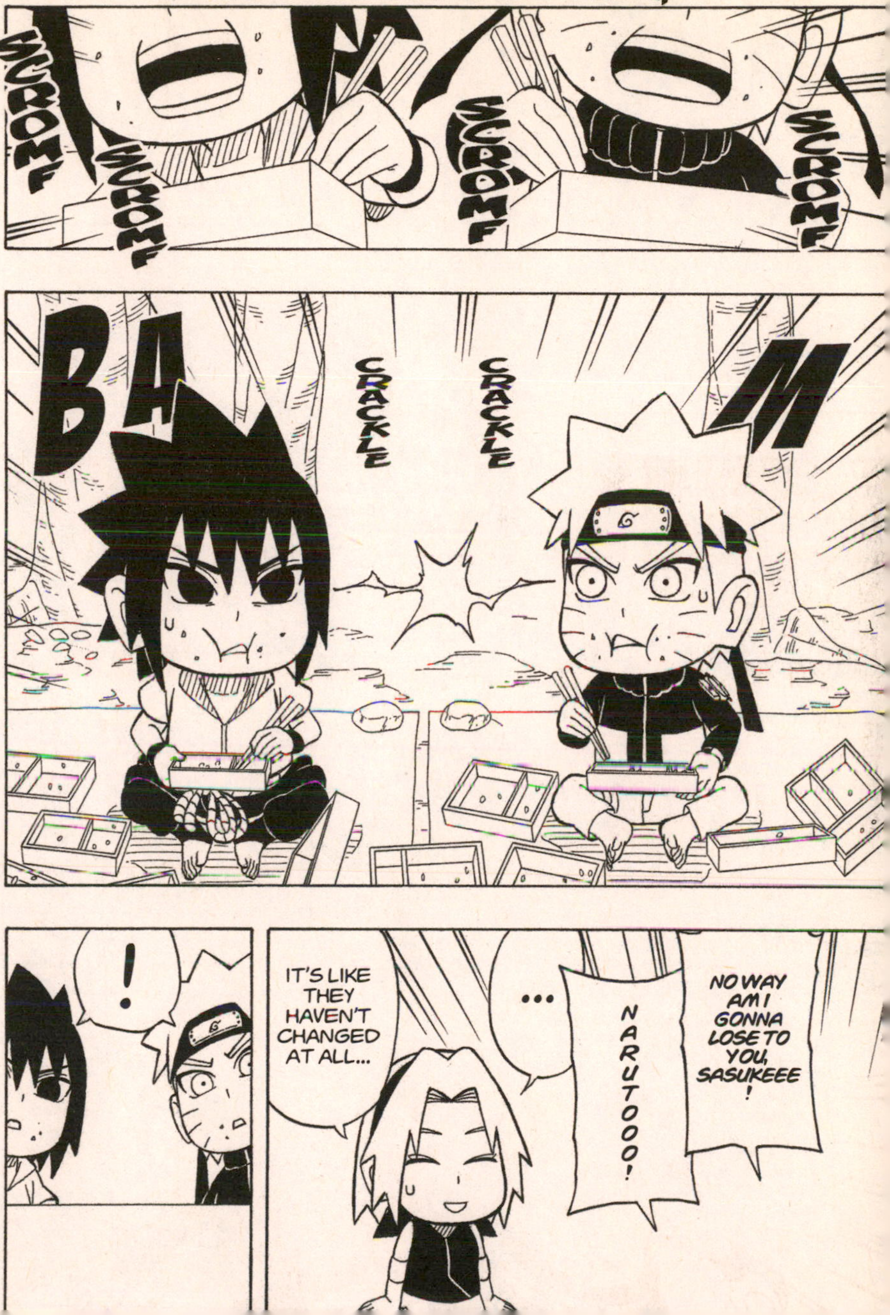
SCROMF
SCROMF
SCROMF
SCROMF
BAM
CRACKLE
CRACKLE
NO WAY AM I GONNA LOSE TO YOU, SASUKEEE!
NARUTOOOO!
...
IT'S LIKE THEY HAVEN'T CHANGED AT ALL...
!

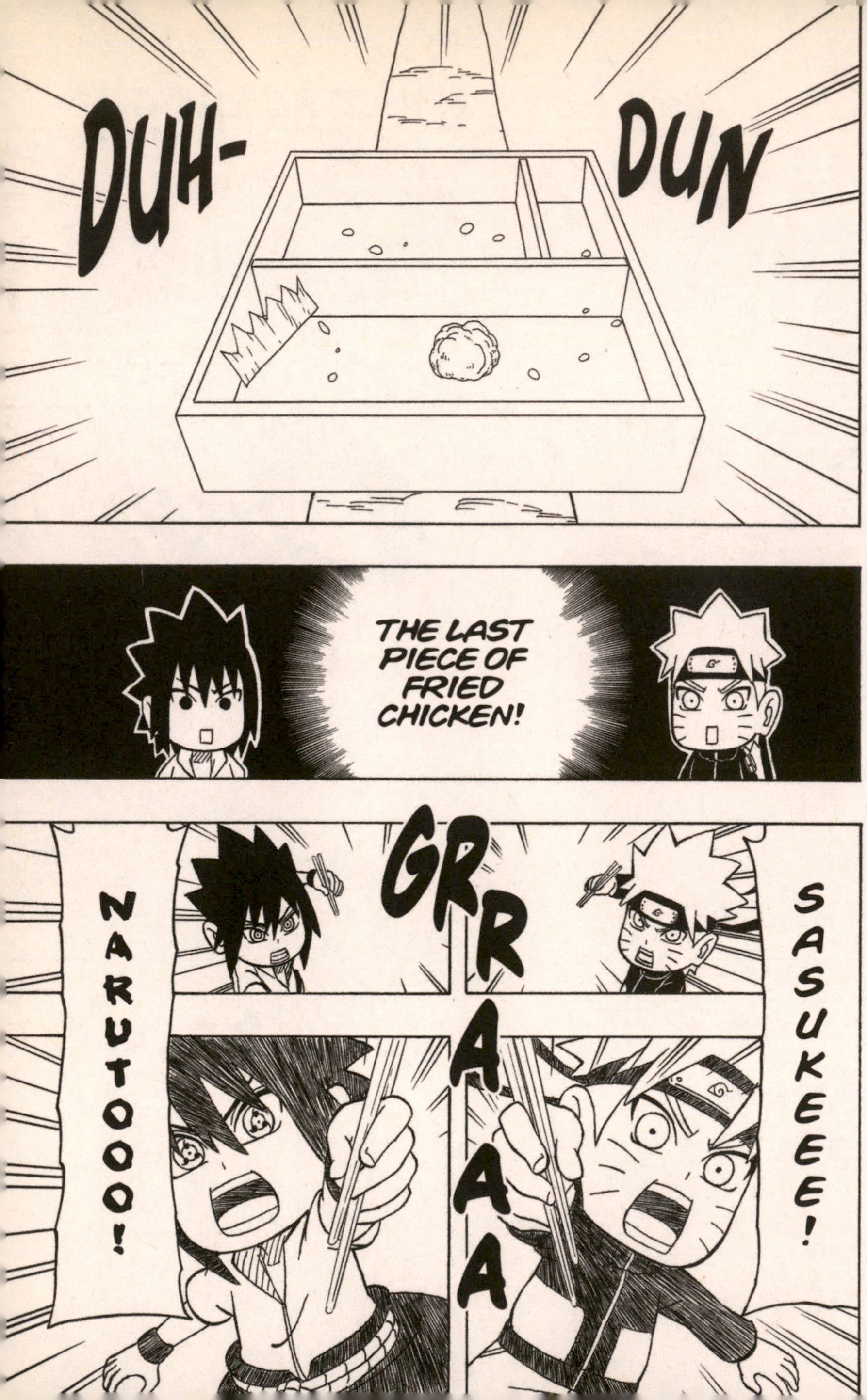
DUH-
DUN
THE LAST PIECE OF FRIED CHICKEN!
SASUKEEE!
GRRAAAA
NARUTOOO!

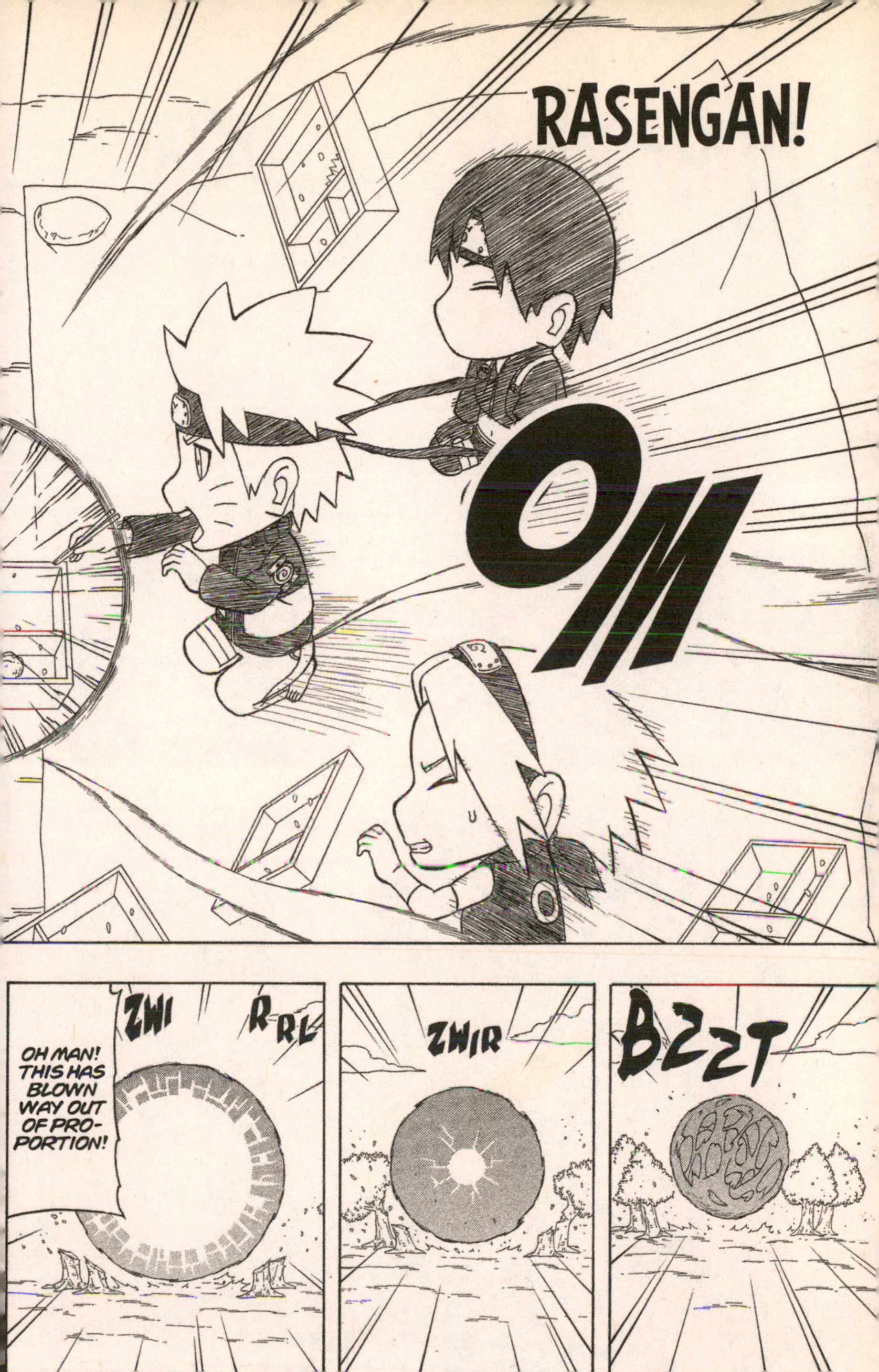
RASENGAN!
OM
BZZT
ZWIR
ZWI RRL
OH MAN! THIS HAS BLOWN WAY OUT OF PRO-PORTION!

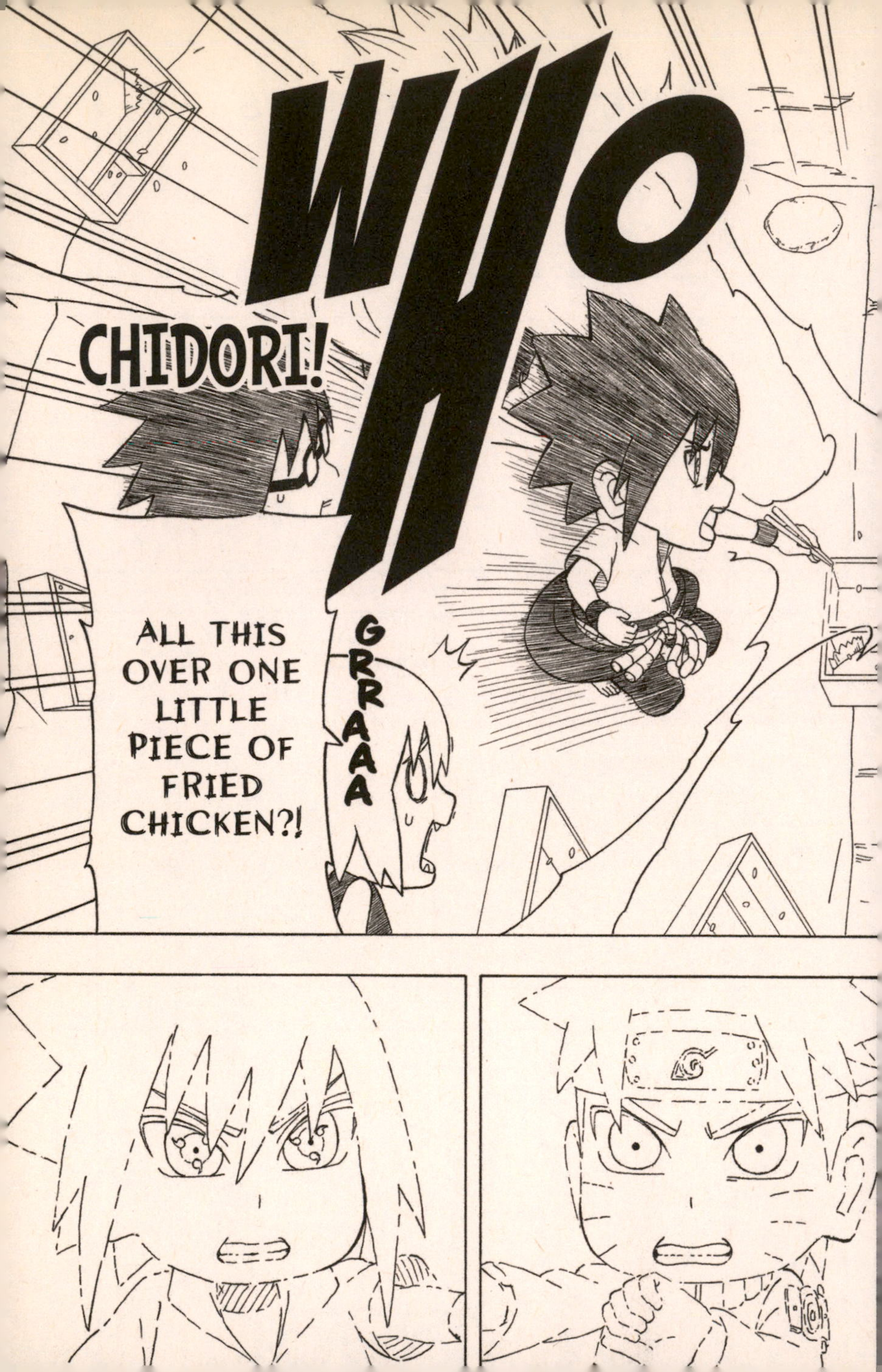
WHO
CHIDORI!
GRRAAA
ALL THIS OVER ONE LITTLE PIECE OF FRIED CHICKEN?!

DEEPEST THOUGHTS

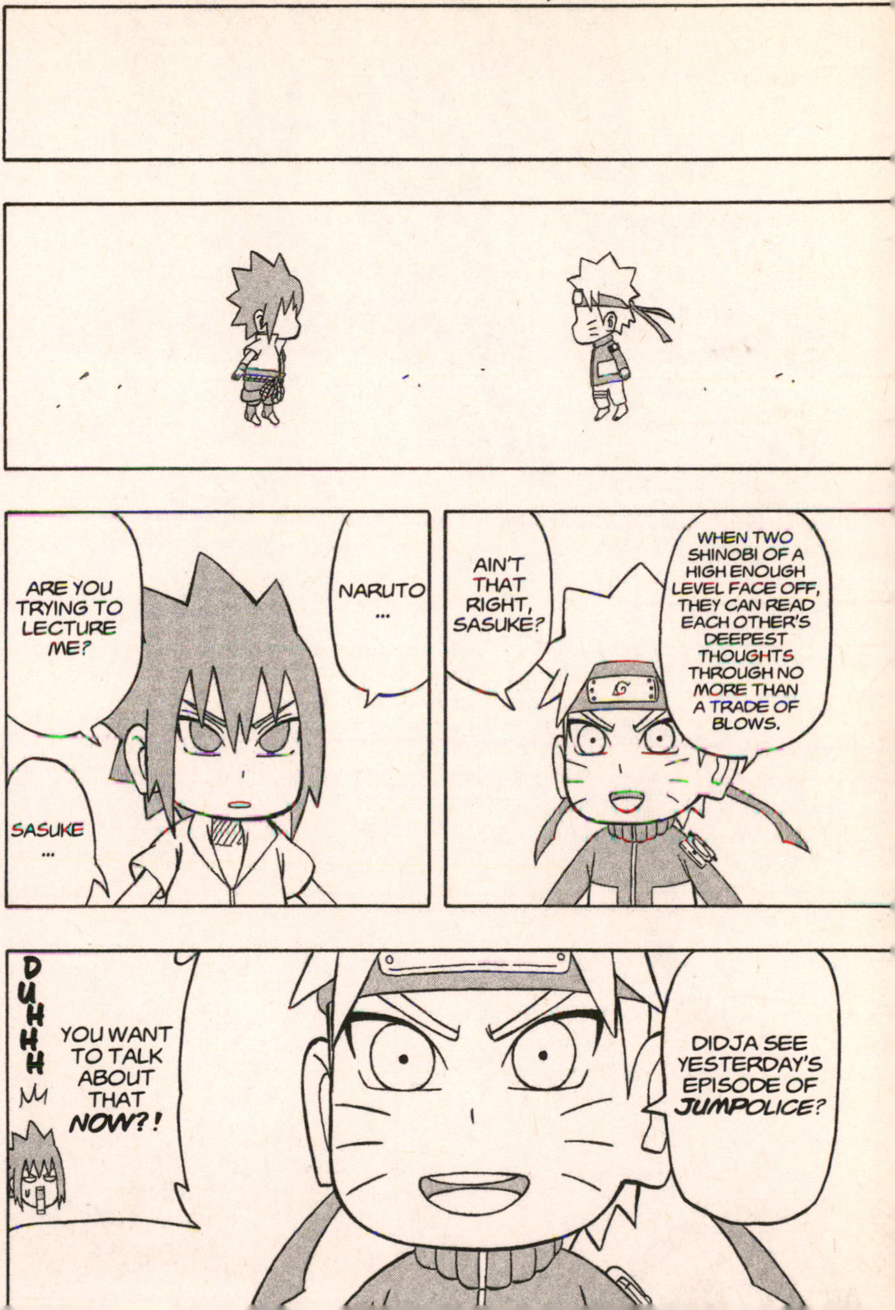
WHEN TWO SHINOBI OF A HIGH ENOUGH LEVEL FACE OFF, THEY CAN READ EACH OTHER'S DEEPEST THOUGHTS THROUGH NO MORE THAN A TRADE OF BLOWS.
AIN'T THAT RIGHT, SASUKE?
NARUTO ...
ARE YOU TRYING TO LECTURE ME?
SASUKE ...
DIDJA SEE YESTERDAY'S EPISODE OF *JUMPOLICE*?
YOU WANT TO TALK ABOUT THAT *NOW*?!
DUHHH

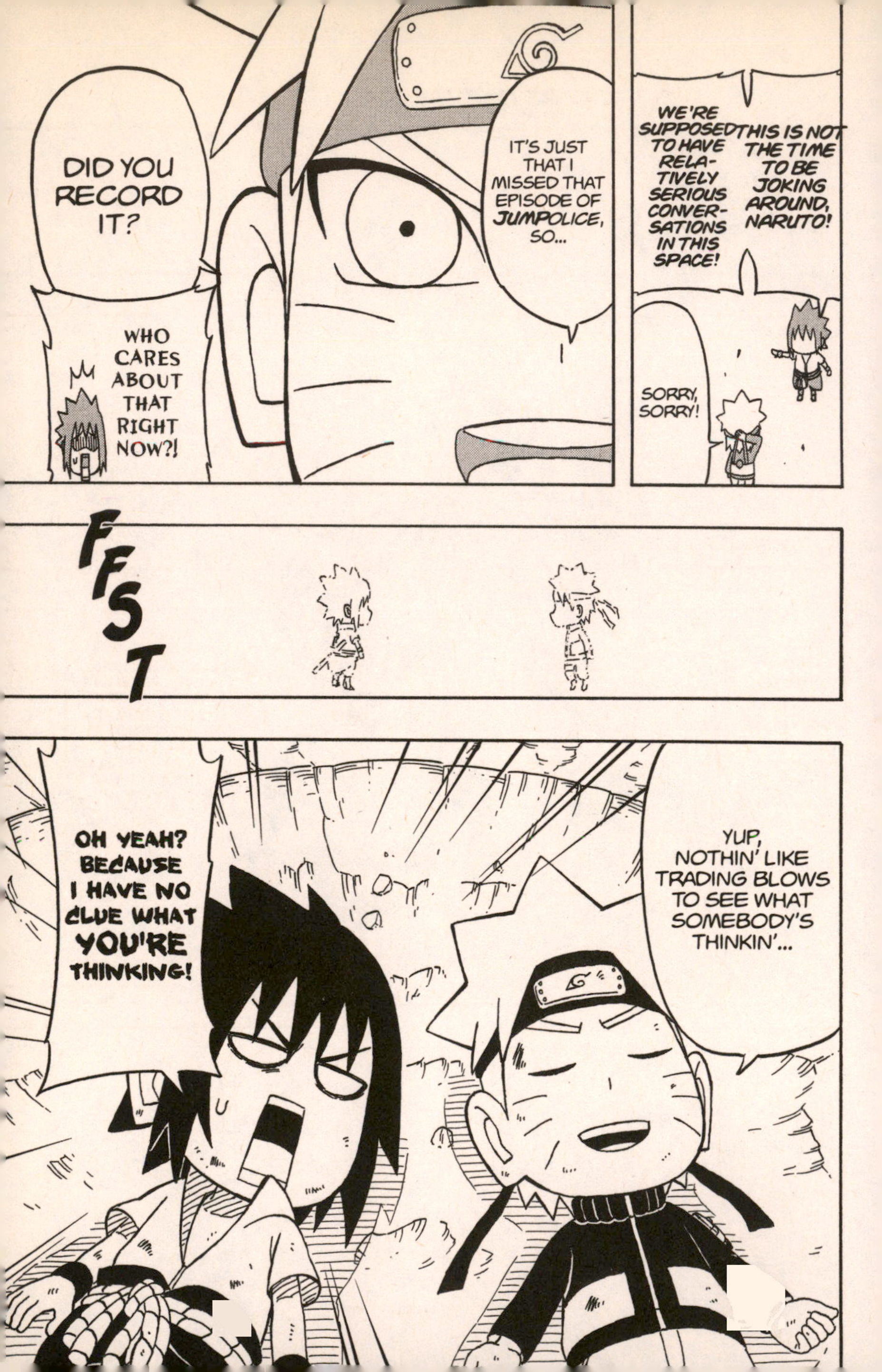
THIS IS NOT THE TIME TO BE JOKING AROUND, NARUTO!
WE'RE SUPPOSED TO HAVE RELA-TIVELY SERIOUS CONVER-SATIONS IN THIS SPACE!
SORRY, SORRY!
IT'S JUST THAT I MISSED THAT EPISODE OF JUMPOLICE, SO...
DID YOU RECORD IT?
WHO CARES ABOUT THAT RIGHT NOW?!
FFST
YUP, NOTHIN' LIKE TRADING BLOWS TO SEE WHAT SOMEBODY'S THINKIN'...
OH YEAH? BECAUSE I HAVE NO CLUE WHAT YOU'RE THINKING!

KAKASHI

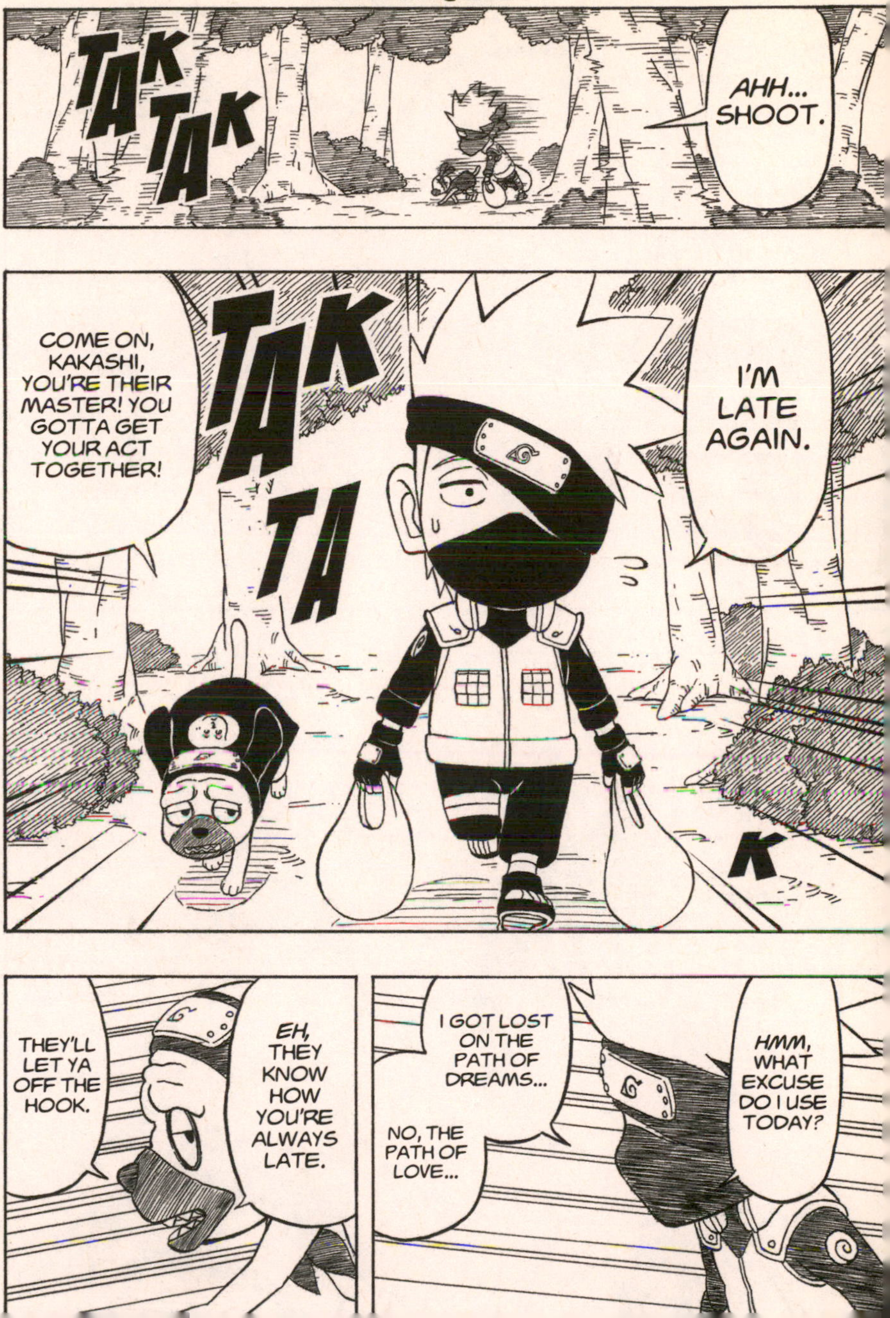
AHH... SHOOT.
TAK TAK TAK TAK
I'M LATE AGAIN.
TAK TAK TA TA
COME ON, KAKASHI, YOU'RE THEIR MASTER! YOU GOTTA GET YOUR ACT TOGETHER!
K
HMM, WHAT EXCUSE DO I USE TODAY?
I GOT LOST ON THE PATH OF DREAMS...
NO, THE PATH OF LOVE...
EH, THEY KNOW HOW YOU'RE ALWAYS LATE.
THEY'LL LET YA OFF THE HOOK.

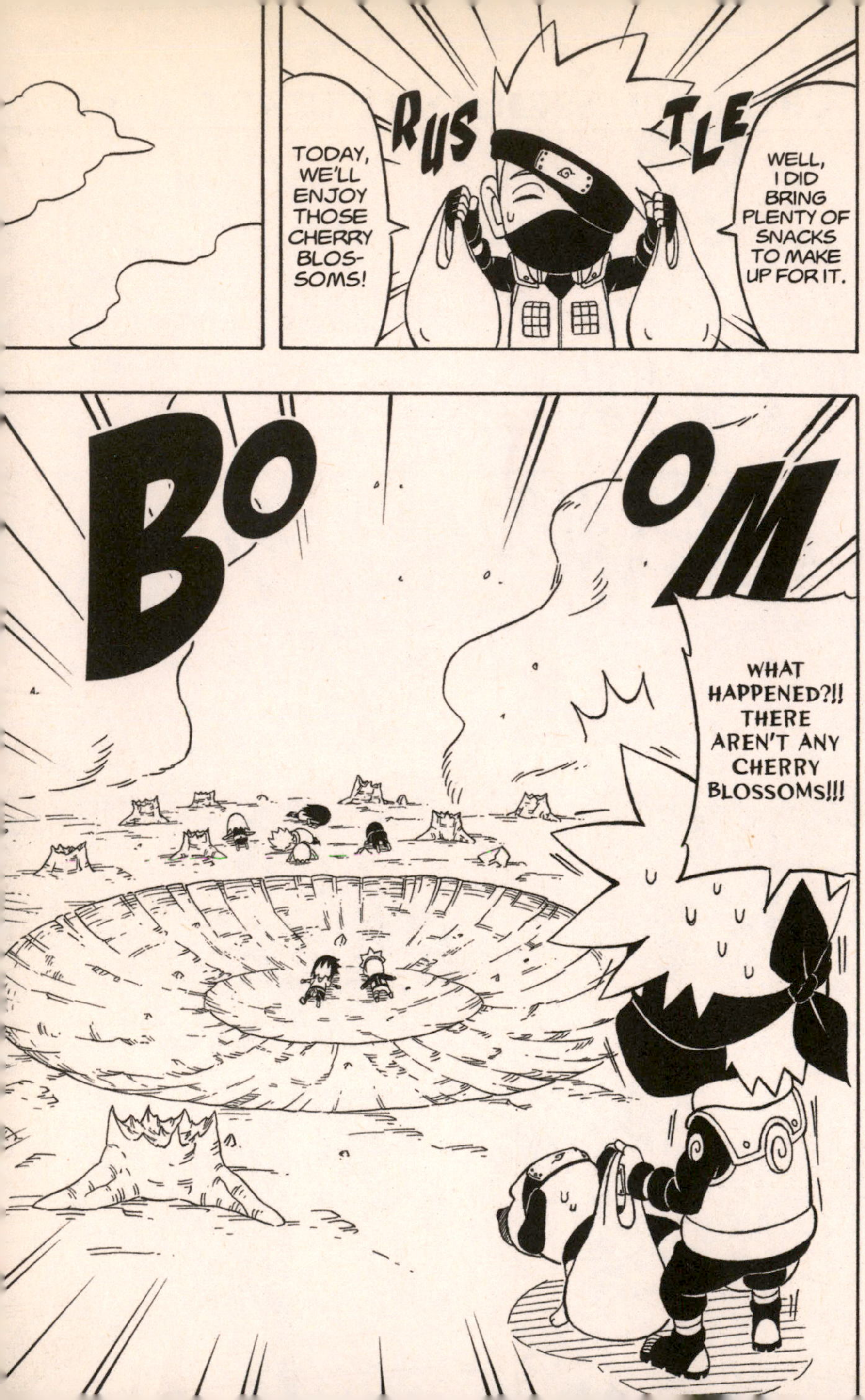
RUSTLE
WELL, I DID BRING PLENTY OF SNACKS TO MAKE UP FOR IT.
TODAY, WE'LL ENJOY THOSE CHERRY BLOSSOMS!
BOOM
WHAT HAPPENED?!! THERE AREN'T ANY CHERRY BLOSSOMS!!!

CHERRY BLOSSOMS FOR THE AKATSUKI

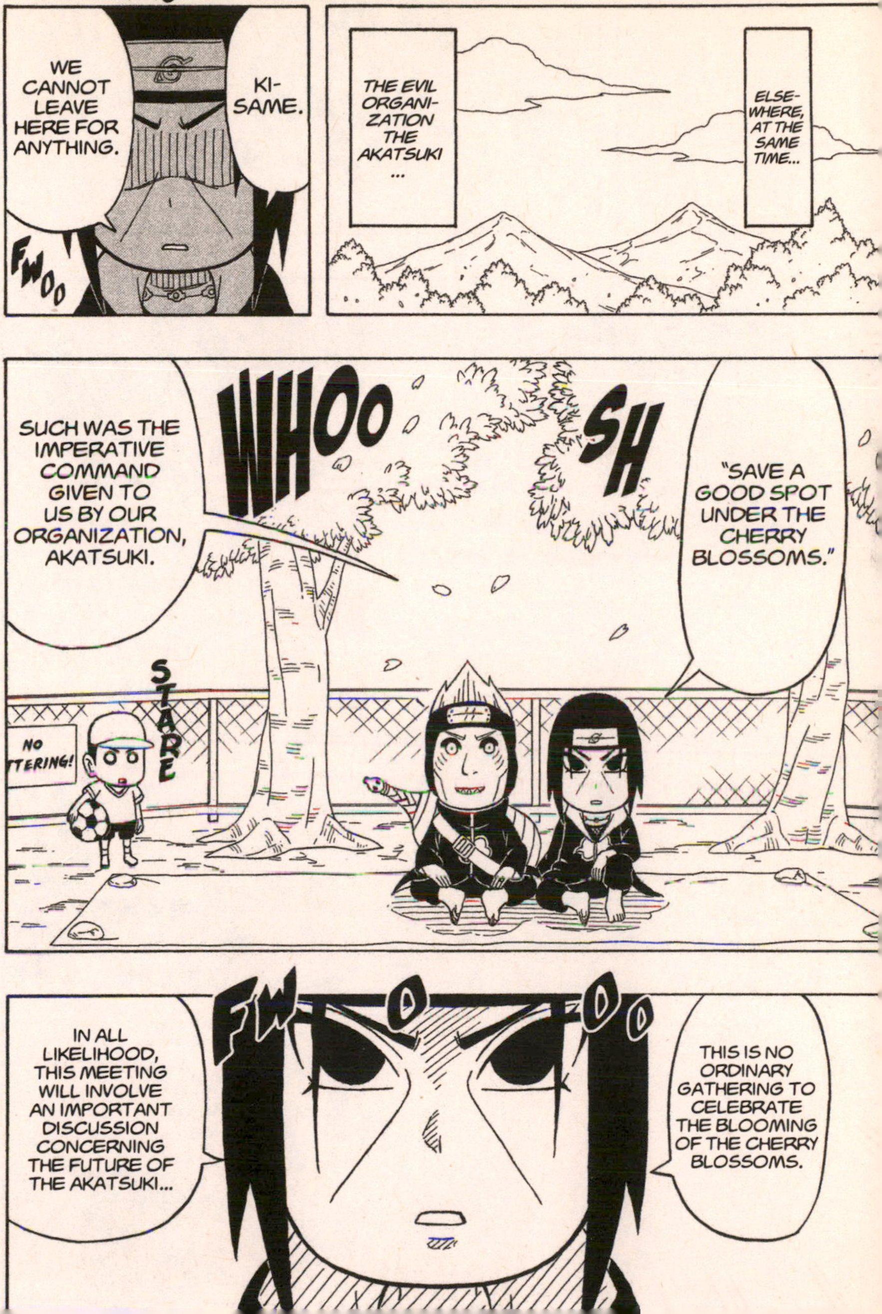
ELSEWHERE, AT THE SAME TIME...
THE EVIL ORGANIZATION THE AKATSUKI ...
KI-SAME.
WE CANNOT LEAVE HERE FOR ANYTHING.
FWOO
"SAVE A GOOD SPOT UNDER THE CHERRY BLOSSOMS."
WHOOSH
SUCH WAS THE IMPERATIVE COMMAND GIVEN TO US BY OUR ORGANIZATION, AKATSUKI.
STARE
NO
TTERING!
THIS IS NO ORDINARY GATHERING TO CELEBRATE THE BLOOMING OF THE CHERRY BLOSSOMS.
FWOOO
IN ALL LIKELIHOOD, THIS MEETING WILL INVOLVE AN IMPORTANT DISCUSSION CONCERNING THE FUTURE OF THE AKATSUKI...

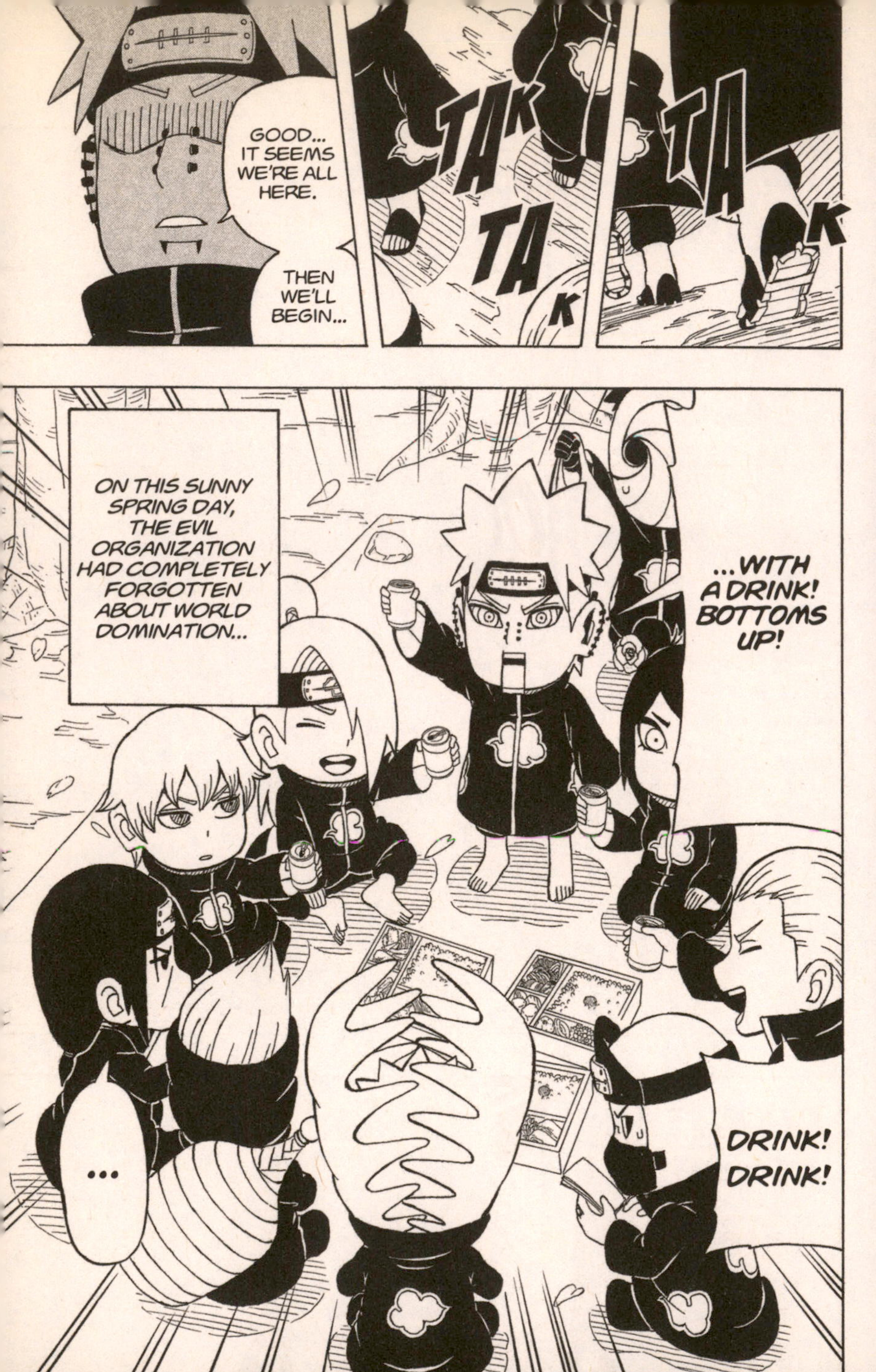
TA TAK
TAK TA TAK
GOOD... IT SEEMS WE'RE ALL HERE.
THEN WE'LL BEGIN...
...WITH A DRINK! BOTTOMS UP!
ON THIS SUNNY SPRING DAY, THE EVIL ORGANIZATION HAD COMPLETELY FORGOTTEN ABOUT WORLD DOMINATION...
DRINK! DRINK!
...

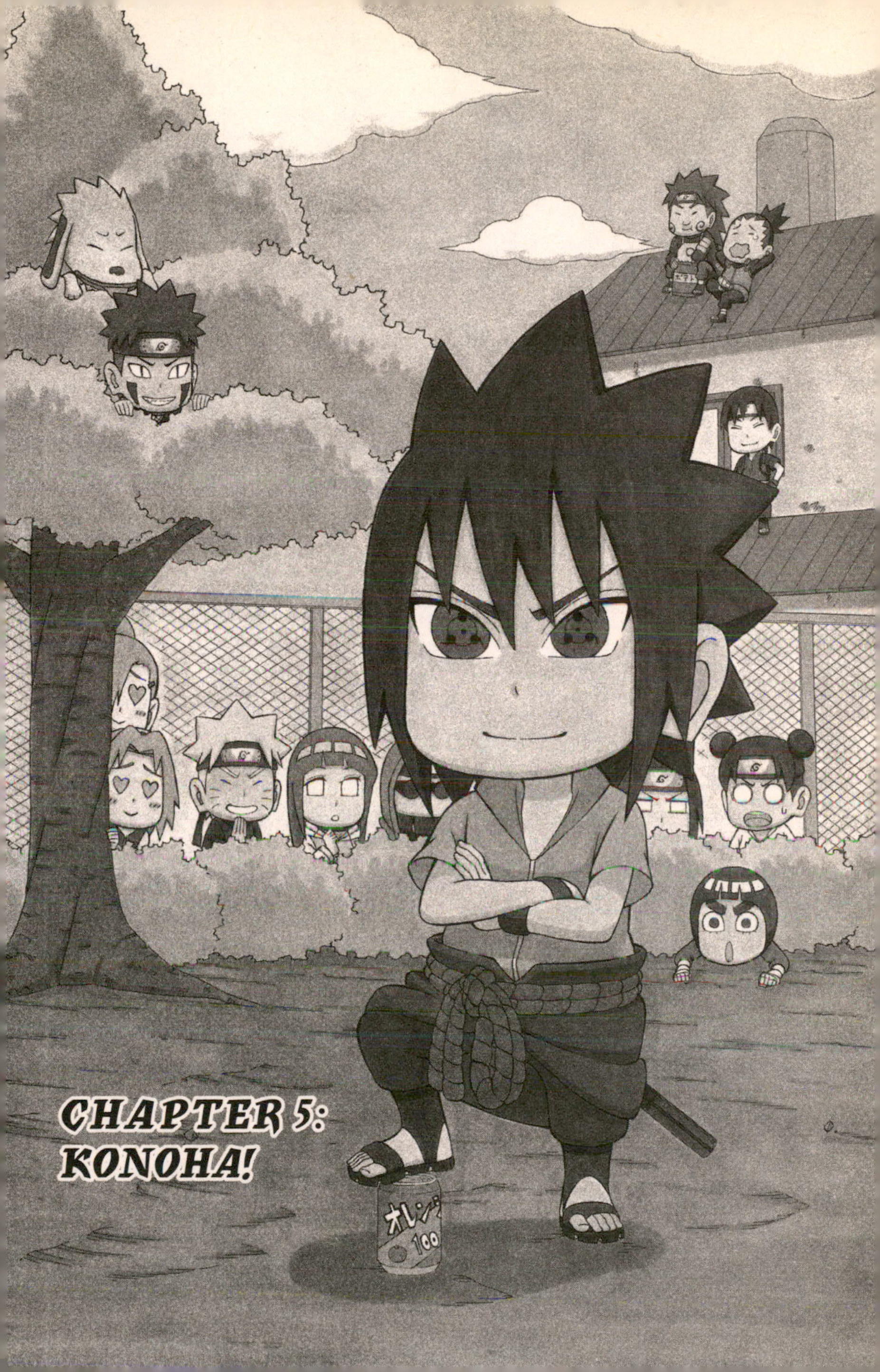
CHAPTER 5:
KONOHA!

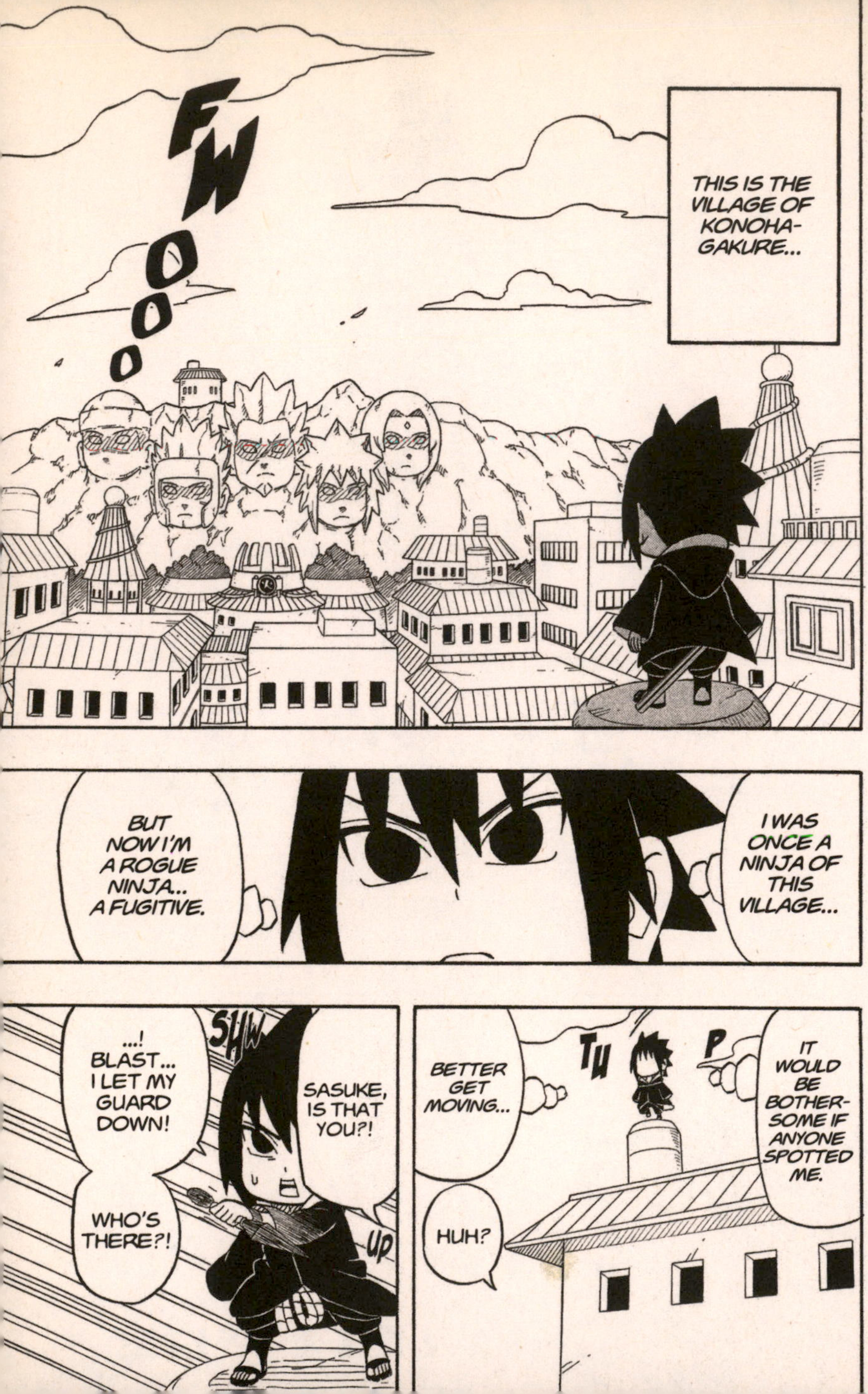
THIS IS THE VILLAGE OF KONOHA-GAKURE...
FWOOO
I WAS ONCE A NINJA OF THIS VILLAGE...
BUT NOW I'M A ROGUE NINJA... A FUGITIVE.
IT WOULD BE BOTHER-SOME IF ANYONE SPOTTED ME.
P
TU
BETTER GET MOVING...
HUH?
SASUKE, IS THAT YOU?!
SHW
...! BLAST... I LET MY GUARD DOWN!
WHO'S THERE?!
UP

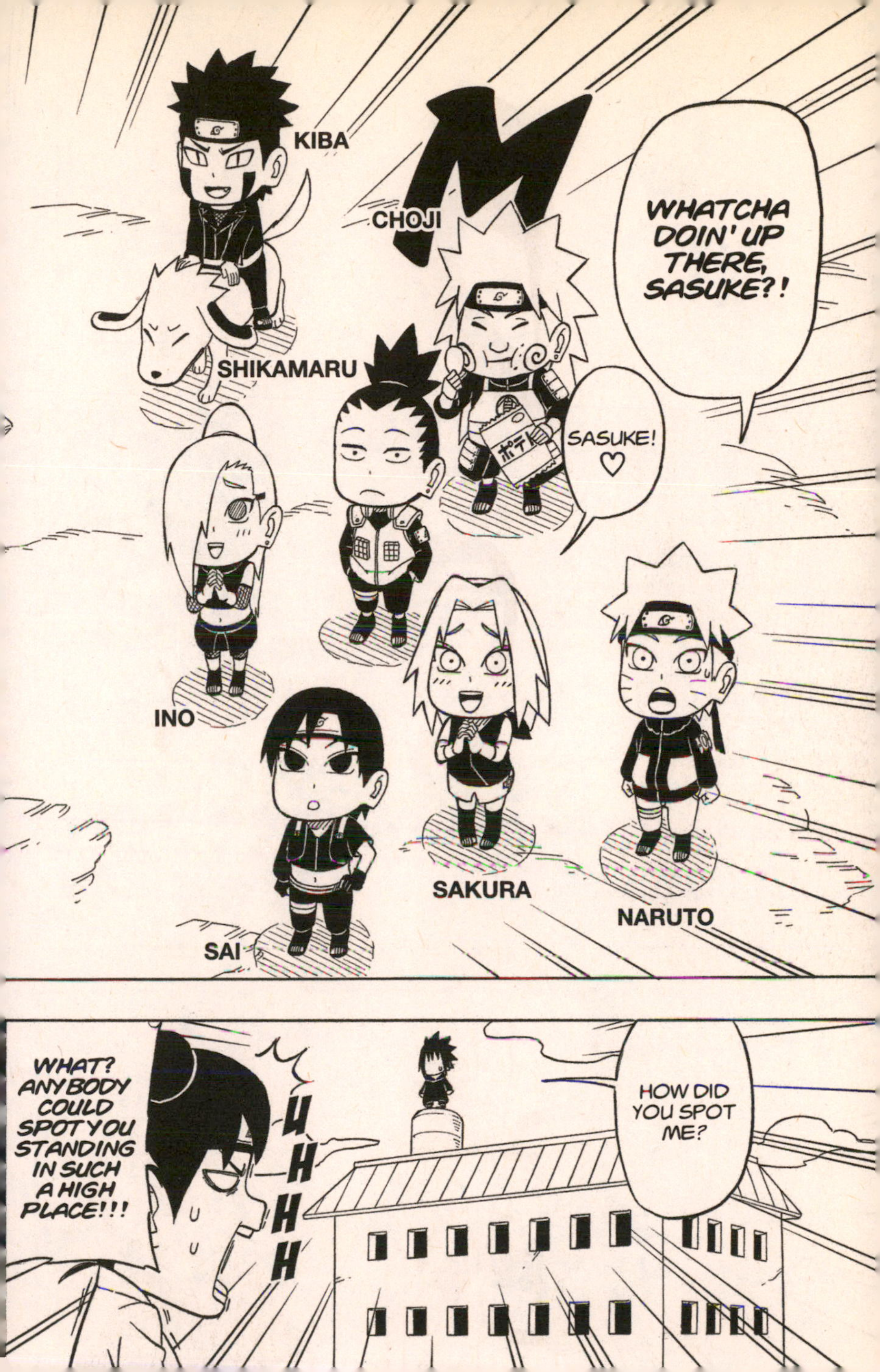
WHATCHA DOIN' UP THERE, SASUKE?!
M
KIBA
CHOJI
SASUKE! ♡
SHIKAMARU
NARUTO
SAKURA
INO
SAI
HOW DID YOU SPOT ME?
UHHHH
WHAT? ANYBODY COULD SPOT YOU STANDING IN SUCH A HIGH PLACE!!!

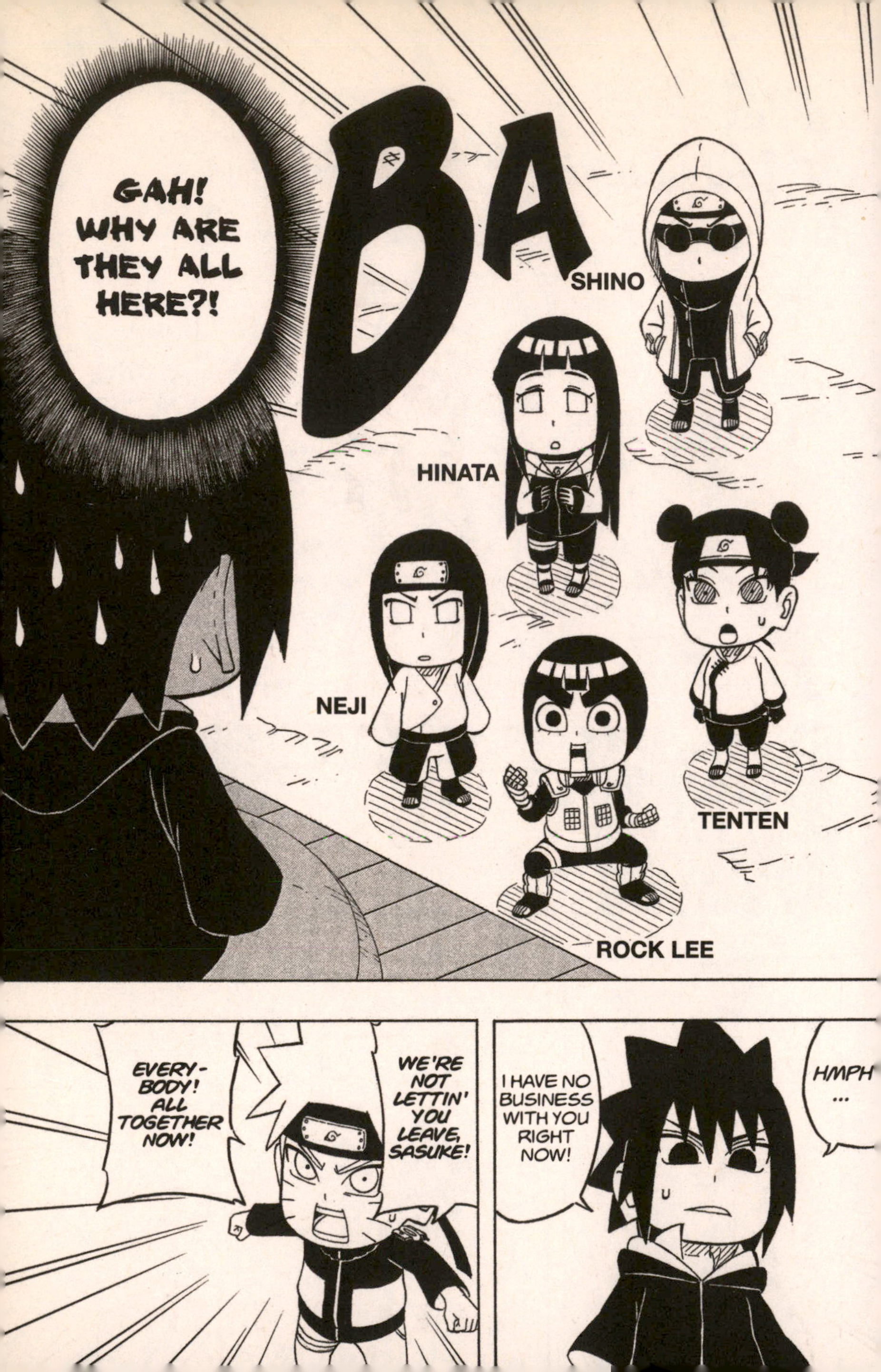
BA
SHINO
GAH! WHY ARE THEY ALL HERE?!
HINATA
TENTEN
NEJI
ROCK LEE
HMPH ...
I HAVE NO BUSINESS WITH YOU RIGHT NOW!
WE'RE NOT LETTIN' YOU LEAVE, SASUKE!
EVERY-BODY! ALL TOGETHER NOW!

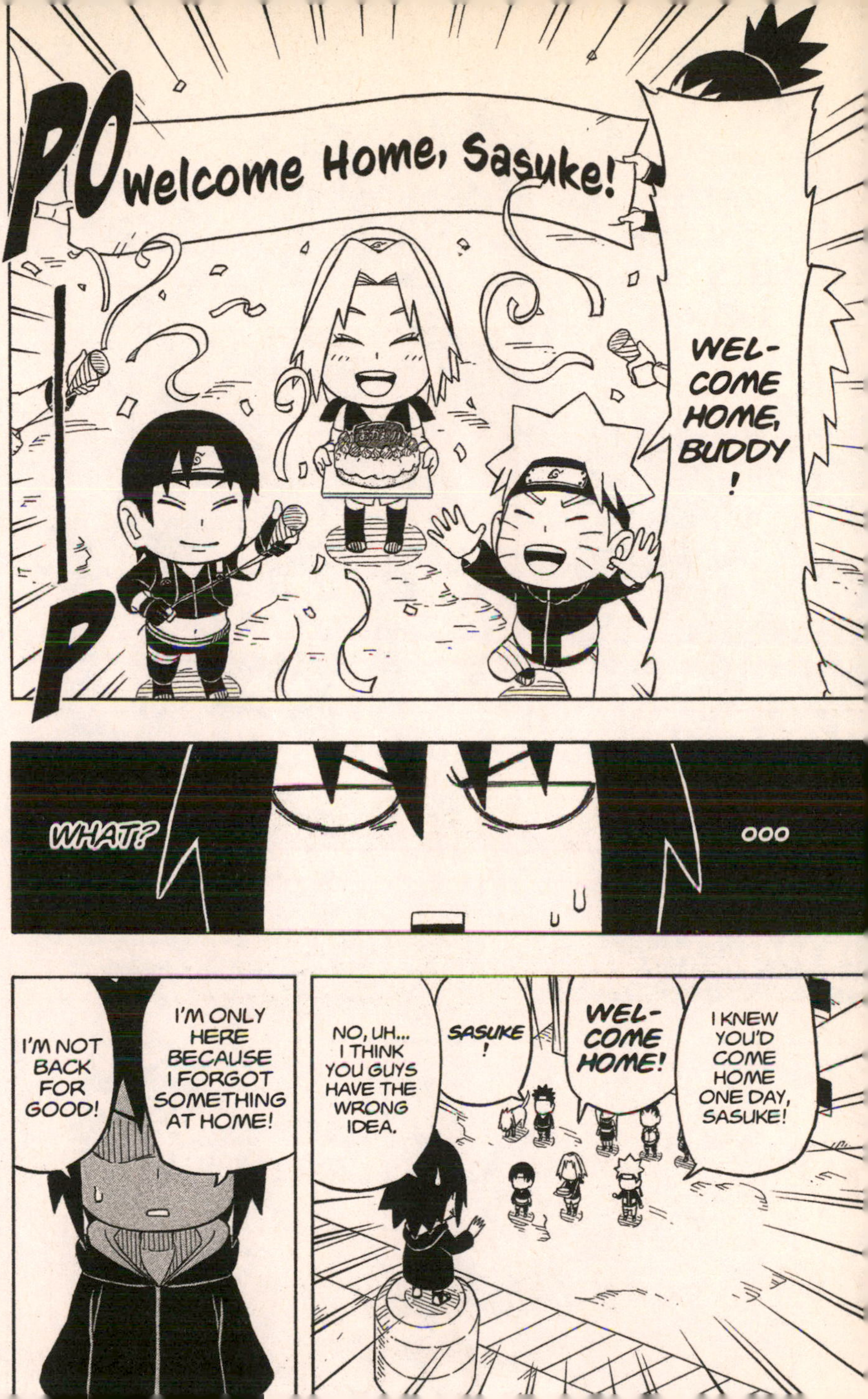

WEL-COME HOME, BUDDY!
Welcome Home, Sasuke!
POP
...
WHAT?
I KNEW YOU'D COME HOME ONE DAY, SASUKE!
WEL-COME HOME!
SASUKE!
NO, UH... I THINK YOU GUYS HAVE THE WRONG IDEA.
I'M ONLY HERE BECAUSE I FORGOT SOMETHING AT HOME!
I'M NOT BACK FOR GOOD!

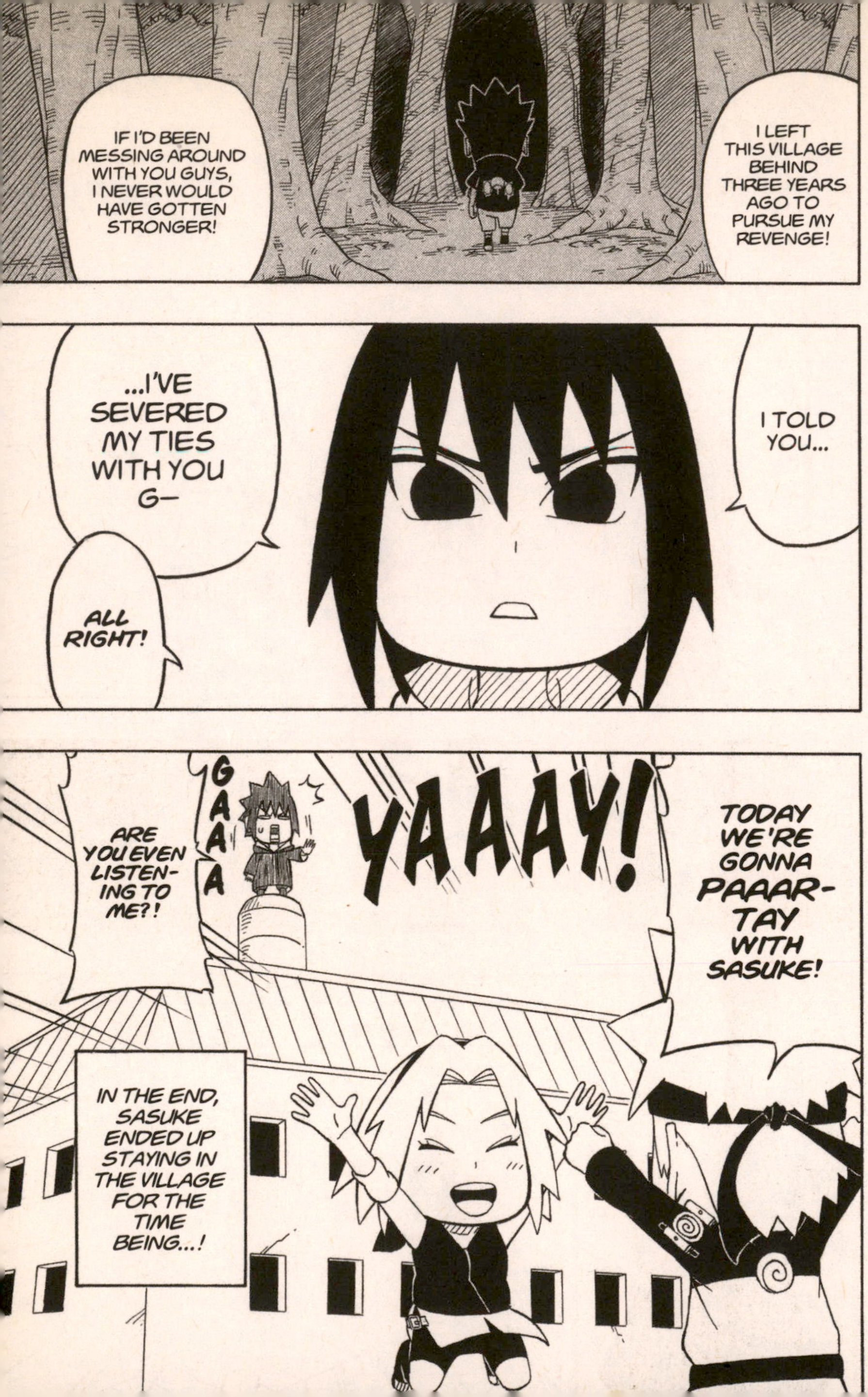
I LEFT THIS VILLAGE BEHIND THREE YEARS AGO TO PURSUE MY REVENGE!
IF I'D BEEN MESSING AROUND WITH YOU GUYS, I NEVER WOULD HAVE GOTTEN STRONGER!
I TOLD YOU...
...I'VE SEVERED MY TIES WITH YOU G—
ALL RIGHT!
TODAY WE'RE GONNA PAAAR-TAY WITH SASUKE!
YAAAY!
GAAAA
ARE YOU EVEN LISTEN-ING TO ME?!
IN THE END, SASUKE ENDED UP STAYING IN THE VILLAGE FOR THE TIME BEING...!

SASUKE'S HOUSE

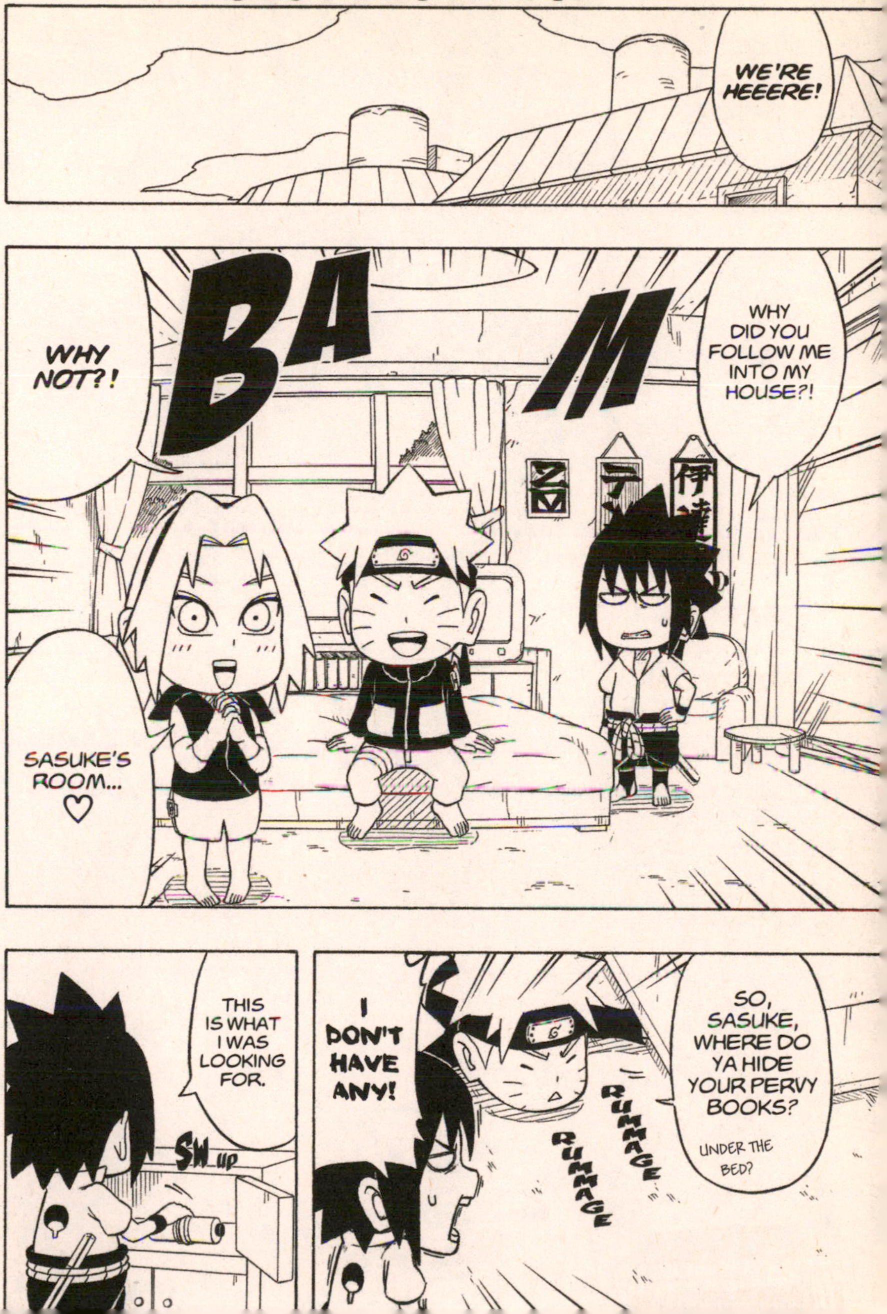
WE'RE HEEEERE!
WHY DID YOU FOLLOW ME INTO MY HOUSE?!
BAM
WHY NOT?!
SASUKE'S ROOM... ♡
SO, SASUKE, WHERE DO YA HIDE YOUR PERVY BOOKS?
UNDER THE BED?
RUMMAGE
RUMMAGE
I DON'T HAVE ANY!
THIS IS WHAT I WAS LOOKING FOR.
SWUP

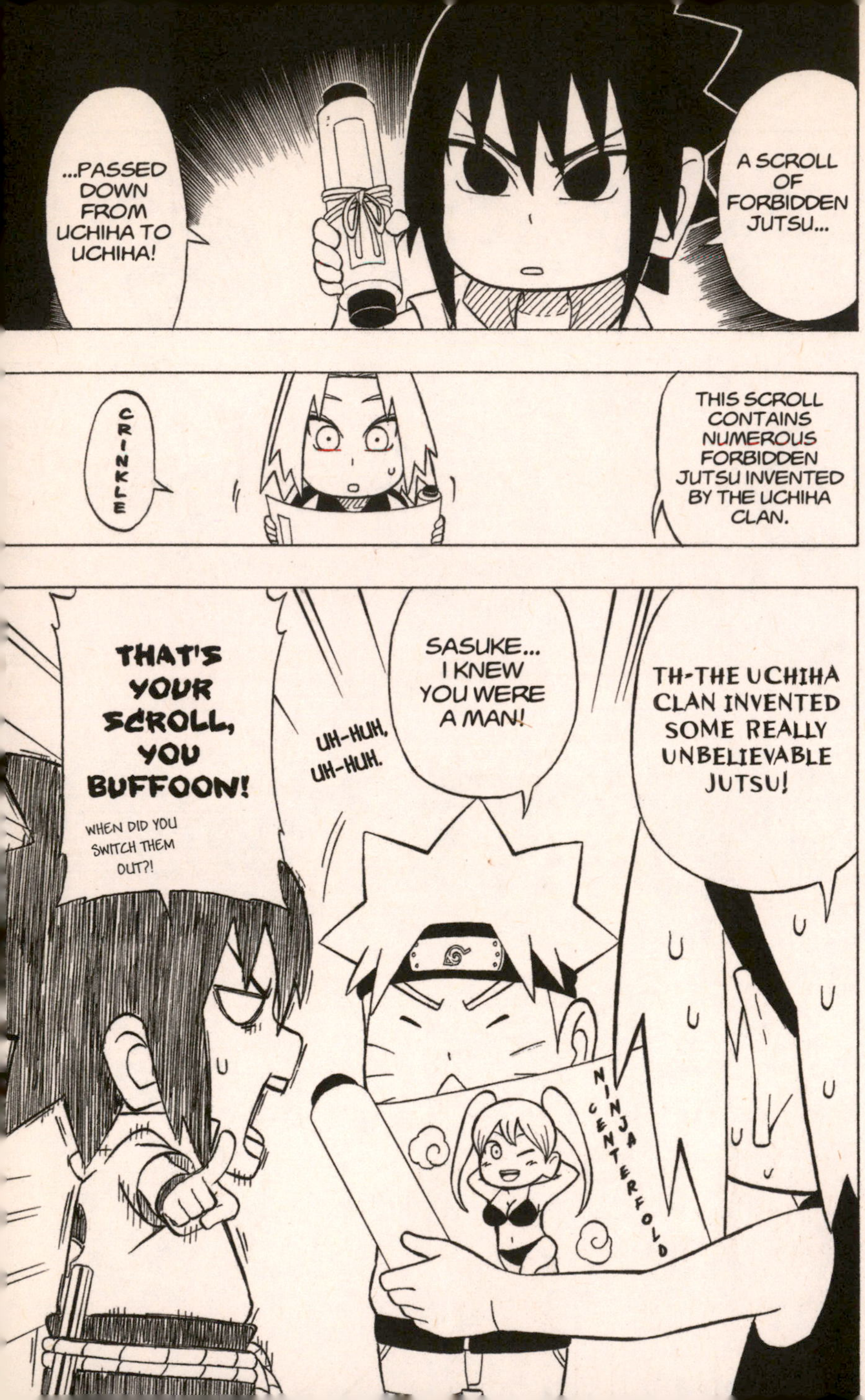
A SCROLL OF FORBIDDEN JUTSU...
...PASSED DOWN FROM UCHIHA TO UCHIHA!
THIS SCROLL CONTAINS NUMEROUS FORBIDDEN JUTSU INVENTED BY THE UCHIHA CLAN.
CRINKLE
TH-THE UCHIHA CLAN INVENTED SOME REALLY UNBELIEVABLE JUTSU!
SASUKE... I KNEW YOU WERE A MAN!
UH-HUH, UH-HUH.
THAT'S YOUR SCROLL, YOU BUFFOON!
WHEN DID YOU SWITCH THEM OUT?!
NINJA CENTERFOLD

IQ 200

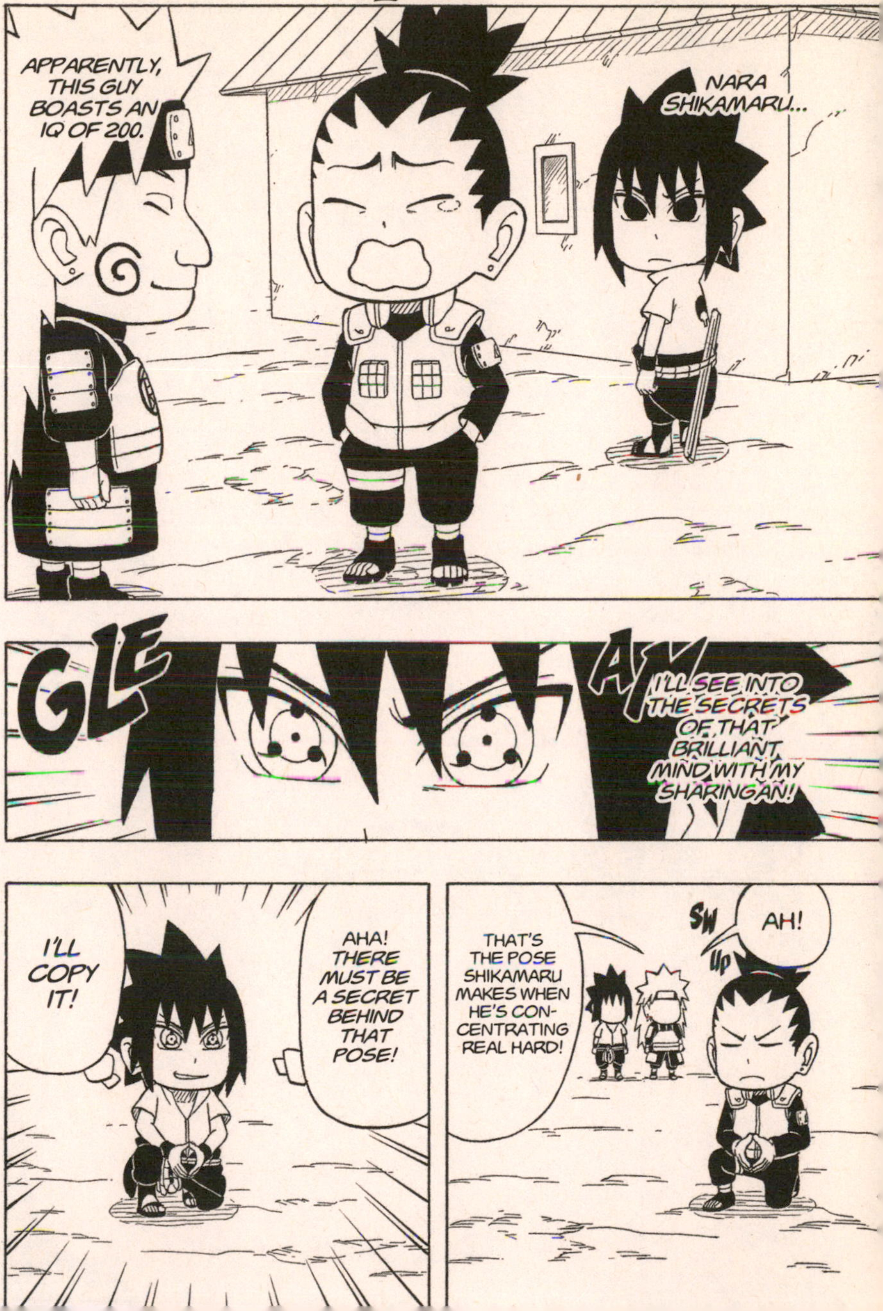
NARA SHIKAMARU...
APPARENTLY, THIS GUY BOASTS AN IQ OF 200.
I'LL SEE INTO THE SECRETS OF THAT BRILLIANT MIND WITH MY SHARINGAN!
GLEAM
AH!
SWUP
THAT'S THE POSE SHIKAMARU MAKES WHEN HE'S CON-CENTRATING REAL HARD!
AHA! THERE MUST BE A SECRET BEHIND THAT POSE!
I'LL COPY IT!

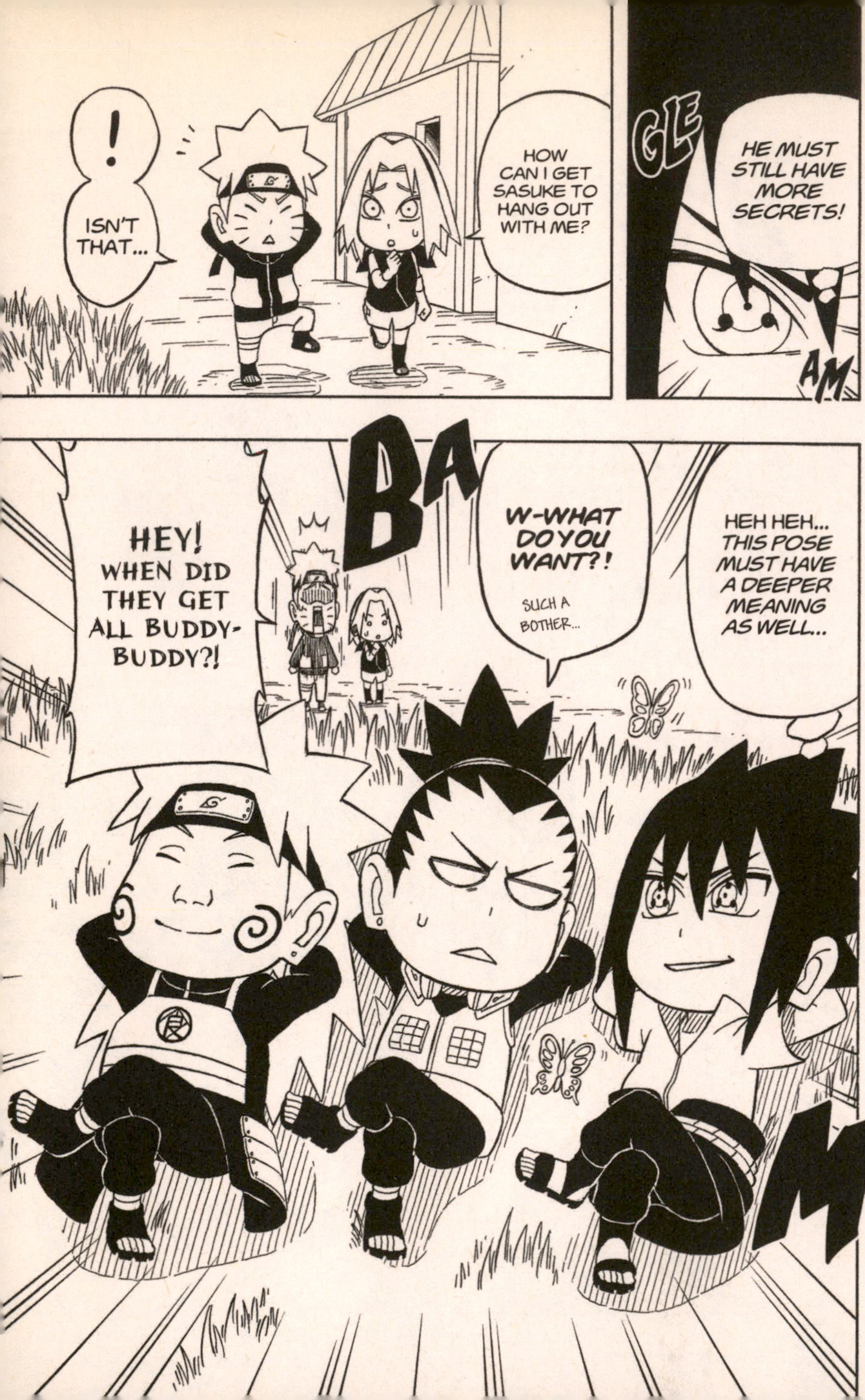
GLE
HE MUST STILL HAVE MORE SECRETS!
AM
HOW CAN I GET SASUKE TO HANG OUT WITH ME?
!
ISN'T THAT...
HEH HEH... THIS POSE MUST HAVE A DEEPER MEANING AS WELL...
W-WHAT DO YOU WANT?!
SUCH A BOTHER...
BA
HEY! WHEN DID THEY GET ALL BUDDY-BUDDY?!
M

SASUKE VS. CHOJI!!

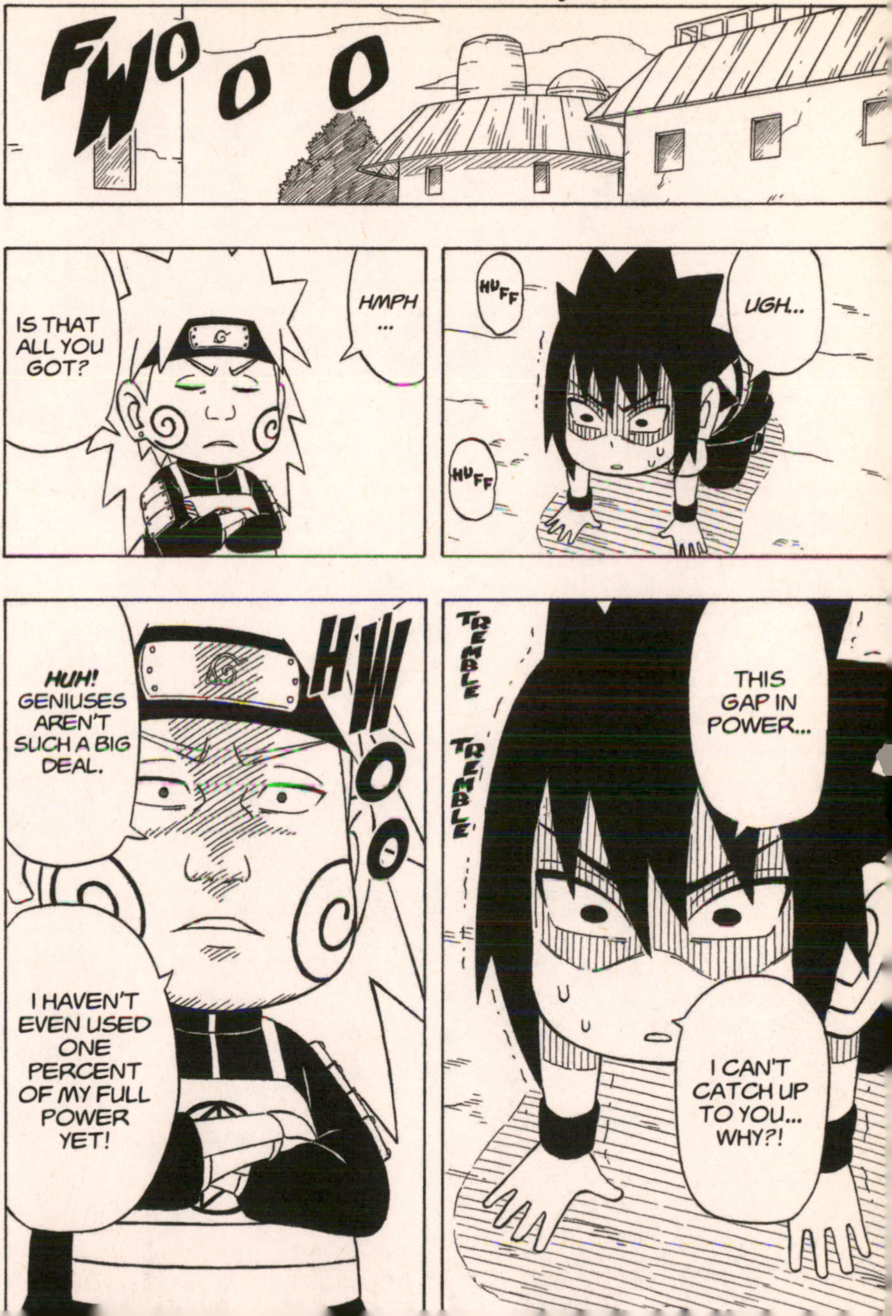
FWOOO
UGH...
HUFF
HUFF
HMPH...
IS THAT ALL YOU GOT?
THIS GAP IN POWER...
TREMBLE
TREMBLE
I CAN'T CATCH UP TO YOU... WHY?!
HWOOO
HUH! GENIUSES AREN'T SUCH A BIG DEAL.
I HAVEN'T EVEN USED ONE PERCENT OF MY FULL POWER YET!

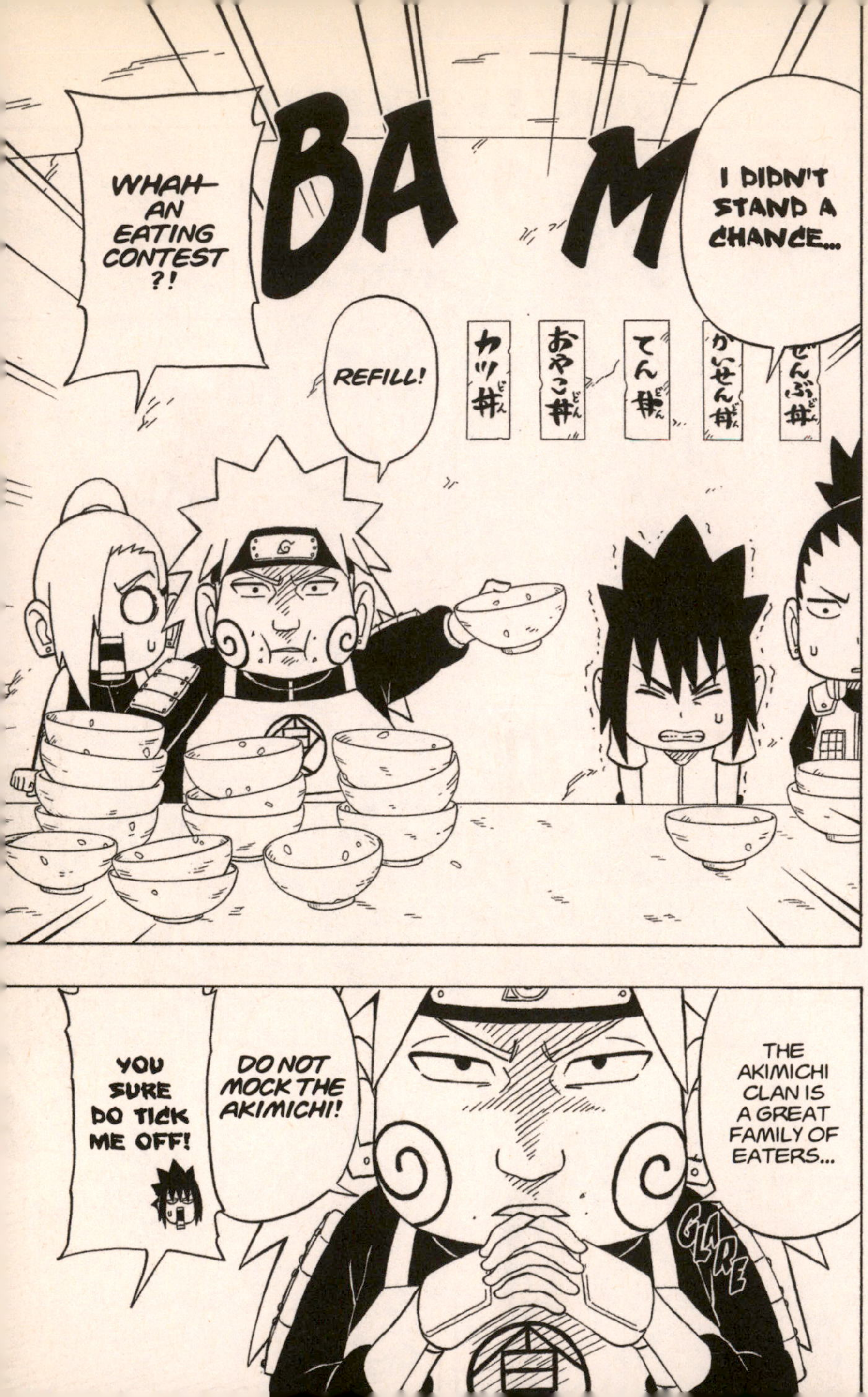
I DIDN'T STAND A CHANCE...
BAM
WHAH— AN EATING CONTEST?!
ぜんぶ丼
かいせん丼
てん丼
おやこ丼
カツ丼
REFILL!
THE AKIMICHI CLAN IS A GREAT FAMILY OF EATERS...
GLARE
DO NOT MOCK THE AKIMICHI!
YOU SURE DO TICK ME OFF!

SASUKE VS. ROCK LEE!!

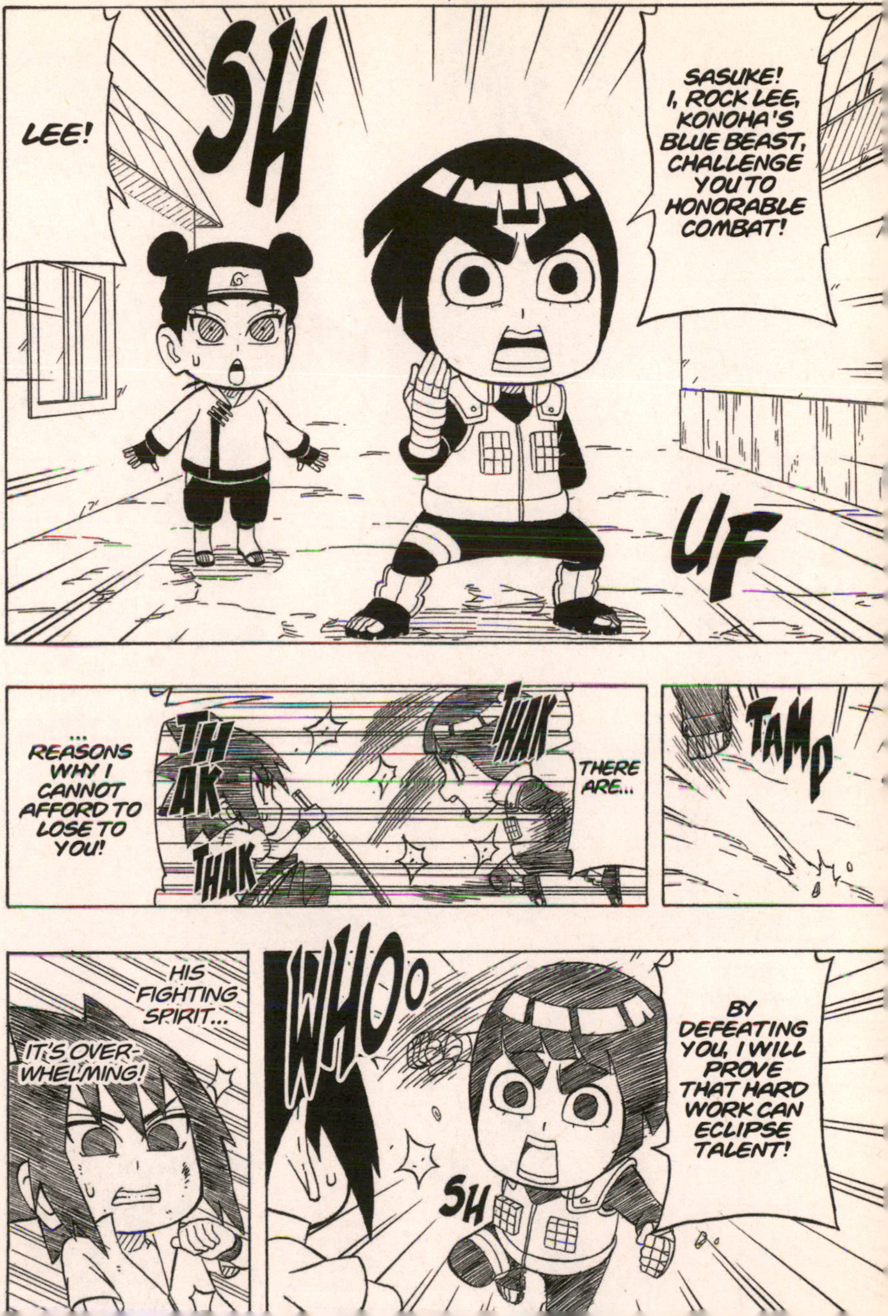
SASUKE! I, ROCK LEE, KONOHA'S BLUE BEAST, CHALLENGE YOU TO HONORABLE COMBAT!
SH
LEE!
UF
TAMP
THAK
THERE ARE...
THAK
... REASONS WHY I CANNOT AFFORD TO LOSE TO YOU!
THAK
BY DEFEATING YOU, I WILL PROVE THAT HARD WORK CAN ECLIPSE TALENT!
WHOO
SH
HIS FIGHTING SPIRIT...
IT'S OVER-WHELMING!

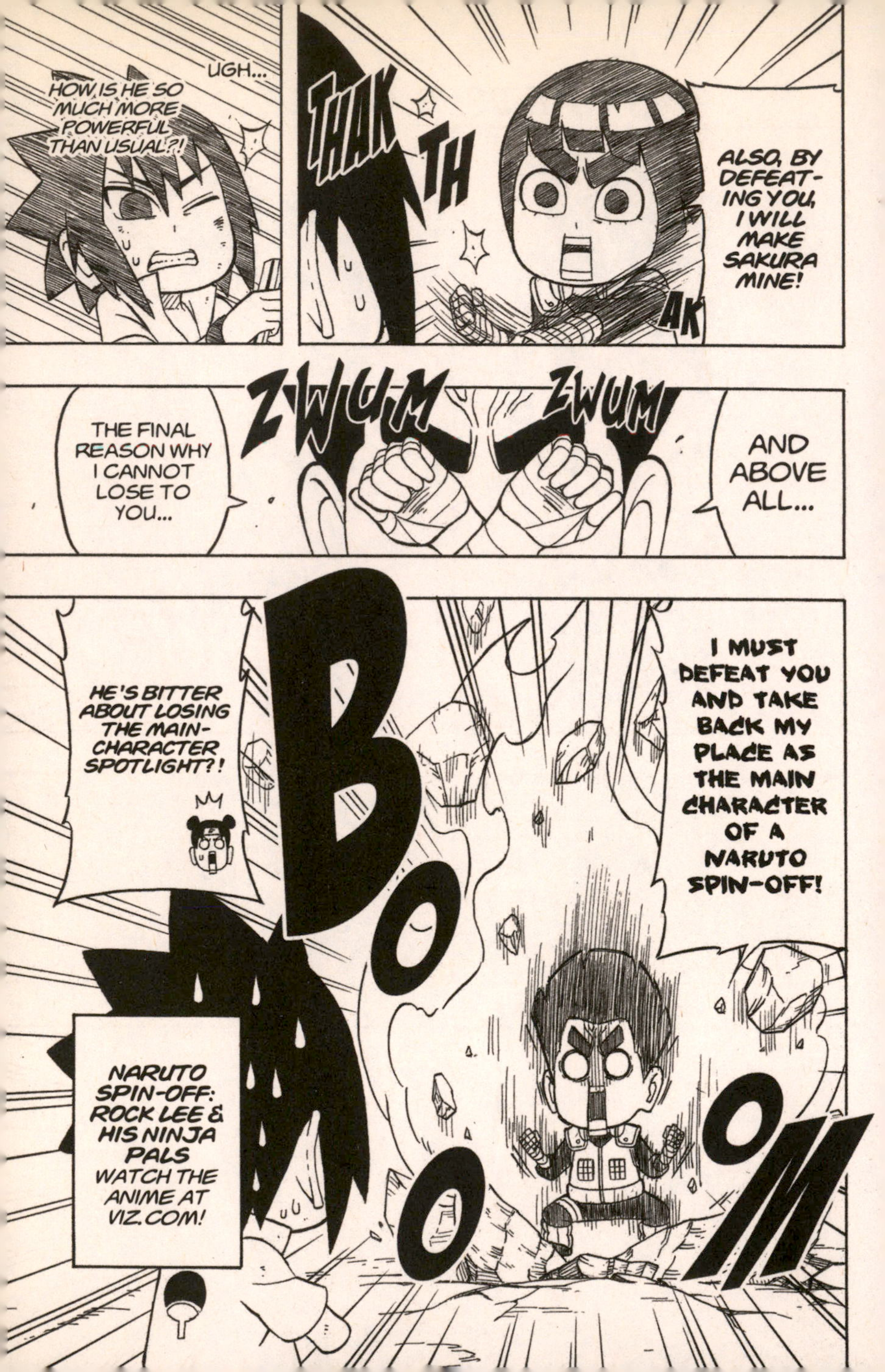

ALSO, BY DEFEATING YOU, I WILL MAKE SAKURA MINE!
THAK
TH
AK
UGH...
HOW IS HE SO MUCH MORE POWERFUL THAN USUAL?!
AND ABOVE ALL...
ZWUM
ZWUM
THE FINAL REASON WHY I CANNOT LOSE TO YOU...
I MUST DEFEAT YOU AND TAKE BACK MY PLACE AS THE MAIN CHARACTER OF A NARUTO SPIN-OFF!
BOOOM
HE'S BITTER ABOUT LOSING THE MAIN-CHARACTER SPOTLIGHT?!
NARUTO SPIN-OFF: ROCK LEE & HIS NINJA PALS WATCH THE ANIME AT VIZ.COM!

SASUKE VS. NEJI!!

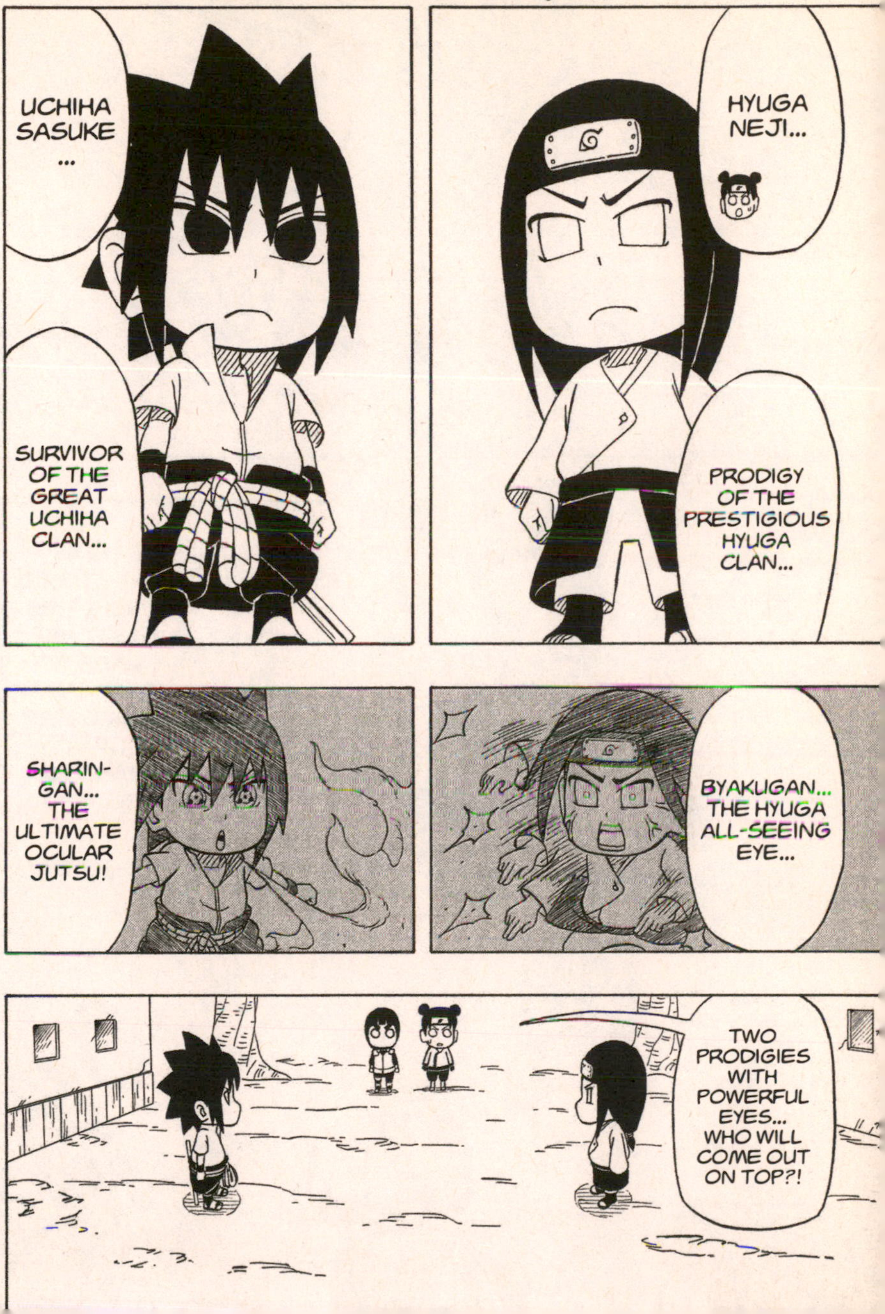
HYUGA NEJI...
PRODIGY OF THE PRESTIGIOUS HYUGA CLAN...
UCHIHA SASUKE ...
SURVIVOR OF THE GREAT UCHIHA CLAN...
BYAKUGAN... THE HYUGA ALL-SEEING EYE...
SHARIN-GAN... THE ULTIMATE OCULAR JUTSU!
TWO PRODIGIES WITH POWERFUL EYES... WHO WILL COME OUT ON TOP?!

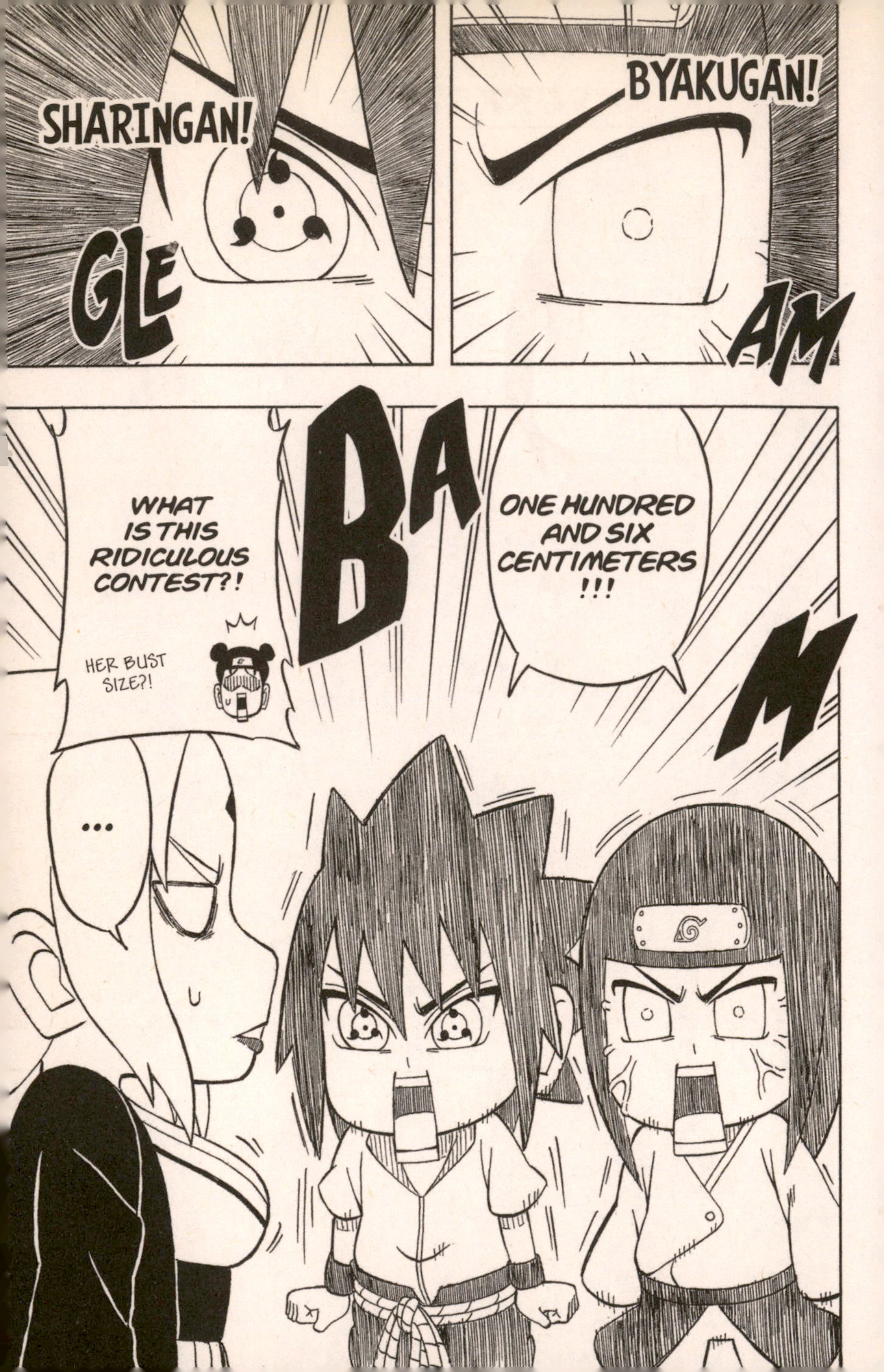
BYAKUGAN!
AM
SHARINGAN!
GLE
ONE HUNDRED AND SIX CENTIMETERS !!!
BA
M
WHAT IS THIS RIDICULOUS CONTEST?!
HER BUST SIZE?!
...

INO'S LOVE

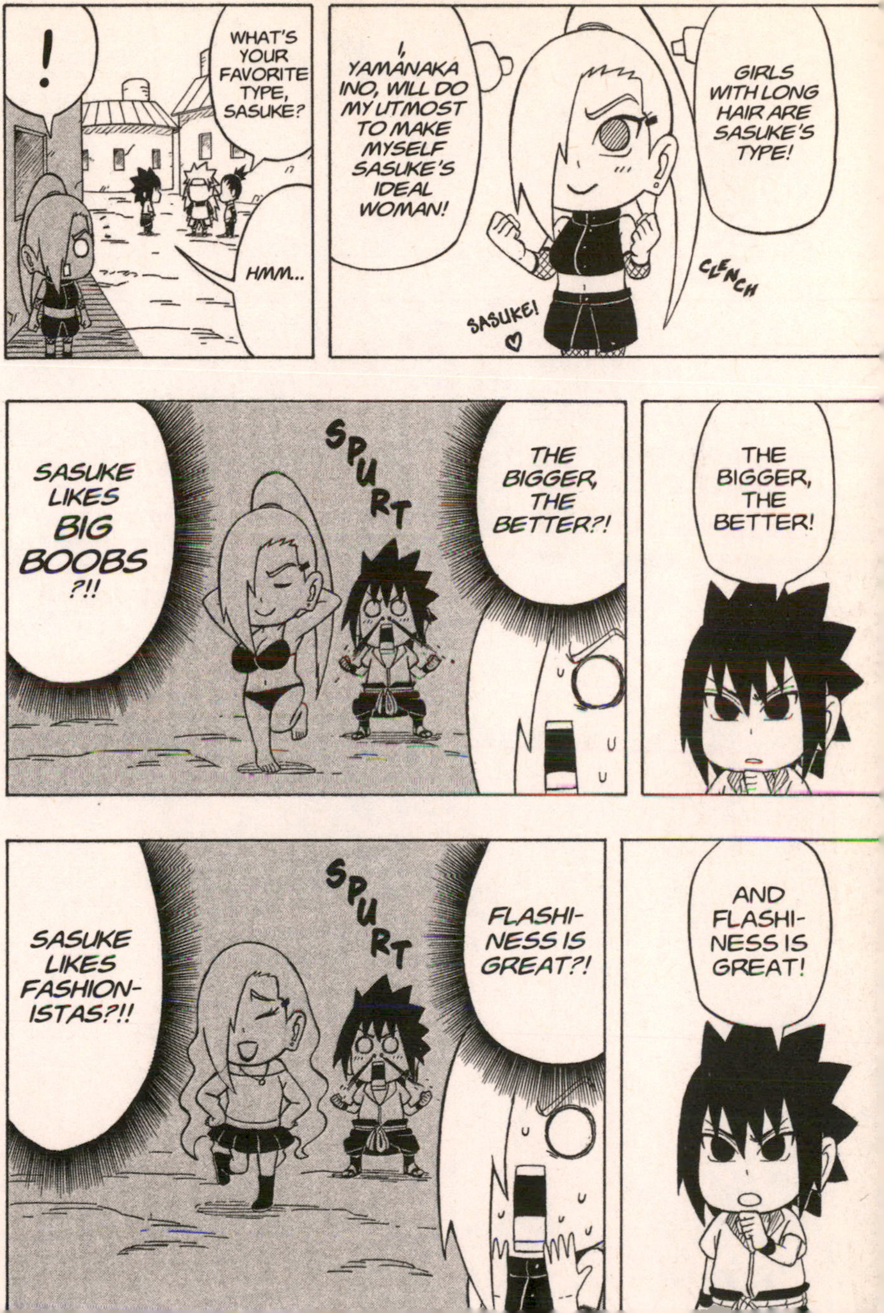
GIRLS WITH LONG HAIR ARE SASUKE'S TYPE!
I, YAMANAKA INO, WILL DO MY UTMOST TO MAKE MYSELF SASUKE'S IDEAL WOMAN!
CLENCH
SASUKE! ♡
WHAT'S YOUR FAVORITE TYPE, SASUKE?
HMM...
!
THE BIGGER, THE BETTER!
THE BIGGER, THE BETTER?!
SPURT
SASUKE LIKES BIG BOOBS?!!
AND FLASHINESS IS GREAT!
FLASHINESS IS GREAT?!
SPURT
SASUKE LIKES FASHIONISTAS?!!

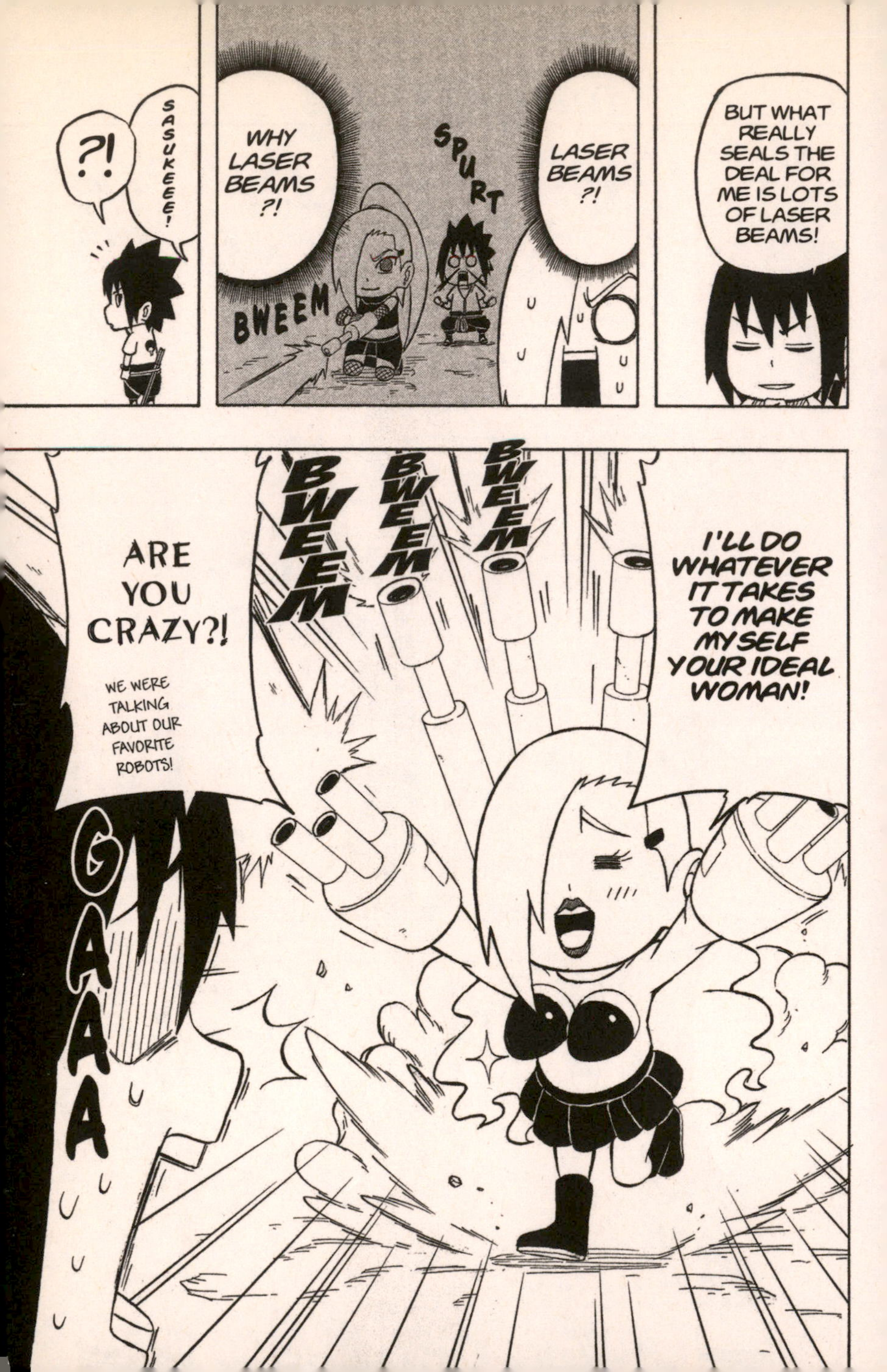

BUT WHAT REALLY SEALS THE DEAL FOR ME IS LOTS OF LASER BEAMS!
LASER BEAMS?!
SPURT
WHY LASER BEAMS?!
BWEEM
SASUKEEEE!
?!
I'LL DO WHATEVER IT TAKES TO MAKE MYSELF YOUR IDEAL WOMAN!
BWEEM
BWEEM
BWEEM
ARE YOU CRAZY?!
WE WERE TALKING ABOUT OUR FAVORITE ROBOTS!
GAAAA

HINATA'S LOVE

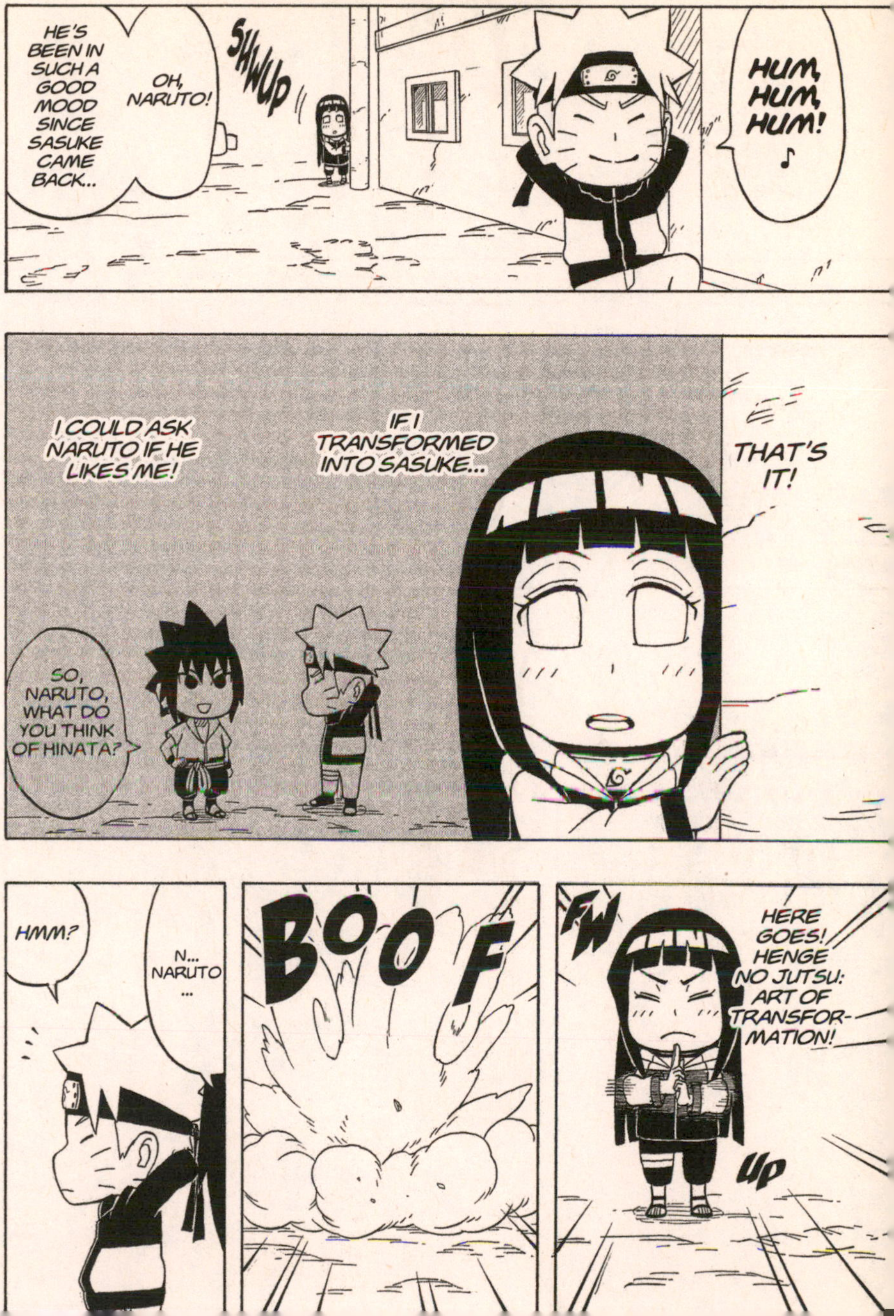
HUM, HUM, HUM! ♪
SHWUP
OH, NARUTO!
HE'S BEEN IN SUCH A GOOD MOOD SINCE SASUKE CAME BACK...
THAT'S IT!
IF I TRANSFORMED INTO SASUKE...
I COULD ASK NARUTO IF HE LIKES ME!
SO, NARUTO, WHAT DO YOU THINK OF HINATA?
FW
HERE GOES! HENGE NO JUTSU: ART OF TRANSFORMATION!
UP
BOOF
N... NARUTO ...
HMM?

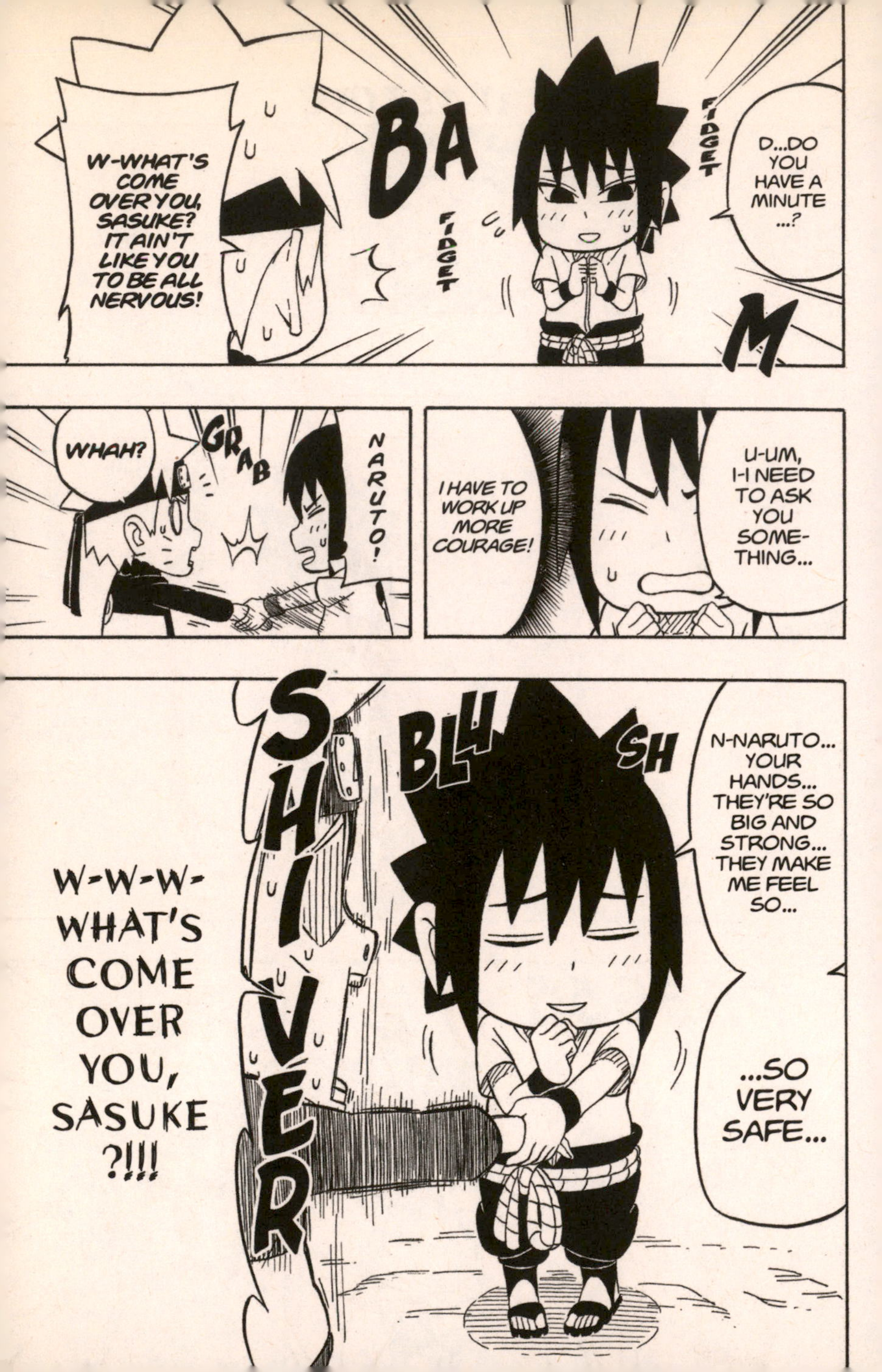
D...DO YOU HAVE A MINUTE ...?
FIDGET
M
BA
FIDGET
W-WHAT'S COME OVER YOU, SASUKE? IT AIN'T LIKE YOU TO BE ALL NERVOUS!
U-UM, I-I NEED TO ASK YOU SOME-THING...
I HAVE TO WORK UP MORE COURAGE!
NARUTO!
GRAB
WHAH?
N-NARUTO... YOUR HANDS... THEY'RE SO BIG AND STRONG... THEY MAKE ME FEEL SO...
SH
BLU
...SO VERY SAFE...
SHIVER
W-W-W-WHAT'S COME OVER YOU, SASUKE?!!!

DOG WALKING

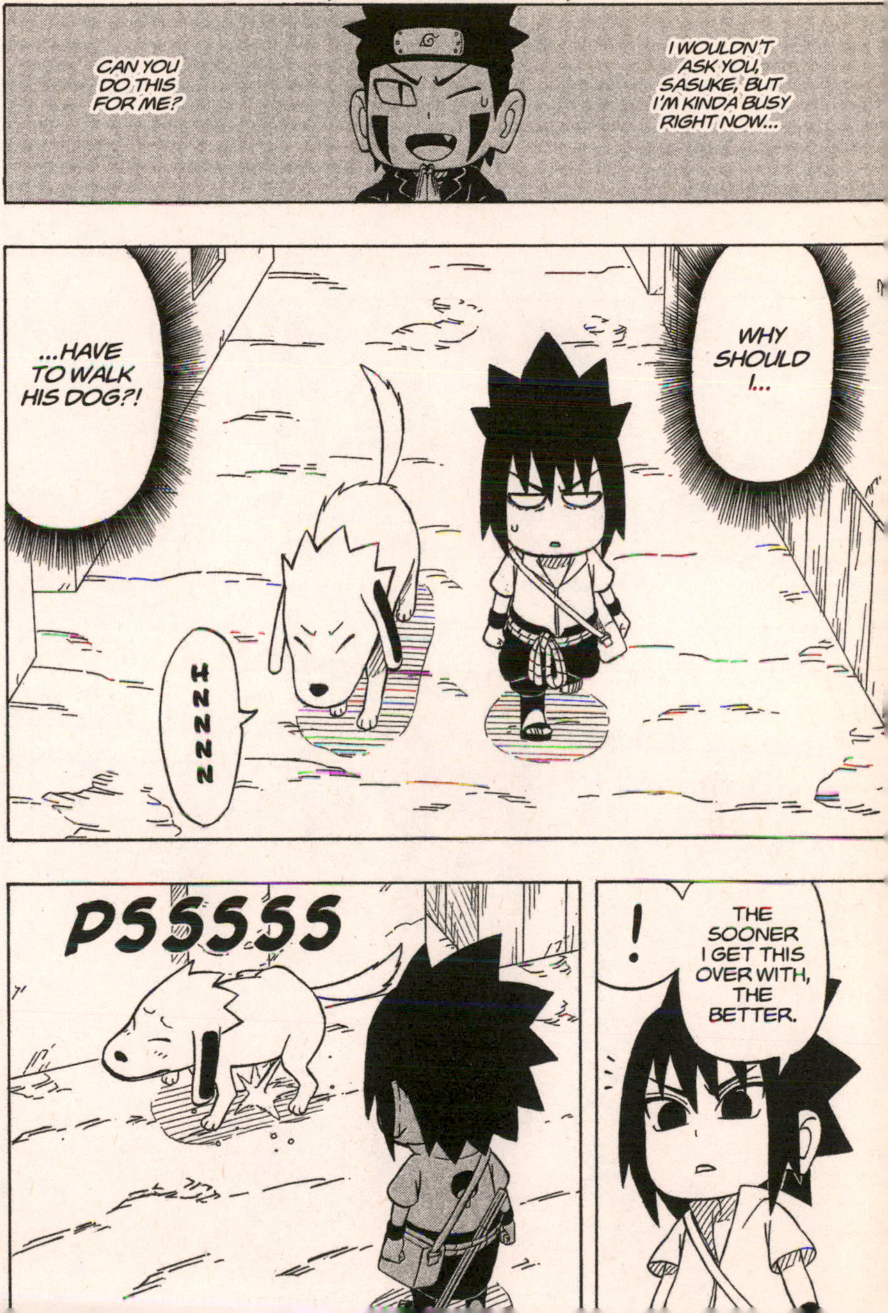
I WOULDN'T ASK YOU, SASUKE, BUT I'M KINDA BUSY RIGHT NOW...
CAN YOU DO THIS FOR ME?
WHY SHOULD I...
...HAVE TO WALK HIS DOG?!
HNNNN
!
THE SOONER I GET THIS OVER WITH, THE BETTER.
PSSSSS

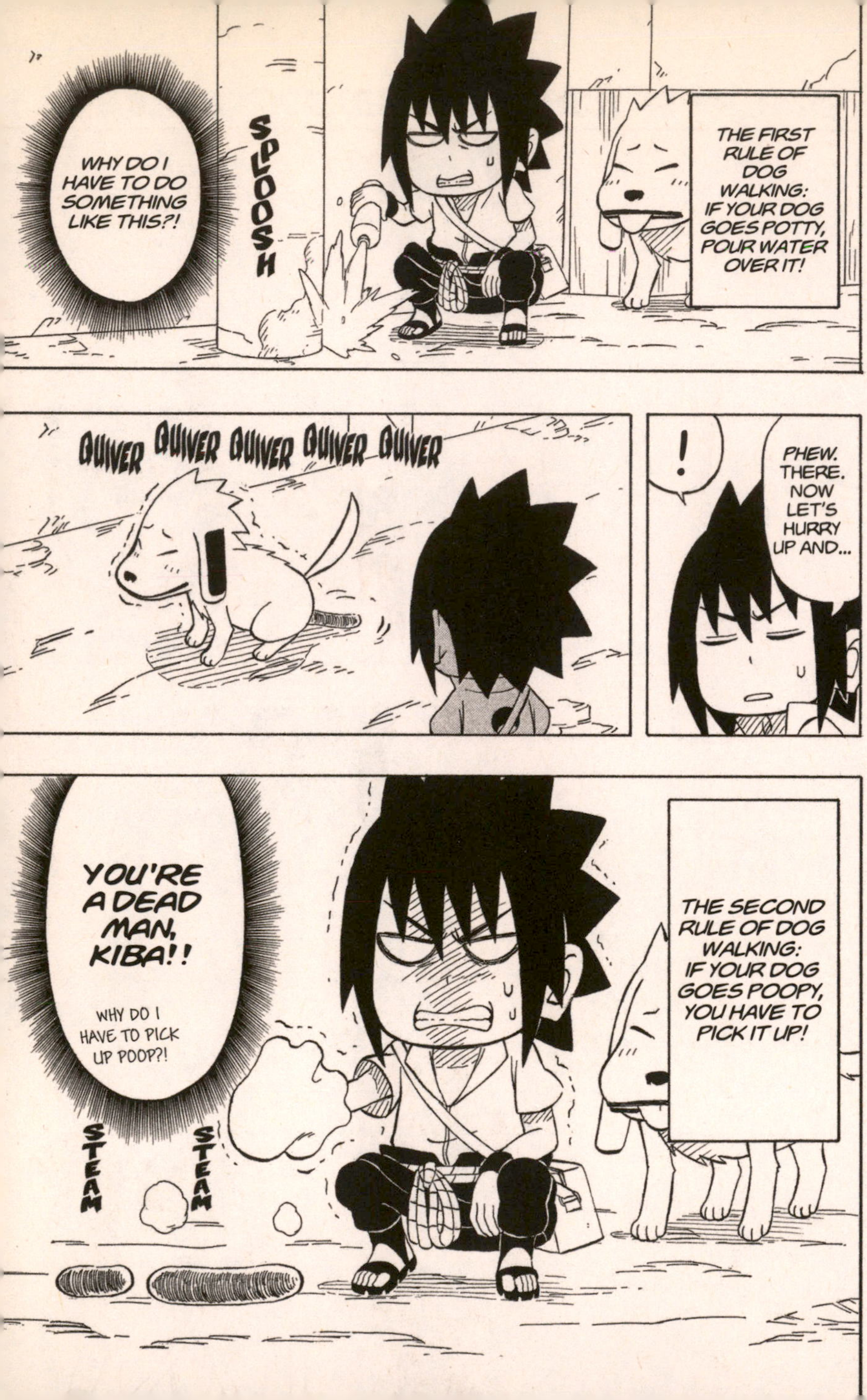
THE FIRST RULE OF DOG WALKING: IF YOUR DOG GOES POTTY, POUR WATER OVER IT!
SPLOOSH
WHY DO I HAVE TO DO SOMETHING LIKE THIS?!
!
PHEW. THERE. NOW LET'S HURRY UP AND...
QUIVER QUIVER QUIVER QUIVER QUIVER
THE SECOND RULE OF DOG WALKING: IF YOUR DOG GOES POOPY, YOU HAVE TO PICK IT UP!
YOU'RE A DEAD MAN, KIBA!!
WHY DO I HAVE TO PICK UP POOP?!
STEAM
STEAM

SASUKE VS. THE DREADED COCKROACH!

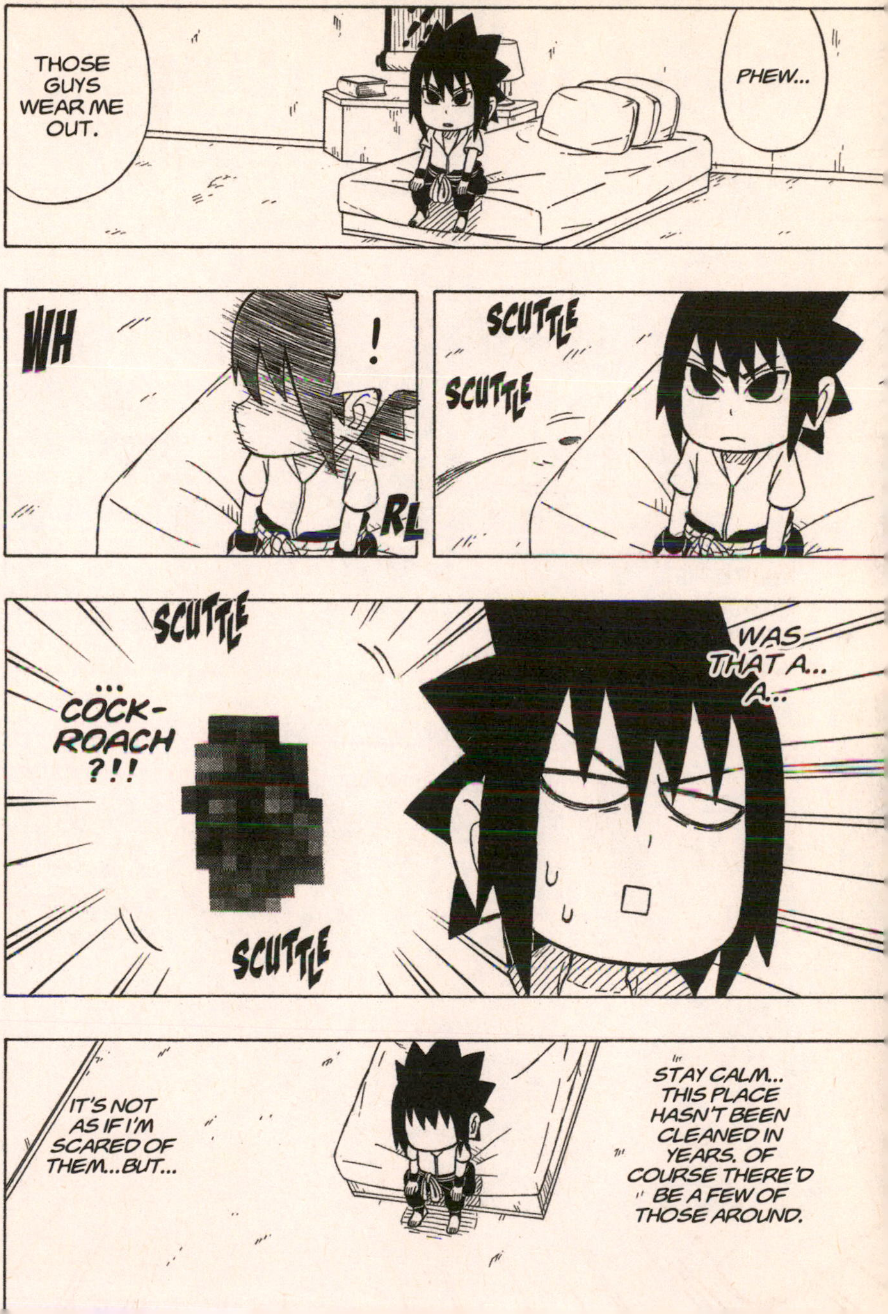
PHEW...
THOSE GUYS WEAR ME OUT.
SCUTTLE
SCUTTLE
!
WH
RL
WAS THAT A... A...
SCUTTLE
...COCK-ROACH?!!
SCUTTLE
STAY CALM... THIS PLACE HASN'T BEEN CLEANED IN YEARS. OF COURSE THERE'D BE A FEW OF THOSE AROUND.
IT'S NOT AS IF I'M SCARED OF THEM...BUT...

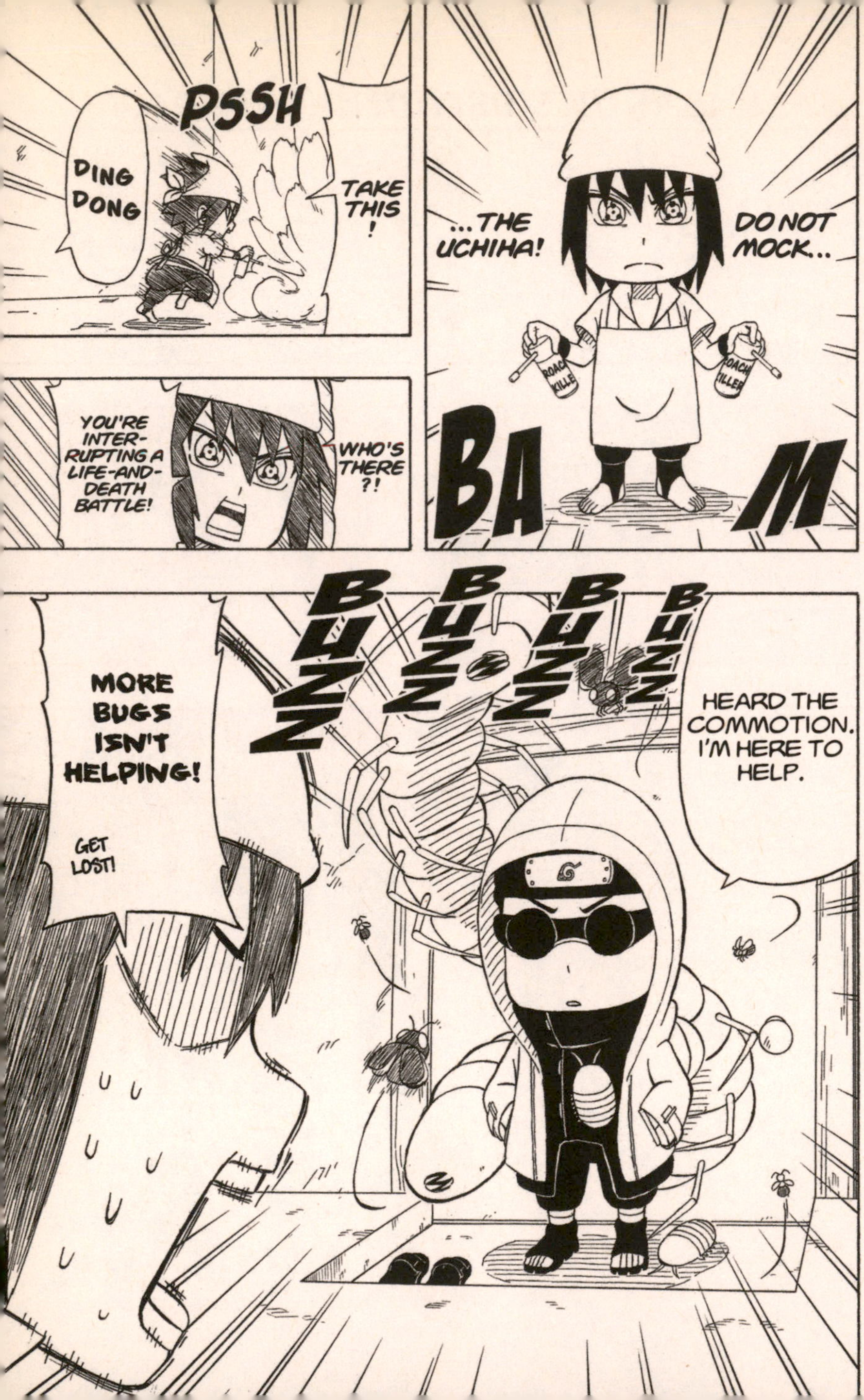
DO NOT MOCK...
...THE UCHIHA!
BAM
ROACH KILLER
ROACH KILLER
TAKE THIS!
PSSH
DING DONG
WHO'S THERE?!
YOU'RE INTERRUPTING A LIFE-AND-DEATH BATTLE!
BUZZ BUZZ BUZZ BUZZ
HEARD THE COMMOTION. I'M HERE TO HELP.
MORE BUGS ISN'T HELPING!
GET LOST!

SASUKE VS. KONOHA?!

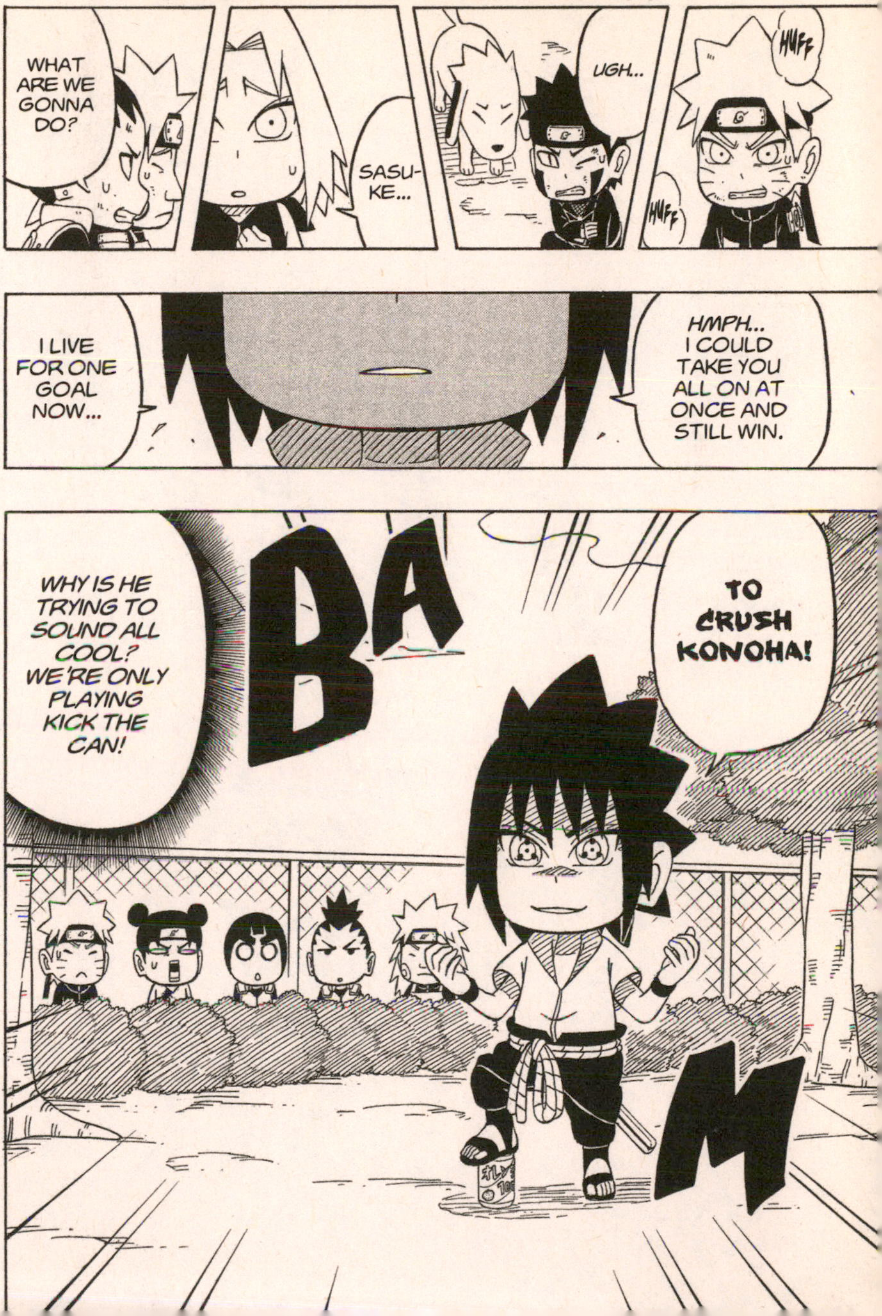
HUFF
HUFF
UGH...
SASU-KE...
WHAT ARE WE GONNA DO?
HMPH... I COULD TAKE YOU ALL ON AT ONCE AND STILL WIN.
I LIVE FOR ONE GOAL NOW...
TO CRUSH KONOHA!
BAM
WHY IS HE TRYING TO SOUND ALL COOL? WE'RE ONLY PLAYING KICK THE CAN!

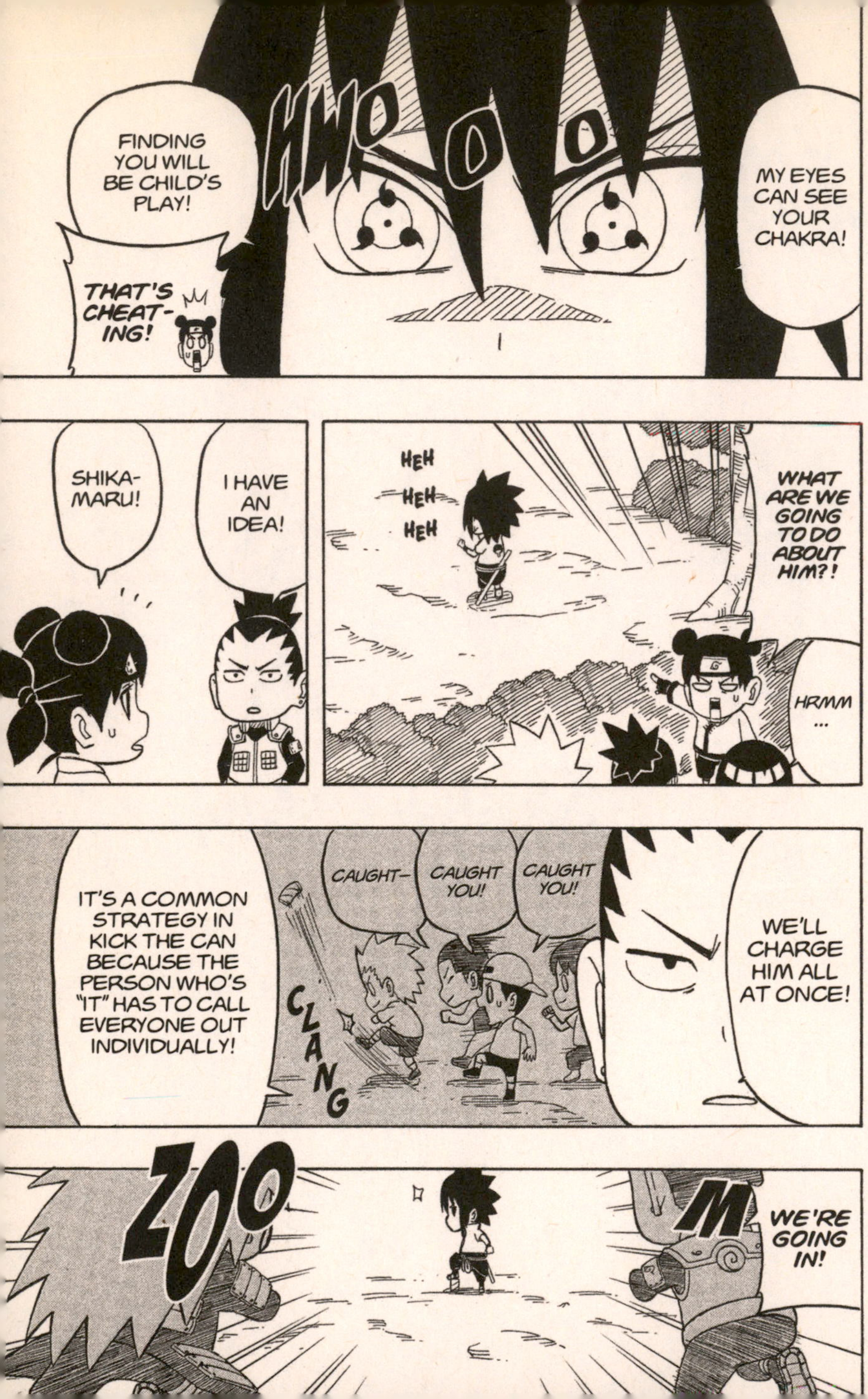
MY EYES CAN SEE YOUR CHAKRA!
HWOOO
FINDING YOU WILL BE CHILD'S PLAY!
THAT'S CHEAT-ING!
WHAT ARE WE GOING TO DO ABOUT HIM?!
HEH HEH HEH
HRMM ...
I HAVE AN IDEA!
SHIKA-MARU!
WE'LL CHARGE HIM ALL AT ONCE!
CAUGHT YOU!
CAUGHT YOU!
CAUGHT—
IT'S A COMMON STRATEGY IN KICK THE CAN BECAUSE THE PERSON WHO'S "IT" HAS TO CALL EVERYONE OUT INDIVIDUALLY!
CLANG
WE'RE GOING IN!
ZOOM

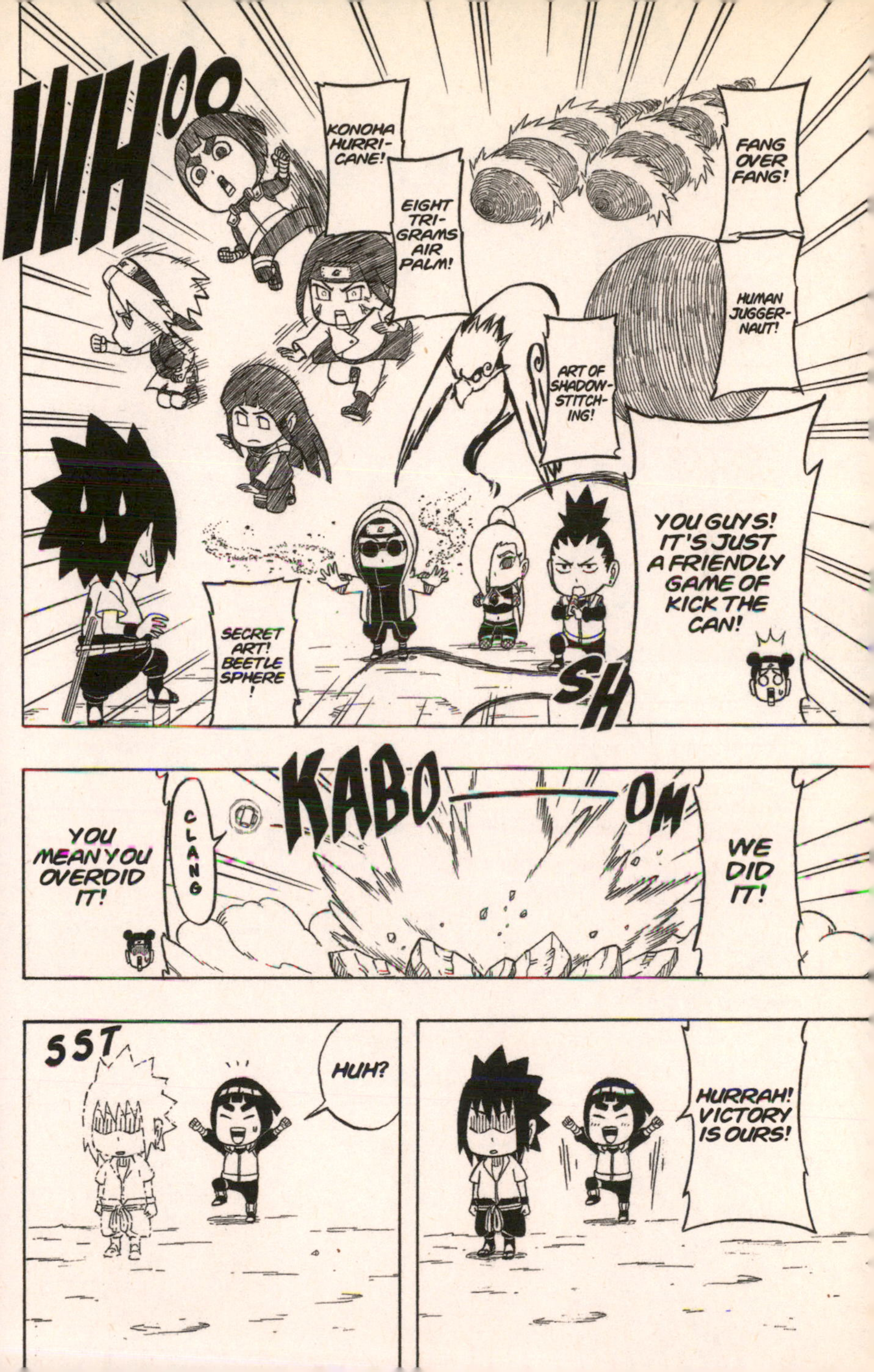
FANG OVER FANG!
HUMAN JUGGERNAUT!
KONOHA HURRICANE!
EIGHT TRIGRAMS AIR PALM!
WHOO
ART OF SHADOW-STITCHING!
YOU GUYS! IT'S JUST A FRIENDLY GAME OF KICK THE CAN!
SH
SECRET ART! BEETLE SPHERE!
KABO——OM
WE DID IT!
CLANG
YOU MEAN YOU OVERDID IT!
HURRAH! VICTORY IS OURS!
HUH?
SST

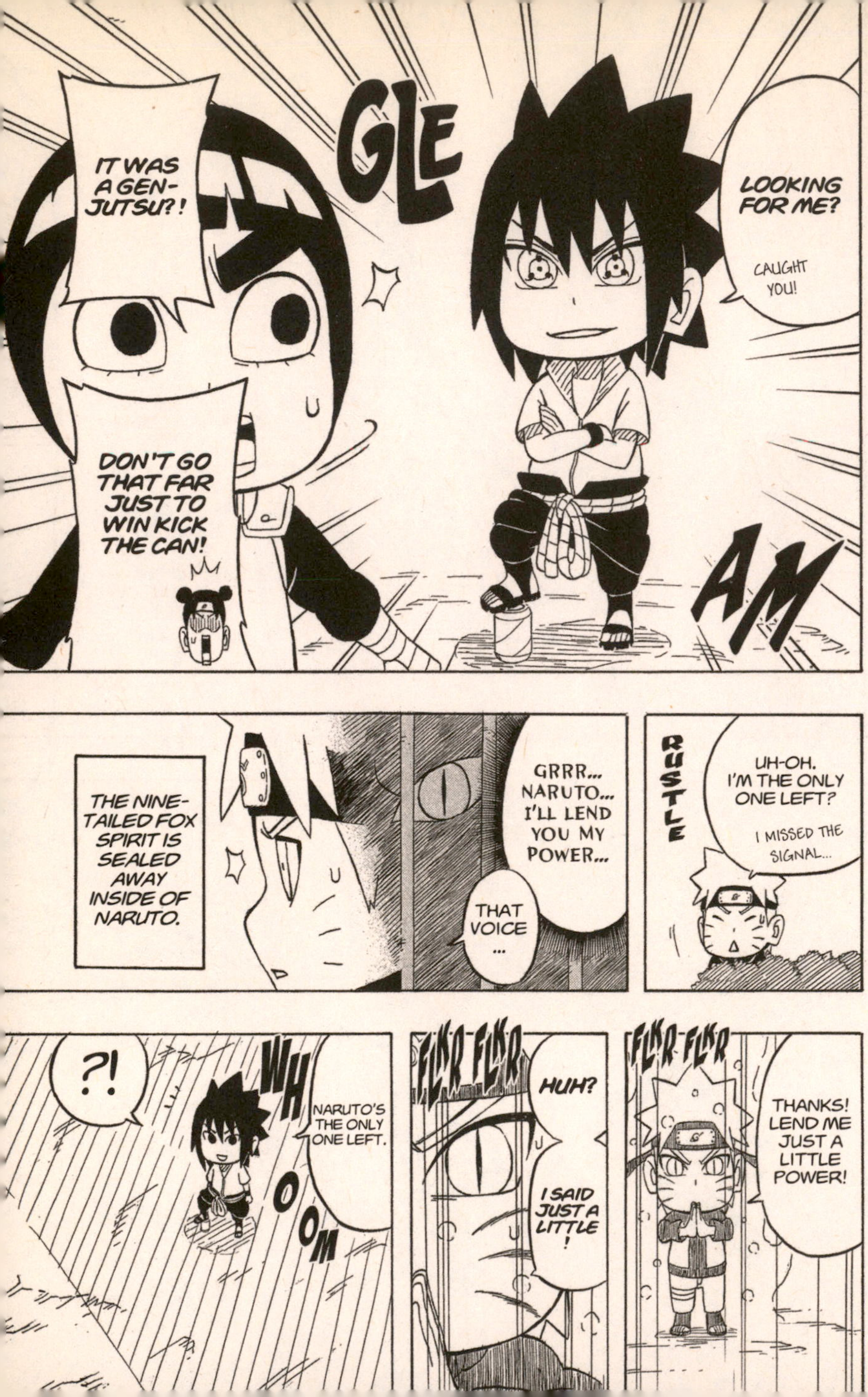
LOOKING FOR ME?
CAUGHT YOU!
GLE
IT WAS A GEN-JUTSU?!
AM
DON'T GO THAT FAR JUST TO WIN KICK THE CAN!
RUSTLE
UH-OH. I'M THE ONLY ONE LEFT?
I MISSED THE SIGNAL...
GRRR... NARUTO... I'LL LEND YOU MY POWER...
THAT VOICE...
THE NINE-TAILED FOX SPIRIT IS SEALED AWAY INSIDE OF NARUTO.
FLKR-FLKR
THANKS! LEND ME JUST A LITTLE POWER!
FLKR-FLKR
HUH?
I SAID JUST A LITTLE!
NARUTO'S THE ONLY ONE LEFT.
WHOOOM
?!

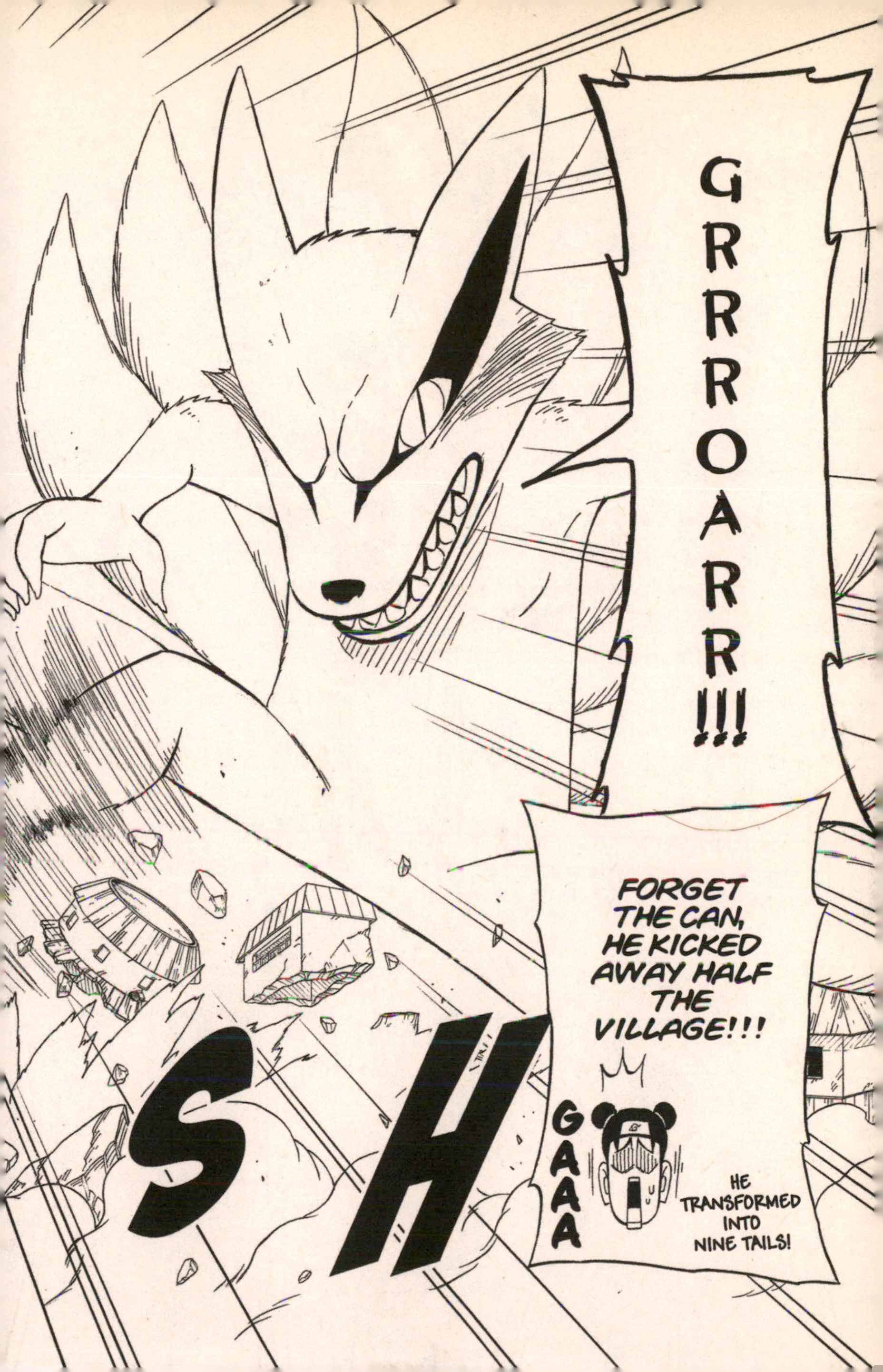
GRRROARRR!!!
FORGET THE CAN, HE KICKED AWAY HALF THE VILLAGE!!!
GAAAA
HE TRANSFORMED INTO NINE TAILS!
SH

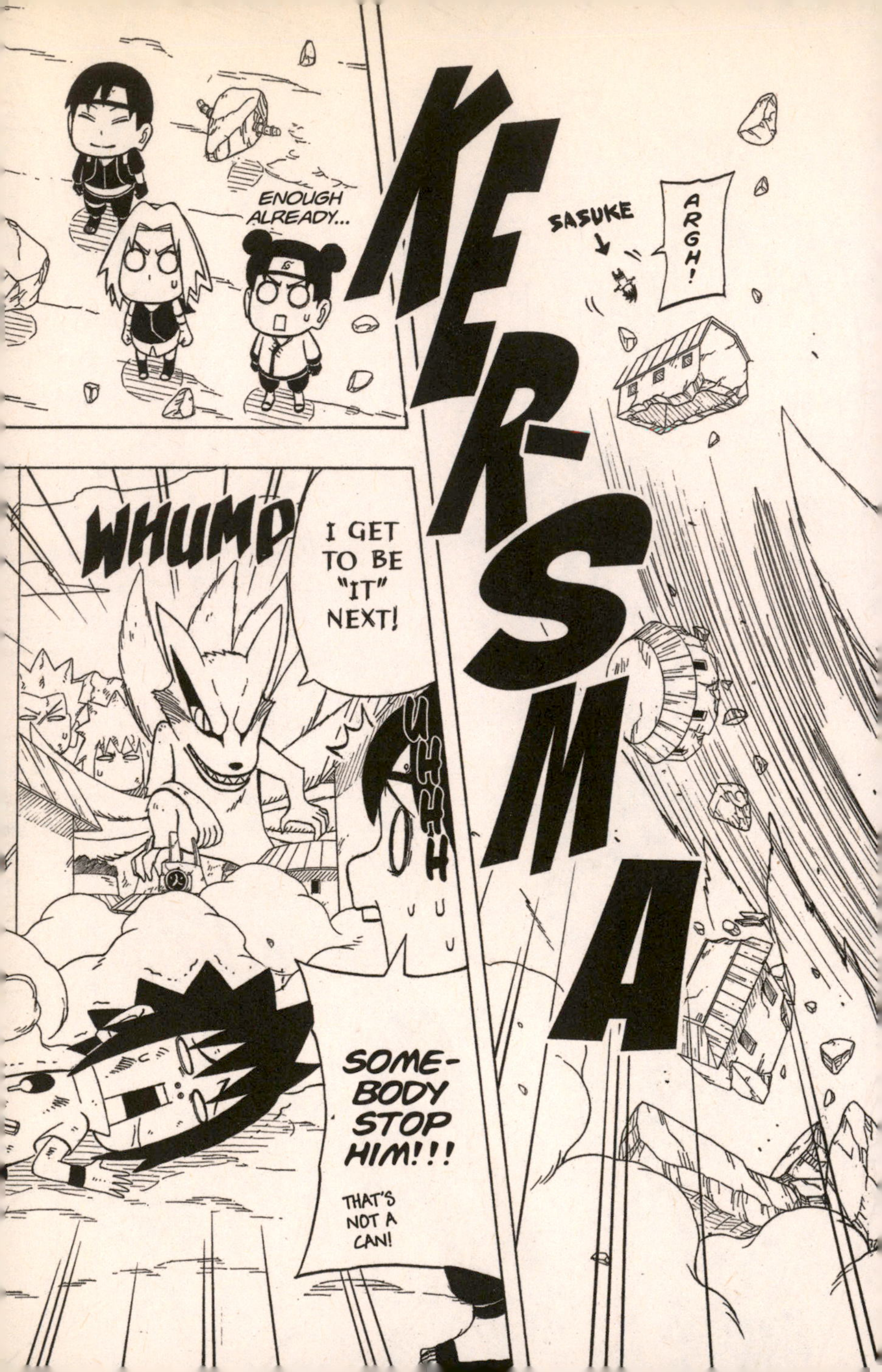
KER-R-SMA
SASUKE
ARGH!
ENOUGH ALREADY...
WHUMP
I GET TO BE "IT" NEXT!
UHHHH
SOMEBODY STOP HIM!!!
THAT'S NOT A CAN!

SETTING OUT

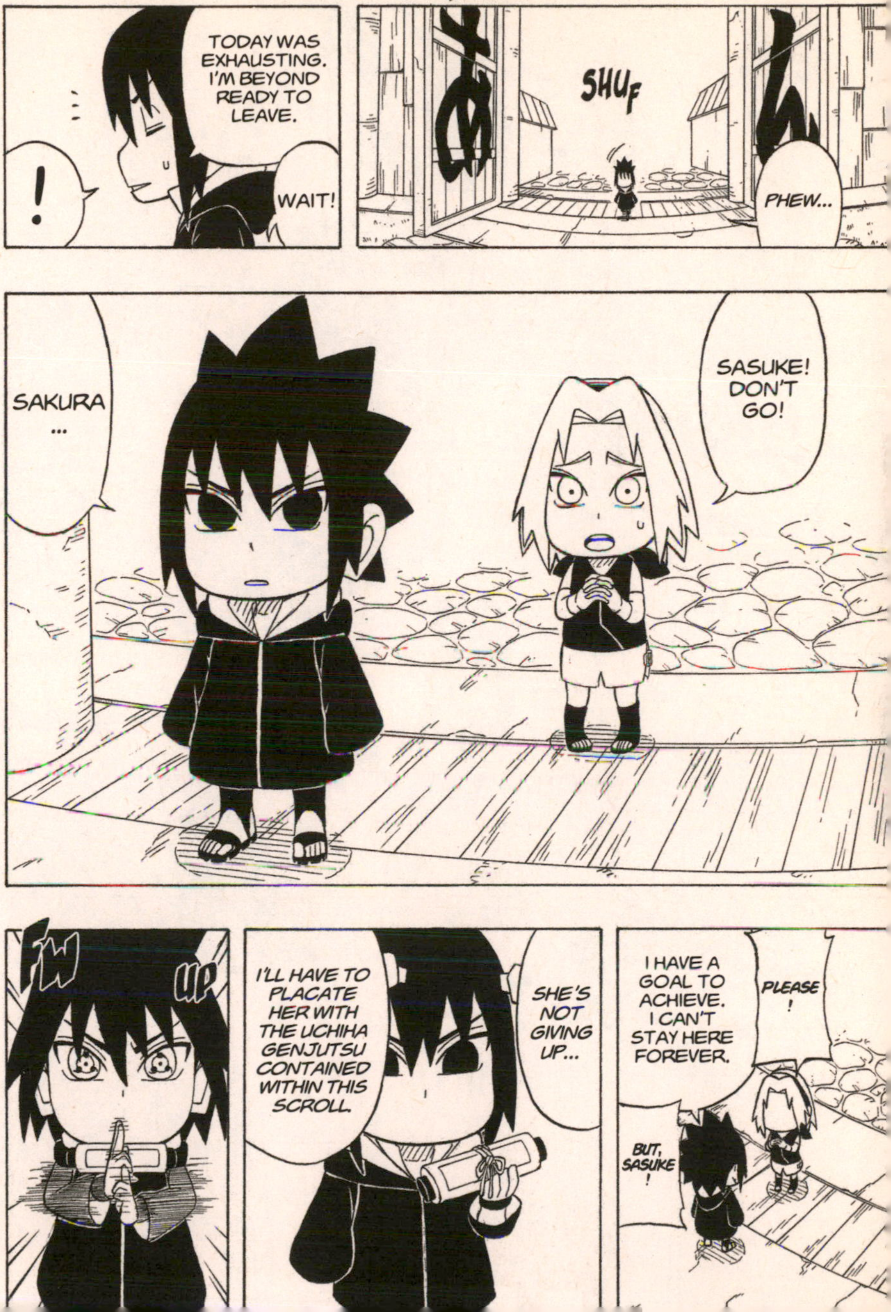
SHUF
PHEW...
TODAY WAS EXHAUSTING. I'M BEYOND READY TO LEAVE.
WAIT!
!
SASUKE! DON'T GO!
SAKURA...
PLEASE!
I HAVE A GOAL TO ACHIEVE. I CAN'T STAY HERE FOREVER.
BUT, SASUKE!
SHE'S NOT GIVING UP...
I'LL HAVE TO PLACATE HER WITH THE UCHIHA GENJUTSU CONTAINED WITHIN THIS SCROLL.
FW
UP

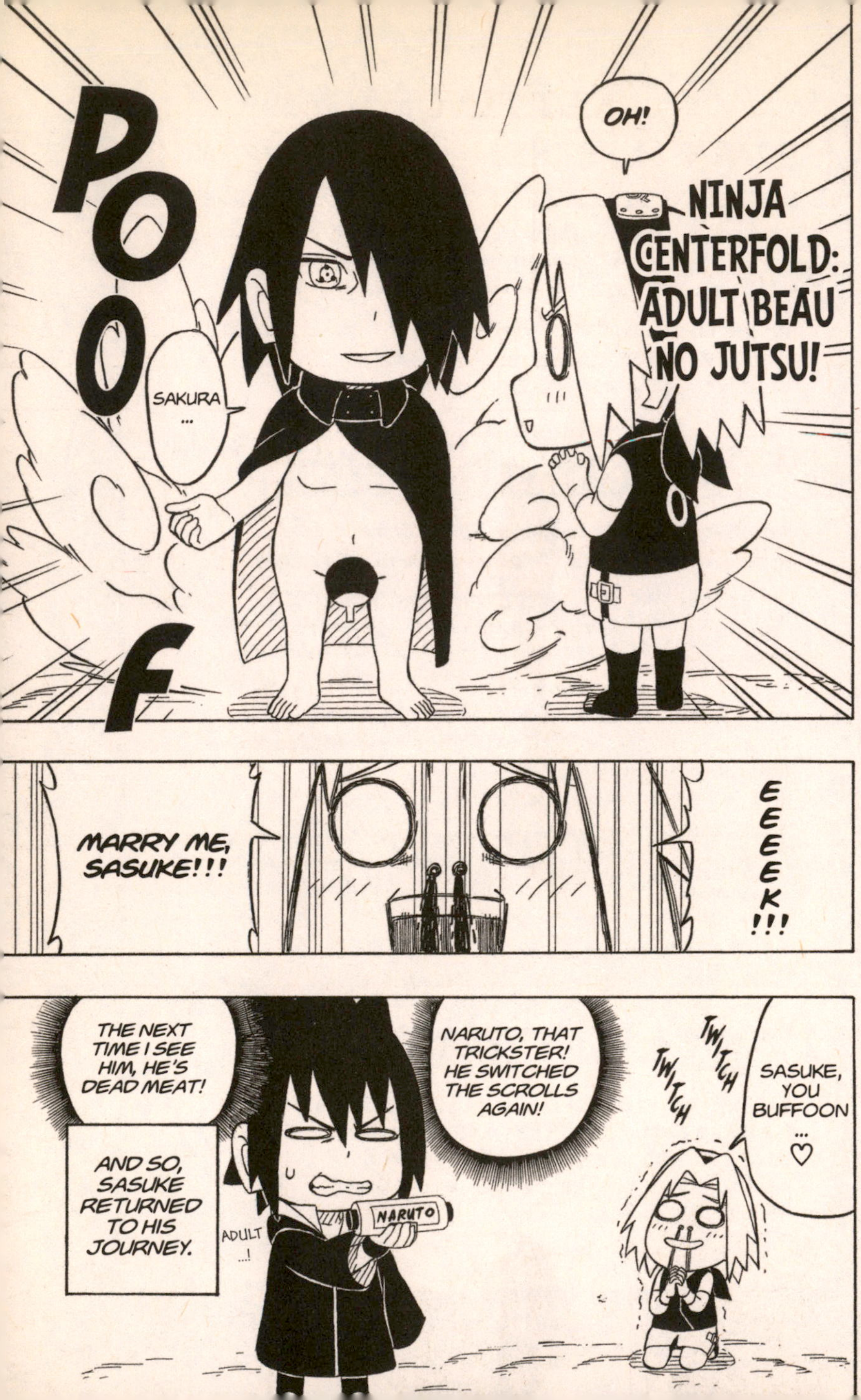
OH!
NINJA CENTERFOLD: ADULT BEAU NO JUTSU!
POOOF
SAKURA ...
EEEEEK!!!
MARRY ME, SASUKE!!!
SASUKE, YOU BUFFOON ... ♡
TWITCH
TWITCH
NARUTO, THAT TRICKSTER! HE SWITCHED THE SCROLLS AGAIN!
THE NEXT TIME I SEE HIM, HE'S DEAD MEAT!
NARUTO
ADULT ...!
AND SO, SASUKE RETURNED TO HIS JOURNEY.

BONUS MATERIAL MINI MANGA CHAPTERS

MINI MANGA 1: SASUKE VS. THE VENDING MACHINE!!

A special chapter published in *Weekly Shonen Jump*.
Check out Sasuke's ridiculous battle!
(from *Weekly Shonen Jump* 2014 No. 45)

MINI MANGA 2: SASUKE VS. THE MASSAGE CHAIR!!

Another of Sasuke's ridiculous battles!
(from Jump Festa 2015 *Jump Special Comics for Kids*!!)

MINI MANGA 3: LET'S GO TO THE NARUTO ART EXHIBIT!

Information on the *Naruto Art Exhibit*. At the exhibit,
you could see the original manuscript pages for the
very first chapter of *Naruto*, exclusive illustrations
and more. It was inspiring!
(from *Weekly Shonen Jump* 2015 No. 13)

MINI MANGA 4: LET'S GO TO THE NARUTO ART EXHIBIT! PART 2

More about the *Naruto Art Exhibit*.
Sasuke and friends go to Roppongi Hills!
(from *Weekly Shonen Jump* 2015 No. 21)

MINI MANGA 5: JUMP FESTA 2015 RULES & GUIDELINES

This manga explains the rules and guidelines
for Jump Festa 2015. The rules differ every
year, so if you're attending Jump Festa, be
sure to check out the current year's rules!
(from *Saikyo Jump* 2015 No. 1)

SASUKE...

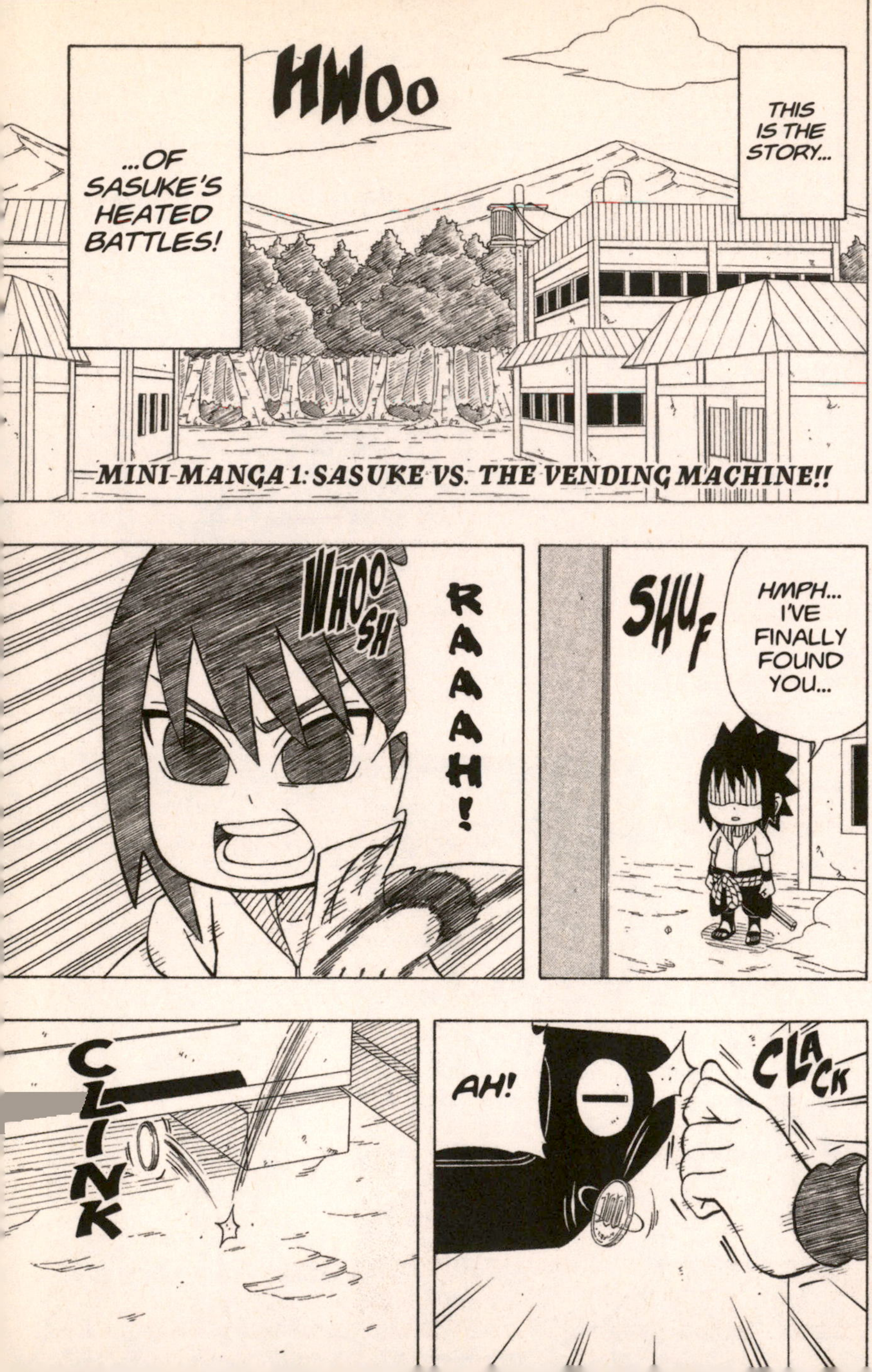
THIS IS THE STORY...
HWOOo
...OF SASUKE'S HEATED BATTLES!
MINI-MANGA 1: SASUKE VS. THE VENDING MACHINE!!
SHUF
HMPH... I'VE FINALLY FOUND YOU...
RAAAAH!
WHOOSH
CLACK
AH!
CLINK

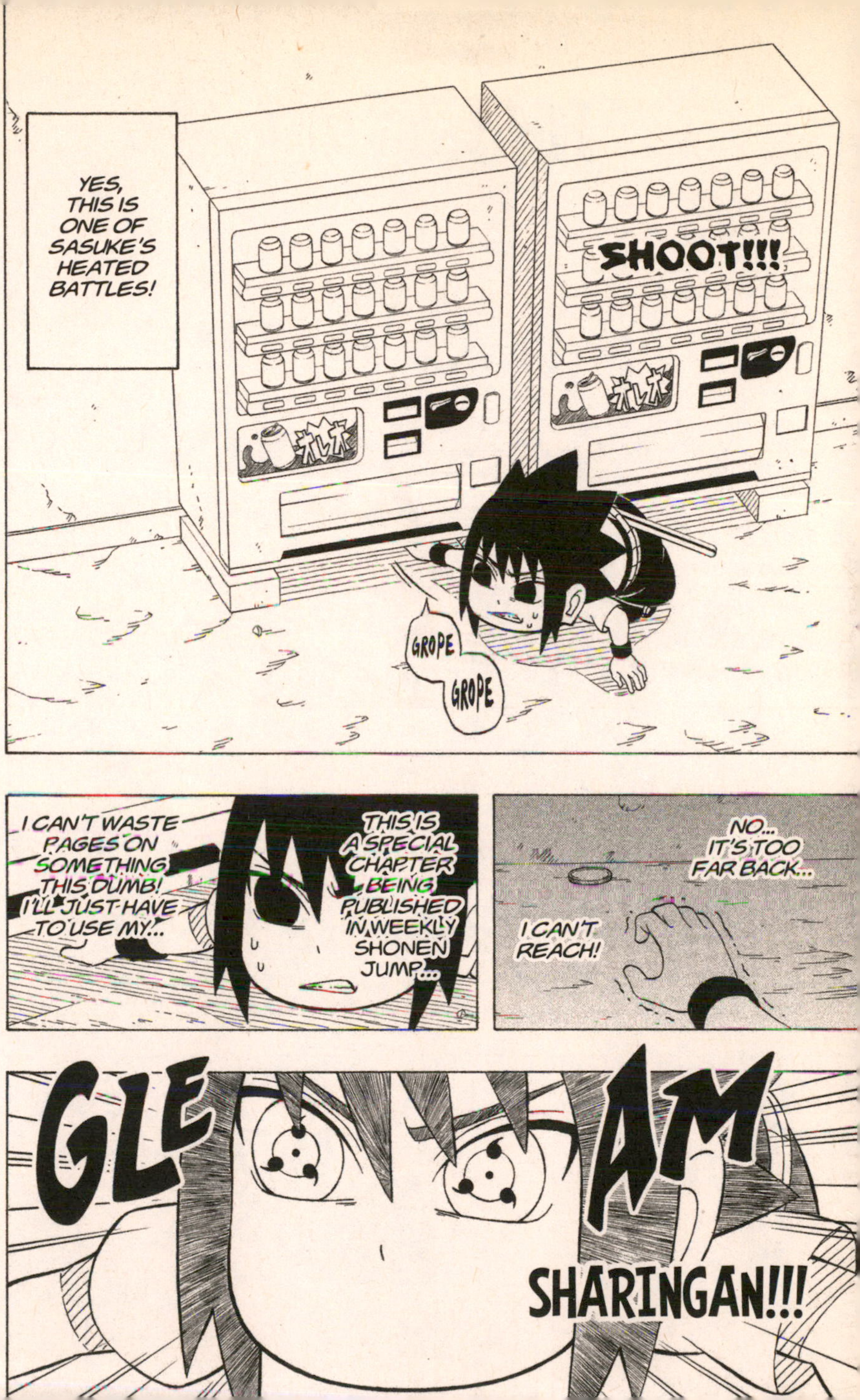
SHOOT!!!
YES, THIS IS ONE OF SASUKE'S HEATED BATTLES!
GROPE
GROPE
NO... IT'S TOO FAR BACK...
I CAN'T REACH!
THIS IS A SPECIAL CHAPTER BEING PUBLISHED IN WEEKLY SHONEN JUMP...
I CAN'T WASTE PAGES ON SOMETHING THIS DUMB! I'LL JUST HAVE TO USE MY...
GLEAM
SHARINGAN!!!

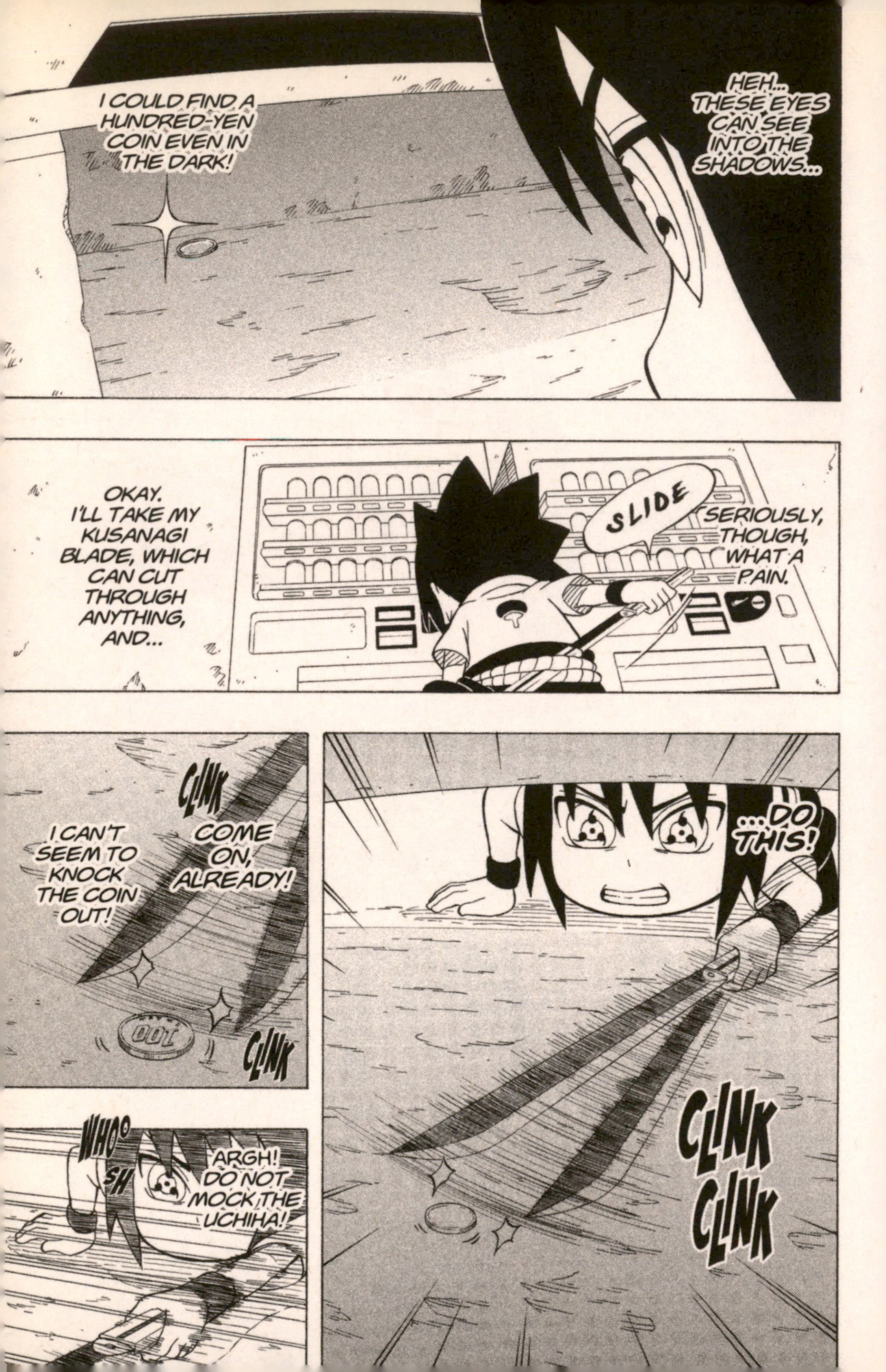
HEH... THESE EYES CAN SEE INTO THE SHADOWS...
I COULD FIND A HUNDRED-YEN COIN EVEN IN THE DARK!
SLIDE
SERIOUSLY, THOUGH, WHAT A PAIN.
OKAY. I'LL TAKE MY KUSANAGI BLADE, WHICH CAN CUT THROUGH ANYTHING, AND...
...DO THIS!
CLINK CLINK
CLINK
COME ON, ALREADY!
I CAN'T SEEM TO KNOCK THE COIN OUT!
100
CLINK
WHOOSH
ARGH! DO NOT MOCK THE UCHIHA!

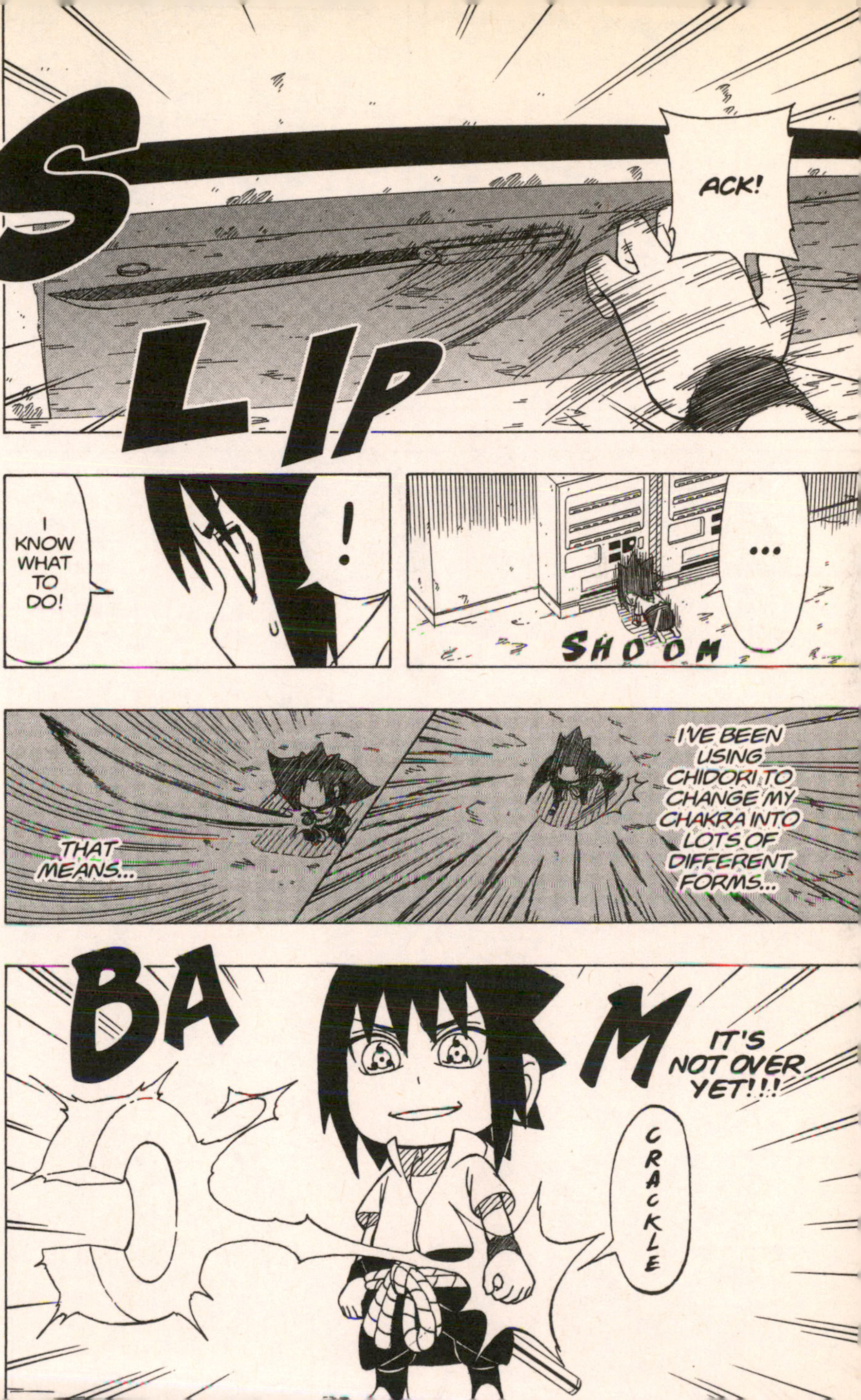
ACK!
SLIP
...
SHOOM
!
I KNOW WHAT TO DO!
I'VE BEEN USING CHIDORI TO CHANGE MY CHAKRA INTO LOTS OF DIFFERENT FORMS...
THAT MEANS...
IT'S NOT OVER YET!!!
CRACKLE
BAM

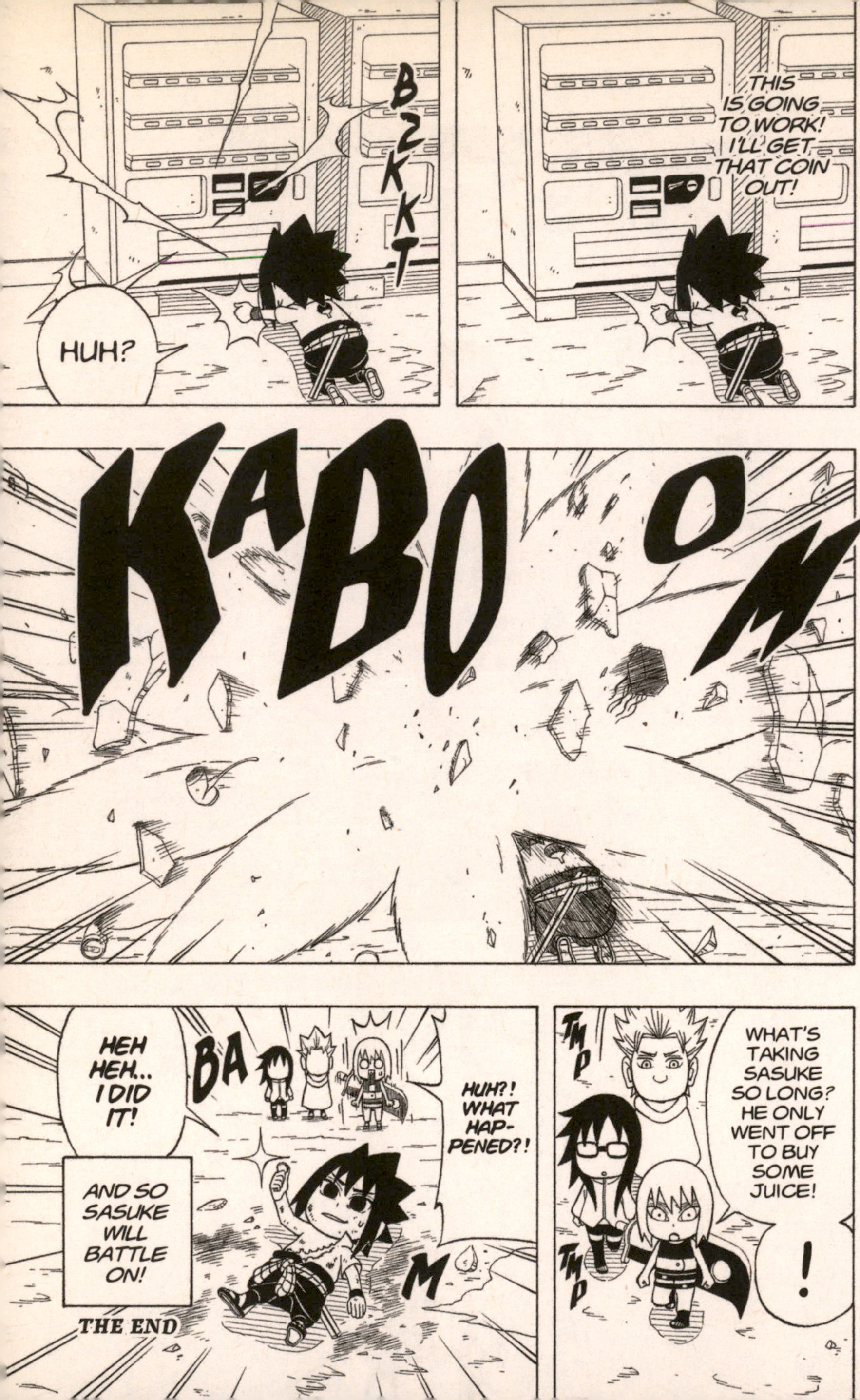
THIS IS GOING TO WORK! I'LL GET THAT COIN OUT!
BZKKT
HUH?
KABOOM
TMP
TMP
TMP
WHAT'S TAKING SASUKE SO LONG? HE ONLY WENT OFF TO BUY SOME JUICE!
!
BA
M
HUH?! WHAT HAP-PENED?!
HEH HEH... I DID IT!
AND SO SASUKE WILL BATTLE ON!
THE END

MINI MANGA 2: SASUKE VS. THE MASSAGE CHAIR!!

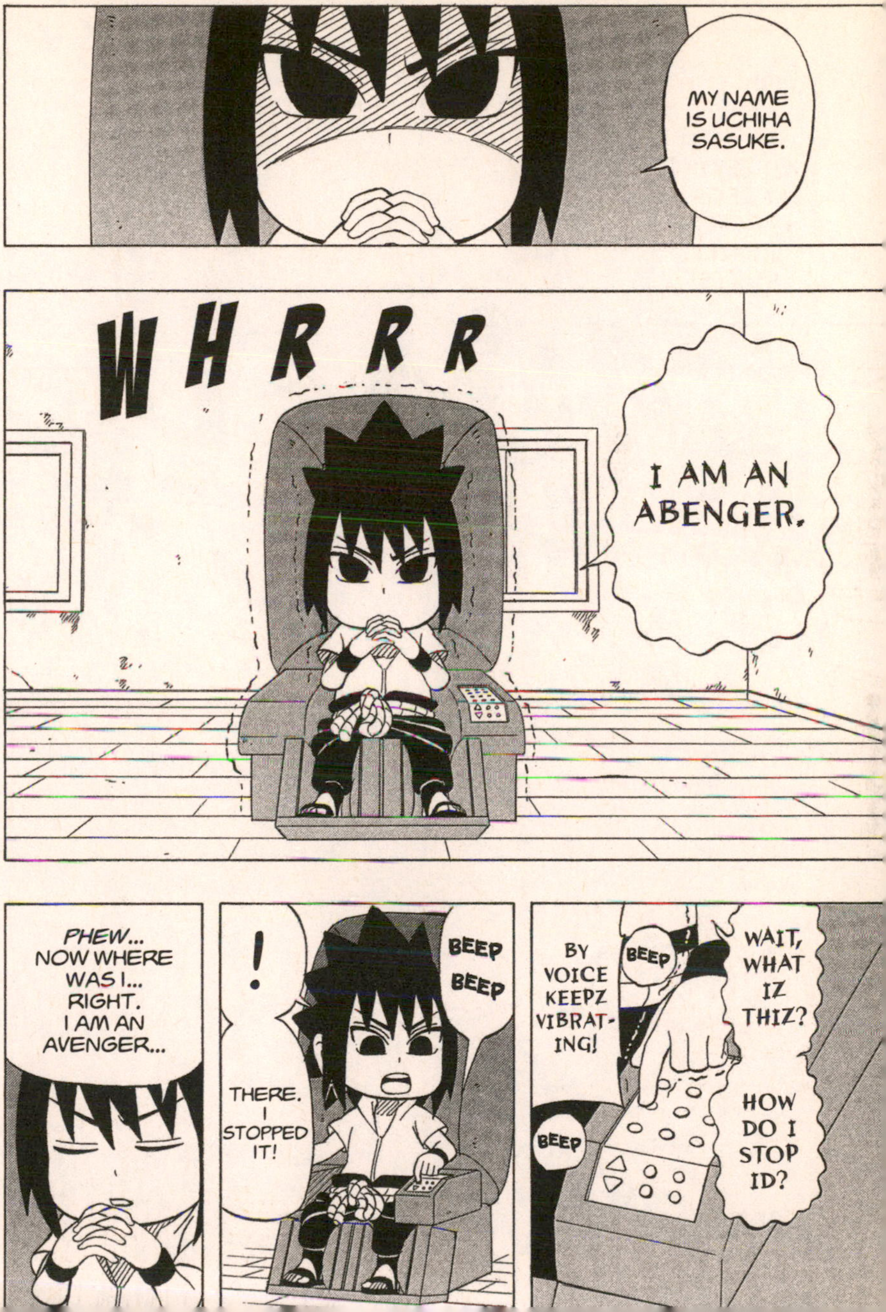
MY NAME IS UCHIHA SASUKE.
WHRRR
I AM AN ABENGER.
WAIT, WHAT IZ THIZ?
BEEP
BY VOICE KEEPZ VIBRAT-ING!
HOW DO I STOP ID?
BEEP
BEEP BEEP
!
THERE. I STOPPED IT!
PHEW... NOW WHERE WAS I... RIGHT. I AM AN AVENGER...

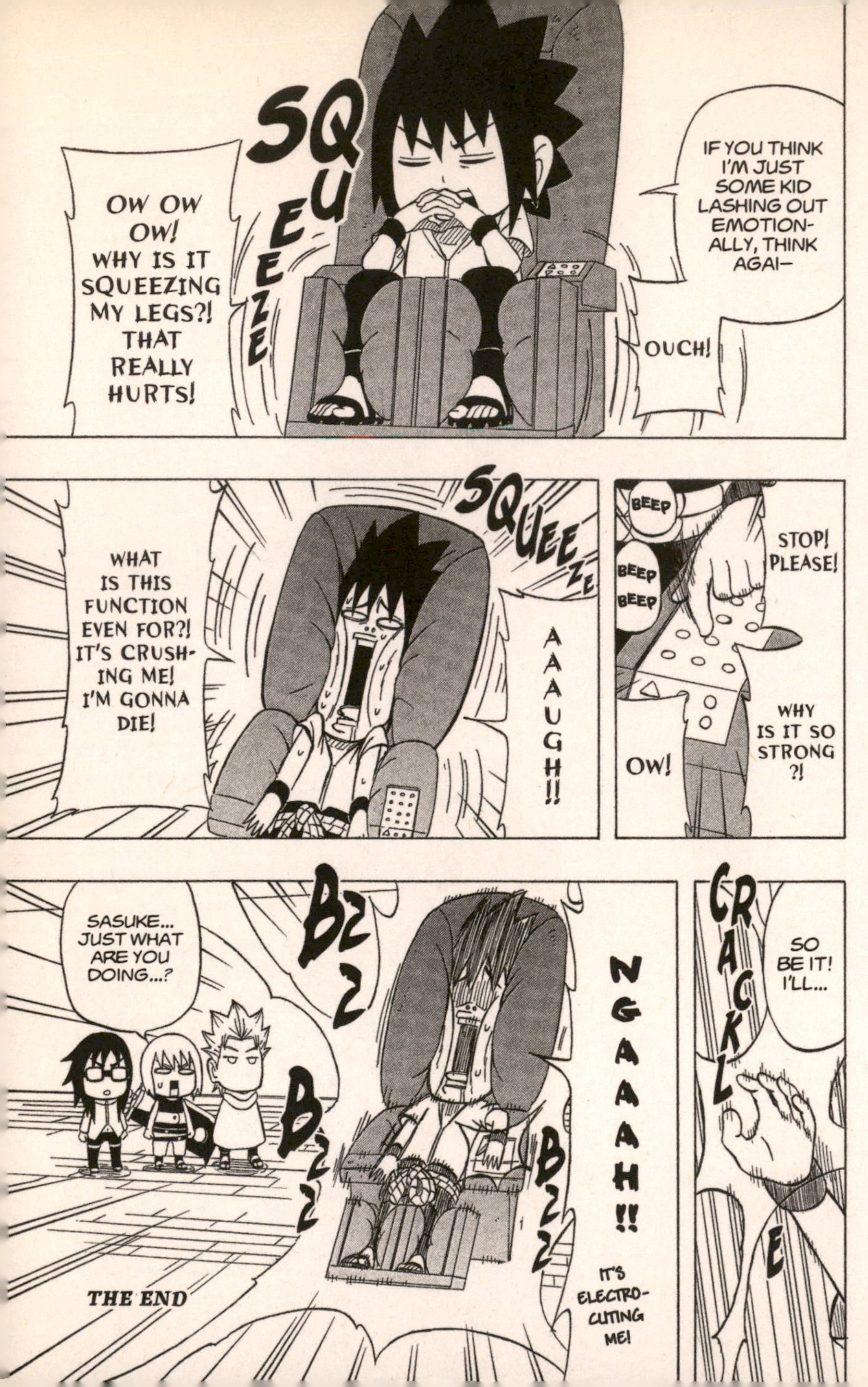
IF YOU THINK I'M JUST SOME KID LASHING OUT EMOTION-ALLY, THINK AGAI—
OUCH!
SQUEEZE
OW OW OW! WHY IS IT SQUEEZING MY LEGS?! THAT REALLY HURTS!
STOP! PLEASE!
BEEP
BEEP BEEP
WHY IS IT SO STRONG?!
OW!
SQUEEZE
AAAAUGH!!
WHAT IS THIS FUNCTION EVEN FOR?! IT'S CRUSH-ING ME! I'M GONNA DIE!
CRACKLE
SO BE IT! I'LL...
BZZ
NGAAAAH!!
BZZ
IT'S ELECTRO-CUTING ME!
BZZ
SASUKE... JUST WHAT ARE YOU DOING...?
THE END

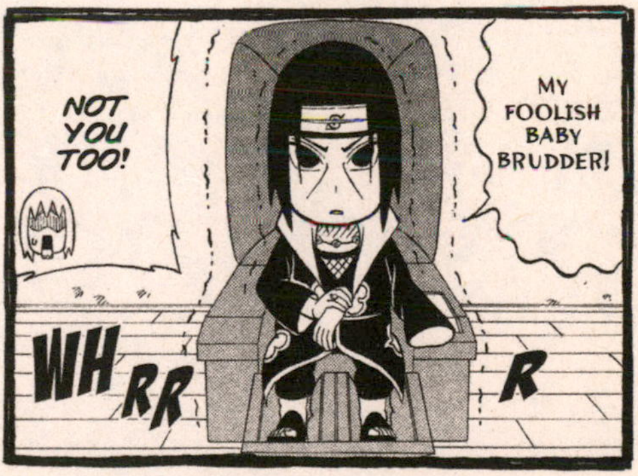
MY FOOLISH BABY BRUDDER!
NOT YOU TOO!
WHRRR

MINI MANGA 3: LET'S GO TO THE NARUTO ART EXHIBIT!

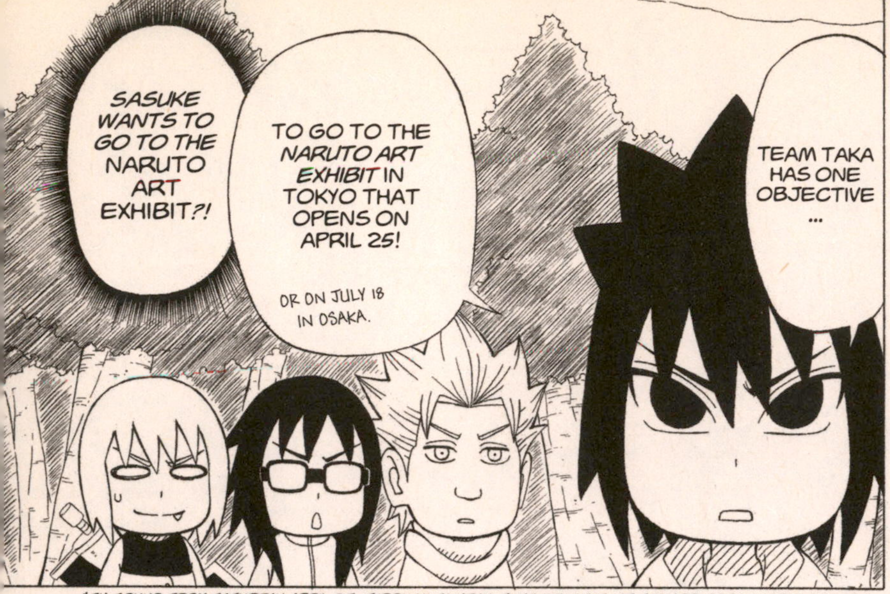
TEAM TAKA HAS ONE OBJECTIVE ...
TO GO TO THE NARUTO ART EXHIBIT IN TOKYO THAT OPENS ON APRIL 25!
OR ON JULY 18 IN OSAKA.
SASUKE WANTS TO GO TO THE NARUTO ART EXHIBIT?!

*IN TOKYO FROM SATURDAY, APRIL 25, THROUGH SUNDAY, JUNE 28, 2015, AT THE MORI ARTS CENTER GALLERY (ROPPONGI HILLS MORI TOWER FLOOR 52)

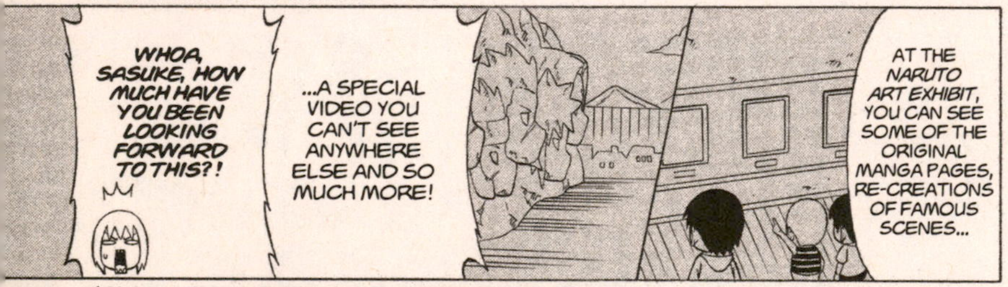
AT THE NARUTO ART EXHIBIT, YOU CAN SEE SOME OF THE ORIGINAL MANGA PAGES, RE-CREATIONS OF FAMOUS SCENES...
...A SPECIAL VIDEO YOU CAN'T SEE ANYWHERE ELSE AND SO MUCH MORE!
WHOA, SASUKE, HOW MUCH HAVE YOU BEEN LOOKING FORWARD TO THIS?!

*IN OSAKA FROM SATURDAY, JULY 18, THROUGH SUNDAY, SEPTEMBER 27, 2015, AT THE OSAKA CULTURARIUM AT TEMPOZAN (NEXT TO THE OSAKA AQUARIUM)

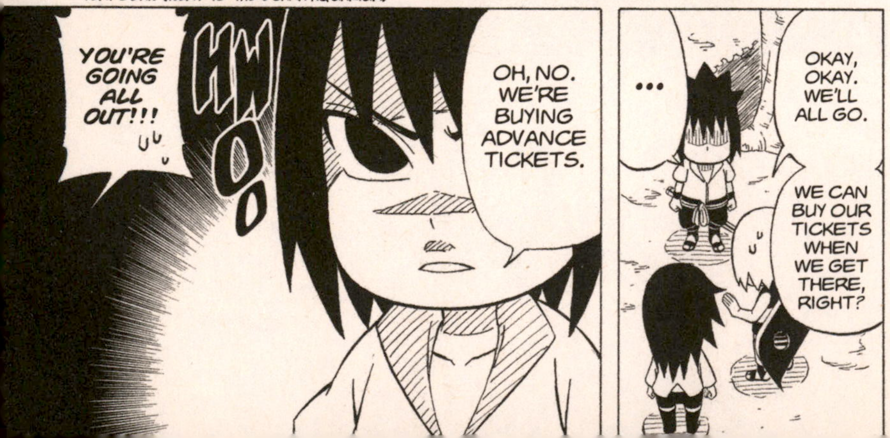
OKAY, OKAY. WE'LL ALL GO.
...
WE CAN BUY OUR TICKETS WHEN WE GET THERE, RIGHT?
OH, NO. WE'RE BUYING ADVANCE TICKETS.
YOU'RE GOING ALL OUT!!!

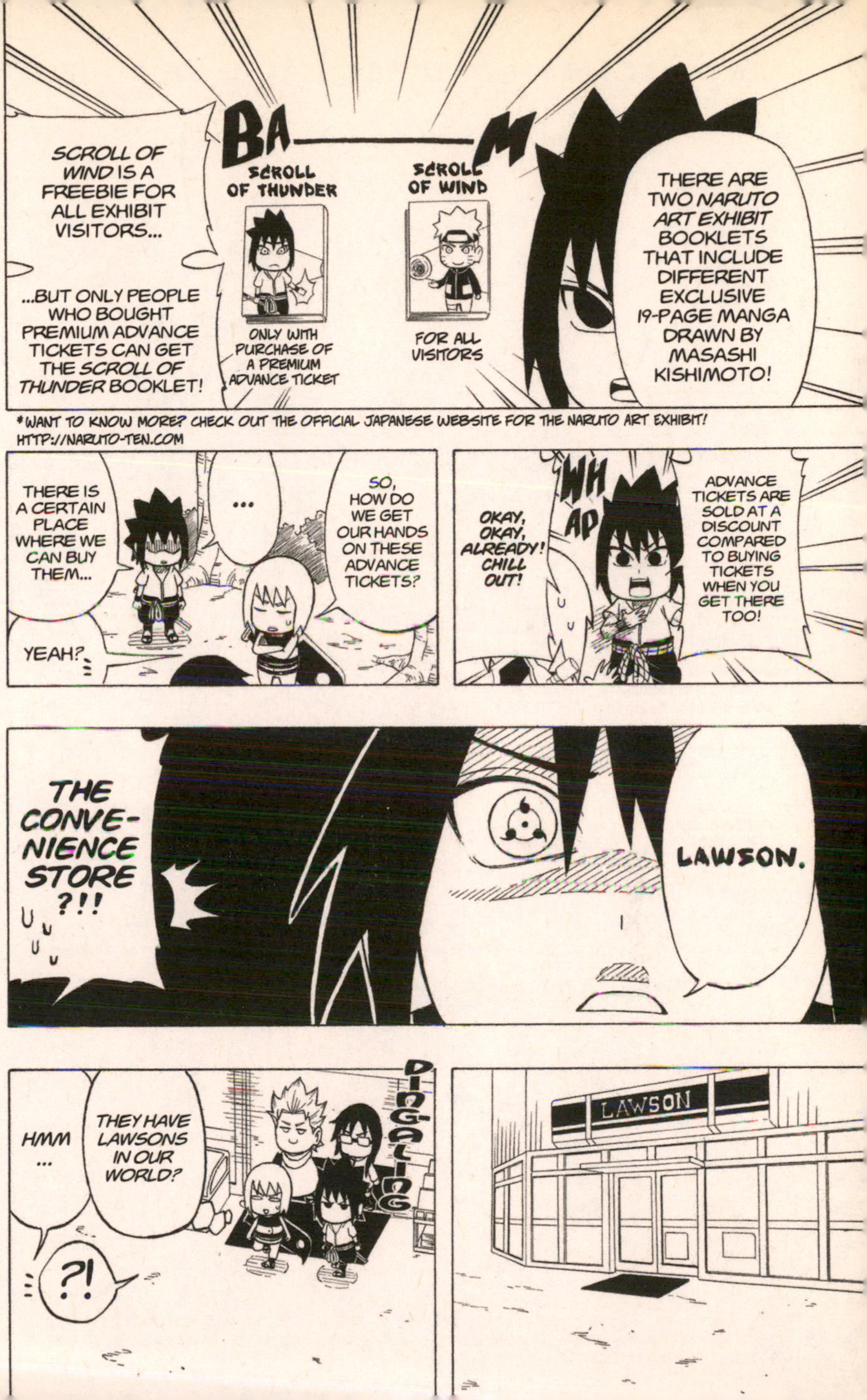
THERE ARE TWO NARUTO ART EXHIBIT BOOKLETS THAT INCLUDE DIFFERENT EXCLUSIVE 19-PAGE MANGA DRAWN BY MASASHI KISHIMOTO!
BA——M
SCROLL OF WIND
FOR ALL VISITORS
SCROLL OF THUNDER
ONLY WITH PURCHASE OF A PREMIUM ADVANCE TICKET
SCROLL OF WIND IS A FREEBIE FOR ALL EXHIBIT VISITORS...
...BUT ONLY PEOPLE WHO BOUGHT PREMIUM ADVANCE TICKETS CAN GET THE SCROLL OF THUNDER BOOKLET!
*WANT TO KNOW MORE? CHECK OUT THE OFFICIAL JAPANESE WEBSITE FOR THE NARUTO ART EXHIBIT! HTTP://NARUTO-TEN.COM
ADVANCE TICKETS ARE SOLD AT A DISCOUNT COMPARED TO BUYING TICKETS WHEN YOU GET THERE TOO!
WHAP
OKAY, OKAY, ALREADY! CHILL OUT!
SO, HOW DO WE GET OUR HANDS ON THESE ADVANCE TICKETS?
...
THERE IS A CERTAIN PLACE WHERE WE CAN BUY THEM...
YEAH?
LAWSON.
THE CONVENIENCE STORE?!!
LAWSON
DING-A-LING
THEY HAVE LAWSONS IN OUR WORLD?
HMM...
?!

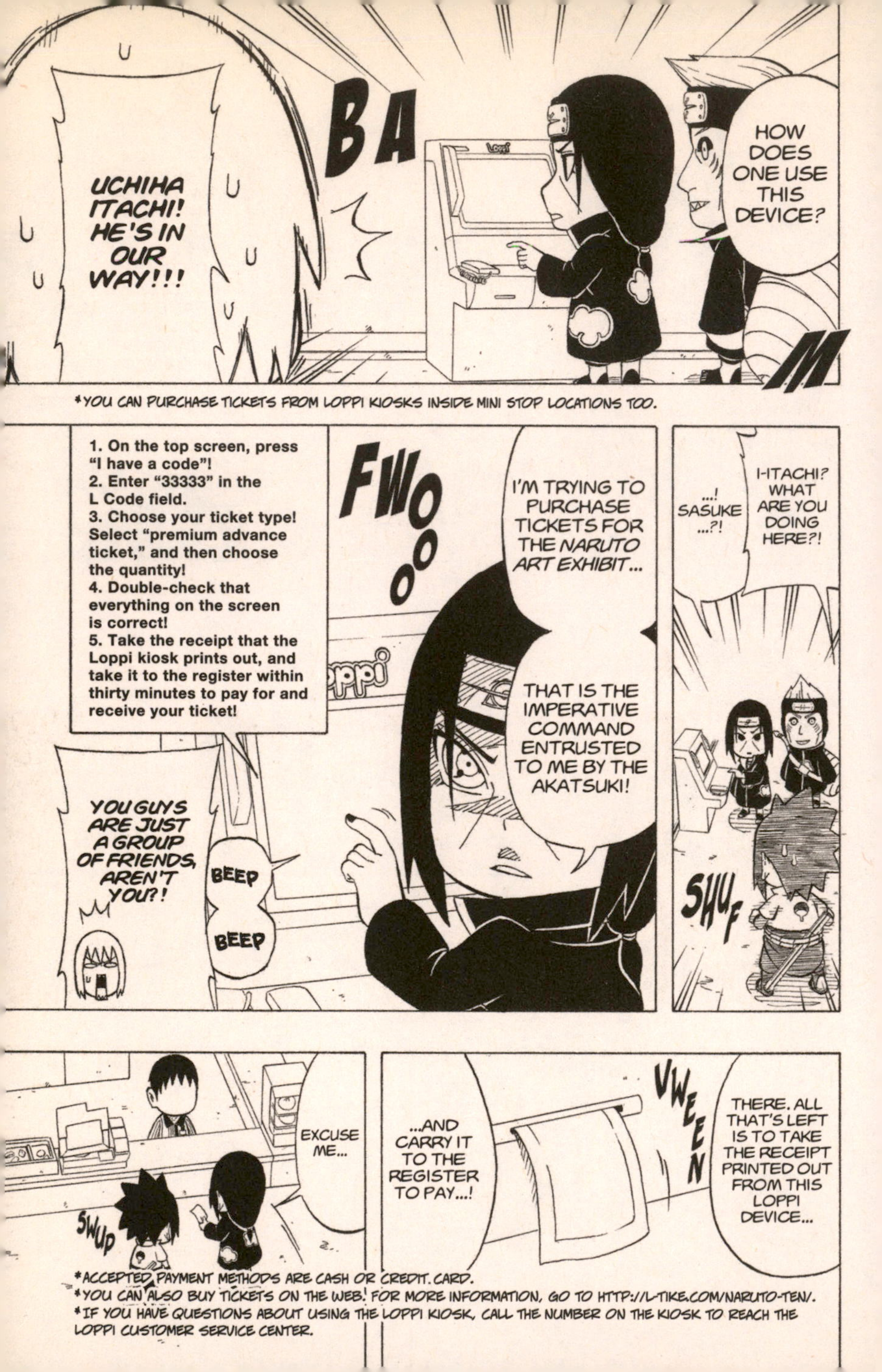
HOW DOES ONE USE THIS DEVICE?
BA
M
UCHIHA ITACHI! HE'S IN OUR WAY!!!
*YOU CAN PURCHASE TICKETS FROM LOPPI KIOSKS INSIDE MINI STOP LOCATIONS TOO.
I-ITACHI? WHAT ARE YOU DOING HERE?!
...! SASUKE ...?!
SHUF
I'M TRYING TO PURCHASE TICKETS FOR THE *NARUTO* ART EXHIBIT...
FWOOO
THAT IS THE IMPERATIVE COMMAND ENTRUSTED TO ME BY THE AKATSUKI!
1. On the top screen, press "I have a code"!
2. Enter "33333" in the L Code field.
3. Choose your ticket type! Select "premium advance ticket," and then choose the quantity!
4. Double-check that everything on the screen is correct!
5. Take the receipt that the Loppi kiosk prints out, and take it to the register within thirty minutes to pay for and receive your ticket!
YOU GUYS ARE JUST A GROUP OF FRIENDS, AREN'T YOU?!
BEEP
BEEP
THERE. ALL THAT'S LEFT IS TO TAKE THE RECEIPT PRINTED OUT FROM THIS LOPPI DEVICE...
UWEEN
...AND CARRY IT TO THE REGISTER TO PAY...!
EXCUSE ME...
SWUP
*ACCEPTED PAYMENT METHODS ARE CASH OR CREDIT CARD.
*YOU CAN ALSO BUY TICKETS ON THE WEB. FOR MORE INFORMATION, GO TO HTTP://L-TIKE.COM/NARUTO-TEN/.
*IF YOU HAVE QUESTIONS ABOUT USING THE LOPPI KIOSK, CALL THE NUMBER ON THE KIOSK TO REACH THE LOPPI CUSTOMER SERVICE CENTER.

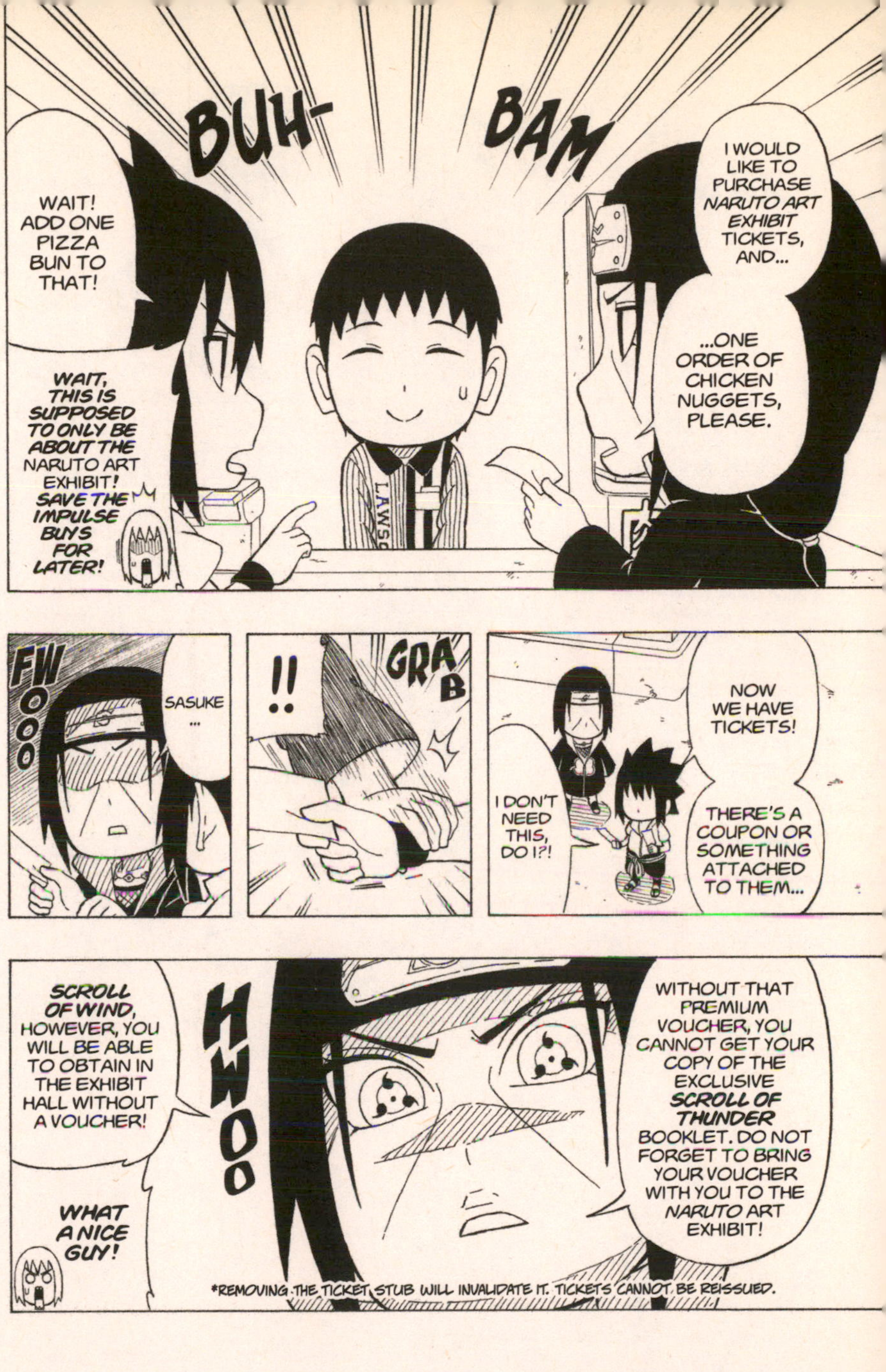
I WOULD LIKE TO PURCHASE NARUTO ART EXHIBIT TICKETS, AND...
...ONE ORDER OF CHICKEN NUGGETS, PLEASE.
BUH-BAM
WAIT! ADD ONE PIZZA BUN TO THAT!
WAIT, THIS IS SUPPOSED TO ONLY BE ABOUT THE NARUTO ART EXHIBIT! SAVE THE IMPULSE BUYS FOR LATER!
NOW WE HAVE TICKETS!
THERE'S A COUPON OR SOMETHING ATTACHED TO THEM...
I DON'T NEED THIS, DO I?!
GRAB
!!
FWOOO
SASUKE...
WITHOUT THAT PREMIUM VOUCHER, YOU CANNOT GET YOUR COPY OF THE EXCLUSIVE SCROLL OF THUNDER BOOKLET. DO NOT FORGET TO BRING YOUR VOUCHER WITH YOU TO THE NARUTO ART EXHIBIT!
HWOO
SCROLL OF WIND, HOWEVER, YOU WILL BE ABLE TO OBTAIN IN THE EXHIBIT HALL WITHOUT A VOUCHER!
WHAT A NICE GUY!
*REMOVING THE TICKET STUB WILL INVALIDATE IT. TICKETS CANNOT BE REISSUED.

THAT IS ALL... UNTIL WE MEET AGAIN, SASUKE...
FLAP
FLAP
GAH!
STOP, ITACHI!
FLAP
FLAP
KAW
KAW
BAM
YOU'RE MAKING A MESS!
TUMBLE
PLEASE REFRAIN FROM USING NINJUTSU INSIDE STORES.

ADVANCE TICKETS ARE ON SALE THROUGH APRIL 24, 2015!
BE SURE TO GET A PREMIUM ADVANCE TICKET!

Tickets on sale at Loppi kiosks inside Lawson and Mini Stop locations nationwide, or on the web at http://l-tike.com/naruto-ten/!
Use the L Code "33333"!

Sales Period for Tokyo	2/7 through 4/24		4/25 through 6/28
Ticket Type	Premium Advance Tickets	Regular Advance Tickets	At the door
Adults	¥1900	¥1800	¥2000
Middle/High Schoolers	¥1400	¥1300	¥1500
Children over 4	¥600	¥500	¥800

*Dates for the sales period of tickets for the Osaka location will be announced on the *Naruto Art Exhibit* website at a later date.

Caution:
*Taxes included in the price.
*This L Code applies only to the Tokyo location.
*Advance tickets sold only through Lawson Tickets.
*Please be advised that advance tickets are issued only at Loppi kiosks, and will not be delivered.
*At-the-door tickets are also available at the Mori Arts Center Gallery ticket counter.
*Premium booklet not for sale.
*Both the Tokyo and Osaka locations will offer the same premium booklet.
*Booklet design and contents subject to change.
*To receive your premium booklet, please present your voucher at the exhibit location during the Tokyo exhibit.
*Depending on crowding, there may be a wait time, or you may be unable to enter.

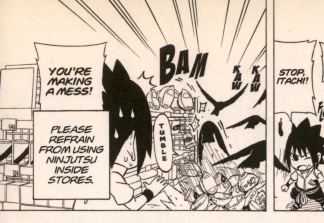

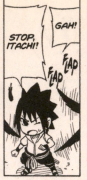

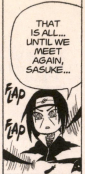

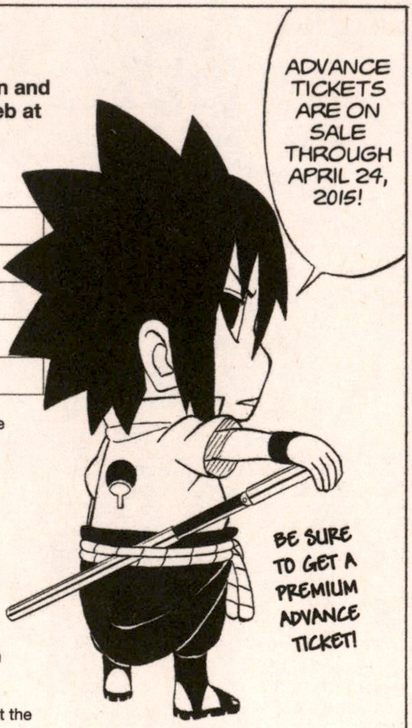

THE END

MINI MANGA 4: LET'S GO TO THE NARUTO ART EXHIBIT! PART 2

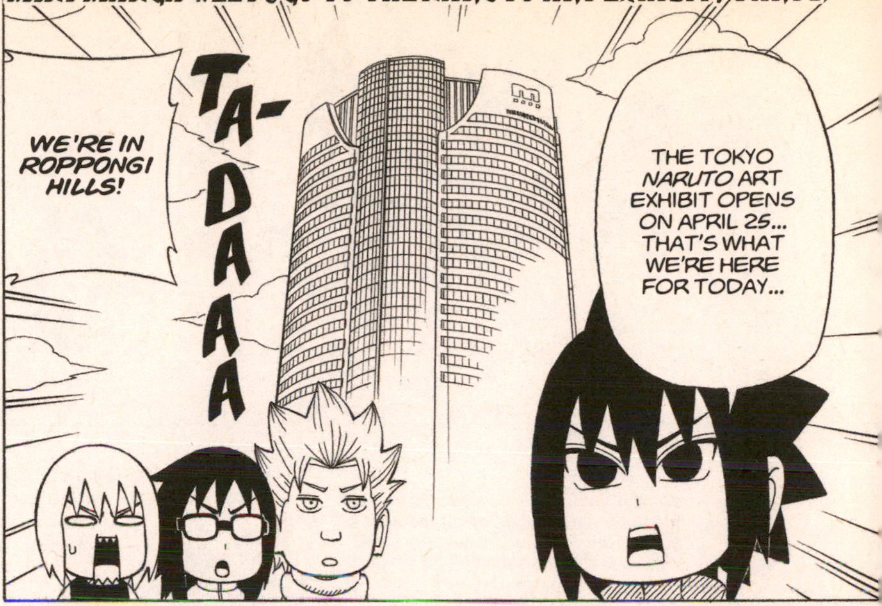
THE TOKYO NARUTO ART EXHIBIT OPENS ON APRIL 25... THAT'S WHAT WE'RE HERE FOR TODAY...
TA-DAAAA
WE'RE IN ROPPONGI HILLS!

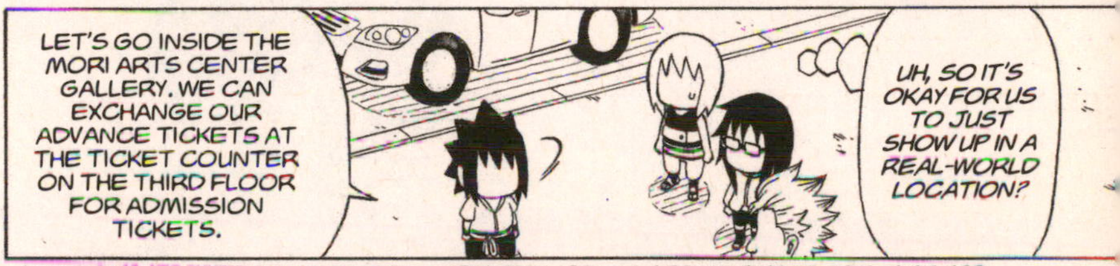
UH, SO IT'S OKAY FOR US TO JUST SHOW UP IN A REAL-WORLD LOCATION?
LET'S GO INSIDE THE MORI ARTS CENTER GALLERY. WE CAN EXCHANGE OUR ADVANCE TICKETS AT THE TICKET COUNTER ON THE THIRD FLOOR FOR ADMISSION TICKETS.

*THE NARUTO ART EXHIBIT TOKYO LOCATION IS OPEN FROM APRIL 25 THROUGH JUNE 28, 2015, IN THE MORI ARTS CENTER GALLERY (ROPPONGI HILLS MORI TOWER FLOOR 25).

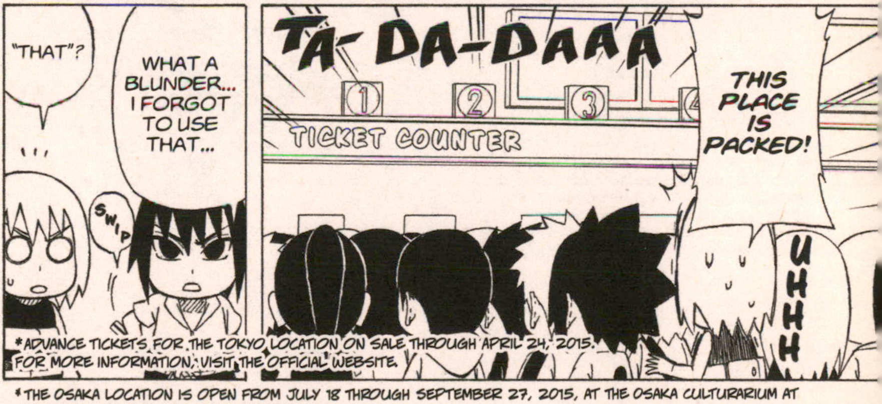
TA-DA-DAAAA
1
2
3
TICKET COUNTER
THIS PLACE IS PACKED!
UHHHH
WHAT A BLUNDER... I FORGOT TO USE THAT...
"THAT"?
...
SWIP
*ADVANCE TICKETS FOR THE TOKYO LOCATION ON SALE THROUGH APRIL 24, 2015. FOR MORE INFORMATION, VISIT THE OFFICIAL WEBSITE.

*THE OSAKA LOCATION IS OPEN FROM JULY 18 THROUGH SEPTEMBER 27, 2015, AT THE OSAKA CULTURARIUM AT TEMPOZAN (NEXT TO THE OSAKA AQUARIUM).

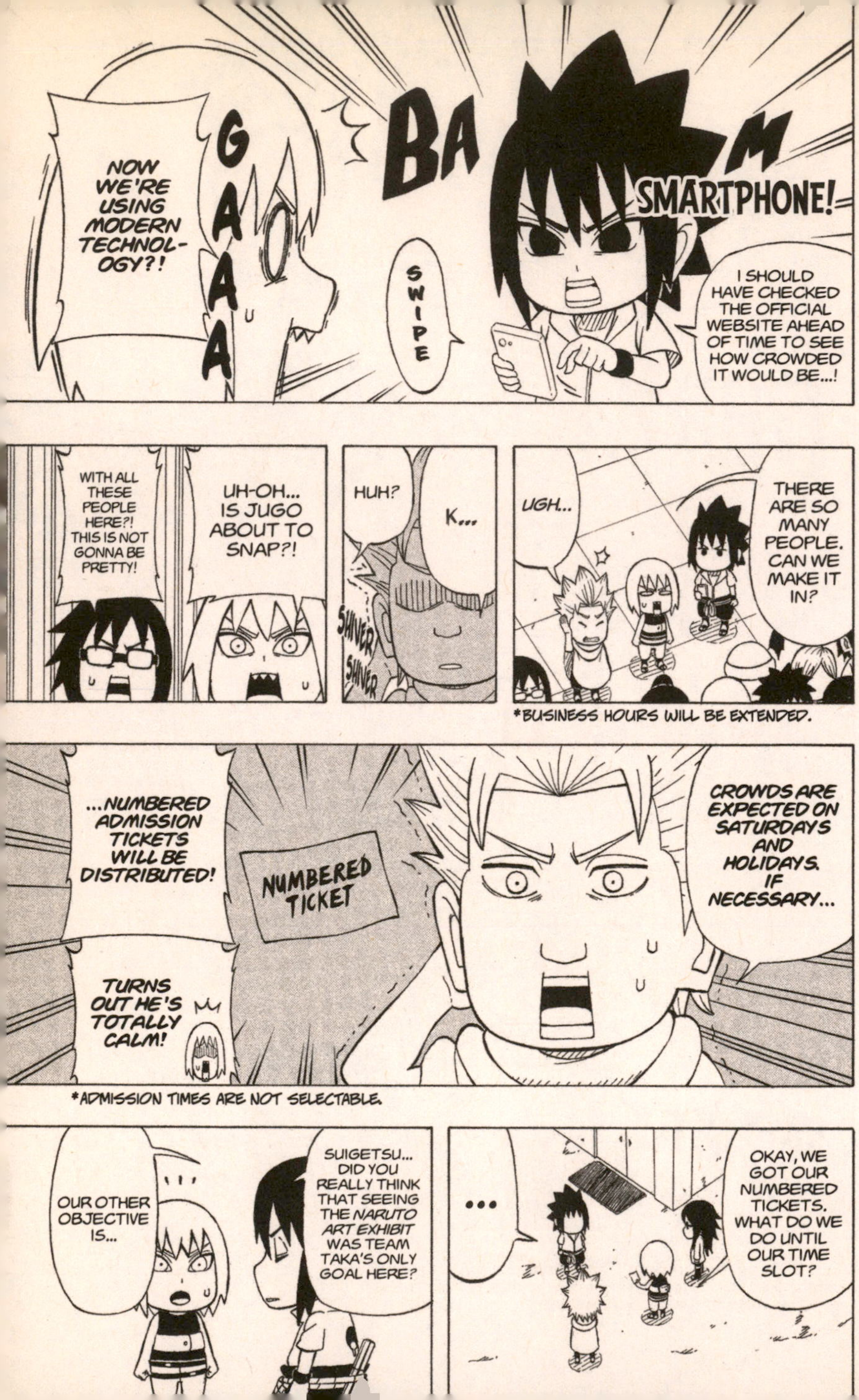
BAM
SMARTPHONE!
I SHOULD HAVE CHECKED THE OFFICIAL WEBSITE AHEAD OF TIME TO SEE HOW CROWDED IT WOULD BE...!
SWIPE
GAAAA
NOW WE'RE USING MODERN TECHNOL-OGY?!
THERE ARE SO MANY PEOPLE. CAN WE MAKE IT IN?
UGH...
K...
HUH?
SHIVER SHIVER
UH-OH... IS JUGO ABOUT TO SNAP?!
WITH ALL THESE PEOPLE HERE?! THIS IS NOT GONNA BE PRETTY!
*BUSINESS HOURS WILL BE EXTENDED.
CROWDS ARE EXPECTED ON SATURDAYS AND HOLIDAYS. IF NECESSARY...
NUMBERED TICKET
...NUMBERED ADMISSION TICKETS WILL BE DISTRIBUTED!
TURNS OUT HE'S TOTALLY CALM!
*ADMISSION TIMES ARE NOT SELECTABLE.
OKAY, WE GOT OUR NUMBERED TICKETS. WHAT DO WE DO UNTIL OUR TIME SLOT?
...
SUIGETSU... DID YOU REALLY THINK THAT SEEING THE NARUTO ART EXHIBIT WAS TEAM TAKA'S ONLY GOAL HERE?
OUR OTHER OBJECTIVE IS...

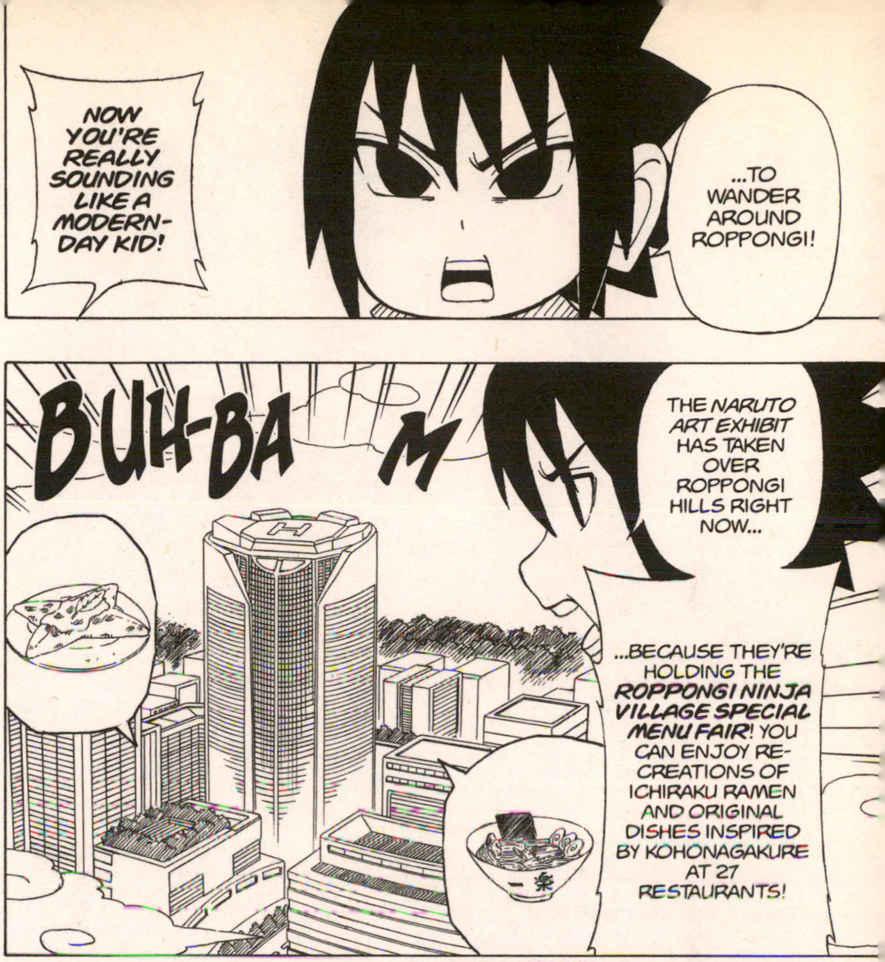
...TO WANDER AROUND ROPPONGI!
NOW YOU'RE REALLY SOUNDING LIKE A MODERN-DAY KID!
BUH-BAM
THE NARUTO ART EXHIBIT HAS TAKEN OVER ROPPONGI HILLS RIGHT NOW...
...BECAUSE THEY'RE HOLDING THE ROPPONGI NINJA VILLAGE SPECIAL MENU FAIR! YOU CAN ENJOY RE-CREATIONS OF ICHIRAKU RAMEN AND ORIGINAL DISHES INSPIRED BY KOHONAGAKURE AT 27 RESTAURANTS!

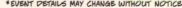

*EVENT DETAILS MAY CHANGE WITHOUT NOTICE.

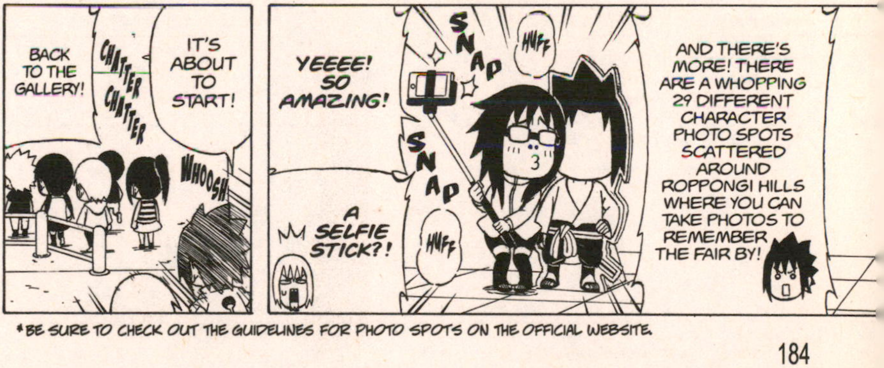
AND THERE'S MORE! THERE ARE A WHOPPING 29 DIFFERENT CHARACTER PHOTO SPOTS SCATTERED AROUND ROPPONGI HILLS WHERE YOU CAN TAKE PHOTOS TO REMEMBER THE FAIR BY!
SNAP
HUFF
SNAP
HUFF
YEEEE! SO AMAZING!
A SELFIE STICK?!
IT'S ABOUT TO START!
CHATTER CHATTER
BACK TO THE GALLERY!
WHOOSH

*BE SURE TO CHECK OUT THE GUIDELINES FOR PHOTO SPOTS ON THE OFFICIAL WEBSITE.

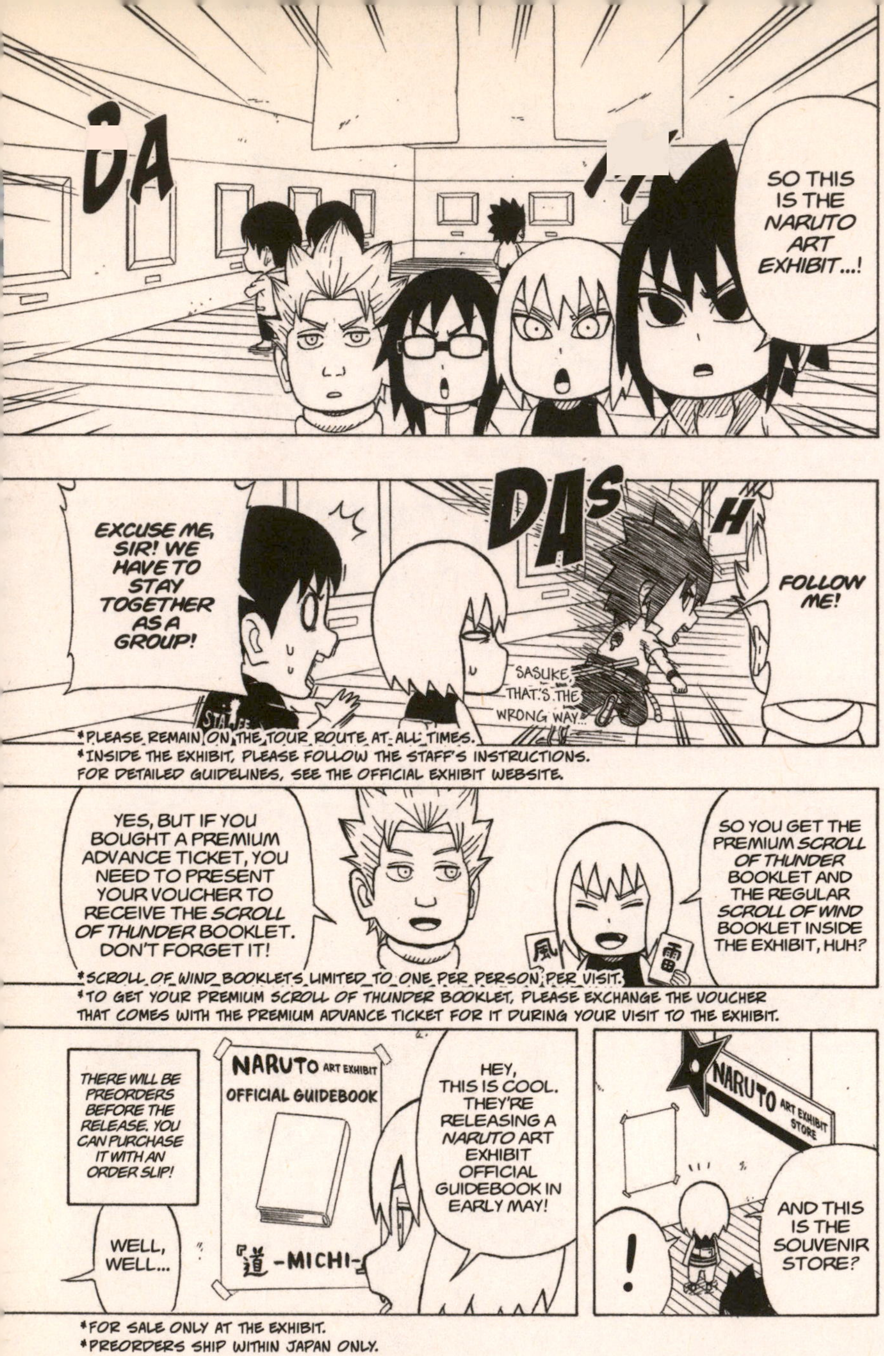

SO THIS IS THE NARUTO ART EXHIBIT...!
DA
FOLLOW ME!
DASH
SASUKE, THAT'S THE WRONG WAY...
EXCUSE ME, SIR! WE HAVE TO STAY TOGETHER AS A GROUP!
STAFF
*PLEASE REMAIN ON THE TOUR ROUTE AT ALL TIMES.
*INSIDE THE EXHIBIT, PLEASE FOLLOW THE STAFF'S INSTRUCTIONS.
FOR DETAILED GUIDELINES, SEE THE OFFICIAL EXHIBIT WEBSITE.
SO YOU GET THE PREMIUM *SCROLL OF THUNDER* BOOKLET AND THE REGULAR *SCROLL OF WIND* BOOKLET INSIDE THE EXHIBIT, HUH?
風
雷
YES, BUT IF YOU BOUGHT A PREMIUM ADVANCE TICKET, YOU NEED TO PRESENT YOUR VOUCHER TO RECEIVE THE *SCROLL OF THUNDER* BOOKLET. DON'T FORGET IT!
*SCROLL OF WIND BOOKLETS LIMITED TO ONE PER PERSON PER VISIT.
*TO GET YOUR PREMIUM SCROLL OF THUNDER BOOKLET, PLEASE EXCHANGE THE VOUCHER
THAT COMES WITH THE PREMIUM ADVANCE TICKET FOR IT DURING YOUR VISIT TO THE EXHIBIT.
NARUTO ART EXHIBIT STORE
AND THIS IS THE SOUVENIR STORE?
!
HEY, THIS IS COOL. THEY'RE RELEASING A *NARUTO* ART EXHIBIT OFFICIAL GUIDEBOOK IN EARLY MAY!
NARUTO ART EXHIBIT
OFFICIAL GUIDEBOOK
道 -MICHI-
THERE WILL BE PREORDERS BEFORE THE RELEASE. YOU CAN PURCHASE IT WITH AN ORDER SLIP!
WELL, WELL...
*FOR SALE ONLY AT THE EXHIBIT.
*PREORDERS SHIP WITHIN JAPAN ONLY.

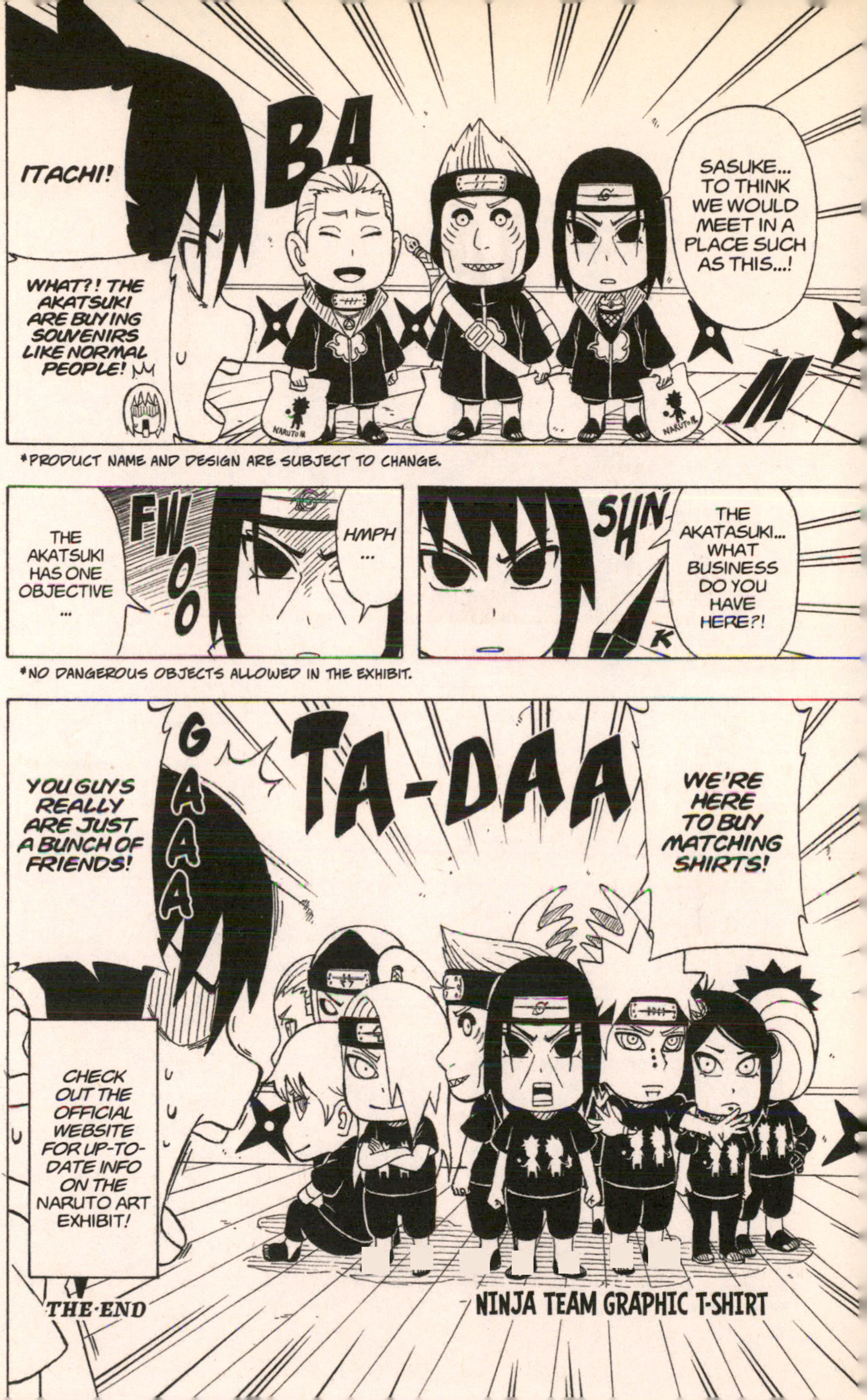
SASUKE... TO THINK WE WOULD MEET IN A PLACE SUCH AS THIS...!
BA
M
ITACHI!
WHAT?! THE AKATSUKI ARE BUYING SOUVENIRS LIKE NORMAL PEOPLE!
*PRODUCT NAME AND DESIGN ARE SUBJECT TO CHANGE.
THE AKATASUKI... WHAT BUSINESS DO YOU HAVE HERE?!
SHN
K
HMPH ...
FWOO
THE AKATSUKI HAS ONE OBJECTIVE ...
*NO DANGEROUS OBJECTS ALLOWED IN THE EXHIBIT.
WE'RE HERE TO BUY MATCHING SHIRTS!
TA-DAA
GAAAA
YOU GUYS REALLY ARE JUST A BUNCH OF FRIENDS!
NINJA TEAM GRAPHIC T-SHIRT
CHECK OUT THE OFFICIAL WEBSITE FOR UP-TO-DATE INFO ON THE NARUTO ART EXHIBIT!
THE END

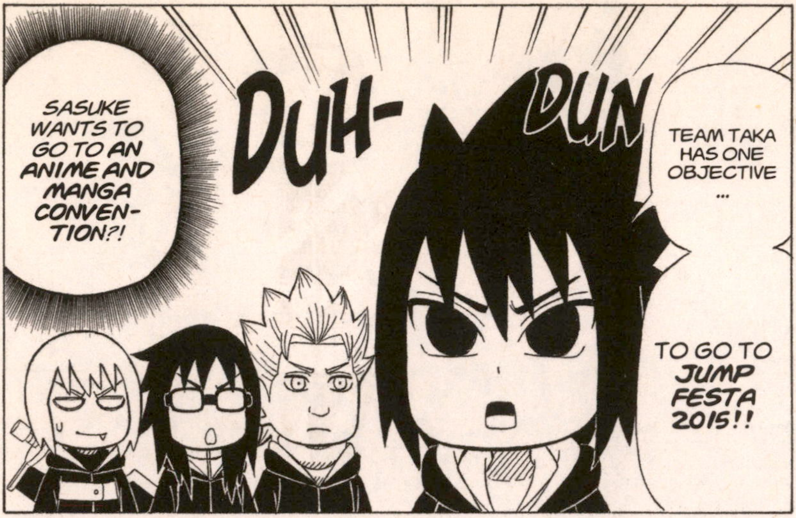
TEAM TAKA HAS ONE OBJECTIVE ...
DUH-DUN
TO GO TO JUMP FESTA 2015!!
SASUKE WANTS TO GO TO AN ANIME AND MANGA CONVENTION?!

MINI MANGA 5: JUMP FESTA 2015 RULES & GUIDELINES

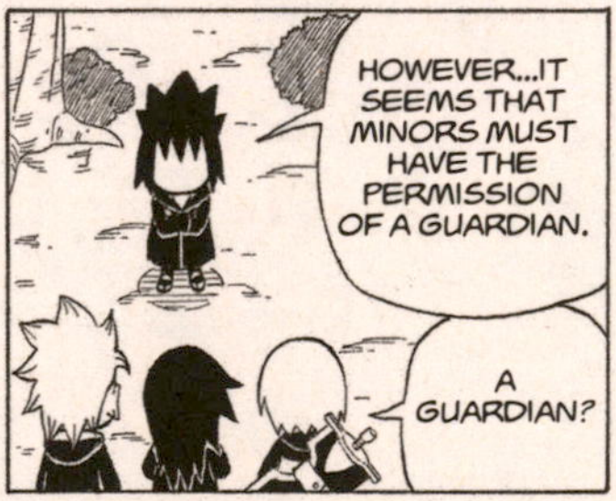
HOWEVER...IT SEEMS THAT MINORS MUST HAVE THE PERMISSION OF A GUARDIAN.
A GUARDIAN?

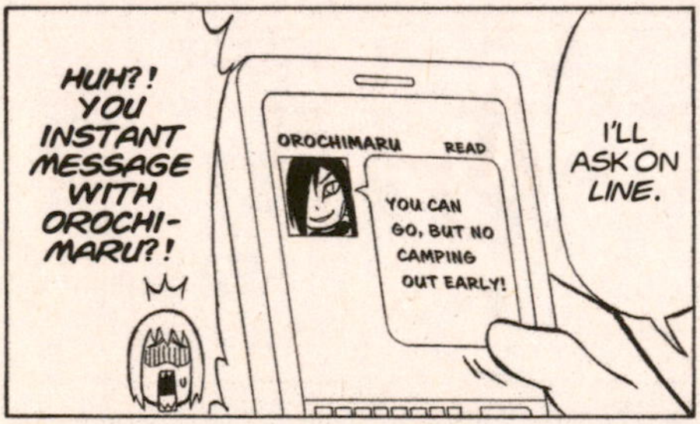
I'LL ASK ON LINE.
OROCHIMARU
READ
YOU CAN GO, BUT NO CAMPING OUT EARLY!
HUH?! YOU INSTANT MESSAGE WITH OROCHIMARU?!

*IN ACCORDANCE WITH CHIBA PREFECTURE'S HEALTHY YOUTH UPBRINGING ORDINANCE, PLEASE DO NOT CAMP OUT OVERNIGHT FOR THE CONVENTION. MINORS WHO LINE UP OVERNIGHT MAY BE COUNSELED BY THE POLICE.

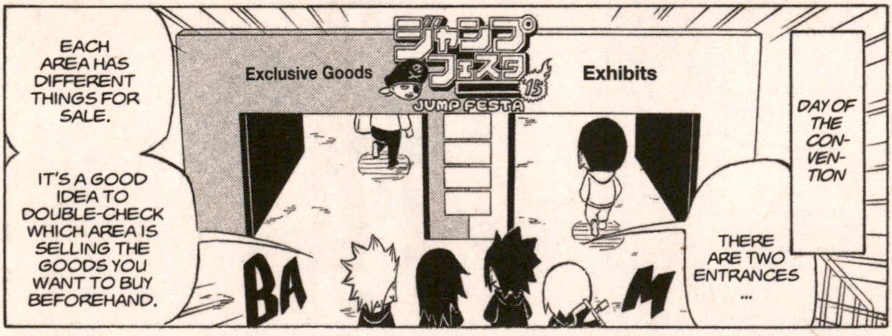
DAY OF THE CONVENTION
THERE ARE TWO ENTRANCES ...
ジャンプフェスタ '15
JUMP FESTA
Exhibits
Exclusive Goods
EACH AREA HAS DIFFERENT THINGS FOR SALE.
IT'S A GOOD IDEA TO DOUBLE-CHECK WHICH AREA IS SELLING THE GOODS YOU WANT TO BUY BEFOREHAND.
BAM

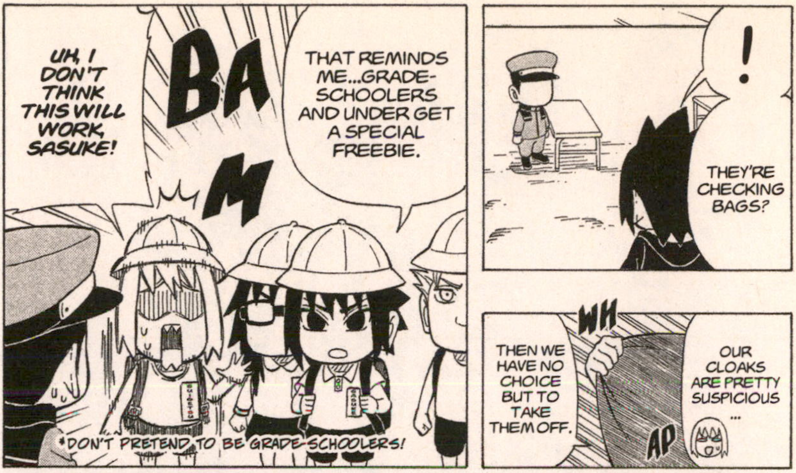
!
THEY'RE CHECKING BAGS?
OUR CLOAKS ARE PRETTY SUSPICIOUS...
WH
AP
THEN WE HAVE NO CHOICE BUT TO TAKE THEM OFF.
THAT REMINDS ME...GRADE-SCHOOLERS AND UNDER GET A SPECIAL FREEBIE.
BAM
UH, I DON'T THINK THIS WILL WORK, SASUKE!
*DON'T PRETEND TO BE GRADE-SCHOOLERS!

*THE JF 2015 STAFF PERFORMS BAG CHECKS FOR THE SAFETY OF ATTENDEES. FOR A LIST OF PROHIBITED ITEMS, PLEASE CONSULT THE OFFICIAL JF 2015 WEBSITE.

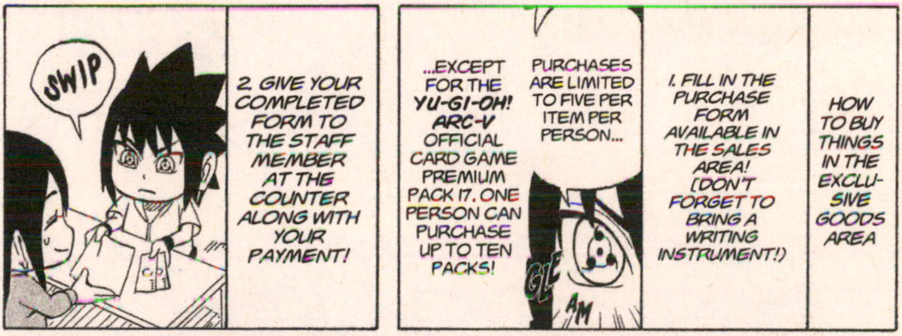
HOW TO BUY THINGS IN THE EXCLU-SIVE GOODS AREA
1. FILL IN THE PURCHASE FORM AVAILABLE IN THE SALES AREA! (DON'T FORGET TO BRING A WRITING INSTRUMENT!)
PURCHASES ARE LIMITED TO FIVE PER ITEM PER PERSON...
...EXCEPT FOR THE YU-GI-OH! ARC-V OFFICIAL CARD GAME PREMIUM PACK 17. ONE PERSON CAN PURCHASE UP TO TEN PACKS!
GLEAM
2. GIVE YOUR COMPLETED FORM TO THE STAFF MEMBER AT THE COUNTER ALONG WITH YOUR PAYMENT!
SWIP

*THE FREE GIFTS ARE AVAILABLE FOR CHILD ATTENDEES IN GRADE SCHOOL OR YOUNGER. LIMITED TO ONE GIFT SET PER CHILD.

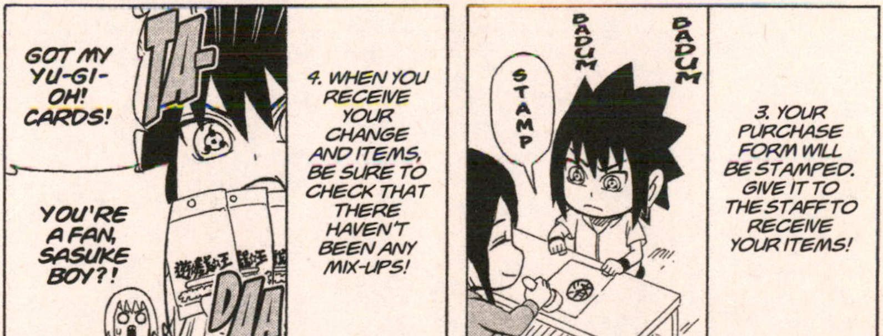
3. YOUR PURCHASE FORM WILL BE STAMPED. GIVE IT TO THE STAFF TO RECEIVE YOUR ITEMS!
BADUM
BADUM
STAMP
4. WHEN YOU RECEIVE YOUR CHANGE AND ITEMS, BE SURE TO CHECK THAT THERE HAVEN'T BEEN ANY MIX-UPS!
TA-
DAA
GOT MY YU-GI-OH! CARDS!
YOU'RE A FAN, SASUKE BOY?!

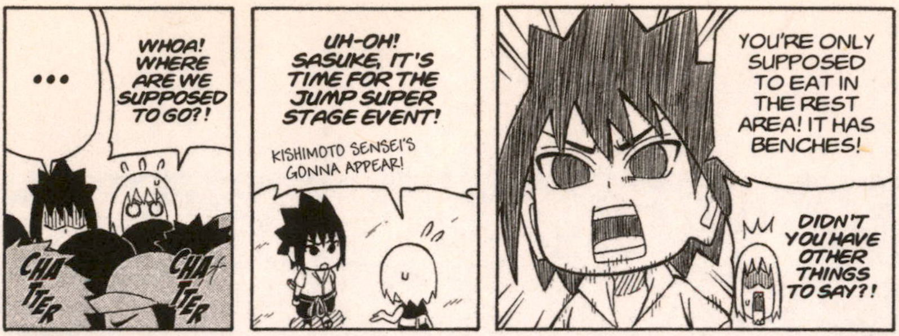
YOU'RE ONLY SUPPOSED TO EAT IN THE REST AREA! IT HAS BENCHES!
DIDN'T YOU HAVE OTHER THINGS TO SAY?!
UH-OH! SASUKE, IT'S TIME FOR THE JUMP SUPER STAGE EVENT!
KISHIMOTO SENSEI'S GONNA APPEAR!
WHOA! WHERE ARE WE SUPPOSED TO GO?!
...
CHATTER
CHATTER

*PLEASE SHARE THE REST AREA WITH OTHERS AND REFRAIN FROM STAYING TOO LONG SO THAT OTHERS MAY USE IT AS WELL.

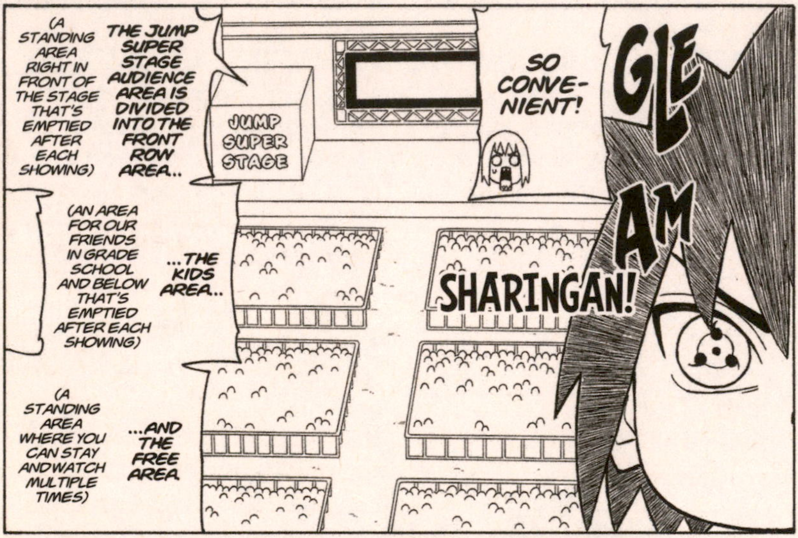
GLEAM
SHARINGAN!
SO CONVENIENT!
JUMP SUPER STAGE
THE JUMP SUPER STAGE AUDIENCE AREA IS DIVIDED INTO THE FRONT ROW AREA...
(A STANDING AREA RIGHT IN FRONT OF THE STAGE THAT'S EMPTIED AFTER EACH SHOWING)
...THE KIDS AREA...
(AN AREA FOR OUR FRIENDS IN GRADE SCHOOL AND BELOW THAT'S EMPTIED AFTER EACH SHOWING)
...AND THE FREE AREA.
(A STANDING AREA WHERE YOU CAN STAY AND WATCH MULTIPLE TIMES)

*FOR MORE INFO ON THE AUDIENCE AREA, VISIT THE JUMP FESTA WEBSITE!

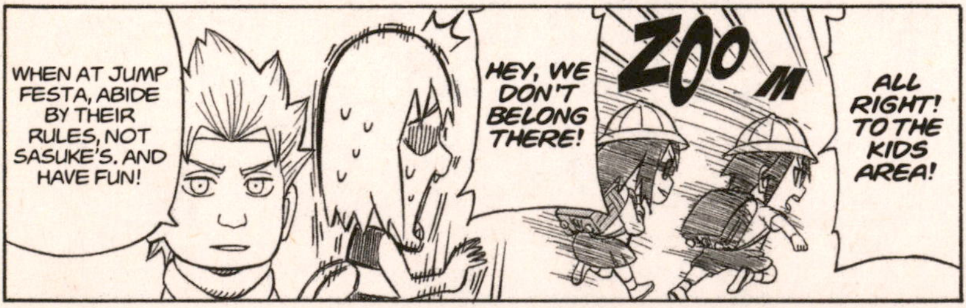
ALL RIGHT! TO THE KIDS AREA!
ZOOM
HEY, WE DON'T BELONG THERE!
WHEN AT JUMP FESTA, ABIDE BY THEIR RULES, NOT SASUKE'S. AND HAVE FUN!

THE END

*MINI MANGA 3 THROUGH 5 HAVE BEEN INCLUDED AS THEY WERE ORIGINALLY PRINTED IN MAGAZINES IN JAPAN.

You're Reading the WRONG WAY!

NARUTO: CHIBI SASUKE'S SHARINGAN LEGEND reads from right to left, starting in the upper-right corner. Japanese is read from right to left, meaning that action, sound effects and word-balloon order are completely reversed from English order.

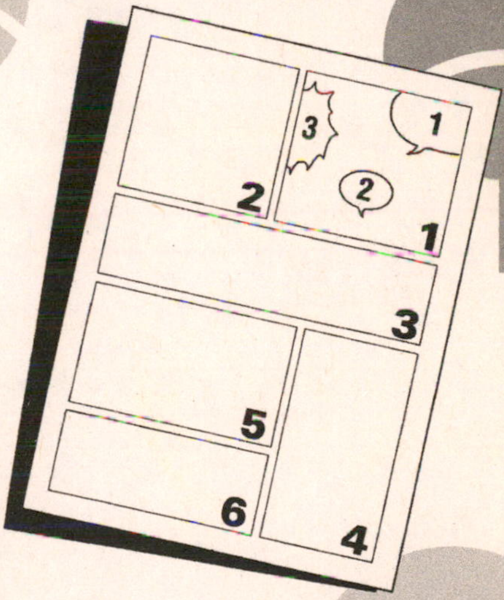
1
2
3
1
2
3
4
5
6

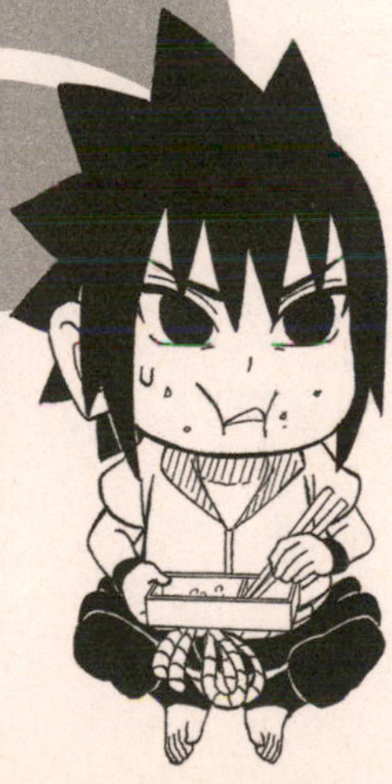

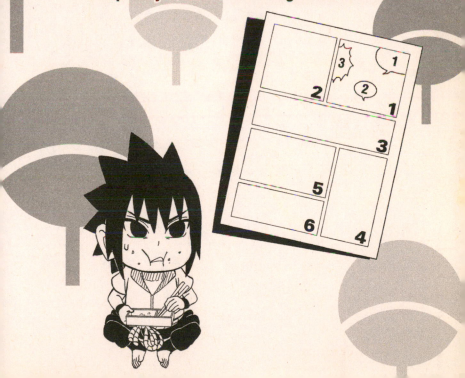

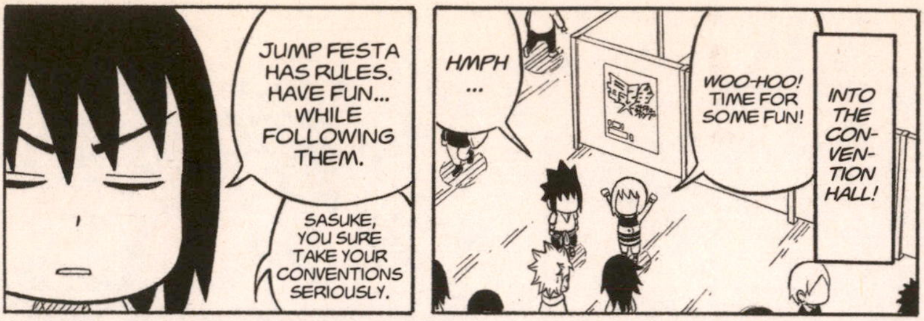
INTO THE CON-VEN-TION HALL!
WOO-HOO! TIME FOR SOME FUN!
HMPH ...
JUMP FESTA HAS RULES. HAVE FUN... WHILE FOLLOWING THEM.
SASUKE, YOU SURE TAKE YOUR CONVENTIONS SERIOUSLY.

*INSIDE THE CONVENTION AREA, EXCHANGES AND RESALE OF CARDS AND/OR OTHER GOODS BETWEEN ATTENDEES IS STRICTLY PROHIBITED.

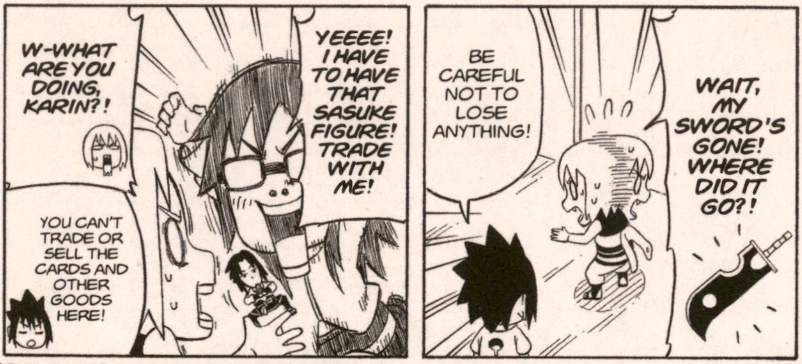
WAIT, MY SWORD'S GONE! WHERE DID IT GO?!
BE CAREFUL NOT TO LOSE ANYTHING!
YEEEE! I HAVE TO HAVE THAT SASUKE FIGURE! TRADE WITH ME!
W-WHAT ARE YOU DOING, KARIN?!
YOU CAN'T TRADE OR SELL THE CARDS AND OTHER GOODS HERE!

*DON'T BRING A SWORD IN THE FIRST PLACE!

*PLEASE KEEP A CLOSE EYE ON YOUR BAGS, VALUABLES, ETC. THE CONVENTION IS NOT RESPONSIBLE FOR ANY THEFT OR LOST ITEMS.

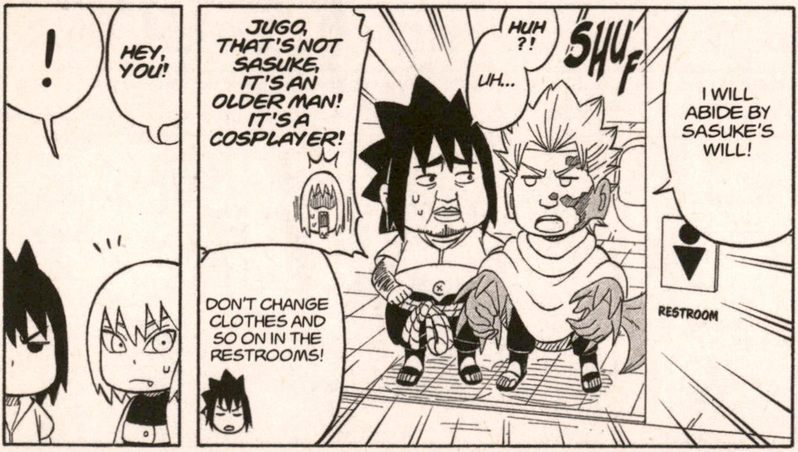
I WILL ABIDE BY SASUKE'S WILL!
SHUF
HUH ?!
UH...
JUGO, THAT'S NOT SASUKE, IT'S AN OLDER MAN! IT'S A COSPLAYER!
RESTROOM
DON'T CHANGE CLOTHES AND SO ON IN THE RESTROOMS!
HEY, YOU!
!

*PLEASE REFRAIN FROM SETTING UP IN THE AREAS AROUND OR WITHIN THE CONVENTION CENTER (PARTICULARLY IN RESTROOMS) TO CHANGE CLOTHES, ETC.

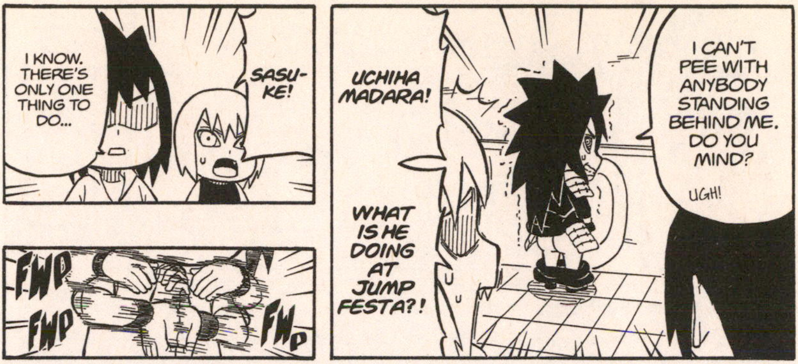
I CAN'T PEE WITH ANYBODY STANDING BEHIND ME. DO YOU MIND?
UGH!
UCHIHA MADARA!
WHAT IS HE DOING AT JUMP FESTA?!
SASU-KE!
I KNOW. THERE'S ONLY ONE THING TO DO...
FWP
FWP
FWP

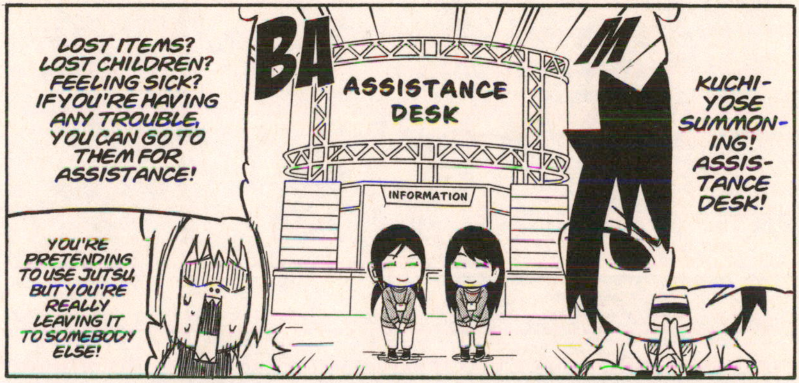
BAM
KUCHI-YOSE SUMMONING! ASSISTANCE DESK!
ASSISTANCE DESK
INFORMATION
LOST ITEMS? LOST CHILDREN? FEELING SICK? IF YOU'RE HAVING ANY TROUBLE, YOU CAN GO TO THEM FOR ASSISTANCE!
YOU'RE PRETENDING TO USE JUTSU, BUT YOU'RE REALLY LEAVING IT TO SOMEBODY ELSE!

*SECURITY GUARDS PATROL THE CONVENTION CENTER. IF YOU SEE ANY SUSPICIOUS PEOPLE OR ITEMS, PLEASE ALERT THE NEAREST SECURITY GUARD OR STAFF MEMBER, OR THE ASSISTANCE DESK.

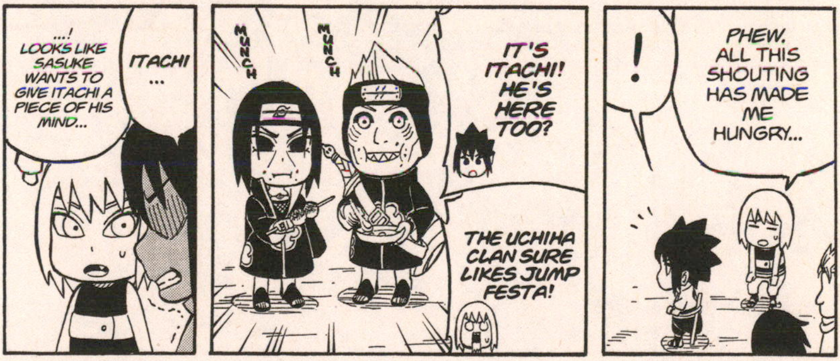
PHEW. ALL THIS SHOUTING HAS MADE ME HUNGRY...
!
IT'S ITACHI! HE'S HERE TOO?
MUNCH
MUNCH
THE UCHIHA CLAN SURE LIKES JUMP FESTA!
ITACHI ...
...! LOOKS LIKE SASUKE WANTS TO GIVE ITACHI A PIECE OF HIS MIND...